Women Who Venture

You can't be what you can't see

Renata George

Design: Dejan Nikolic
Editing: Lee-Anne Weston-Ford
Publisher: BSMRT
Photos provided by the persons featured
in the book and their affiliates

ISBN 978-0-578-44994-4

First edition: June 2019
Printed in the United States of America

CONTENTS

To all women, people of color, and LGBTQ people
who make investment decisions in venture capital

To all men who make decisions in favor of women,
people of color, and LGBTQ people

To my family, colleagues and partners who helped me finish this
book, or were patiently waiting until it was finished

As an avid writer and reader, I feel that a book is a unique medium that serves a different purpose than the other written media that we consume regularly. A book can display a variety of perspectives at once, providing enough details on the subjects it explores, while giving us space to contemplate.

When Renata George told me she was going to write a book about Women Who Venture, featuring around a hundred female investors of different generations, I immediately said I'd be supportive. Renata told me that she wanted to do in-depth individual interviews, to both learn and explain the true state of affairs in the venture capital, while celebrating women who best reflect this industry.

The existing bias in the venture capital industry is multidimensional and implicates career challenges not only for women, but also for other underrepresented groups. Many of the investors interviewed for this book, offer advice and solutions to address this issue. Their ideas are bold, opinions are candid, and the narrative sometimes goes against what we are used to reading in popular media.

Having unconventional perspectives to consider is helpful in understanding what true diversity looks like. By being exposed to it, we can identify particular actions that each of us, male or female, can take to generate positive change. It's the critical mass of all the tiny changes that we can each make daily, that will eventually change the perception, and reality, of diversity in venture capital.

This book is an essential read for aspiring female venture investors who want to be inspired by the life stories of women who made it all the way to the top in venture capital. It is also a valuable resource for male investors interested in increasing diversity. Institutional investors can benefit from learning more about their investees, as well as find new general partners to consider investing in. Finally, entrepreneurs can benefit from the book by learning how the investors featured in it make investment decisions.

Fixing the diversity problem in venture capital will take a long time and require a continuous and steady pace of activities and changes. With Women Who Venture, Renata is helping us all along that journey.

Brad Feld,
Managing Director at Foundry Group
Co-Founder of TechStars

This remarkable book, Women Who Venture, provides important guidelines for women who want to work in venture capital and private equity. It is also a vital read for men seeking a place in the industry, and for those already working there, because it is a harbinger of what is coming to the business at an increasing pace as women become vital to the venture capital world.

The book's author, Renata George, has had years of experience as an entrepreneur and venture capitalist in Eastern Europe, China and Singapore, as well as in the USA where she formed a successful venture capital fund.

Renata compiled a list of a hundred women who are active in decision-making roles in venture capital firms around the world, although most of them invest in the United States. Each chapter of the book is dedicated to just one female venture capitalist — her story, lessons learned and advice to the readers. Please, do pay attention to the key points that emerge in the book — in particular, the following, which I find significant:

- Men will find greater success for their firms and themselves if they appreciate, and cooperate with women when making and implementing decisions:
- Women should assertively be the women they are, in appearance and demeanor, and at the same time understand and appreciate the views of the men with whom they work.
- Success in venture, for men and women, depends on very hard work.
- Finally, there are certain character traits inherited by many of these women, which led them to success in the industry, helped them influence people and make good deals, and get guidance and support from others.

Franklin 'Pitch' Johnson,
Founder at Asset Management Co.
Pioneer venture capital investor since 1962

When I learned about the book Women Who Venture, it took me back to my time as Chairman of the National Venture Capital Association (NVCA) and my focus on increasing diversity in the industry during my tenure. I was reminded of the efforts we made and the lessons I learned from them.

In 2014, we had decided to set up a special working group — a diversity task force — to discover and understand the best practices for increasing diversity in other industries, and to bring them to venture capital. Our objective was to help VC firms be successful in recruiting more diverse partner groups, and to create the kind of environment that would help a more diverse workforce thrive.

When I asked the members of the NVCA board for volunteers to join the diversity task force, women and underrepresented minorities were quick to raise their hands. We could have been done with the formation of the task force right there, but I felt that the group was not diverse enough. We did not have any white men among those who had volunteered.

Since the VC industry is still predominantly white male, I knew that if we wanted to make the biggest difference the fastest, we needed white male representation. Happily, it was not difficult to recruit white men who wanted to become actively involved in the effort.

Lesson to learn: we should be proactive and get the current decision-makers bought into the process early on, to make the greatest impact.

We then looked at the board of the NVCA and realized that it was not as diverse as we would like it to be. We had historically elected six new board members every year, who would serve for four years. In addition to gender diversity, we wanted to have representation from other underrepresented groups as well, but with only six seats per year, we were not going to move the needle very quickly on a board with 24 members.

Then, Bobby Franklin, President of the NVCA, reminded us that our bylaws did, in fact, allow us to increase our board beyond 24 members and suggested we elect a larger board to achieve a more diverse board faster. We did just that! That year we elected 10 new directors, including a wonderful selection of women and other minority groups representatives.

Lesson to learn: there are ways of accelerating a change — we just have to deliberately look for them.

Earlier during my time on the board, we had a panel discussion on diversity at the NVCA annual meeting. There was an older Indian gentleman on the panel who told us about his personal experience when he came to Silicon Valley in the 70s.

At that time, he noted that it was really hard for Indians to be hired as CEOs, because Indians were usually only recognized for their engineering talent. So this gentlemen had experienced quite a lot of discrimination in his career.

I sat in the audience and thought how ironic this was when you consider the prevalence of Indian CEOs at the helm of Silicon Valley's top tier companies today. It was a reminder of how far we have come since then.

Lesson to learn: social progress can happen for underrepresented groups, and I am confident that it will be the same for women.

The question is, how do we nudge the change, so it happens faster?

While it is true that women have been underrepresented in the venture capital industry, it is also true that there are some women who have been outstanding investors for quite a long time. Early in their careers, these women had far fewer role models to follow, if they had any at all. Today, because of books like this one, there are stories to inspire the next generation of women, reminding them that it can be done, that they can be successful in this business, and that it's worth the extra effort to overcome the obstacles that still remain.

At NEA, we have been very deliberate about hiring women. To achieve that, several years ago, we adopted a variation of the Rooney Rule, which is a National Football League policy requiring league teams to interview ethnic-minority candidates for coaching jobs.

We stipulate that we want to see as many diverse candidates in the final applicant pool as we'd like to see in our general partners group in 10 years. Regardless of how few diverse candidates we get at the top of the funnel, we want to make sure that some of them will be advanced to the next stages of this funnel. The more of them that get to the bottom of the funnel, the more likely it will be that some will get hired. With this approach in mind, we have substantially changed the makeup of our partner group within the last few years. It will take time before these newer hires move up to the general partners group, but a quick glance at our website will quickly reveal that it is every bit as hard to be hired as a white male today as any other profile.

It is not easy to find a job in venture capital, but it is a wonderful occupation where you can truly do good while doing well. I wish all the readers of this book the very best luck in finding a great home in this amazing industry.

Scott Sandell,
Managing General Partner at
New Enterprise Associates (NEA)

It wasn't until I published my first book that I stopped thinking it was something that anyone could do. Not all athletes can become coaches, not all practitioners can teach. It's the same with books. Writing a book is a full-time job that requires a lot of commitment. However, after sending more than a hundred emails to the investors nominated for this project — right after the New Year holidays in January 2019 — I realized that it would be more than just a book. Firstly, it wouldn't be about me or the things I had to say, but rather about a hundred other people who I personally knew or would become acquainted with, and *their* stories. Secondly, I became conscious of the fact that it would be a platform with which I could reach other venture capitalists around the world who make hiring and investment decisions; the institutional investors who will be funding some of the women featured in this book; and the aspiring investors and entrepreneurs who have been looking for role models and mentors. So many stakeholders were involved that this not-your-typical book came with a great deal of responsibility, and I figured that I'd need a lot of patience to make it happen. But as Margaret Thatcher said, "I am extraordinarily patient, provided I get my own way in the end." So let me tell you how I got here.

I first came up with the idea for a book about women in venture capital in 2017 after I had accumulated enough data about the place of women in the industry worldwide. Among all other discoveries, I had seen a lot of books written by and about male investors, but just a couple that mentioned female VCs. It was obviously yet another channel that women hadn't harnessed for their own benefit. At that point, however, the stars didn't align for it to happen for different reasons, and instead of giving up on the idea, I took that as an invitation to do more work on the concept of the book. I invested my time in talking to the target audience — investors, entrepreneurs, and limited partners of both genders — to find out what they'd like to read about, what value a book like this could create for each of them personally, and how the information should be presented. It became clear that aspiring investors among the potential readers were interested in the career stories and tricks that helped women who are now well-known venture capitalists break into the industry. General partners and VC executives wanted to meet and network with fellow investors and get to know their personal and professional points of view. Limited partners were interested in the same, but from an asset allocation perspective. And entrepreneurs were, of course, curious to know what place diversity held in the investment theses of the investors featured in the book.

Was there a way of satisfying all these audiences at once? There was! I started investing as an angel investor back in 2009, after I sold my publishing house that had four print magazines in its portfolio. It had originated from just one of them, called Lighthouse, that was built entirely on stories told by people or about them. It was the most impactful product we had, and our readers loved it to the moon and back. All of a sudden, I knew what the book would look like. However, aside from the entertainment factor, I also wanted to add some academic value to the book. In my mind, it shouldn't be only an object of art for which I could pick people according to my personal taste and write about what I'd subjectively be interested in. So I decided to make it a part of the regular research that we've been doing through our international think tank, Women.VC, for the last five years. We've been busy. But as many other investors have confessed in this book, I recognize now that I was also making mistakes that we teach female founders not to make, such as not releasing a product to the public before perfecting it. Some of the women who I interviewed for the book convinced me that it was time to summarize the work we'd been doing behind the scenes. I'd like to thank you for this (you know who you are!). This is how I know that through the immense moral support that all of the investors expressed in this book, many more people — men and women — will be inspired to pursue their next greatest achievements.

Back in 2014, when I almost fully deployed the capital of the early-stage venture capital fund that we'd raised with my European partners, I felt that I was in a position to do something for the industry and give back to the community. The internet still hasn't figured out who the author of this famous quote is: "You make a living by what you get; you make a life by what you give," but it's nevertheless a good one. I asked my long-time mentor, Michael Halloran, ex-advisor to the Chairman of the Securities and Exchange Commission, and then partner of one of the iconic law firms in the United States, Pillsbury, about where he thought I could make the most impact. It didn't take him long to reply, "You should look at where and how women fit, in the venture capital industry."

As with many other people of both genders, it didn't occur to me at that time (which was only a few years ago), that there weren't that many women in venture capital firms, both on the associate and partner levels. Michael quickly made some introductions and there I was — figuring out the relationships between women and venture capital before this topic got really hot on the news. So Women.VC was born in 2014 as a project dedicated to women in venture capital, with the goal of researching the issue and developing solutions along the way. By the end of that year, the National Venture Capital Association (United States) had announced their Diversity Task Force to foster diversity and inclusion in venture capital. The timing was right. I knew that if it wasn't treated as a token project, Women.VC would require a lot of resources — team, time, and money. So I committed to this long-term endeavor. I have learned a lot since then and would like to share the most critical learnings with you before you start reading the stories of the women featured in this book to show you the full picture of what is happening to women in the venture capital industry.

It was possibly due to my undergraduate studies in life sciences that the only appropriate way of approaching the issue of the lack of women in venture capital I saw was through profound research. Question by question, assumption by assumption, I've been unfolding the underlying reasons holding women back in venture capital ever since. I started with a simple question: **how many women are making investment decisions in the United States?**

Back then, there was no data on that, and the media only listed one or two dozen women who were investment partners, but I couldn't believe that there were that few of us, so I decided to check for myself. My team and I scanned all the venture capital firms in the United States, and found all female investment partners, as well as executives, who held different titles, e.g. Principal or Vice

President, but had equity in partnerships, were sourcing deals, voting on investment committees, and taking board seats. We found almost 300 such women, and sorted them according to their investment focus, which brought us to ~250 women investing in tech (after excluding biopharma, life sciences, and other non-tech investment verticals).

We studied just over 1,000 US-based venture capital firms, and even a rough estimate showed that 250 women in that group of investment decision-makers, was too few for the industry at its stage. But they were there — startups could practically pitch one woman every weekday in the United States alone, which gave us a much better understanding of the scale.

So why had the media ignored the other two hundred female investors who had been out there for years? We women always tend to find things to do that are more important than self-promotion. Even if the media had wanted to feature more women in venture capital, it wouldn't have been easy to detect them. There was no public list of female investors out there, and we decided to create such on our website — www.women.vc — so that not only journalists, but also entrepreneurs could easily find them, sort them by investment focus, and reach out to them. We also tried to proactively connect female investors with different media outlets, and were even doing some publicity work for them ourselves. When we saw that the topic had reached a certain critical point and the media was eager to write about not-so-famous female investors on their own, we celebrated that our work as a middleman was done!

In the meantime, Michael Moritz, a legendary partner of equally as legendary VC firm, Sequoia Capital, said, "What we're not prepared to do, is to lower our standards," answering a question about the lack of women in the firm, and the fact that there were zero US female investment partners in Sequoia's 40-year history. Many women were irreparably offended by his statement, and he got a lot of heat in the media for saying that. Four years later, he's still quoted every once in a while. Even I couldn't avoid doing that, although I do have an excuse: his words became the inspiration for my next research.

My father had a PhD in physiology, and most of my other family members were or currently are psychiatrists. As a result, it's in my blood to never blindly trust a third party's diagnosis without my own examination, and I'm also an inherently analytical listener. Instead of rushing into judgment, I listened to Michael's interview to the end, in order to understand what he really meant.

Unlike Michael Moritz himself, who was a reporter for Time before joining Sequoia, many venture capitalists were traditionally coming into the industry after being entrepreneurs. There had been very few women in the tech arena, so it was definitely not the obvious path for sourcing more female investors, hence, it was hardly the same bar for them to get into venture capital at all. More likely, it should have been an entirely different kind of sport. I also learned that there was no hard data behind his words, so it made me curious as to **whether those ~250 female tech venture capitalists that we had found, make good investment decisions**. It might be an interesting issue to explore, so we decided to find out. I must admit that it was a little scary to do, because there was only a 50/50 chance that female VCs provided good returns to their limited partners.

We found more than 3,000 startups that these female VCs had invested in through the venture capital funds they represented (let's call them female VCs' portfolios). By 'invested', we meant that these women had either sourced these deals in the first place, and/or voted on investment committees and led them, and/or taken board seats. We calculated the return on investment (ROI) from those companies that had already exited, and the paper value of the companies that were still private. We included all the failed companies from this list in our calculations, and the losses incurred by the VC firms with which these female VCs were associated. The overall result showed that the return on investment on the female VCs' portfolios was on par or better than the average in the industry, which depended on the scenario that we used in our calculations.

One of the main difficulties of this research was that there's no accurate data when it comes to valuations, the investment amounts, and the exit numbers. While we used several databases to source this information, even there it might vary or not be available at all. That is why we cross-checked these numbers with the VC firms and startups in personal interviews, where possible. We had to calculate several scenarios, in order to benchmark and find the margin of error. So, if you trust the numbers that were available through different sources, you can confidently state that female VC portfolios perform better than the average in the industry. If you want to be conservative, then saying that it's on par with the average, is absolutely fair, if we take into consideration the highest margin of error we calculated. It took us a year to do this research, and the data we relied on was as good as it gets.

When we published the results of the study, I sent an abstract of it to Michael Moritz in a cold email, so that he could consider them when making his next hiring decision. I assumed that he wouldn't want to discuss the topic at all to avoid any further backlash on what he had said, and didn't expect any reply. Much to my surprise, he invited me to meet to discuss the study. We had a very professional conversation where he challenged its results due to another factor that's even less transparent than the financials of private companies — how the said women actually relate to the startups we included in our study. For example, people listed on boards of directors might not be connected to a deal at all in any other way, meaning that they might neither have discovered a particular company, nor made an investment in it. However, we had considered that, and it was another reason why we tried to cross-check all the information with the investors or entrepreneurs in the manual mode.

We also knew that even though some women *had* sourced particular companies and *made* the respective investment decisions, their male colleagues might have convinced them to not be listed as lead partners on the deals and to give up their board seats to more senior partners of their VC firms, who, unsurprisingly, would be men. In this case, the women would have gotten no public credit for these deals at all, and we couldn't have linked them to the companies in any other way, except through personal interviews. Moreover, these women would not have any official record of such work, which they could then present to limited partners, should they decide to raise their own VC funds in the future — in such cases, their performance as investors would effectively be stolen. This scenario is rarely spoken of, however, we knew of enough real cases where this had happened and took them into consideration too.

With all these limitations and manual digging for data, our findings were accepted by the professional media and limited partners. As a matter of fact, it became the foundation for the investment thesis of Plexo Capital, a spin-off from GV (Google Ventures), that invests in early-stage startups, as well as gender-diverse seed fund managers. The fund has raised capital from some of the most venerable names in technology, financial services, and family offices.

Once the issue with 'lowering the bar' was settled, I started asking myself another question: **what is the most common way for women to get into investment decision-making positions?** We turned to our database again and found out that more than a third of all US female investment partners were founders or co-founders of their own VC firms. Ironically, the path that was commonly regarded as being the hardest, turned out to be the most realistic. Corporate venturing was second in popularity among female investors — it was apparently a really female-friendly environment. Growing within one VC firm, or between several, to the investment partner level was the last of the top three ways to become a decision-maker in venture capital.

My next question was: **what can we do to help women start their own venture capital firms, since it's the most likely way to increase the number of female investors in the industry, based on our findings?** Everybody knew that the Kauffman Fellowship Program was the main dedicated source of education for venture capital investors. After I talked to the Kauffman team, their alumni, as well as those who couldn't afford it for one reason or another, it became clear that the Fellowship Program addresses a more sophisticated audience of current and aspiring investors. Many of its fellows already work for VC firms, which more often than not sponsor their education.

However, those aspiring investors who needed a more thorough academic approach, and who wanted to save the money that would otherwise be paid to the Program as a tuition fee for launching their own funds, had no place to go. First-time general partners with limited financial resources, younger staff — like analysts and associates — as well as people from other countries, who aren't able to travel to the United States for short-term courses, are a huge audience that weren't previously served by any comprehensive, convenient, and affordable educational program. A program that would teach them the nuts and bolts of venture capital, train them to do the daily job of a venture capital investor, and explain the current trends happening in the market, in real time. So we decided to create such a program and called it VC Academy, www.vc.academy.

With the help of a dozen venture capitalists and industry professionals — lawyers, accountants, and coaches — we created a blended course consisting of more than 300 lectures to cover the entire venture investing process — from finding a job in venture capital, to deal-sourcing and deal-making, portfolio management and exit strategies, to fund formation, fund management and fund liquidation, as well as developing a personal profile, coaching skills, and leadership qualities important for a venture capitalist. It was a first of its kind program, which we kept low-key for the whole of 2018, and the only channel we used for the beta run, internationally, was my timeline on LinkedIn.

In just one year, with basically no marketing, we served shy of 1,100 students from the following countries: Australia, Canada, Finland, France, Germany, Greece, India, Ireland, Israel, Italy, Lebanon, Russia, Singapore, Spain, Thailand, Ukraine, the United States, and the United Kingdom. The level of response was unbelievable! We haven't taken this for granted, however, and have been improving the program ever since the first student signed up. Flexibility, affordability, and convenience are the cornerstones of VC Academy. Although we decided to make it the cheapest among comparative educational programs and courses, we also provided female applicants with special scholarships. Aside from all the content improvements that we've done, and will be doing continuously, we were thinking about what other features would make sense. I asked myself again: **what can we do to help our students find jobs in venture capital?**

A niche recruiting platform became the next logical step. We all know that VC firms are looking for a set of very specific knowledge, skills, and backgrounds that are not obvious on the candidate profiles, nor are they listed on any of the existing recruiting platforms. For that reason, many capable candidates are disregarded at the very top of the hiring funnel and never make it to an interview. Whether it's LinkedIn or Indeed, the only way to find all the people with specific experience is to search with keywords, and to hope that the candidates mentioned those particular words in their resumes. For example, we cannot find all the applicants with consulting experience, or those who have already done early-stage deal-sourcing and investing — this could only be done by looking through each and every candidate's profile and sorting them manually. We decided to build a platform that would allow recruiters to search for candidates according to industry-specific requests — whether it's previous work experience in a startup or a corporation, or a personal investment portfolio, etc. We've been testing the platform in a private mode with several venture capital firms for the last couple of months. Please reach out to me if you'd like to become a beta-tester as well.

We didn't stop there, and also added an internship placement option for our students who scored highest with their practical assignments. We wanted to experiment with skill-based recruiting in venture capital — a new trend spreading across many industries, which is also appreciated by some of the VCs featured in this book, and often spoken about in private conversations. We've signed up almost 50 VC firms in different countries to provide our students with internships and welcome any other VCs willing to be truly progressive and implement new tools in their hiring practices.

A lot has been happening for my team behind the scenes, and although we haven't marketed anything broadly yet, it feels like we're not in beta mode anymore and actually running at full speed. Most recently, the impact of our efforts was appreciated by the Canadian investment community, and we were officially invited to permanently move our team to Canada.

All of this grew out of a simple website www.women.vc with a list of almost

300 female venture capitalists. We were psyched to see the growing number of women in investment positions from 2014 through 2018, and recognize some of the graduates of VC Academy among them. It's an amazing feeling to know that we contributed to that not just by talking, but by doing. However, we also know that women leave the industry, and it's too early to decamp. The media doesn't count those 'losses' when reporting the numbers. I'm not sure that any organization out there actually sees the real picture precisely, because so far, we've been the only team tracking venture capital firms of all sizes, with no exceptions, to make sure that we don't exclude anyone from our research. Let me explain why this is important.

No matter who and how we count women in venture capital, there are too few of them, and that's a fact. Conducting studies on the issue has become a popular publicity tool. However, before consuming any such data, I always recommend reviewing the sample used in the study before citing it. The numbers we see most often in the media, say that between 7 and 12% of all the investment partners (or sometimes just partners) in the United States, are women, depending on the study. Why would they differ almost twice as much? Firstly, some studies don't investigate whether a person with a partner title actually has equity in the partnership and makes investment decisions. This alone significantly skews the results. I'd say that the higher the reported percentage of female partners, the more likely this study analyzed the titles alone, and not the actual investment powers.

Secondly, the problem with most of the studies is that all of them (to my knowledge) limit the group of venture capital firms they survey by some parameter, whether it's the amount of capital under management, the funds' performance, membership of certain organizations, or anything else. The truth is that most of the diverse and female fund managers don't belong to any of these samples — they either manage too little money, or they don't yet have enough exits, or they don't do lobbying, due to the early stage of their journey. More often than not, they fall into the micro VC category, which is typically defined as sub-$50 million VC funds. However, they can go as low as $5 or even $3 million under management for proof-of-concept funds. There are more than 600 micro VCs in the United States alone, so you can imagine the distribution of capital among them and the number of those excluded from the studies. The last time I checked, the lowest threshold for a diversity research in the venture capital industry in the United States was at $25 million, meaning that all VC funds and their managers who raised less than that, were excluded from the sample. Why?

The emerging managers raise such small amounts, not only for proof-of-concept funds, but also because they simply can't raise more than that, due to the reluctance of limited partners to fund first-time managers. Raising a $5 million fund for a first-time manager is as difficult — or even more so — as raising a $100+ million fund, so I could never quite understand the logic behind the limitation of a sample by the amount of assets under management, other than that it would just be too much work. Since the inception of Women.VC, it was our goal to not exclude anyone based on the size of their funds, and yes — it *is* a lot of work.

When you look at funds of all sizes, you get many more partners to include in your calculations, and the more people you have, the lower the percentage of female investors among them. According to our data throughout funds of all sizes in the United States, only less than 5% of all the investment partners are women. It's remarkable that some of the investors I interviewed for the book and who hadn't seen our study before, intuitively felt that this was a more realistic percentage of female investors, despite the higher numbers reported by other studies.

The same concept of absolute inclusion was the foundation for this book. I didn't want to pick the women featured in it myself, so I asked entrepreneurs in my network to nominate their favorite women VCs. I also got some nominations from other investors — both male and female. My only job was to make sure that the final list of nominees included female investment decision-makers of all generations — the very first venture capitalists, seasoned and celebrated in the community, as well as lesser known general partners, and brand new names in the industry. I also wanted to show that there are a lot of female investors beyond the United States, so I reached out to the communities across the Pacific and Atlantic to cover as many countries as was practically possible. Obviously, I couldn't care less about the amount of assets under management — quite the opposite. I wanted to show more female general partners who are, or will be, fundraising, to introduce them to institutional investors and wealthy individuals who will read this book. So please, do the international venture capital industry a favor and send this book to some of your limited partners who'd be interested in backing more female investors. **Thank you!**

The time I allocated for developing the concept for this book and surveying my network was well spent: I found that X factor that united more than a hundred people around it. It was of paramount importance to me to involve male VCs in this project as well, so I'm very grateful to three dedicated women's advocates who contributed a foreword to the book — Brad Feld, Pitch Johnson, and Scott Sandell. Out of the 118 nominated women VCs, I managed to reach out and interview 99 of them, as well as Beezer Clarkson, who represented the limited partner side through Sapphire Ventures, and Shelly Porges, who consolidates capital allocated for female founders as pledges to the Billion Dollar Fund for Women. All of them got a dedicated chapter in the book in alphabetical order. There's no rule for the length of the chapters — the amount of material I ended up with for each depended merely on how long we talked on this or that topic with each nominee. All of them were asked an almost identical set of questions, unless I already knew the answers to some from other sources. My main goal was to have an intimate talk, to hear candid opinions, and to get raw confessions, and I'm thankful to everyone who trusted me with those. Call after call, meeting after meeting, it was a very humbling experience, which has definitely become a milestone in that part of my venture capital career that I've dedicated to advancing women in the industry. It feels as good as the exits I had!

I recorded more than 3,000 minutes of interviews, with the average interview lasting 27 minutes. I spent two whole months writing more than 150,000 words, which were effectively trimmed to fit 300 pages, and yet, we ended up with more than that. All of this doesn't include at least half of the time that each of my team members spent helping me bring this book to life. Yet, the book Women Who Venture, wouldn't have happened if not for the 101 extraordinary women who found time to chat with me! Who made it part of their personal and professional missions to tell me their stories, to give advice to the readers on how to get into venture capital, what to learn at each stage of their careers, and how to navigate the industry with all its good, bad, and ugly. Each chapter is filled with valuable advice, but I didn't want to influence the reader's perception by my own choices, so I decided not to point to any of it, except for, maybe, in the table of contents.

I fell in love with this book very early on because once all the chapters were in the making, I realized how powerful it would be.

Firstly, we now have a collection of 101 role models to learn from — this number is far lower than the actual number of brilliant female VCs out there, but much higher than anything that the media has ever delivered in a single publication. I know that aspiring female investors will no longer experience a lack of role models to follow, and I hope that each of the featured women will become a mentor to a young investment professional — a female or person of color, or LGBTQ person.

Women Who Venture is also a great networking tool for women VCs themselves because I discovered that many of them don't know each other. I learned who has had similar experiences, or have the same views, who could become best friends, and who would benefit from co-investing. I've introduced some of them to each other, and hope the book will make more introductions!

I also wish to draw the attention of institutional investors, endowments, family offices, high-net-worth individuals, and other potential limited partners, to the variety of female general partners and their investment strategies. If you're eager to diversify your portfolio, listen to their voices, and learn from them about how you can get better returns.

This book is an invaluable source for entrepreneurs who want to develop a personal connection with their potential investors, to learn their investing principles, and to see for themselves whether having more female venture capitalists will bring more funding to female entrepreneurs.

Finally, all diversity advocates, as well as those people who are starting to recognise the power of diversity (because I don't believe that anyone would prefer to stay away from making better returns), can learn a thing or two about what we, as a professional community, are failing to achieve, how we can advance the venture capital industry, and where we should look for unconventional solutions to do so.

I have much more to say, but it's time for me to introduce you to Women Who Venture!

Renata George
Author

Jenny Abramson

Founding Partner, Rethink Impact, United States

If you think that venture capital firms first started focusing on investing in women a few years ago, you would be wrong. The first significant female-centric VC firm was created back in 1997 by Patty Abramson, Jenny's mother. She had worked a lot with female-owned businesses in various capacities and found that there was a big gap in their ability to access funding. So she started Women's Growth Capital — a fund that invested in female leaders. After raising sizeable capital from individual and institutional investors, they also got Small Business Administration (SBA) as a Limited Partner that matched the capital they had raised 2:1. "I was in college when I saw my Mom on a magazine cover. It was a picture of her with a cigar superimposed in her hand and the title 'Welcome to the Club,'" Jenny recalled. "I remember being surprised that they saw a female in venture capital as such a big deal." When the partners realized the effect of the dot-com implosion, they knew they might need to wait several years before the economy recovered, so that they could keep investing. They decided to return some of the remaining capital to investors and focus on their also successful angel fund called WomenAngels.net. "My Mom has always been a firm believer that if you see a problem, it's your responsibility to solve it. That's clearly what she was trying to achieve with her fund," Jenny added.

When I was doing my research on this story, I found a Washington Post article from 1998, stating the following: 'Studies show that less than 2% of venture capital each year goes to female-owned businesses'. Its author also offered the following explanations for this fact: 'Women typically don't have the necessary contacts at traditional venture capital firms, whose employees are overwhelmingly male; they, historically, have run retail and service businesses, which often aren't high-growth enough to attract investors; and the high-tech companies that make venture capitalists salivate, are rarely run by women, who still go into science and engineering in lower numbers than men.' The article also quoted an expert, who said, 'This is not a feminist thing or a cause thing, this is an investment niche that meets multiple causes.' It is very ironic that we still use all of these same arguments and numbers more than 20 years later.

Jenny Abramson, however, wasn't planning on following her mother's mission until she emerged in the startup world herself. After earning her Harvard MBA, she spent eight years as an executive at the Washington Post Co. She then became the CEO of a security tech startup called LiveSafe, which was helping to prevent school shootings and sexual assaults on college campuses by using mobile technology. "It wasn't until I became a CEO that I noticed how few of my peers were also women. As any good Stanford data nerd would, I decided to turn to numbers for the answer," she said. "I found that despite recent studies showing that female-led and diverse companies outperform their all-male counterparts and the fact that nearly 40% of tech businesses are started by women, female-led companies were still only getting a tiny amount of venture capital dollars in 2015.

"When you see study after study showing the outperformance of gender diverse teams, you start to realize that investing in women isn't just good for the world — it's also good business. Our industry has been in the headlines for all the wrong reasons lately. We have the opportunity to level the playing field in a way no one else is really doing now."

With this in mind, Abramson and her partners began to raise a female-led VC firm dedicated to investing in women — mainly in Series A and B rounds. Jenny chose this strategy due to another finding of hers: the amount of seed and angel money available to women was growing, however, once female entrepreneurs got to a later stage, it became harder and harder for them to raise capital. Abramson and her partner Heidi Patel believe that their team will create a stronger impact by playing at these stages.

"Our belief is that the biggest opportunities out there are created by diverse teams — not only in terms of gender, but also ethnicity, and background, etc. We are convinced that diversity in leadership at any company creates a positive impact on business in general, and, if anything, this approach opens new opportunities for us. The more diversity you have, the better!

"I was speaking at the United Nations about gender lens investing, and my Mom said, after listening to it, 'So much of what you're sharing, shockingly, hasn't changed in the past 20 years! And yet, there is something so promising about what you are building that became possible with the technology changes.'"

We all know that venture investing relies on pattern recognition a lot, which is a way for investors to de-risk things. But there are very few venture capitalists who are actually conscious about the fact that diverse teams provide more patterns to work with, which is ultimately beneficial for VC firms as a business. In that regard, Jenny Abramson is indeed rethinking diversity, but she is also a dedicated impact investor who knows first-hand from her work experience, that one doesn't always have to trade off between profits and a social or environmental impact. "What's really exciting is that impact investing and sustainable investing have become some of the fastest growing trends," she declared. "I see more and more investors who now see social impact not just as philanthropy, but as one of the key criteria for investment. Katharine Graham, The Washington Post's famous CEO, said it best: '[You have to] do well in order to do good.'

Smita Aggarwal

Director, Omidyar Network, India

Every time I look through the team section of the website for Omidyar Network, I am blown away by the number of women on the investment team. "I think that Omidyar Network has succeeded in creating an open and safe space for every employee, in which they can thrive and grow, based on their own merits. This approach is reflected in the kind of people that the company is able to attract, retain, and grow," Smita Aggarwal explained this phenomenon.

Throughout her career, she has worked in the financial services sector in India. Whether it was banking or corporate finance, Smita did the whole gamut of things, including the treasury routine, and consumer banking. About 15 years ago, when the financial inclusion trend took over many countries — and India in particular, where economic exclusion was quite rampant — Smita was one of the first market guards who worked to make sure that banking was available to all.

Aggarwal worked for the largest private bank in India for many years, before she set up a rural financial services business. She then spent a few years as part of a think tank of the Reserve Bank of India, the country's central bank, where she saw a completely different perspective in terms of how policy-making and regulation happen in the country, and what the impact of all of that was on the end consumers.

"By that point, while I wanted to stay in the sector where my competencies were, I also wanted to do something different. Omidyar Network offered me the perfect opportunity to use my experience and expertise in financial services and financial inclusion, to back innovative and bold entrepreneurs who have a vision for building new business models that can serve consumers better and create social impact," Aggarwal outlined.

Women in banking and financial services is a common thing in India, however, Smita doesn't observe many people transitioning into private equity and venture capital from these sectors. "I think venture capital requires a set of skills that doesn't come from just one occupation, whether it's investment banking or operations. For those who have worked with mature companies, risky investing — especially in early-stage companies — is a whole different world. While growth-stage companies have a lot of history you can actually go by, early-stage investors like us, are betting on the potential of what a company could become. One has to be able to actually build that vision based on tiny pieces of data, and very often there aren't many of them. Early-stage investors take a lot of leaps of faith when there is not enough evidence, and not many people are comfortable with this.

"If you are an operator or entrepreneur, there is another barrier in venture investing that you need to overcome: you have to hold yourself back and not tell a founder, 'I'll show you how to do this', let alone do it yourself. That's the first big thing that you have to be very conscious about when you are an investor, because it's the entrepreneur's vision, it's the entrepreneur's business, and it's the founders who are running and managing it with all their wins and failures — not you. Bringing in operating experience is tremendously helpful and useful for founders — because you've actually worked in the trenches — but it takes a lot of effort to switch over to the role of an investor, and you have to be very clear in your mind that you're not running your portfolio companies."

I can totally relate to what Smita was saying, because this part was the hardest for me personally when I was switching from being an entrepreneur to an investor. I know people who decided to not continue their VC careers because of being unable to make this switch, and it's a good thing — some roles aren't for us. We will talk more about this in the book. When I coach aspiring VCs, I always start with assignments and experiments that will help them understand whether venture investing is for them in the first place.

At Omidyar Network, Smita invests in startups in the financial services sector, and 50% of her portfolio companies have at least one female founder. This ratio, in the fintech field, is very impressive compared to the US statistics, so I asked Smita what her secret sauce was.

"We invest based on merits — not on gender or any other personal characteristics, so at the investment committee level, we don't do anything specific. However, I personally feel a natural connection between myself and female founders — not only due to our gender, but also because I have a lot of operating experience and, in a way, I am more empathetic to the realities of what they would be going through. I think I am very proactive, and often come up with different suggestions and solutions when they're stuck, which may be that bridge to establishing better connections with female entrepreneurs.

"I do observe, however, that in India, women in general, think very differently from men. Female founders relate better to female VCs than to male VCs, but I cannot say that the latter do anything specifically wrong to create this situation. We aren't discussing the gender disparity in the startup and VC worlds on a greater scale in the country yet, so I don't think that many Indian VCs are doing anything explicitly to bring more women into the industry today," Smita concluded. It may happen that doing nothing is what keeps women away from venture capital in India and the world.

Marie-Helene Ametsreiter

Partner, Speedinvest, Germany

When I was developing the concept of this book, I wanted to include women from as many different countries, cultures, and ethnicities as I would be able to reach, in order to provide different perspectives on the issues we care about. Marie-Helene Ametsreiter gave her sound opinion on gender equality that definitely deserves your attention.

"I don't believe in total equality of the genders, because we don't start in the same place and we have different needs, which is for the better. I think each gender has some strengths and weaknesses, and that is exactly what creates diversity in the first place. So, I prefer focusing on leveraging the strengths of both genders, to level the playing field, which creates equity for everyone's success," she said.

Before joining Speedinvest, Marie-Helene worked in the telecommunications industry for almost two decades. "At some point, I realized that there wasn't much I could do for the company, as it all boiled down to the pricing game in the industry," she recalled. When her first daughter was born, she decided that it was time for her to do something that would impact society at large. After testing herself in a couple of different capacities, and consulting young companies along the way, she then got invited to join Speedinvest to build an early-stage venture capital fund in Austria. "I had no idea what venture capital was, but when I familiarized myself with the concept, I realized that it was the innovation engine of the future, which was much needed in Europe at that time. I learned about American companies that were considered innovative leaders, and wanted to become a part of that movement in Europe."

We then talked about European startups and the venture capital market, and Ametsreiter shared some concerns. "The European venture capital industry has grown significantly in the last several years. We are well-equipped with capital from pre-seed through Series A, and even Series B stages, but later than that, when tech companies start generating real value, they have to turn to foreign investors for expansion and growth capital.

"Europe still lacks later-stage investors due to the regulatory restrictions. For example, big European pension funds, which are one of the main sources of institutional capital in the United States, are not yet allowed to invest in venture capital here. I think that everyone is aware now that we lost a couple of really good, successful companies like Spotify, which were significantly financed in the US at their later stages, meaning that European investors didn't benefit much from its IPO due to dilution. The community and regulators are trying to change the framework for venture capital in Europe, but it's happening very slowly.

"On the other hand, I am very proud of our educational system and tech talent. Traditional industries that have a long heritage — like the automotive, manufacturing and production industries — generate a lot of talented people who are respected worldwide. That is also recognized by the US investors who are very active in Europe due to the great quality of talent available, with much lower valuations than in the US market."

When we started discussing gender equity in Europe, Ametsreiter highlighted that we cannot generalize. "I feel like in Germany, gender discrimination is much stronger than in Eastern Europe. Having worked in Croatia for many years, I saw that women in leadership are much more accepted there. Many women in Germany don't work, and stay at home for two years when they have children. It's very hard to get back on a career track after that.

"Governments and corporations are talking a lot about bringing more women into executive roles, but in reality, very little progress has been made. Until we collect a critical mass to make the necessary changes at the state and industry level, the best we can do is to change women's attitudes. Let me explain how.

"The very first thing that we should do immediately, is to help women stop thinking that they are not good enough. It makes me very upset when I see how many women underrate their expertise and the value they can bring to the table.

"Secondly, there is this social phenomenon that many women feel guilty if they go to work right after giving birth, or don't spend enough time with them later on. Our society is still very traditional, and 'mompreneurs' cannot avoid judgment when they rarely attend teacher/parent conferences or send nannies to pick up their kids. Being a 'mompreneur' is a daily struggle and it is exhausting — that's a fact and everything else is simply a lie. But the tip is to be proud and convinced to work, and to not feel guilty. We have to be role models for our kids.

"I have two daughters and I want them to learn from my example that having both parents working is the most natural thing, so they don't feel guilty when they grow up. In order to change society as a whole, we need to educate the next generation of women that both partners have the right to work or socialize, and both have an obligation to play their part in raising kids.

"I know in myself, that I'm not a happy person if I do not work. I love my work and I need it because it gives me energy, positive vibes, and ultimately, allows me to be a good mother. I know that this may sound very contrarian, but it's true. I tried to work part-time, so that I could spend more time with my children, but I realized that it didn't make me happy. More often than not, when we compromise between our job and family, we get second-tier jobs with little room to grow. That is not what I wanted," Marie-Helene passionately inferred.

Janet Bannister

General Partner, Real Ventures, Canada

People who know Janet Bannister, say that she's a ball of fire, and I could even feel her bottomless energy here in San Francisco, while talking to her over the phone when she was driving home in Toronto, Canada. "Venture capital is a very demanding job. You have to have lots of energy if you want to bring your best self to work every day," she elucidated.

An athlete from her early childhood, Janet still wakes up every day before five o'clock and exercises for an hour or more. She is a General Partner at one of the most active early-stage VC firms in Canada, but is also a dedicated Mom to her 13-year-old son. When I asked how she achieved that mythological work/life balance, she replied, "I prioritize and I am 100% focused on whatever I am doing at that moment: if I am at work, I am all in; if I am at home with my family, I don't think about work. I deeply love both parts of my life and I am at my best when I have energy and focus for each. You need to stay fully engaged in whatever you're doing, in order to do it well and do it efficiently. For that, you need to have physical stamina so that you can stay focused and energized throughout the day.

"One of the most formative things in my life that made me the person I am today, is that I ran long-distance competitively from a young age and was on the national triathlon team later in life. It taught me determination, goal setting, persistence, discipline, and mental strength. My experiences in sport strongly affected my personality and approach to work. I know that I need to work very hard to achieve my goals. I understand that, as in sport, we all go through ups and downs. Not every day is going to be great — we'll have injuries and setbacks, but it is all just a part of life and we'll get up and try again," Janet spelled it out.

Bannister started her entrepreneurial journey quite early — at age 15, she launched her own healthy baking business. She wrote a business plan for a

muffin operation, with the help of her father; costed out ingredients, researched flavours, learned how to prepare financial statements, and built a special muffin carrier for her bicycle. That summer she convinced 15 shops near her home to stock her muffins. She would wake up at 1 am to bake 25-30 dozen muffins and leave the kitchen spotless by 7 am. Later that summer, she worried that she wouldn't reach her $2,000 profit goal for the season, so she started making lemon cakes too, and exceeded her goal by 20%.

Her professional career started in operations and consulting at Procter & Gamble and McKinsey in Canada. Then, she decided that she wanted to work at a fast-growing tech company in California, United States. Despite having no prior tech experience and no US work visa, she went on a quest to find a way to make it happen.

Janet compiled a list of top venture capital firms in Silicon Valley and read the bios of all their partners, to find someone who had a similar experience to hers and could relate. She was planning to reach out to them and find some company in their portfolio that she could join. Among other attempts, she was very persistent in reaching out to Bob Kagel of Benchmark, a packaged goods and consulting veteran, by sending multiple emails and leaving voice messages on his cellphone. He never replied, but his assistant called Janet and said that Bob had received all of her messages, but had nothing to offer at the moment.

Bannister continued chatting with her, describing her background and experience, and Bob's assistant promised to arrange a meeting with him when Janet would come to the Bay Area in the future. Not surprisingly, it didn't take long for Janet to come up with a reason for the trip to San Francisco, and she informed Kagel's assistant that she would be arriving next week.

She got to meet Kagel, who was quite a legend in Silicon Valley. "I was well prepared for the meeting and we had a great conversation. He told me that I hadn't experienced enough failure in my life, because people learn a lot more from their failures than their successes," she remembered.

At the end of the meeting, he suggested that Janet meet with eBay to explore their opportunities, and the next thing she knew, she got invited to move to California to work for eBay on transforming them from a collectibles marketplace to a mainstream marketplace.

"I'm a big believer in the notion that people control their own destinies and make their own opportunities. I always advise people to be deliberate about what they want and motivate them to find courage to set ambitious goals and determination to see them through. Tenacity and grit go a long way."

eBay wasn't the only example of Janet creating opportunities for herself. Among other instances where she did the same, is her creation of Kijiji.ca, a classifieds site that grew to become one of the most visited websites in Canada and deserves a special attention.

After four years in Silicon Valley, she decided to move back to Canada, and was transferred to the local office of eBay. The new role wasn't exciting for her, but she took it on anyway, because she knew that she'd find a new one along the way. When she started benchmarking the e-commerce market in Canada, she soon figured out that although eBay in Canada had plenty of visitors, they were very reluctant to convert into buyers. Rather than trying to adapt Canadians to eBay, she suggested that eBay should adapt to the local preferences of making purchases offline. She came up with the idea of building an online classifieds site, similar to Craigslist.org, which was dominating the US market and had launched in Canada. Nobody at eBay's head-office believed that a new classifieds site would be successful in the country. Bannister was persistent, as always, and eventually launched Kijiji.ca, which became a great success.

"I have learned to be ambitious and to dream big. Being audacious is critically important for any entrepreneur. Always follow your passions, because when you work on what you care about, you will be happy and find maximum success. I also learned to have high standards and to treat people well — not only because it is ethically important, but also because the world is small and life is long, and you will never rise above your reputation," Janet added a coda to this story.

When Kijiji.ca became strong enough to sail without Bannister, she left eBay to take a break from her career and spend time with her family. "I really loved my work, but my son was a priority at that moment. Too often we idealize the sacrifice of one's personal life in pursuit of financial gain, but the truth is that your job does not define you, it is simply something you do. We are more than the prestige of our titles or the salaries that come with them. I believe that we should make the biggest decisions in life with our hearts, not our heads," she added, something you don't hear too often from venture capitalists. Maybe that is because she never planned on becoming one.

At that point in her career, she had that mythical mix of experience that VC firms are typically looking for: she had been in consulting, worked for a tech company, and had even been a successful entrepreneur herself. However, venture capital was never on her radar.

"I had this image in my mind of venture capital being a very unfriendly, male-dominated industry, where cutthroat and ruthless people give entrepreneurs a hard time," she laughed. "Then a friend of mine introduced me to Real Ventures — a VC firm that was looking to hire a partner in Toronto with a background like mine. One conversation led to another, and I quickly realized that I had been wrong about most investors! I realized that their job is to actually *help* entrepreneurs become successful. Instead of being taboo, venture capital seemed like a perfect match for me, because I was at a point in my life where I wanted to help other people succeed.

"I love the entrepreneurial spirit and the speed at which they move along their business journeys. I like the fact that entrepreneurs put everything on the line and work hard every day in order to build their businesses. I like that they are driven by desire to see their dreams come true. It has been five years since I joined Real Ventures, and I have never been happier in my career than I am now! I feel extremely privileged to be able to meet entrepreneurs who are doing innovative things every day, to work with our portfolio companies and help them achieve their full potential. Not only is it rewarding, but it is also fascinating from an intellectual standpoint — I keep learning and growing every day," she threw another ball of energy into our conversation.

I couldn't help but ask Janet whether men in venture capital gave her a hard time, and she said, "Truth be told, I have never felt intimidated by men — even as a child. When I was just starting my running career, I saw how girls were pushed to the sidelines by better performing boys. But the only thought I had back then was, 'I'm going to keep up with those guys. There's no way they're dropping me! I'll give these guys a run for their money!'" Janet laughed. "I also grew up with two older brothers and I was always trying to keep up with them and do whatever they were doing. So, from a young age, I've never thought too much about gender dynamics. When I walk into a room full of men as the only woman, it doesn't even register in my mind.

"I think, among other things that helped me to develop this attitude, was my love for reading biographies. I saw women and men achieving great results in life, business and politics, and I thought that I could do that too. That's why I think that what you are doing, Renata, by writing this book about a hundred of successful women-investors, is so terrific! It is much needed today, to show current and aspiring investors what is possible. Your book will tell the stories of venture capitalists who have very different sets of experiences and approaches — stories about how they shaped their careers and achieved their success. Page after page, this book will give confidence to other women who want to work in venture capital. By the time they finish reading the book, I hope that they get the feeling of: 'If they could do it, I can do it too!'

"To bring more women into startups and venture capital, we need to create a self-reinforcing network — a 'snowball effect' — whereby the more female role models we have, the more women will get the desire and confidence to join the group," Janet rounded off.

Amy Banse

Managing Director,
Comcast Ventures, United States

When I learned that Amy Banse loves to play bridge, I knew that we would have a lot to talk about. We, indeed, ran out of time when we first talked and had to schedule the continuation of our conversation, for which I am most grateful.

They say it's healthy to change jobs every four years to advance your career. Amy has stayed with Comcast Corporation for almost 30 years — the longest of all the careers I've seen while interviewing for this book. What fascinated me was the fact that she made bold transitions within the company while staying interested, passionate, and never bored. I wanted to know how Banse made her moves, continually adding value to the company in new roles.

"I joined Comcast in 1991, when it was a smaller company growing very fast. There was plenty to do and various holes to fill. I am a firm believer in doing what you are hired to do extremely well, while always being on the lookout for additional opportunities to learn, to build, and to lead. Find those stretch projects. Raise your hand for challenging initiatives. Surround yourself with great teammates and mentors. That's what I did. And that's what helped me grow throughout my career. That's what has made my long journey ever-changing and exciting."

Her favorite advice to young professionals is: "Find a growing company in a dynamic industry with a small but excellent management team and get in any way you can."

Amy Banse started as a lawyer, transitioned to corporate development, and now, she helms the corporate venture fund Comcast Ventures. Her career gained momentum quickly in the 90s, as the internet, broadband, and cable business started growing.

She focused on content programming, eventually becoming Senior Vice President of Programming Investments from 1996 to 2004. She oversaw the development of Comcast's cable network portfolio, leading investments in E!, The Golf Channel and the company's regional sports networks. She also launched Sprout, which is now Universal Kids.

In 2004, Amy was tapped to head up Comcast Corporation's digital strategy. As founder and president of the company's digital media division Comcast Interactive Media, she drove the acquisition of a number of digital properties, including Fandango, a movie ticketing company. Her team was also responsible for overseeing the development of Xfinity TV. Through it all, Amy continued to look for those opportunities to learn more and do more to drive innovation within the company.

Perhaps the most courageous jump she made was moving her family across the country to head up Comcast Ventures in 2011, which has grown to become one of the country's most active corporate venture arms. The team invests in early- and later-stage companies across a wide spectrum of categories and industries, complementing the cash with the opportunity to leverage the full breadth of the company's platform including Comcast, NBC Universal, and Sky.

One of her colleagues likened Banse to an air traffic controller. She sees and manages all of the moving parts while keeping an eye on the horizon. In her role, she manages an investing team and day-to-day operations of the firm, which has four offices in San Francisco, Los Angeles, Philadelphia, and New York. Comcast Ventures has grown the size and diversity of its portfolio to include startups focused on commerce, digital media, cybersecurity, SaaS, enterprise, autonomous vehicles, frontier technologies, and more.

Banse has to stay informed, ahead of trends, and adopt new methods of competing for deals in this new, more crowded venture landscape. She doesn't get rattled. I believe this is, in part, due to her unique background as an investor with a law degree. "Lawyers are trained to lay the facts out a linear manner, and then evolve a strategy and construct a story that fits the facts. It's that skill of thinking in systems that helps me in venture investing," she attested to the importance of system thinking.

"It's also important to remain grounded in real relationships and interactions. We live in a world of screens today where we're constantly looking down at our devices and communicating digitally. I fear we have lost the art of rapport with the people we work with, negotiate against, and invest in."

I recognized a bridge player in her when Amy said that. Indeed, this card game is based on bidding, which depends on how well you communicate with your game partner at the table without disclosing too much information to your opponents. You should really be in tune with your partner to understand how strong the cards that you both have are. It's that type of communication when there is more information between the lines than in actual words that are articulated, so you learn not just to listen, but to hear. And that's a very important skill in any part of our lives — whether we negotiate with a business partner or discuss home errands with a life partner. It's that rapport and trust that Amy Banse finds important. "I think we need to spend more time and more focus on connecting with each other and establishing the trust that's critical to a successful relationship," Amy continued. "Investors and an entrepreneurs engage in a long relationship. It's not just about investing capital. We are investing in an idea, a dream, and a vision. It's a huge responsibility and significant endeavor that works best when founded on trust."

Stacey Bishop

Partner, Scale Venture Partners, United States

You won't find much about Stacey Bishop on the internet, but her story is one of the most educational for aspiring venture capital investors. "We have a pretty hard-working, humble culture at Scale Venture Partners. That is probably why you couldn't find as much on our firm as what we have to tell, or maybe we are not as bold as we could be, given our performance," she smiled humbly.

Although her personal investment performance was also pretty impressive, it took her nearly 10 years to grow from an associate to a partner position within one VC firm, so I had a lot of questions to ask about her career.

"Partner roles open up very slowly. Venture capital is not a large industry — its partnership dynamics are very conservative. For a younger team member to become a partner at a VC firm, there should be a seat at the table," she started. "Bringing a new partner into a partnership is always a big change, including the share distribution. Typically, new partners are welcome when the fund is growing, and the existing partners can voluntarily give away a portion of their shares to a new partner, without losing the overall monetary value. Alternatively, when a partner leaves the firm, their seat becomes available for a new investor. So, even if a junior team member is ready, but there is no room for another partner, little can be done at that point," Stacey explained.

"Scale Venture Partners were doing reasonably well during my first ten years there, but in those intervening years, there were two downturns — in 2001, and then in 2008. Today, we have been experiencing basically a bull market for almost a decade, and that's why we see so many new VC firms in

the market. People are moving up to partners quickly, and principals and even associates are getting checkbooks sooner — it's a good time to be in the venture capital industry.

"But at that point, we were happy that we had jobs at all, because there were lots of people who didn't make it. I knew that I needed to wait for my turn to get the opportunity of becoming a partner, so I wasn't wasting my time. It was clear to me that I had to prove to the partners that I was a good investor, and I was looking for great investments to get a checkbook for myself.

"I started doing due diligence on the companies I found, as if I would be leading the deals and getting them to the finish line. I was working with founders closely and even got a note from one of them that said, 'You've been so helpful to my company, you know so much about our market — I want you to join our board'. It really helped me to establish myself among partners, because entrepreneurs were asking me to lead their deals.

"I glommed onto the digital marketing trend as my investment theme, and started working with entrepreneurs that then ended up being great successes. I had an almost $2 billion exit with a company called Omniture, which was sold to Adobe, with a really great return for Scale VP. Another digital marketing company called ExactTarget also ended up with a $2.6 billion exit. Then, I led my first investment in a social media management company that we exited fairly quickly (in just 15 months, which isn't typical) with a good return from the $320 million exit. It kept happening to me thereafter, and we ended up with five exits across the digital marketing team," Bishop chronicled.

In an analytical manner, Stacey addressed the downside of staying with one VC firm for long too. "I can see how growing within one firm from the entry level can be a challenge. You join as a 20-something-year-old associate and it's pretty difficult to make the partners see you in a different way — as an investor who has matured over the years. So it may take a little longer to prove to them that you have risen to the partner level within your 5-10 or whatever years at the firm. For VC firms, it's typically much more natural to hire someone from outside, who has a little more experience or comes from a position of authority, which would definitely look unfair to you.

"It takes a long time to see results in venture capital, and if you are not an investment partner, how can you evaluate yourself as an investment professional at all? The best thing one can do in this situation, is to track one's work in great detail: write down everything you think about a company that you are doing due diligence on — what opportunity it presents, what risks it bears, and if you would invest in the company or not and why, etc. And then over time, you watch what happens to those companies and go back to your notes to calibrate your judgment: which of your assumptions were right and which were wrong, and why. Try to reflect back on what might have affected your thinking, what you might have missed or what created your concerns.

"It may take three, five, even seven years to see whether you were right or wrong about a company. But sometimes it takes just 6-12 months to get a sense of whether it is going to take off or not."

Stacey's career trajectory to venture capital was pretty straightforward. She spent very little time at a startup and Morgan Stanley before joining Bank of America's Corporate Development Group to do M&A transactions. "Back then, there were a lot of big banks that had venture capital arms, and so did Bank of America. They had a $5 billion venture capital fund, of which we allocated a small piece for our buyout group. After the restructuring, I joined their venture capital group as an associate on a two-year contract. I was thinking that I would do that for a couple of years, and then I would figure out what to do next. Two years turned into three years, four years, five years... And then, somewhere along the line, I was promoted to a Principal. I wasn't sure how long I was going to stick with it, but I always had this mindset that I would work for any company, for as long as I enjoyed what I was doing. So I stayed. And here I still am!"

In 2006, the group spun out of Bank of America as Scale Venture Partners, and became an entirely independent entity. The firm raised outside capital for the new fund, unlike the previous funds that had been funded entirely by the Bank.

I asked Stacey if she had ever thought about starting her own VC firm. "Oh no, because I'm super happy at Scale VP! We've got a really good dynamic. I invest in what I love and know best, and I don't feel that I need a change. I think in most of the cases, people spin off to go on their own for two reasons. They either want to invest in something outside of the firm's investment focus or more narrow than it is, or they are just unhappy with where they are — they may not have enough autonomy or ability to affect change."

And then our discussion took an unexpected turn. "I don't think that being a general partner of your own VC firm should be the ultimate goal," Bishop contemplated. "Raising your own fund entails a lot of work, because you have to set all the infrastructure, raise the capital, and you also have to operate the firm as a business founder. You basically steal the time from your main investing job for fundraising and operations. That is why many investors prefer joining an established platform — a brand that helps you get access to the best deal flow, a well-oiled machine that is already operating and functioning smoothly. All you have to do is entirely focus on investing.

"I just recently heard from an investor, who was very qualified to raise his own fund, but he chose to join an established firm. His rationale was, 'I just want to invest. At this firm, I can start writing checks the moment I join'. Whereas if he decided to set up his own firm, it might take him a couple of years to write that first check."

We also talked about people leaving the venture capital industry. "I've seen people who try working in venture capital and then decide that it is not for them. They really wanted to do it, but for whatever reason, they were not super successful at it. I've seen entrepreneurs and operating executives who kind of dabbled in it, but then realized that it was not a good fit.

"We had an executive-in-residence who tried to work with us for about five months, but then said, 'Nope, it's not for me. I want to be an operator, I want to be in the middle of the action, to work with companies daily, to be at executive meetings, to drive the change. I don't want to be the outsider that VCs are — I just don't like this.' So he found that sometimes venture capital can be very lonely, that most of the time you are an observer, and it wasn't right for him.

"Some VC firms operate in small, pretty close-knit teams, but in some partnerships, each partner is kind of a one-man band. You can have weekly partnership meetings, but you work alone the rest of the time. You can have influence at the board level, but you're not actually operating your portfolio company, and your advice can go unnoticed. That feeling alone that you cannot really effect any sort of change, can be pretty depressing. So venture capital job is not for everyone, and you should really understand the culture and structure of a VC firm before joining it, so that you don't get disappointed later."

Speaking about women in venture capital, Stacey said, "I was lucky to have women in executive positions on the team from the day I joined. Scale VP has always been open to women on any level — from associate to partner, and over the years, the culture hasn't really changed significantly.

"Although I don't have any personal stories to tell, I think there has always been a lack of diversity in venture capital, and there has been discrimination by gender. Back then, we knew what was happening around us, but we put our heads down and focused on our work, in order to get to somewhere by doing our jobs and working hard to try to get ahead. I hate to say this, but our generation just sucked it up. The younger generation is more vocal about it, and there are definitely many more discussions about diversity and women in venture capital, in particular, so this is a great momentum to band together and call out everything that we think is wrong with the industry."

Andrea Böhmert

Co-Managing Partner, Knife Capital, South Africa

I named this chapter 'Venturing in the dark' for a reason: when I called Andrea Böhmert in South Africa, she had candles lit because the national utility service company had implemented load shedding, only supplying power during certain hours due to operational difficulties.

"South Africa is a fascinating place, because it is a first world and third world country at the same time. It has absolutely all the components of an emerging market, but I can honestly say that there are also some areas where South Africa is more advanced than the United States or Europe. It's a very nice feeling to be solving third world problems by investing in first-rate technologies, and having a deep understanding of both. Our technology gets underestimated because 'they are from Africa', but they compete globally against the best and come out on top. To be honest, my biggest competition as an investor is not local — it's international venture capital that is coming into the market to fill the financing gap, because foreign investors see great opportunities and strong technologies in South Africa at lower valuations. Many of them have realised that not only can they provide good returns, but they can also make a difference to society here. This first world/third world emerging market contrast can offer many benefits, but it does come with challenges, like for example having no electricity," Andrea laughed.

Böhmert grew up in a small town in Germany and got the equivalent of a master's degree in economics with a focus on marketing and technology innovation. At the end of her studies, she decided to go and get some real international business experience and accepted an internship in South Africa.

"While I was working in Cape Town, my boyfriend got a job offer here during one of his visits, and we decided to stay in Africa for a year or so longer. We were young and wanted to experience something different from the life we were used to."

After her internship, Böhmert got a job at the local branch of Siemens as an assistant in their strategic planning department. "When a big multinational company invites you to work for them, you don't say no. I thought that I would accept their offer and then ask them to transfer me back to Germany in a couple of years."

But Andrea's plans definitely made God laugh. After seven months of working at Siemens, her boss took on a new role and the person who was supposed to replace him, declined the job offer. The company's next choice was Böhmert, who became the head of strategic planning for Siemens Southern Africa after being an assistant for less than a year.

"All of my counterparts in other Siemens offices around the world had 20+ years of experience, held PhDs and whatnot, and there I was — fresh off the boat from Europe, reporting directly to the CEO of the multinational corporation. I spent five good years with Siemens, instead of fulfilling my original short-term plans."

After a few other jobs, Andrea started her own consulting company to help young companies succeed. "I saw all the great things that startups could do in South Africa and beyond, but none of them were really making money, so I thought that I could leverage all of the experience that I had, for good. I realized that these companies could do much better if they had access to venture capital, of which there was none in South Africa, aside from a couple of government funds that were very reluctant to invest in risky businesses.

"Very naively at that point in time, I decided that I should start my own venture capital fund. I built a team with strong credentials and pitched every single potential local investor I could find. Nobody laughed in my face, but they were all very clear that venture capital was too risky an asset for them, and that it only worked in Silicon Valley and wouldn't work in South Africa.

"One Sunday, I was sitting at home and thinking that if I couldn't raise money in South Africa, maybe I should raise the capital from someone else that might be interested in South Africa. So I asked Google and identified some individuals who might be interested in supporting a South African VC fund."

One of the potential investors on Andrea's list was Dr Hasso Plattner, co-founder of software company SAP and a German billionaire.

"I found out that he owned real estate in South Africa and had just started a venture capital fund in Berlin, Germany — he was a perfect match! I wrote a nice long email through the company's website, which basically said, 'Dear Dr Plattner, if you are interested in supporting entrepreneurship in South Africa, please help me, so I could start a venture capital firm,'" Andrea laughed proudly. "I never expected him to reply, but he did respond to me three days later and asked me to pitch the head of their fund in Germany. I met him in Berlin and pitched the whole idea."

Andrea Böhmert found herself in the right place at the perfect time. What was happening in the background of this story, is that Nelson Mandela, then President of South Africa, was in talks with Dr Plattner about supporting the country. Dr Plattner liked the idea and wanted help South Africa become famous, not only for its wine and natural beauty but for technology as well. He didn't have a ready solution of how to do that, so Andrea's proposition came in handy and this was the start of Hasso Plattner Ventures Africa, her first fund. Years later she moved on and joined Knife Capital, where she is now one of the co-Managing Partners.

"One can't compare the Southern African venture capital arena to Silicon Valley. First of all, we only have a few investors whose investment mandates don't necessarily overlap. That is the main reason why every local investor must be prepared to be the only *first* investor in any given startup. We rarely syndicate in South Africa just because of that.

"The next big difference is that we have some early-stage investors, but almost no later-stage investors. So when backing a startup, we also have to assume that we will be the *only* investor that will ever fund it in its lifetime and we need to make sure that we have enough money to keep the company funded and take it to exit. Only the very best startups make it to raise international funding as a follow-up.

"Both of these realities of the local venture capital market create a foundation for a very different approach to investing than in pretty much any other part of the world. When you are investing in Africa, you are on your own. However, the opportunities outweigh the challenges.

"Finally, until recently there weren't many high-profile exit opportunities in Africa, so you also need to plan your exit strategy beforehand, understanding how to position South African businesses to be attractive to international acquirers," Andrea described local market challenges.

"To our knowledge we are currently the only VC fund in South Africa that has completed the full cycle — from raising a fund to fully investing it, to fully exiting its portfolio to the likes of Visa, General Electric and Uber, generating significant returns for the investor and earning carried interest. We have proven that venture capital in South Africa can work."

Böhmert says that venture capital as an asset class in South Africa is in its infancy. Her previous fund — Hasso Plattner Ventures Africa — had €25 million under management, which made it the largest VC fund at that point in time. Even today, most of the other VC funds in the region do not manage more than $15-20 million, so it's fair to say that the entire market is populated with micro VCs, compared to venture capital markets in other countries.

When we talked about entrepreneurs, Andrea surprised me with the biggest challenge they experience in South Africa, which is not what we would think. "There are plenty of entrepreneurs in South Africa, but mainly in lifestyle businesses, generating the employment that South Africa so desperately needs. However, these are not VC-fundable businesses. If you look at scalable technology-enabled companies, the typical profile of a tech entrepreneur in South Africa is a white male. And in a country where the population is predominantly black, that is a huge problem. There is a lot of criticism and plenty of discussions around it, and we also call this problem a diversity issue. We are, honestly, less concerned about the lack of female entrepreneurs than about the lack of black entrepreneurs. But recent trends are very encouraging.

"Many of the white technology entrepreneurs have gained deep knowledge and experience by working for international corporations. They then leave corporate careers and use the acquired skills to start their own businesses. There is a lot of talent here in South Africa and the products that they develop can easily compete in the European and US markets. However, South Africans are not always the best sales and marketing people. They prefer talking about the technology, but are reluctant and even shy to promote themselves and their companies as boldly and loudly as American entrepreneurs do."

As for female entrepreneurs, Böhmert once analyzed 1,000 companies that approached her fund, to draw a founder's profile. "Only eight of them were founded by women," she revealed. "If you ask me how many female tech founders I know locally in general, I'd have to really think about it and then I'd probably only come up with five names of female CEOs or tech founders. Most women still choose traditional lifestyle businesses — like services industries, marketing agencies, or consultancies — but when it comes to VC-fundable companies, you'll find very few. I think we are 5-10 years behind the growth of female tech entrepreneurship that I see in Europe and the United States. We talk the talk at different events about women in business, but not much is being done about it. One of the reasons is that we desperately need more role models of successful business women to motivate other women to go into tech in the first place, because we cannot force them to do so without their desire.

"I don't believe that we, as the South African VC industry, discriminate against female founders, because many VC decision-makers in South Africa have studied or traveled abroad, and it makes them more open to having diverse teams that include women. However, I have to say that Africa is a huge continent, and what's true for South Africa may not be true for other countries and cultures here. There are still regions of Africa where women are perceived as inferior."

When I asked about women in venture capital in South Africa, Andrea could only remember a handful of other female investment partners. "I don't think that it happens because the men don't want to have women in their VC firms. I think it is because there are no women coming into the industry, especially because there are no women in tech, so they don't have any foundation to follow a common path into venture capital. You will also barely find women at an analyst level as well, so they can't even come up through the ranks. I see women in private equity, but there is much more money there, so they aren't rushing to trade that off for the venture capital industry, at this point.

"Every person who is in this ecosystem in South Africa is an activist, because we have to be such to develop and grow the industry. We understand our role in it and try our best to create those role models we desperately need by creating successful entrepreneurs. I think it will take several years and many more stories like those in your book for the venture capital and startup industry to mature. But it's great to be part of this movement today and hopefully make a little bit of a difference in the country — one entrepreneurial success story at a time." I must admit that Andrea's excitement about South Africa is very contagious.

Sara Brand

Founding Partner, True Wealth Ventures, United States

Sara was exposed to tech since her early childhood because her father was a mechanical engineer and her family strongly encouraged her academically. "I was told by my parents that I could do anything, and although I believed in that, I didn't actually have any role models who could show me how to do that. In our very traditional household, my dad was the sole breadwinner and my mom stayed home and raised the kids."

Sara got her MS and PhD in engineering at the University of California, Berkeley, while working at tech companies in Silicon Valley. She worked in technical roles at Intel, Sematech, and Applied Materials, and then moved on to management consulting at McKinsey & Company.

Years in consulting made her realize that, although this job exposed her to a great variety of businesses and problems to solve, it didn't quite add much to her technical expertise. She thought that venture capital looked like the perfect blend of leveraging (and not losing) her tech background, as well as her management consulting experience: she could meet entrepreneurs and understand their attempts to solve big challenges with new technologies every day, and help portfolio companies with any business challenges they had. "I learned that Fremont Ventures was named as one of the top 10 venture capital firms in the US for adding value to portfolio companies, and decided to join them, because I wanted to be a hands-on investor," she explained her next career choice.

Over a decade later, when Brand, and her partner Kerry Rupp, raised True Wealth Ventures that invests solely in female-led companies, they ended up with 80% of their limited partners being women. "We expected quite the opposite of that, given what we had been told when we started fundraising. We had heard that women were more risk-averse and focused on their philanthropic interests, while delegating wealth managers to oversee their financial investments. When we conducted the first close of our fund, we didn't even really notice that half of our investors were women. When we realized that, we decided to double down on female investors, and the network effect snowballed."

Sara didn't pay attention to their limited partner gender initially, because she had often been the only woman in the room, as have many other women featured in this book. "I was really blind to any gender-related experiences, because I had always been surrounded primarily by men in my career. The reason why I loved math and engineering so much is that I didn't have to worry about bias in the grade because it was either the right answer or it wasn't!

"The one gender-specific, self-induced challenge I had, was the feeling that I only had about 5–7 years to significantly advance my career and pay rate in order to make getting a PhD worthwhile, before having kids. I believed that I had to be high enough up in an organization to be valuable enough that I could continue working when having kids. No one ever told me that, but it was in the air."

When I asked Sara why the growing number of female investors hasn't changed the amount of funding for female entrepreneurs much, she declared, "I'm not actually sure that we see a lot more women making investment decisions than years before. There sure is a lot more talk about it in the press, but I think the real situation at the partner level has not changed for a lot of VC firms. Adding a token woman to the table doesn't change the decision-making process. Catalyst Research revealed that it actually takes three women on a board of directors to really accelerate a company's financial performance, because that's when the behavior change really happens. I think the same can be applied to VC firms.

"Many people assume that with such a spotlight on the industry, the reality is naturally getting better, but it's not yet. Unfortunately, we're even seeing the pendulum swinging the other way after all the sexual harassment scandals, because a lot of male decision-makers are being coached to not even meet with women, to avoid the risk of damaging their reputations. Most young men and women entering tech workplaces today, believe that the gender-based obstacles have been removed, and that's part of the challenge.

"The younger generation of men has lost a lot of the traditional biases, but they sometimes still don't see inherited bias existing in the workplace because they aren't on the receiving end of those, oftentimes subtle, situations. It's naturally difficult for men to realize an issue until their daughters are old enough to complain about similar circumstances in the workplace, and that's the first time when they really become aware of the problem.

"As for millennial women, I think they largely think that they won't have to deal with those obstacles, so when they don't get a promotion and their male colleagues do, they take it personally, since they think that bias is gone. This can really exacerbate confidence issues."

After identifying specific issues, I always ask for possible solutions. "Showing more success stories of women is both the quickest and most powerful way to make lasting change," Sara suggested. "Having people who'd advocate for you is another critical component. I am not a huge fan of mentoring, as I think it is often sloppy and inefficient, but advocates who are senior to you can open up new opportunities for you, push you to pursue them, and put your name on the table in conversations you are not a part of. I was very lucky to find such people for myself — they were all men due to the nature of the industry, but they were great! These people have been more important to my career than mentors ever could be."

Sonya Brown

General Partner,
Norwest Venture Partners, United States

Sonya Brown is a growth equity investor — a different breed of investors who are more often than not drawn as the opposite of venture capitalists. Unlike the latter, who often invest in crazy ideas with unclear future, growth equity investors are keen on more mature companies, preferably market leaders with proven business models and a clear plan for achieving profitability. In addition to these differences, Brown adds another one. "Different types of financing have different risk/return profiles, which is critical for you to understand before you commit to a career in investing. Growth equity investing was better suited for me personally, in terms of how much risk we take for the size of the returns that we may get. I prefer to rely on numbers, while VC investors, especially those who invest in pre-revenue startups, rely mainly on gut feeling," she outlined.

With a bachelor of science degree from Northwestern University and a Chartered Financial Analyst designation, Sonya began her career at Bear Stearns, a New York-based global investment bank. She then joined a fast-growing internet services company — iXL — where she had a chance to learn about venture capital from interaction with investors of the company. "It was the end of the 90s, when every large company started investing in startups and creating corporate venture groups. So did we, with the investment focus on internet services. We helped build many notable names in the industry, and I led about 10 investments before the bubble burst," Sonya recalled.

I wondered if the investment banking background that is so highly sought after in Silicon Valley, helped Sonya become a growth equity investor. "I don't think many people realize that investment banking has little to do with investing, because it is basically a service for companies that go public or conduct M&A transactions. Venture capitalists or private equity firms are the clients of investment bankers, but that's where it pretty much ends. An investment banking background helps to build a foundation in finance, which is instrumental in any kind of investing, but there is much more to learn besides that," she clarified.

When the tech bubble burst, Sonya decided not to waste time during the economic downturn and pursued an MBA at Harvard. "I intended to build my career in venture capital, but I was also learning about different investment approaches. I realized that there was an entire spectrum of them, starting from early-stage investing, to later-stage and growth equity, and then, what we identify as private equity, all the way to leveraged buyouts. On that spectrum, growth equity seemed like the best match for me."

After she got her MBA, Sonya joined Summit Partners, a private equity firm with over $11 billion under management, where she was responsible for leading the firm's Consumer and Internet Industry Group. She was later recruited to co-head a newly created growth equity team at Norwest Venture Partners, a premier multi-stage investment firm managing more than $7.5 billion in capital.

Throughout her career, Brown has never been solely focused on investing in Silicon Valley, and that helped her see the investment landscape from a very different perspective. "The majority of venture capitalists traditionally build their strategies around Silicon Valley. It's largely true for tech investors, but since growth equity typically has a much broader investment focus, I have seen a lot of great companies outside of Silicon Valley, as well as many companies founded by women.

"I always advise women who want to advance their careers, that the fastest way to become a CEO is to start a company. A lot of women are doing that, but they don't show up in the statistics that we are discussing in the media, because they're not sitting in Silicon Valley and not raising venture capital. They bootstrap taking loans from their families, mortgaging their houses, using credit cards. They're looking for profitable business models and don't chase big checks to fuel growth blindly, but rather prefer growing their companies methodically over time. Female-led companies open up tremendous opportunities."

Sonya was raised in a male-dominated household led by her father and grandfather. "Their strong personalities helped form me into the person I am today. I owe them both a great deal for shaping my expectations of the world and how I fit into it, how to find a comfort level in business and how to work most effectively with different kinds of people. Nevertheless, I faced some men who challenged me in my career as any woman has. The good news is that the investment industry is a very transparent in terms of results — your returns are black and white. You invest money, and you return money — no other factors are included in the mix, and definitely not gender.

"With that in mind, I want more women to have the confidence to speak up, because we won't be heard if we're not speaking up — you can't be a wallflower and hope to make a career. Women have to speak up about their achievements, instead of keeping their heads down and waiting until their success speaks for them. We have to be vocal about the work we're doing, be very present about it, and even humblebrag if necessary. And if our contributions still aren't being appreciated, we should have the courage to find another place where we fit best."

Sonya Brown is not the only investor in this book who is not afraid to brag a bit. After all, if we love what we are doing and we are doing it well, to be good role models, we should tell the world about it, so that the next generations can follow.

Malin Carlstrom

Senior Vice President, ABB Technology Ventures, Sweden

Malin Carlstrom warned me at the very start of our conversation that she doesn't like talking about the gender issue. I wondered why. "When I was a part of a female network, I noticed that most of the discussions we had about gender equality were held by women or by representatives of minority groups, and no white males were involved. I found that ineffective, because white men still have most of the power. Not involving them in the conversation about these issues leads us nowhere," she answered with a European kind of candor.

"I also wish we relied more on numbers than feelings in such conversations. I keep seeing all these wonderful studies and reports on female funders and founders conducted in the United States, but we have very little of that in the Nordic region. Most of the talks that we have are based on assumptions rather than numbers, and at the end of the day, are emotion-driven.

"After 15 years in my career, I have seen it all — bad bosses, jealous male colleagues, narcissistic behaviors, but I never felt that it gave me the right to put men into buckets and then generalize and apply individual experience to all the males out there. The fact remains that examples of badly behaving individuals are exceptions. As an engineer, I don't buy sensitivity arguments at all. Whenever we have a serious discussion, it always seeks factual and quantitative data. I am sure that if we relied on at least one good piece of research, it would increase the quality of that discussion significantly."

Malin studied engineering with a strong conviction. "When I was younger, I was an environmentalist by heart and by brain. I was very focused on saving the planet, and that was my biggest mission. So I studied energy technology and received a bachelor's degree and a master's in science. At that time, environmental issues were deemed to be 'soft problems'. Everybody was thinking about them as just a cushy subject that doesn't really play into any major financial consequences. Not surprisingly, most of the environmental managers were females. However, when I took my master's, I realized how these issues affect our wealth."

Malin went to the UK to get her MBA, with the intention of becoming either a management consultant or a management trainee. She then enrolled in a trainee program with a large Northern European bank, to work on a lean banking concept. "Banks' 'costs over income' indexes were very high back then, so all banks were concerned about increasing the efficiency of their processes.

"When I applied, I didn't know whether banking would be interesting to me, as that was not really what I was looking for. But during my training program, I got the chance to spend a couple of weeks at the bank's venture capital division.

"With my background, which was mostly technical and not so much financial, I found my home, because in venture capital, the financial performance depends

on the right implementation of technology. In my investment vertical, you have to understand the tech side of the business first and work with engineers closely. You also have to work with customers, which are typically companies that want to improve the world through smarter, more efficient technologies, decrease the consumption of resources, and so on. After that year, I just wanted to continue working in venture capital, and so the department invented an analyst role specifically for me, because there were only senior people working in it, but they wanted me on board.

"That lasted several years until I realized that there was limited opportunity for growth. Banks are still very conservative organizations and it takes years for junior professionals to climb the career ladder. Although the HR department was flattering me to stay, saying that they always find opportunities for prodigies like me, I wanted to grow and develop faster."

Malin's venture capital career started early, and after leaving the bank, she worked for several different organizations deploying private and public venture capital to tech companies of different investment verticals.

"I remember my mother said to me, 'Malin, you need to find a job where results matter, because they can't take that away from you. Don't choose work and assignments that are more about politics and processes, than actual results.' She supported me being a consultant, because it's pretty clear how to make a contribution in that role. She also agreed that I could achieve measurable results in venture investing if I stayed in the industry for long enough. Her advice made so much sense over the course of my career.

"When I ended up managing larger amounts of money, my mom also said, 'You are a woman who represents the largest buckets of cash. You will become a threat, you're going to face uncomfortable situations more and more often — but don't let it stop you.' And she was right there too.

"Whenever I found myself in a challenging situation, when I could feel in my stomach that the problem would not go away, I was always ready to quit. If something happened once, there was a chance that it was a misunderstanding, but if it happened twice, it would likely keep happening, and accelerate thereafter. Oftentimes, we are not able to move other people from where they stand and it has nothing to do with gender. There is no sense in waiting around and hoping that people or company culture will change or that the situation will improve. It may become a slippery slope. So a timely exit is critical in this case, because when you are in control of it, you are able to take the power of the situation and utilize it. You won't have to fight and compromise your reputation over time. You won't have to exit with an excuse. You have to choose your battles.

"Such situations may happen not only in regard to your own job, but also, for example, in a boardroom. When I make investments and work with portfolio companies, I always pay a lot of attention to the executive team and board composition. Sometimes you can see that the chief officers or board members will do more harm than good, from day one. Then, you need to make an important decision in terms of changing the management of the company, or balancing the board, because it's very unlikely that people will change and start doing better all of a sudden. As an investor, I am responsible for the outcomes of my investments, therefore, I have to prevent or exit harmful situations as soon as possible, in order for the company to perform well."

Our discussion inevitably turned to the gender topic and wound up being very educational. "We have a so-called Nordic gender equality paradox. From the outside, Nordic societies seem to have it all: a historic tradition of female entrepreneurship, modern welfare states that provide support to working parents, outstanding participation of women in the labor market, and populations that strongly support the idea of gender equality. Yet, Nordic countries have very few women among top managers and business owners compared to other countries. Even our neighbors — three Baltic countries that have more conservative societies and a more small-government approach than us — have more female managers, top executives, and business owners," Malin intrigued me.

"The robust research conducted on this issue showed that the Nordic welfare system unintentionally holds women back. For example, public sector monopolies and substantial tax wedges limit women's progress in the labor market. An overly generous parental leave system encourages women to stay at home rather than work. Welfare safety discourages them from self-employment.

"Sweden is one of the most compressed and dense countries in the world when it comes to income equality. We have just a few super-rich people, and also a few super poor people. This apparently doesn't motivate enough people to stand out and take the risks involved with starting their own business.

"That said, I must admit that we have no shortage of ethnic diversity in the country. My last investment happened to go to a team consisting of a refugee from Syria and a Swede — both males. It's unusual for me to see all white male teams here in Sweden. Most often, I see companies that have mixed teams of people of different ages, different nationalities, and different experiences. But when it comes to female entrepreneurs, we still have too few of them.

"I believe that we need to start involving girls in STEM as early as in school. We need to teach them to code, we need to make them comfortable with technology, and we need to develop their engineering skills. It may be a boring answer, but it's critical for Sweden, as well as for the venture capital ecosystem as a whole. The majority of women here prefer typically 'female' professional fields, such as marketing or recruiting. At some point, we also started seeing more female physicians than male. And what do you think happened? The salaries of medical personnel dropped! The same happened with teachers. Back in the day, teachers had very high salaries in Sweden, but when it became a 'female job', the average teacher's salary dropped as well. It may be the result of excess labor, but it may also be happening because women are typically paid less, which affects the entire category, and over time, these professions become less prestigious due to low salaries. So from all standpoints, we need more women in tech and entrepreneurship, because this is what keeps society moving ahead."

Carlstrom also enlightened me that the United States is not the first country that legally required businesses to have a certain number of women on corporate boards. "There is some buzz going on about supporting women in executive roles, but there's not much action yet. For example, Sweden rejected a bill introducing quotas for women on the boards of public and state companies. Our neighbor, Norway, however, became the first country in the world to introduce a gender quota for corporate boards. In 2007, they passed a law requiring that all companies listed on exchange have at least 40 percent of their boards being made up of women. The expectation was that it would also create a ripple effect to top management teams, which, unfortunately, didn't happen. Go figure! I'm not sure whether it's men who don't hire women, or women themselves who are not willing and persistent enough to serve in the C-suite.

"I started advocating for such quotas for women in 2000. I think that in order to make a change, each team needs to have at least two women in it. It can't be one, because one person alone can't move things and just becomes an exotic token. So you need at least two diverse people in any group structure. When I wrote an article about it back then, I received a lot of feedback saying that hiring decisions are based on the competencies of candidates — not on gender. But the fact is that this is not the case today — we all know many males that are holding their seats at the table, bringing everything from amazing to a very low value. Therefore, this argument about merit-based hiring decision, oftentimes, has no hard evidence."

Other women featured in the book also spoke about these quotas. I didn't survey them on this matter, but it feels like the camp that is against the quotas is larger than the one that supports them. Norway is a great example of this experiment. If their law that requires 40 percent of board directors to be female, didn't lead to a global change of women's place in the C-suite across the country, let's see how the Californian law that requires locally incorporated public companies to have at least one woman on a corporate board, will work out.

Tracy Chadwell

Founding Partner, 1843, United States

When I asked Tracy Chadwell about the number one quality that a person needs, in order to become a successful venture investor, she said, "I think if you want to really excel in venture capital, you can't have an attitude. Just because you have a checkbook, you cannot sit back and relax. Your job is not simply to judge, but rather to discover. It is a very different approach. You have to be out there sourcing really interesting deals and building your deal flow around the thesis that you have developed. You have to be persistent and work with your portfolio companies when a deal is done — helping them with customer acquisition, keeping them focused, and following the strategy. I've seen people who start feeling way too comfortable after they have gotten those checkbooks — they enjoy their lives to the fullest, thinking that their job is done by just writing a check. That's not how you build really successful companies."

Tracy sets her standards high for entrepreneurs as well. "So many people are too transactional these days. Sometimes they'll be on the phone with me pitching their company, and if in the first 20 minutes they sense that I'm not going to write them a check that week, I can feel how they want to get off the phone really quickly.

"I am surprised each time I face this phenomenon, although so much has been said and written about entrepreneur-investor relationships, that it should be a startup 101 type of thing. I really mean it when I say, 'I like your company, and I find it very interesting, but you're super early for us, because we need more proof points instead of merely plans. Can you please

send me quarterly updates, nevertheless?'. Many entrepreneurs, however, take that to mean that I want them to never show up again, and so they disappear. They get very upset later on when they have to start building a relationship with me all over again, when they call me while raising their next financing round. How am I supposed to fund a company that I haven't heard from after that one call?

"Somebody told me the other day that I should write a book, and I said it would be a very short one — it would just say: 'Follow up'. I take every meeting as an opportunity to either learn something, to start building a new relationship, or to gain a new introduction. And I find that many people are very short-sighted about that," she sighed.

Tracy was lucky to work in private equity early in her career, when she was a practicing attorney. Although she was mainly involved in real estate transactions, they were primarily done through private equity funds, which led her to venture capital. She then joined an investment bank on the West Coast and worked with their in-house venture capital fund, Crosslink Capital, started by Mike Stark and Sy Kaufman. The fund won big when Pandora went public about owning half a billion in shares of the company. With that background, Tracy moved on to becoming a partner at one of the first billion-dollar funds — Baker Capital.

Despite that impressive resume, Tracy Chadwell has remained very humble. She admitted that she faced some challenges, regardless. "Being the only woman in the room a lot of the time, was an interesting challenge. Also, socializing with startups and other investors has never been a woman's strong suit, and it was a delicate matter for me for quite a while."

Tracy raised her first VC fund back in 2016 and named it '1843', inspired by Ada Lovelace, a 19th-century mathematician who has been called the first computer programmer. In 1843, Lovelace published a transcript that some have dubbed the first computer program. Besides popping up among the first VC firms on alphabetized lists, due to its numerical name, the fund differentiates itself primarily by looking to invest in companies with diverse leadership teams that include at least one woman. In deep tech — which 1843 is focused on — this investment strategy narrows it down significantly, or so I thought. I was truly curious as to whether Tracy is contemplating a change in her investment approach.

"It actually has been a great advantage!" exclaimed Chadwell. "We don't experience a lack of female leaders in our investment verticals at all. In fact, we're completely overwhelmed with the deal flow. People have a perception that there are few to no women in highly technological spaces. In fact, this perception is mostly formed by whatever we see on the surface — not many tech women founders are being seen at demo days and on Techcrunch.com, but that doesn't mean that there are none. We work through our networks very thoroughly and unearth some interesting companies that other investors have never seen," she added.

This is something that I don't hear often. Most of the venture investors I've talked to — male or female — said that they wish they had more female founders in their deal flow. So I asked Tracy to share her secret sauce for these amazing results with me and my readers.

"I think, because women have so few places where the doors are open to them, we can see an increased number of female entrepreneurs knocking on these doors, compared to all the others. My partner and I are both women, so that, coupled with our proactive female founder-friendly position, means that we attract a watershed of fabulous deals. We also leverage our networks to the maximum and receive, I would say, 60% of the deals through referrals. Another 40% would just come through our website. We try to get back to each and every founder that contacts us, but we invest in less than 1% of what we see. So, unfortunately, for every one company we invest in, we have to turn down 99 other companies," Tracy diligently explained.

1843 is a relatively small fund, so they always co-invest, but try to only join deals where the leading investor has experience in deep tech. Tracy said it would be tough for them as a specialized VC firm to participate in a round led by just a generalist investor. "We'd like to follow someone who has the strength and specific expertise in the space, rather than just capital."

Deep tech is one of the favorite investment verticals of large VC firms, and male investors are the most common lead partners on such deals. I was curious if they warmly welcome female tech founders and are proactively interested in them. "No, I wouldn't say there's a steady interest. We work very hard with our companies to make sure that they're well-positioned for raising the next round and that they are seen in the best light by big VC firms," Tracy replied.

"Female founders do still struggle to (A) get meetings with venture capitalists, and (B) to actually secure funding. We all know the statistics that female founders receive a much lower total dollar amount of venture capital. So even though they are getting the money, maybe they get just $1 million, where a male-only team in the same position would receive $2 million.

"The bias in funding still takes place more often than not. In fact, I did have one meeting recently where we discussed a female-founded company with another investor, and his comment to me was, 'I'm not sure I could see her running this company, because I knew her when she had a ponytail and wore a baseball cap,'" Tracy paused for a second to let this quote sink in.

"On the other hand, I'm now going through the round with a female-founded company that was wildly oversubscribed, and it's going to be an all-female board, interestingly enough. I think there are a couple of reasons for their success.

"First of all, it was a Series A round, so we saw the traction and proof points. I think, with each subsequent round, it gets easier and easier for women-entrepreneurs to raise capital, because they have delivered results, instead of just telling a big story. In this particular case, the company was growing 1000% year over year, so it was clear that the founder had a rapidly accelerating growth rate. That result was also coupled with the fact that she'd been extremely conservative and capital efficient in the past, which makes the ROI look very attractive."

I was talking with Tracy about how female entrepreneurs could improve their positions, and I mentioned that sometimes women say that they would prefer to not adapt to other people, with their argument being: 'Why should we change ourselves? Why can't men adapt to us?' Chadwell agreed, "I've heard this argument about the outfits, among other things too. Like, 'Why should we have to cover up and wear a button-down shirt? Why shouldn't we be able to wear short shorts and a tight blouse, because men should treat us with respect anyway?'

"And while in a perfect world, I would love for every person to be naked and be treated with respect, quite honestly, men are very visual people, and hoping to avoid bias in this scenario is not where we are at this point. Besides following a basic business dress code, we also have to meet people where they are, and we can't expect them to change overnight. Why would someone provoke an unfavorable perception just because we are now not afraid to speak out? There is no argument that men should treat women with respect, regardless of the outfit, but we all have our own inherent biases.

"Let's not put this just on the men — we women have biases as well. It happens to me quite often when young founders seem too young to me, and I check myself and say, 'Oh Tracy, just because she's under 30, doesn't mean she can't build a really great business.'"

Carmen Chang

General Partner,
NEA, United States

Carmen Chang came to the United States from Taiwan and studied first in college and then in graduate school, to earn a doctorate in Modern Chinese History. However, after leaving without completing her dissertation, she instead earned a degree from Stanford Law School, and went on to work for Wilson Sonsini Goodrich & Rosati, an iconic Silicon Valley law firm.

At the time when Chang began her legal career, she was one of very few lawyers who were bilingual in Chinese and English, and had an understanding of Chinese history, politics and institutions. Carmen was a lawyer for some of the first US investments in China — such as Goldman Sachs' investment in China Netcom — as well as to many US companies who wished to grow their footprint in Asia, such as Google. Setting up Uber's operations in China, helping its founder Travis Kalanick to hire the right person to run the business there, and then facilitating its sale to their rival, Didi, is one of Carmen's recent advisory work.

Most of Chang's career was unplanned. When she went to work for a law firm, it was for the practical experience everyone had told her was required to become a law professor. She also hadn't thought about utilizing her academic knowledge of modern China to build an Asia-focused legal career. However, there was a need for lawyers with her particular skills and she found herself fascinated by the growth of so many companies, the transformation taking place in China, and the complexities of cross-border transactions. One year turned into another, and she ended up becoming a partner and staying in law for more than 25 years.

Carmen started planning to retire from the partner position at a law firm, but still wanted to stay active and work on something equally exciting. The now Managing General Partner of New Enterprise Associates (NEA), Scott Sandell, who had known Carmen for a long time, asked her to lead the firm's deals in Asia as an advisor. By that time, she had become known in Silicon Valley as the 'China whisperer'. This role evolved to where she is today — a General Partner of the firm. "Lawyers in Silicon Valley are so much more than just lawyers," Chang said. "They are early mentors to entrepreneurs, they are advisors, they wear many hats. That's why lawyers play such a significant role in the Silicon Valley ecosystem."

When I asked Carmen what the most useful skill that she had obtained as a lawyer was, she highlighted a challenge that the legal profession imposes on venture capitalists, instead. "Lawyers are trained to be risk-preventive, while investors need to be able to live with uncertainty and take risks, albeit calculated. The art is in balancing both — being detailed-oriented and comfortable with risk."

She named strong human skills, analytical ability, and having experience in both large and small companies as the most important skills that are crucial for a venture investor. But she also thinks that the importance of a technological background is hard to underestimate. "In the past, Silicon Valley was almost entirely deep tech. Most of the companies I worked with were founded by professors, engineers, biologists, doctors or tech graduates. Today, many of the changes in consumer products are also fueled by new technology, so for everyone — even people without a tech education — understanding technology on some level is important, regardless of the investment sector."

The lack of technical background is the most common challenge that female entrepreneurs and investors face on their paths, so we moved onto the issue of diversity in venture capital. "Steps are being taken to increase opportunities for women. NEA and many other firms are implementing strategies to ensure that their hiring pool is diverse. Besides that, the opportunities for women in venture capital today are no longer limited to larger firms, but now includes new venture firms, corporate VCs, micro VCs, super angels, and accelerators. That said, there are still fewer job openings in venture capital than notable talents in the market, and diversity among investment partners is still very low.

"To change this, we should stay consistent and admit that data is just as important for this issue as it is for making investment decisions, and the more accurate data we have, the better we are able to understand the real situation. For example, I have suspected that there is a much smaller share of female investment partners among all the VC firms in the United States than often cited, and that has been confirmed by your research. The fact that your WomenVC think tank studies all the venture capital firms, regardless of the amount of assets under management, is really important because most of the diverse first-time managers start as micro VCs, and we must not ignore this group."

I asked Carmen what she thinks about token hires among women. "There are so many talented women out there that I don't think there is a need to hire tokens! I think it really is a question of how much people recognize the value that women can bring to the table, and that includes both the hiring male VCs and the female candidates themselves. Women tend to be less confident than they should be, and thus they create a barrier in their minds that they are being hired merely as token hires and not because they are truly valuable additions to the teams. That, in turn, sends a signal to other people that encourages them to doubt women as well. We really need to not create room for mistreatment and misperception by others. There's a perception that women are supposed to be nice and aren't allowed to have sharp elbows — something that is often considered acceptable for men. Yes, it's not fair, but all female VCs I know have figured out how to adjust to the reality and turn it to their favor. Venture capital is a lot about how we carry ourselves, and it's not a bad thing."

Joanne Chen

Partner, Foundation Capital, United States

There is nothing I like more than a raw, candid talk. When Joanne made a statement early on in our conversation, "I didn't put venture capital on a pedestal. For me, it was just another asset class," I knew it was going to be an interesting one.

Prior to joining Foundation Capital, Joanne spent many years working on Wall Street and helping tech companies go through their IPO and M&A processes, as well as advising venture firms on their own fundraising processes. She helped to raise Atomico, a VC firm founded by Niklas Zennström, the founder of Skype, and Revolution of Steve Case, the co-founder of AOL. "I thought that venture capital was a fascinating place to work, but because I was on the other side of the table, it didn't happen to intimidate me in the first place," she added.

We jumped straight to the good and bad of venture capital, as she saw it from that other side. "The greatest thing about venture capital, for me, is that people in the industry are very optimistic about the future and are taking risks around that. If you look at the top tier Silicon Valley firms in general, you will see that the quality of people has been consistently very high in that dimension.

"The other strength of the venture capital industry, is that many people were operators prior to becoming investors, and have very strong networks due to that. Once you get into their company, you automatically find yourself in the 2nd-degree circle of pretty much anyone in the VC and tech industries.

"Finally, I think venture investors have a rare combination of resilience, and yet, the ability to improve themselves in an inward position, because the amount of external validation is relatively limited in venture capital. You put your money in with no guarantees, and it may take 10 years until you know that you have done a good job, because only one of all your investments worked. It takes a great amount of resilience, and a strong personality, to be able to have a career like that. So I've been largely impressed with the people in the industry in general," Joanne shared.

"In terms of weaknesses, I would say that VCs are far less strategic, realistically, than they position themselves to be. You need to know how to separate the wheat from the chaff.

"Another thing is that there is a constant argument about who's a better venture investor — former founders, operators, or investment bankers and PE managers. These different kinds of people come into venture capital in waves, and each wave argues that they are better positioned to be venture investors than the others. This argument is mainly based on a misconception that investment decision-making in venture capital is somehow an innate or talent-driven ability. However, what I've observed is that it is very much a learned skill, instead. It does require quite a long time to learn and master, so it may take years of mentorship, honing, observing, and self-reflection to become really good at that, but it's nevertheless an acquired skill. I put this argument to rest for myself, because this is just one of the myths created around venture capital.

"Finally, diversity has always been a concern in the industry. It wasn't very noticeable in the early days of venture capital, but it certainly is today. Compared to what I saw in venture capital before I joined the tribe, not only was it a white-male-dominated industry, but it was also very homogenous in regards to educational background. Today, it's much more diverse in all dimensions, but there's still a long way to go. I do think that diversity improves the odds of making good investments in general, if you think about it from a purely ROI perspective, and I am sure many venture investors will start seeing and agreeing with it too. I hope that in the next 10 years, diversity will no longer be a topic."

Foundation Capital was co-founded by Kathryn Gould (passed away in 2015) who believed that: "The men who have the guts to do business with you, have the extra self-confidence to be more successful." I asked Joanne what the firm's culture looks like in that regard.

"The main thing that makes the environment at Foundation Capital friendly, is the awareness that everyone has their own communication style. Each team member recognizes that and makes sure that everyone expresses their opinions. I can recall so many situations where someone has remained quiet during meetings, and we proactively give them the limelight to speak up by saying, 'Hey, what do you think?' Simple things like that make a lot of difference, because they happen every day and become a habit throughout everything we do.

"Finally, I must say that I did my due diligence on the team when I was joining the firm, and I found that Foundation Capital had people with high integrity in general. They are genuinely good people with high moral centers doing the right thing. This factor in a partnership is critical, because the hierarchies and dynamics of partnerships are very different from what we are used to in corporations," Chen concluded.

Cheryl Cheng

General Partner, BlueRun Ventures, United States

Cheryl's parents were first-generation immigrants to the United States, and expected her to become a doctor, a lawyer, or an engineer. However, none of those occupations attracted Cheryl. "I wasn't the strongest in math, nor was I interested in engineering, and hospitals scared me," she remembered. "So the only choice left from those defined by my parents, was to become a lawyer. Although I went to college with the determination to choose the legal profession (and even found my first internship by cold calling law firms through the phone book), the jobs I was given were painfully boring. I pored over legal documents written in a very complex, convoluted language, and it was not at all exciting for me.

"I did two summer internships, tried litigation and corporate law, and then I decided to get some mentorship from a law school professor, which would help me fall in love with the law, or so I hoped. I went to Stanford Law School, found a couple of professors who were willing to have coffee with me, and soon realized that I couldn't answer their questions as to why I wanted to be a lawyer, or whether I really saw myself in that career, etc. That seed of doubt really took root in my mind, and so I struck through the last of my parents' planned careers for me, and went on to explore other options."

At Stanford, Cheryl got exposed to the tech world. "The only thing I knew, was that I wasn't going to be an engineer, but I tried to find a kind of fire hose of information and learning experiences that would help me learn more about

technology faster. It was either investment banking or consulting, and I chose the former," she described the life-changing moment.

Through her work at an investment bank, she was hired into an affiliate venture capital firm as a senior analyst. "There I was, a 24-year-old, doing research on enterprise software and analog mixed signal semiconductors, to find the best companies to invest in. It was challenging, because I was doing research on a range of technologies without any context. I had never worked at a company that sold any real products, and had never been on the operating side of business before, so it was really difficult for me to define what 'the best' meant. It felt like studying something very academic in a vacuum.

"After a couple of years, I went to business school with the goal of learning more about business operations and other industries. I moved out of tech altogether and joined Clorox as a member of their product group, where we launched new cleaning products that could be category game-changers. I loved innovation, even those that were very far from the traditional tech world: it was more material science and manufacturing, rather than software."

With her blend of investment banking, venture capital, retail and consumer product management experience, Cheryl later joined BlueRun Ventures. She worked on the operational side of the firm, helping their portfolio companies with marketing and business development, as well as repositioning the firm to be focused on mobile software.

"It was the right time, the right skill set, and the right people. I hadn't planned on going back to venture, but I had differentiated skills that I could bring to the team. In hindsight, I think this approach is generally very important for creating a long-term career path in venture."

Not only had she not planned to return to venture, Cheryl had also never thought of becoming a general partner, or even an investment partner. "My goal was very simple: I wanted to re-immerse myself in the world of technology, similar to the way that I had done at the very beginning of my career, and figure out if there was a company that I'd want to work at, and if that company would have been a match for the BlueRun portfolio."

Over the years since 2008, Cheng took on more and more functions at the firm, and at some point, she stopped introducing entrepreneurs to the firm's partners and started doing deals herself. Finally, one of the senior partners of the firm sat her down and asked if she wanted to move over to the investing side. "I told him, quite frankly, that I hadn't really thought about that, and he said that I could build my path to a General Partner position. He promised to help me along the way, and I really thought of it as a very unique opportunity that I had to seize."

Growing into a General Partner within one firm is the least popular way for women in venture capital. It took Cheryl 11 years to reach that goal, and her appointment to this role was only just announced in January 2019. Her collection of experiences was significantly enriched by almost a decade-long job in venture capital within one firm. So I asked Cheryl if there was anything else left for her to learn before this job would become routine.

"Of course!" she exclaimed. "Every single deal is unique — they are handcrafted for a particular moment by a particular person. There are no two companies that take the exact same path to an exit. There's almost an unlimited number of permutations of things that could go wrong or right, and every single one of those is a scenario that an investor needs to deal with. So even if I invest in a hundred companies, throughout the rest of my career, there will be something that I will learn in every single one of them.

"From a skill and learning perspective, one of the most amazing things about the job that I do at the firm, is that I can learn from every single interaction and transaction that I am involved in. Venture capital is a continuously learning job, indeed."

I asked Cheryl to list the three skills that she has acquired over the course of her career, that are the most helpful in venture investing.

"Firstly, you have to be a good judge of people. Meeting entrepreneurs and figuring out whether a founder is going to build a game-changing company is at the very core of what we do. There are no tests for them to pass, but there is an exhaustive number of factors that can affect the outcome, that we need to consider. It's more an art than a science.

"The second skill is being a really good listener, and being able to hear the signals that your founders are giving you about their businesses. These signals are not obvious, and more often than not, don't come with reports. You have to recognize them between the lines, and align them with the market situation — short- and long-term — as well as with the fund's strategy. All of that helps you to develop the pattern recognition skill that venture investors so often refer to.

"The last, but not least, skill that is really important, is the ability to become an advisor to your portfolio companies, so that you can help them navigate all the ups and downs as a silent leader and a partner, but without making decisions for them. It's not as simple as it sounds, because we work with different companies over the years, and the problems of a three-person company are very different from the problems of a 50-person company. You have to know how to deal with all of them. I will keep improving these skills constantly throughout my life and career," she added on.

I wondered whether Cheryl could highlight any aptitude that had helped her survive in the male-dominated industry, and she replied: "You have to know how to read the person that you're talking to all the time. In every form of communication, you need to recognize what to say and how, so it will be properly perceived by the other side. In my personal and professional life, I have become very attuned to not just what I say, but what other people will hear. I work with plenty of immigrant entrepreneurs, so cultural sensitivity is something that I've developed as well.

"When it comes to the gender issue, I think, it's important for women to understand that the way we speak, and the things we say, may be the most comfortable mode of communication for us, but it may be misinterpreted by men if we don't tune in with them. The onus is not just on women but on everyone to have such sensitivity.

"I can hear your readers thinking now about how we define who's right and who's wrong, but this is not the question to ask. Communication is a two-way street, and people need to be ready to modify the approach on both sides. It's not just about being politically correct — that just keeps you out of hot water. To be effective, you also have to be attuned and aware.

"This skill of being an effective and respectful communicator, is critically important for the success of any business and personal relationship that we want to have. I feel that this is something that has helped me a lot in my career. When I used to lead cross-functional teams, I would have to think about each person at the table and do some modification of the words that I chose, or the way that I presented information, depending on their characters and occupations. To sum it up, I'd say that being an effective communicator is a range of tactics to learn over time."

On diversity in venture capital, Cheryl touched on an important point: "I think we've taken the first step: every second VC firm now wants to hire a diverse person and I'm very encouraged by that. The bigger problem is that once you've hired these people, will you set them up to succeed? Will you actually have an inclusive culture that mentors and teaches them? Will the voices of those bright-eyed and bushy-tailed talents who are coming into this industry, be heard? And that is still to be determined. So I hope that venture capitalists will take this further, because it is that next level that will actually create long-term change."

Tina Cheng

Managing Partner, Cherubic Ventures, Taiwan

Tina Cheng co-founded an education consulting firm with a friend, in order to have a taste of being an entrepreneur. "Starting a company was a great lesson for me. Reading about startups on Techcrunch.com is definitely very different from actually running the business. The media usually just highlights the glamorous side of startups, but it's probably the toughest 'job' out there."

After getting her MBA in California, Taiwan-born advertising major Tina Cheng went to work for Yahoo! and Cisco. "After just three years in Silicon Valley, the entrepreneur bug got me. Being Asian, I thought that the best place for me to start my entrepreneurial journey would be back home, because at the time, China was booming with many interesting opportunities. So I decided to pack up and go back to my hometown to explore entrepreneurship."

While doing all of that, Tina would occasionally assess startups that a prominent super angel investor — Matt Cheng — was considering for investments. He'd send her pitches and ask for her opinion as a Silicon Valley insider, as well as an entrepreneur.

In 2013, Matt decided to institutionalize his angel fund, but more so, he wanted to create a platform that would connect Silicon Valley and Asia. He was on the lookout for a partner who would help him build such a platform, who'd be bilingual and familiar with both Asian and American markets, and also someone who had entrepreneurial experience. He thought that Tina was a great match.

"I did not plan that at all!" she said. "I never had the thought of, 'Oh, I want to become a venture investor'. Instead, when Matt asked me to join Cherubic Ventures, I thought, 'Oh, I want to help bring this platform together, work with entrepreneurs, and assist with their endeavors."

Tina joined the firm as a Partner, and five years later, she was appointed as the Managing Partner, at the end of 2018. Today, Cherubic Ventures manages a total of $300 million, has about 160 portfolio companies across mainly Greater China and the US, including such hits as Hims, Calm, Flexport, and Wish, 19 of which have had exits through IPOs and M&As.

Tina offered an insider view on the differences between American and Asian investing and entrepreneurial approaches. "Venture capital as an industry, in China, is very progressive and fast-paced, so is the startup scene. For many young people in China, becoming an entrepreneur and bringing the company to IPO one day is a common dream, as many of their peers have already done it. The Chinese founders are extremely ambitious and are willing to work very hard for it, as exemplified by the recent buzz around the country's working culture "996" (i.e. working from 9am to 9pm, 6 days a week).

"Chinese entrepreneurs, in general, move much faster than entrepreneurs from any other culture that I've seen. If they have an idea, they will just quickly put together a team, launch a prototype right away, and raise money from friends and family before their pitch is perfect, and the product is completed. Whereas in other countries, including the United States, I see entrepreneurs spending a lot more time on perfecting their pitch and product prior to going out into the world. It's a very different mentality, and I think, in terms of speed and agility, Chinese entrepreneurs are currently ahead of everyone else in the world.

"Another thing that comes easy to them is monetization. I sometimes see identical ideas in China and the US, and Westerners may have a superior product, however, they struggle with sales. Chinese entrepreneurs might present you a product that's less impressive or innovative, but they would be making tons of money with it because they cracked the monetization model. It's a gift that local entrepreneurs have — they're just good at figuring out who will pay for what and how much," Tina assessed entrepreneurs in an impartial manner.

"In venture capital industry, we, in Asia, are very hungry for great ideas, and don't have the luxury of creating barriers for them, whether it's gender, ethnicity, or anything else. When it comes to venture investments, I think, the Chinese culture is very open and flexible. As soon as they see a moonshot idea, they will do whatever it takes to make it happen. People here are very focused on just one thing, which is: how do we become successful? They know that they must move fast to take advantage of an opportunity, so there's no time for bias.

"Speaking of gender, although the VC industry is still predominantly male, I somehow feel that the society here is actually more open-minded than in the West. You do see unapologetically strong female leaders in China, both in the VC and tech worlds. You also see how some women break into the big boys' club. This, of course, differs from industry to industry — however, in general, I think as a society, China has become more modernized. In large cities, women don't feel intimidated by men. In certain parts of China, for example, in Shanghai, women are actually very dominant: lots of the housework is done by husbands, while wives are off-site, socializing. If you look at the history of China, men always had a higher status, but in the past several decades, especially in the last 10 years, women have gotten a much stronger voice and a bigger say.

"We're also seeing that the age of investors is trending down, and that also helps to break the stereotypes. The common perception is that investors are all 40-50-year-old men, however, many VCs in China are in their late 20s or early 30s; they are much more modern, have a different worldview, and are very likely educated overseas," Tina portrayed China in a way that we have never seen before.

Susan Choe

Founding Partner, Visionnaire Ventures and Katalyst Ventures, United States

Susan Choe is one of that particular tribe of women VCs who decided to go on their own and be a sole general partner. Despite this title, she didn't stop being a mompreneur to a five-year-old daughter, and seems to have figured out that elusive work/life balance.

"As all parents know, especially working moms, time is best utilized when managed," she said. "It's integral to have a reliable support network, and in order to be successful and efficient, there can't be a single point of failure in that network. Time can't be managed if any of the pieces are lacking. This is why it is important to plan for hiccups like last minute meetings, sick days and travel issues.

"I always have parallel schedules running in my brain and my duties as a parent translate into my life as an investor. It's a dual universe. Keeping the LPs up to date on developments and milestones, and having reliable colleagues and team members who are at the top of their game, assists in keeping me on track. As a mom, I always have to consider the well-being of my daughter and family too. I realize that you can't always have it all at once; this is necessary for your sanity and the sanity of those around you. My daughter helps me optimize my schedule."

Whenever I meet Susan Choe, a General Partner of Visionnaire Ventures and the newly raised Katalyst Ventures, her smooth manner of speaking makes me think that she's prepared all the answers to whatever it is I want to discuss with her, well ahead of time. The same happened when I went to her new office to talk about this book. We had a short but very intense conversation, and I have selected those of Susan's opinions that simply cannot be ignored.

Susan Choe has a rule that I will be quoting for the rest of my life: don't give the power of judgment to others. I asked her how we can achieve that. "In your head first, and in your heart next. Do whatever it takes for you to feel happy and confident. There is no need to change your voice or persona, etc. We have to forge our own paths and feel comfortable in our skin. Indeed, our authenticity as women-leaders makes it difficult for others, both men and women, to assess and connect with us right away. But the more often society at large sees the positive impacts that women in various walks of life, across media, daily life, and leadership positions, have, the more the image and acceptance will broaden."

Susan's investing philosophy was shaped early in her career when she saw how difficult it was for teachers to work with students who spoke different languages in one classroom. Advancing existing industries by leveraging data-driven tech to optimize time spent on different tasks, is the basis of what Susan's firm targets.

"Time, indeed, is money. Backing teams with ideas for improving quality of life at home and work, while building exponential enterprise value, are key goals for Katalyst. Our mission is simple — profit and purpose," she explained.

Choe became a venture capitalist after being a founder and CEO of her own startup. "There's much I've learned from hiring, fundraising, and board management, that I leverage daily in my work as an investor. Most of all, the appreciation of what it takes to make something from nothing, never leaves me."

She had her stories of being a woman in tech and venture capital, but her attitude is not what you'd expect if you knew them. "Don't reverse discriminate, as in: if men discriminate against me, then I will discriminate against men — it isn't productive," she opened another topic.

"Firstly, you can't change human nature and social tribalism by repeating the model. Our society is still led by traditional men. It will take time for that majority group to change, unfortunately. When they see women having their own careers, it means that men will have to change their lives and make room for female professionals as well. It's not a natural path for established groups to give up some of their privileges to new groups. For that reason, inclusion and creating a solution together with male allies is a solid next step. Gandhi, Martin Luther King, Jr., Rosa Parks, and other changemakers are a persistent, steadfast illustration of the values that they rallied for human nature to rise.

"Secondly, men have been positioned to be providers versus life partners. So there is an implicit understanding that men need to be paid more to support a family. However, this is a lose-lose situation for both genders, in my opinion. We need to get to the point where society at large feels comfortable with female leaders as they are. For that to happen, the media will have to portray more women in leadership, as much as nurturers. Same with men — we need to show them both as leaders and life partners. I do believe with a true life partner role definition, struggles will decrease at home and in society.

"When women try to stand up for themselves today, it often backfires. It happens, because our society is not used to a woman who speaks up. She is deemed 'difficult' or worse. We have to infuse our own female DNA into how leadership in the workspace works. Something I am still evolving myself to. Men and women have to come to terms with how each of our roles progress at work, in families, and community. A life path should be chosen by the individual. Isn't that the basis of democracy and free will that we all advocate for?" Susan shared a lot more wisdom that we decided to save for another occasion.

Maria Cirino

Founding Partner,
.406 Ventures, United States

Ironically, two major events in Maria Cirino's career happened somewhat thanks to men: starting her own company and joining a venture capital firm. "I say this to women all the time: use the fact that men don't hesitate, to your advantage. When they tell you, 'You could do that!' — go ahead and do that!" Maria exclaimed. "Men in my orbit were saying this to me all the time, 'Oh, don't be ridiculous! What a great opportunity — just go do it. Don't talk to me about not being qualified, just get in there and do the job!' I did and look where I am!"

Cirino doesn't hesitate to express her strong and candid opinions, which are sometimes pretty unconventional. However, she is one of those people who also puts a lot of positive energy into her words, so that you just want to go and do it, even if you haven't entirely agreed with her just yet.

Maria was an operator for about 15 years before she started her own company. Coming out of college with an English literature degree, she got lucky to get involved with one tech company after another, and worked her way up — typically through sales and marketing. She worked for Lotus Development, one of the largest software companies in the world at the time. She then left there to move to a startup world, where she worked for companies and grew them from single digit revenue to multi-million and multi-billion exits.

With such a stunning background, Maria was approached by several venture capital firms to join them. However, she declined all the offers, and when she was asked by one general partner she had a meeting with, what she was going to do next, she didn't have a plan and replied with the first thing that came to her mind, 'I'm thinking about starting a cyber security company'. Maria wasn't prepared for what happened next. The partner said, 'That's great! That's exactly our firm's investment focus. Come in on Monday and pitch the partnership'.

"At the time I was like: 'Oh no! I need to really go explore this and build a business plan... I'm not ready to do that. I'll be back in a few months,'" Maria recalled. "But he really pushed me hard to come in that following Monday. So I had to learn an awful lot about cyber security in the next six days!"

Cirino went in and pitched her idea, which was then funded by Charles River Ventures, Sequoia Capital, and New Enterprise Associates. Her company, Guardent, was one of the first security service providers and got acquired by VeriSign just four and a half years later. At the end of her tenure at VeriSign, she was approached by VC firms again, but contrary to the popular advice to take any opportunity one gets to break into venture capital, Maria wasn't rushing.

At a dinner with a former colleague, she was telling him about all the offers from venture capital firms, when he said, 'I want to introduce you to a venture capitalist who is looking to start a new fund. I'm thinking about becoming a founding team member there, and I think you should think about it, too.' That was how .406 Ventures started, back in 2006, and grew over the years into a VC firm with $700 million under management and four vintages of funds.

"My 13 years in venture capital feel like three!" Maria said. "It's been the fastest and most fun ride I could ever have imagined. I have had the good fortune to back talented entrepreneurs who do the greatest things in the world."

Maria's success story is one of the most solid stories I've heard. I, of course, asked for her secret recipe. "A lot of it was finding myself in the right place at the right time. I was very lucky to work with great teams building great companies. However, I was mindful about that luck. Having been part of a couple of very successful companies early on really boosted my career, because it helped me establish a pattern of success. When you have that knowledge, people pay attention to you. They recognize that you have seen successful patterns, which they would want you to bring into their companies or situations, and replicate them in their environment. That will get you in the door, but whether or not you get invited to the next party, is all about what you do when you get in. Are you hard-working? Are you a problem solver? Are you collegial and a team player?

"The greatest compliment that I have received throughout my career, is that I'm a 'gonna make it happen' person. Think about what that means: you don't let anything get in your way, you solve problems — none of them are insurmountable, you figure it out, you take on the toughest task, and no job is too big. You do it with a great attitude, and you somehow get it done," Maria was saying all of this with a hypnotizing conviction, and it strongly resonated with my personal experience.

Cirino was the only female investing partner at .406 Ventures for a long time, and we couldn't help but talk about that. "I started getting asked that question at some point a lot. I was actively involved in the diversity initiatives of the National Venture Capital Association (NVCA), at the board level, and I didn't want to be a hypocrite. So I said to my partners that we should be more mindful about our hiring funnel and make sure that our next hire would bring more diversity into our firm," Maria started another big part of our conversation.

"We absolutely would not have been able to increase our diversity, had we not collectively agreed to do that. Based merely on the numbers in the hiring process, we would very likely have ended up with another white male hire. But we were willing to wait until the right candidate showed up. We made an intentional effort, which came out of the fact that this diversity conversation is happening today across the VC industry... finally! This is long overdue and an exciting evolution for the VC industry as a whole — and kudos to the NVCA in particular, for pushing the agenda and forcing the conversation to happen.

"I remember how many discussions we had at its board meetings a few years ago about what we were doing for women and minorities; why VC firms seemed unconcerned about whether or not their portfolio companies were hiring them; as well as ignorant to their internal diversity. The whole campaign that we launched, was aimed at bringing awareness to this matter, because the NVCA is an organization that's supposed to help VC firms — not police them. So the best thing that they can do is to have a very unemotional data-driven argument about what the industry looks like.

"A lot of that has happened in the last few years and the volume reached a fever pitch with #MeToo. However, this industry is not going to get fixed fast, given that partner hires and internal transitions sometimes take decades in VC firms. The good news, however, is that the lighthouse is shining on firms that have long ignored diversity, and the press attention has made some very senior VCs uncomfortable to the point where they're looking to increase diversity in their firms to avoid negative PR attention. Just based on numerous conversations I've had on this topic with male colleagues from other VC firms over the past couple of years, I guarantee that there are so many more men in venture capital today, who are thinking about making their firms more diverse when the next hiring opportunity arises, and that's progress. That definitely wasn't on people's minds a few years ago. Is it enough? Perhaps not, but it is at least a positive step in the right direction. Sadly, I think we did a better job of hiring more women in technology back in the 90s without as much effort," Maria mentioned quietly.

It was time to talk about female entrepreneurs, and I asked Maria about the ratio of female founders pitching her. "Quite frankly, I am very surprised that we don't see more female entrepreneurs in enterprise IT and deep tech," Cirino shared. "The ones that I see more frequently are working on consumer-oriented startups. They often ask me for advice, and I sometimes find that they take that rule of 'working on a solution for your own pain', too literally. Many of their ideas are shaped by personal experiences, i.e. scheduling their kids' sports events or time-consuming grocery shopping. That's not a world-changing idea, so I am constantly encouraging women to think bigger. Here's what I mean.

"Creating a change-the-world solution or solving a bleeding head wound problem may come because you lived a problem as a practitioner, but it may also result from the experiences of the customers of a business that you work for. Here's what we love to back at .406 Ventures: an individual or individuals who have lived a problem as operators in a technology company, where this company has unintentionally created a pain point, and is ignoring it — or, for a variety of reasons, it is unwilling or incapable of solving it for their own customers. These people have deep and first-hand insights into this pain and can apply some entrepreneurial thinking to solve the problem.

"That is exactly what happened to me before I started my own company. I suggested to the founder of the company I had worked for, that we start a security division, but he was adamantly against it. Thank goodness he was, because otherwise I probably wouldn't have started my company, and would have just stayed working for him. By talking to customers, I understood their unmet needs and had an idea of how to fix them. So, if the reader of this book is working for a business that has customers who have problems that the company is unable or unwilling to solve, leave! Draw up that business plan and come talk to us, whether you're a man or a woman or a purple squirrel!"

Many non-tech female founders would experience one and the same problem in this scenario: they'd have a hard time fundraising, because almost all VCs want to see a team with at least one technical co-founder. I challenged Maria with this fact and she immediately came back at me. "When I started a security company, I couldn't spell 'security' and that's true!" she belly-laughed. "I hired a handful of the smartest security people I could find. My pitch to them was simple, 'I'm starting this company. I have VCs who are willing to back me because I've worked as an executive at four successful startups in a row. I understand what it takes to build a successful company, but I don't understand security.' We taught each other different skills, and it was a very exciting and ultimately very gratifying time.

"When we started, there had already been a couple of other companies founded by security people ahead of us. However, they didn't have a clue about how to build a fast-growing business, which was our magic! We ran right by them, because one thing I knew was how to operate a successful tech startup. Having that pattern recognition, knowing how to find customers, build scalable systems, and create a strong company culture — all of that turned out to be much more important than the actual mechanics of security, which I learned over time.

"So, if you are not a tech founder, team up with tech people! There are a lot of tech founders out there who simply don't have the EQ to lead a company. The majority of women have a high EQ by nature, so they can definitely use that to their advantage, bring this critical piece of the equation to the table, and in the best of scenarios, create a tremendous collaboration. I'm sure Mark Zuckerberg brought Sheryl Sandberg into the company for that reason as well, and that seems to have worked out pretty darn well for them and Facebook!" Maria cheered.

"Entrepreneurs need to understand that most VCs are gender blind. You don't get any extra credit for being a woman, and you don't get any extra credit for being a man. We don't care about gender when it comes to who we are backing, but we care deeply about experience, good DNA, drive, and perseverance. These are the characteristics that make entrepreneurs great.

"We have our fiduciary duty to our limited partners to invest their money wisely. Our job as fund managers is not to solve the sexism problem that's endemic in the venture capital industry. Our job is to provide the biggest return we can. As I said earlier, we're committed to increasing our firm's diversity when hiring investment professionals, and continually remind our portfolio companies that the most successful companies are built by diverse teams and boards. We also know from experience that diversity of opinions is critically important for robust decision-making. Our limited partners are very keen on diversifying their portfolio of general partners as well. But when it comes to investing money, investors will typically invest in an idea that stands on its own merit," Cirino said with conviction.

Elizabeth "Beezer" Clarkson

Managing Director, Sapphire Ventures, United States

Elizabeth Clarkson, or as she prefers to be called 'Beezer', takes the other side of the investment table: in addition to its traditional growth fund, Sapphire Ventures also invests in early-stage VC funds as a limited partner (LP) through the Sapphire Partners platform she leads. It all started as SAP Ventures — a venture arm of the German-based enterprise software and database technology giant — and launched with a growth fund in 1996. In 2011, the investment vehicle became independent of SAP, rebranding as Sapphire Ventures in 2014. The firm's growth platform has invested in more than 100 companies, and helped to create more than $100 billion in enterprise value.

Beezer sees the women in venture capital topic from both the general and limited partner perspective, but we dedicated our conversation to her experience only as a limited partner. "I wish I saw more female general partners of venture funds. Although the surveys show some improvement in the industry, it is still not common to see a woman pitching limited partners," she prefaced the part of our conversation on diversity in venture capital. Along those lines, she shared with me a couple of trends she has observed in the industry today, which we focused on for this book.

"I see a fair number of men and women leaving established VC firms, and raising their own funds as solo general partners. I don't have enough empirical evidence to say whether this is happening more often than in the past, but it definitely feels like it," Clarkson always prefers evidence-based facts to blind assumptions. "I haven't found a great explanation as to why there is more of this activity now, because I've been asking that question myself for a while, but I assume that being a solo GP is the most direct path these days, if you don't want to wait until you find a reliable partner to start a new fund with.

"It's never easy to raise a fund, and finding an **equal partner** to work with is extraordinarily hard. If you're new to venture capital, figuring out who you want to work with, adds a lot of pressure to something that is already complex. So I understand people who decide to do it by themselves, rather than trying to find a partner before they can go and pitch investors. It can take a long time to build a strong partnership and be able to show potential LPs that the partners can work well together. If you do it on your own, you can just hit the ground running and make it happen," Beezer explained the premises of the phenomenon.

"There is a persistent running commentary in venture capital that while an average marriage lasts only seven years, a VC fund's typical life cycle is usually 12 years. Hence, being in a VC partnership will last longer than the average marriage, especially if you're going to raise more than one fund together. It's no wonder that such partnerships should be built over time and with thoughtfulness. Having a partner, at the end of the day, can add some real stability to a VC firm as a business as well, but not everyone wants to wait until they find the right person for that.

"The downside of this speedy solution, is a natural cap on how much and how often you can raise as a single general partner. Due to this one-person GP structure, the amount of money they can raise tends to be small. I keep encouraging people to band together, so that they can raise more money, because it's very hard to get institutional capital into the sub-$125 million funds, let alone sub-$50 million funds. Solo general partners usually end up in this 'large/small numbers' challenge," she broke it down.

"On the other hand, there may be a distinct strategy about going solo at the very beginning. Kirsten Green was a single general partner at her first fund — Forerunner Ventures. Sunil Dhaliwal also raised the first fund for Amplify

Partner all by himself. They both started with sub-$50 million size funds and grew their firms into multi-GP platforms.

"Venture capital is a people's business, both within VC firms, as well as externally. A lot of success and failure comes down to interpersonal dynamics. There does need to be a great deal of compatibility within the partnership, an agreement on how the partners want to work together, and what kind of strategy they want to pursue. As the firm gets growing, how do partners want to evolve? Because it all becomes very personal over the years. People naturally learn and grow over time and at some point their preferences may change — someone might want to keep investing in early-stage startups, while another partner might want to pursue growth stage. How do you deal with that?" Beezer continued.

"It's hard for there to be one right answer to anything, and there are a lot of aspects of managing a VC partnership. That is why limited partners see GPs not only as money managers, but also as actors in a business that is highly dependent on the team. People may wake up in the morning and feel that they don't want to work together anymore, or that they're not working together well, or something else may happen. It is very common, in our experience, that if something breaks in a VC partnership, it's almost always going to be the people.

"I always laugh at the dichotomy between how fast our world is changing these days with all the new tech, sharing and gig economy, and ways of doing bite-size options on things. And yet, venture capital is still the old world where investors are supposed to do what they have been doing every single day, for the next 50 years to come. Nor is venture the job for everyone, and it is quite a challenge for any partnership.

"That is why I am receptive to the idea that some general partners are going to show up one day and say, 'I'm done. This was an awesome run for X number of years, but I am not gonna do it anymore'. I think it would be unrealistic to not expect that. Just think about all the changes in your life that happened within the last 10 years — that's just one fund's average life cycle. You would expect people to evolve, and that can have different ramifications.

"At this point, as a limited partner, I want to know how a VC firm would deal with succession, which is a tricky thing in venture capital. There aren't that many firms that have gone through a whole series of different successions, and still maintained the same performance. This is part of what limited partners are thinking about when they listen to pitches from general partners."

Before switching to the next topic of our conversation, I asked Clarkson whether it makes sense to send cold emails to institutional investors. "I'd like to believe that cold emails work as well as warm introductions, because many first-time fund managers don't have broad networks among limited partners, and this may be their only way of reaching out. However, what I observe is that usually the cold emails we get are under-researched. If an email starts with 'Dear Mr Beezer', it is not an awesome way to open up the dialogue, because you haven't found time to even look at our website, right?" she snickered.

"While I would never close the door on cold calls in general, the majority of cold emailed pitches didn't land on my desk because they just hadn't been thought through well enough. We have a website, we blog, we tweet, we speak at different conferences, we put our information out there, so folks could research us. After all, as an investor, you'll have to do your due diligence on startups as well, so if you fail to do it now on people you are pitching your fund to, what sort of signal does that send?

"On the other hand, not all warm intros are equally warm. For me, the best warm intro is the one that comes from a person who has had a previous relationship with a general partner and can speak highly of them. That's compelling. I'd certainly listen to that. It's super helpful if the warm intro can actually speak to their investing experience or other things of a relevant nature. If an introducing person just says that they know somebody, it is not really a warm intro. It's better than nothing, but it's not as good as a recommendation that can speak to how they are differentiated as a general partner."

Another trend that we discussed with Beezer, is that there is a rarely considered driver of diversity in venture capital and the tech industry as a whole, which is entrepreneurs themselves.

"One of the conversations that I've been hearing in the ecosystem, and find very interesting, is that founders and executives of tech companies want to have diversity among their investors as well, both at the GP and, potentially, the LP levels. For them, diversity is larger than just gender alone, and also includes background, ethnicity, socio-economic factors, and so on. The founder-driven discussion of diversity in venture capital is really interesting, because, essentially, a founder is a client in our industry, and if your client says that they want to see it, you have to pull activity through the system faster." Beezer was one of just a couple of investors who brought up this idea.

"I am hearing founders saying that they would like to see diversity on their boards formed by their investors in large part. They proactively solve problems, they try to tackle them based on real-life experience, and they want to have investors who understand the whole spectrum of needs among their customers. I like this trend, because it comes from an unexpected side of the table and can actually make venture capital firms accelerate diversity faster."

I asked Clarkson about what activities LPs might be doing differently as part of this effort and she replied, "We, unfortunately, don't get to see other LPs' due diligence, but we hear that new questions are being asked when institutional investors make investment decisions. They want to know the GP team's equity composition, and their hiring plans, and how their portfolio companies are doing in terms of diversity and inclusion. These discussions between general and limited partners became a reality due to a whole bunch of activities in the field. Hopefully, the net result will move everybody forward, but we're still in the process.

"No one person holds the key to making an industry-wide change. It's going to involve all parts of the ecosystem, and all the different groups working together to create that change. Entrepreneurs are a really important component in that, because there are many more entrepreneurs and employees in startups then there are venture investors. If diversity is present in startups, and of interest to them and their investors, then all together we are definitely capable of moving the needle."

Lisa Coca

Managing Director, GE Ventures, United States

Lisa Coca spent more than a decade working in real estate in various roles. When the global stock markets crashed in 2011, GE Capital decided to exit the real estate business, and Coca was left to consider 'what's next'. "After the announcement, I began to search for new opportunities and met with a corporate male recruiter who looked at my resume and said, 'You have such deep domain in real estate! Why wouldn't you find a job in the sector?'" Lisa stopped talking for a second to emphasize that she expected a different opinion. "But I was fortunate to secure an informational interview with Beth Comstock, a former vice chair of General Electric, who looked at my resume and didn't comment on the real estate expertise at all. Instead, she said, 'Wow! All the different things you've done and the different skills you have! I can think of a bunch of different places where I could plug you in,'" Lisa recalled.

"I was blown away by her reaction, which to this day is one of the most important and pivotal encounters in my career — not only did it serve as my entrée to venture capital, but it also represented one woman trying to help and elevate another. She looked at what I had accomplished and saw it as an indication of what I was capable of, of my potential and ability to go all in and acquire new skill sets and expertise. And she was willing to take a chance on me."

Coca has an impressive pedigree. After graduating from Wharton's undergraduate program, she started off on Wall Street, obviously became very comfortable with numbers, and subsequently completed her MBA at Stanford. She's done sales and marketing for real estate and private equity

funds, as well as strategy, new products, and new market introduction. But all of this breadth of experience was in a pretty narrow sector, which she was always mindful about — commercial real estate.

"That meeting with Comstock was very much a point of introspection for me, because the easiest path to take would obviously have been to leverage my extensive network in real estate business and find a new opportunity outside of GE. But I knew that if I did that, I would probably stay in this field for the rest of my life. I had demonstrated an ability to successfully acquire new skill sets and decided it was time to leverage that ability to move into a new domain. So I ventured. I knew that there were a lot of challenges around working in a very large organization, but there are also plenty of opportunities. I decided to take that chance to find a new path for my career.

"This story changed a lot in my life. I now like to describe myself as a Jack of all trades, and unlike the common opinion that says that a Jack of all trades is a master of none, I know for certain that a Jack of all trades can also be a master of many!" Coca triumphantly declared.

GE Ventures started as a project, and Lisa received her first 'bubble assignment' — a part-time project-based assignment that could go somewhere or... nowhere. The project got approved and Lisa joined it as one of the very first employees. When I asked her about the learning curve and skills she had or didn't have for a job in corporate venture capital, she gave another bold answer.

"I had worked on Wall Street, so I brought a background steeped in complex financial models, which I, honestly, never used. Venture capital is not rocket science. It's less about finance and more about soft skills. I found that it's critically important for a successful venture capitalist to be curious and passionate, to develop domain expertise, and to build a network of relationships. In my opinion, those are the table stakes in venture capital.

"I am a naturally very curious person and have a passion for excellence. If I say that I'm going to do something, I'm going to do it really well. With only these two pillars, you can learn everything else. I learned to identify the signals of a successful startup, and the red flags of a weak team and operations. And my background in strategy has been a point of leverage in identifying new market opportunities. I worked closely with Karen Kerr, who mentored me through all the deal-making processes, coupled with whatever I learned from reading, seminars and my participation in Kauffman Fellowship Program. I also religiously attended our investment committee meetings from day one, even when they were dedicated to deals outside of my investment focus.

"I probably needed to work harder, and to be as well-equipped and informed as my male peers, if not more so, but I never considered it a barrier. I jumped in with both feet, and the experience has exceeded my expectations. I sit on boards with some of the most prominent and successful male VCs in the industry. I've worked with successful serial male CEOs and entrepreneurs. And I can honestly say that I have never felt marginalized, never felt that my voice was not heard — neither in the boardroom nor anywhere else — in the eight years that I've been in the industry. I am not a fan of the blanket use of the word 'meritocracy', but I do think that I've earned respect solely because of my contribution," Lisa said humbly.

"When I invest in a company, the most important thing is how much value I bring to that business. I want the CEO to know that whatever he or she needs, I'm there to assist. I want co-investors to know that I'm doing everything I can to help the company scale and grow. That is the most important thing that builds my brand — not the fact that I am a woman."

Lisa opened the door to my favorite question about the reasons why we keep hearing the stories about male VCs being less respectful towards female VCs, which is contrary to her experiences. "There's definitely a spotlight on the industry right now, because of the lack of diversity and inclusion. But the reality is that most industries are male-dominated, because most companies are managed and controlled by men at the top. Each of them has gone, or will go, through a change, to become more diverse than they were. What's happening in the venture capital industry is similar to what happened on Wall Street decades ago. I've earned my recognition in both industries, regardless, because I've always worked hard. If we want to excel in these industries, we need to promote equality for the future, but we also need to accept the reality of today. If you can't — just opt out. But the change we want, will not happen overnight, let's be real.

"If we force this change from within, we risk causing more damage than good. For example, we can call VC firms out and compel them to hire more women. We can see how everyone is focused on talent acquisition these days and getting those diverse numbers up to show a change. But ultimately, it is about more than the raw numbers. If the culture of those firms is not fundamentally changing, the numbers we are celebrating today will flatline and eventually go down. Women will start to opt out and we'll get back to the status quo. We need to remember that venture capital has a very long-tailed financial cycle. It's hard to quit without losing your share. And if the culture of the firm isn't changing, women will have to leave and lose or stay and struggle. None of the outcomes is what we fight for.

"It'll be interesting to see how everything plays out. A lot of effort is made today to step up the recruiting, and I hope that an equally strong effort is being made within those VC firms to change their 'bro culture' and the mindset, so that the women they hire can actually succeed after all. However, I think the greatest change will likely come from outside the walls of today's VC firms — from women launching their own funds and from increased funding to startups with diverse teams."

We also touched upon competition in the tribes of first-time general partners and younger investment professionals. "It's absolutely there," Lisa was certain. "There are men out there who are threatened by the fact that more and more intellectual women are surrounding them, but there are also women who are threatened by other women as well. Internal competition is the reality of business in general and is not exclusive to venture capital. You just gotta put your big girl pants on and deal with it!"

Before we finished our conversation, I asked Lisa what she has learned about female entrepreneurs as a VC. "The upsetting thing is that we are battling for equality as females, but when we stand in the limelight, individually, we have a tendency to underestimate ourselves. Where does all the confidence go? I don't think there are as many women as there are men who think highly of themselves, their ideas, and their CEO potential, and who are very comfortable going in and pitching hard. The 'imposter syndrome' for women is, unfortunately, all too real.

"In my experience, on average, women's pitches and presentations generally tend to be stronger. Women know what they're up against and do their homework well. The startup world is not for the faint of heart, right? Yet, even among those women who dared to raise venture funding, too few are receiving checks as large as men do. Of course, the explanation of it depends on how you paint it. One can say that women underestimate their potential, others would say that women are being more realistic and practical about their capital needs and, of course, some would say it is the unlevel playing field. I would say that it's all of the above! And regardless of which of these explanations you choose, one thing is obvious - we need to take control of the reins and ownership of our own destiny!"

Vanessa Colella

Head, Citi Ventures,

United States

"She is as strategic as she is bold," said Arvind Purushotham, Managing Director at Citi Ventures in Palo Alto about Vanessa Colella. Indeed, when I asked her about what could be done in venture capital to attract more diverse investors, she described how the industry is changing across the world, thus creating new opportunities that should be taken by women and minorities, rather than expecting that they will be given to them.

"Humans are neurologically wired to react to change that happens quickly. We learn about the 'fight or flight mode' in early science classes, because it is embedded in humans by nature. However, a change that happens slow is harder for people to see and react to," Vanessa's biological background was speaking.

Recognizing such hidden changes is a venture investor's job. That is why I am a big advocate of systems thinking: if you were not schooled in this art, it's never too late to study it on your own. As for Vanessa, not only did she graduate from MIT with a degree in biology, but she also taught courses on the dynamics of complex systems. She always thought long-term, even when she started teaching kids right out of college. "I was interested not only in education but more so in the areas that require large-scale change and transformation. I joined the charter corps of Teach for America, because public education, particularly for the underserved communities that we were working with, was one such area.

"I was a molecular geneticist by training, so I taught science to seventh-graders. I was fascinated by what we could do in the education field that could help change the trajectory for students, but also the system overall. When one works as a teacher, one gets a really great grasp of all kinds of challenges and issues that students and teachers face every day in the classroom. You can get a ground-level view of what works and what doesn't, but you have less — if any — of that bird's eye view of the overall system, and a poor understanding of how the things that work can be scaled," she artfully explained by breaking down complex issues into units, drawing from her own experience.

"I started spending a lot of time in technology and education, with different sorts of tools that could help drive change across the education system. And I realized that I just didn't know enough to drive that kind of transformation from a single classroom. I thought a lot about how behavior and technology are changing, and I needed to learn how those two things can come together to make a systemic change," Vanessa continued.

"I went back to graduate school to learn from Seymour Papert and Mitchel Resnick, pioneers in technology and education, at the MIT Media Lab. One of the really interesting things about studying there was that the corporations were bringing in real-world challenges or problems that they saw, and we were trying to connect those challenges to technology that students at the lab might be exploring. It was a fascinating way to realize how little I understood about corporations."

By her early 30s, Vanessa had never worked for any company, staying in some form of academia — either studying or teaching. She decided to work for McKinsey, for two reasons. "Firstly, the notion of transformational change that consulting companies help their clients overtake, was intriguing. Secondly, I read a lot about how much one learns about the intricacies of business by working in consulting, and I knew nothing."

All of Vanessa's previous years of experience, together with her half a decade tenure at McKinsey, were well spent. She quickly accelerated from there to working at one of the largest tech companies at the time, which was Yahoo!. However, it wasn't a big corporation that intrigued Vanessa. She got really curious about rapidly growing small businesses, aka startups, and how she could help them deal with the management challenges that they had, and how they could achieve their aspirations most effectively. She tested her abilities at US Venture Partners (USVP) as an entrepreneur-in-residence for a while and got recruited by Citibank soon after.

When we were speaking about diversity, Vanessa was fairly optimistic. "Venture capital, as an industry, is undergoing a significant structural change. It is slow and therefore barely noticeable to the untrained eye. When we look back 20 years from now, we will see this time period as a time when the industry probably changed a lot. I think that gives us a lot of opportunities to bring new kinds of people into the field and to change mindsets and behavior. But it won't just happen on its own without enough effort from everyone involved.

"Firstly, we need to expose our own biases, which are natural for both men and women. There are a lot of studies on the matter, but one of them (unrelated to venture capital) by which I, personally, was intrigued, studied the auditioning of musicians for an orchestra. To exclude gender bias, they started auditioning people behind a curtain. However, when people were coming up, the judges could still recognize women walking across the stage in high heels from men walking in shoes. So they had to make the musicians show up in socks, to exclude that factor too! This highlights just how much work we need to do to address bias.

"Secondly, and most importantly, we have to stay focused on the goal of making our environment more diverse, because the biggest danger is that we make a little bit of progress and think that we don't need to do anything anymore, which makes us slide right back to where we were. We need to make it a habit of making sure that the voices around the table are heard and funded."

Barbara Dalton

Senior Managing Partner,

Pfizer Ventures, United States

Barbara Dalton calls herself an accidental tourist in venture capital. She walked out of a research laboratory and moved into VC overnight. She believes that everyone in a venture capital firm has to bring something else to the table, besides an MBA. "I can train a scientist to be a business person, but it's difficult to train someone to do things the way scientists do them. So I do believe that VC firms should hire people with different unique experiences and skills that can't be easily trained," Barbara said.

With a PhD in microbiology and immunology, Dalton got introduced to venture capital in 1993. "It was before the rest of the world really understood venture investing. I had spent 10 years in the research lab of a pharmaceutical company, when their corporate venture capital group called me up and asked me to help them with the due diligence of the companies they were looking at. I did that for them for a couple of years, and then I decided that it was time for me to move out of the lab and do something else," Barbara looked back.

She was planning to find a business development job within the corporation, which was a common track for scientists, when that venture capital group invited her to work with them instead. "I was offered a job because they needed a scientist. They had a lawyer, a finance and a business development professional on the team, and I was that different piece of the puzzle that was missing.

"A lot of people nowadays are trying to chart their career paths to get into venture capital, whereas that was not a planned future for me. I just happened to be in the right place at the right time, with the right background, set of skills, and expertise that proved to be valuable for a member of a corporate venture capital team. But the only reason why they knew about my existence in the corporation at all, was because I took a train to Baltimore one day and happened to bump into the head of that venture capital group and got introduced to him. There was a lot of serendipity, and I stayed in venture capital for more than 25 years already."

Barbara agreed with the notion frequently discussed in this book, that corporate venture capital is friendlier towards women in general. "Throughout my career, I have never felt isolated or separated out, although I'm sometimes the only woman in the room. I think corporations are enlightened to the fact that a diverse workforce makes them stronger, and many of them have done an excellent job of advancing women in different executive positions.

"When we compare corporate businesses with VC firms, we need to remember that most of those corporations are much larger than the average VC firm. Pfizer has close to 100,000 employees, which, I guess, is more than all the staff in the entire venture capital industry in the United States.

"Many VC firms consist of only a couple of buddies who raised money together and agreed to split the profits, so there is not much we can expect from such firms. Larger VC firms nowadays are becoming more formally functioning balanced organizations, and in this case, women naturally become part of the team," Barbara characterized the opposite structures of VC firms.

When I asked what set her apart from male colleagues with similar skill sets, that caused her to be invited by the corporate venture group, instead of them, Barbara said, "I was asking a lot of questions as a scientist, which is quite useful in venture investing in general, and scientists are professionally trained to be curious. I believe I was also perceived as a people person — somebody who could survive with all the schmoozing and cocktail parties that are necessary to be successful in the industry, and someone who had no fear of cold calling."

It was time to talk about other qualities and skills that can help women to get into venture capital and become successful investors.

"Women need to be well-connected. They need to generate a lot of respect in external communities, so that people only speak highly of them, their skill sets, and achievements. I place a high value on women's intuition and gut feelings, coupled with the fact that women are calculated risk-takers. This is quite valuable in venture capital, although it is sometimes misunderstood and called 'risk aversion', when compared to bettors.

"In addition to that, venture capital is a people business. Staying away from people who create problems and gravitating more to those who are going to be successful, is a skill that nobody can teach. I'm going to be biased here, but I think women are better at a lot of those people-oriented skills," Barbara stated.

When answering my question about the things venture capitalists can do better to attract more diverse talent into the industry, Dalton made a great suggestion to all those VCs who won't be 'lowering the bar' for women and diverse candidates. "I think that the older generation of VCs has a responsibility to teach and train the younger generation, whether within or outside of the firms. I see that the younger generation of VCs will bring new skills, new tools, new technologies, new ways of thinking about things, and they are also very welcoming of diversity to change the landscape of the industry in the near future. Every VC firm that doesn't have room for a diverse hire now, can increase diversity indirectly in the long term, by mentoring the new generation of venture investors outside of their firms." In line with that, any VC firm is welcome to offer internships to the students of VC Academy, who we train before placement.

Alda Dennis

General Partner, Initialized Capital, United States

Alda Leu Dennis expressed her somewhat contrarian point of view on building a career in venture capital. "I don't think that apprenticeship is absolutely necessary in venture capital. It is certainly useful to have a mentor — someone who'd help you along the way — but I don't think it's imperative. There are plenty of ways of getting into venture capital, so I wouldn't want anyone to limit their options, even by commonly held opinions." That wasn't the only uncommon sentiment she brought up in our conversation.

In between being an attorney for a prominent VC firm and an investor, Alda had a stop off at Airtime, a social network started by Sean Parker and Shawn Fanning — visionnaire entrepreneurs who built several notable companies. "What working for a startup offered me, was a particular kind of understanding of how products were created, how tech stacks were architected, and how consumer distribution worked, among other things. I developed my knowledge of the struggles that founders go through on a daily basis. When you are an investor and work closely with your portfolio companies as a de facto executive coach or trying to help them with general management, you will be more efficient if your advice is informed by your own experiences. Otherwise, I think you just don't have the same amount of empathy for what they're going through," Dennis expressed her opinion.

After Airtime, she moved on to 137 Ventures, a growth-stage venture firm that provides customized liquidity solutions to founders, investors, and early employees of tech companies. However, early-stage investing was more attractive to Alda, so she joined Initialized Capital, a VC firm founded by Alexis Ohanian (co-founder and executive chairman of the social news website Reddit) and Garry Tan (co-founder of Posterous and Posthaven, and former partner at Y Combinator), where she now serves as a General Partner.

Based on her experience over the years, across different competencies, Dennis shared another interesting point of view. She thinks that the world doesn't appreciate the role of the people beyond the visionnaire founders, in particular, the operating executives who actually make the gears run, 24/7. "I'm seeing more and more venture-backed tech companies, where a visionary CEO works hand in hand with someone who's really good on the execution side. I would be hard pressed to say which one is more valuable, but it's hard to have one without the other.

"If you look in history books, there are a fair number of unicorn startups that had someone with a strong vision, who was very inspirational and great at sales, paired with another person, who was really creative at execution, listening to people's problems, finding solutions, and getting things done.

"In such cases, we should train the limelight a little less on the chief executive officer and a little more on the chief operating officer," she said. "A visionary, charismatic CEO goes a long way. Certainly, you want to have someone who can recruit talents, raise money, and convince strategic partners to work with you... More important than all of those sales attributes, however, is the vision and ability to transform or revolutionize products or services, or even entire industries. But it's absolutely crucial to convert this vision into actions that can actually be accomplished. That is where an operational wiz steps in."

We spoke with Alda when the movie about Theranos, possibly the biggest fraud in Silicon Valley, just premiered, and we discussed this topic.

"I thought a lot about the level of due diligence — especially in early-stage investing — that would be sufficient for an investor, but not excessive. We've heard stories, and I've witnessed first-hand, where startups have presented numbers that were simply not true. I have found that references on the founding team are possibly the most valuable thing we can do, especially if we don't have a pre-existing relationship with the founders. Because ultimately, if someone wants to pull the wool over your eyes, they'll figure out a way to do it. And our job is to spot those falsehoods early on by listening to what other people have to say about them, coupled with enough due diligence to notice red flags."

Lastly, when we were talking about her portfolio, Alda shared another observation — I asked her whether she saw any difference between male and female entrepreneurs, their presentations, and funding requests.

"No, systematic differences are not something that I've observed. As an investor, I can totally affect any situation by simply asking the right questions that don't create the grounds for the wrong impressions in the first place. I can guide the conversation in a way that allows entrepreneurs to feel confident and empowered, instead of being apologetic or timid."

Jesse Draper

Founding Partner, Halogen Ventures, United States

Jesse Draper is the third Draper that I have met. Her father, Tim Draper, and her grandfather, Bill Draper, have never left any of my emails unanswered. I always appreciated how approachable they were, and Jesse turned out to be a true Draper in every way as well. She was busy 'creating female billionaires of the future' when I reached out to her, but saw her contribution to this book as a part of her mission, and we had a fun and inspiring conversation.

It was no surprise that Jesse was nominated by entrepreneurs for this book, because her VC firm, Halogen Ventures, invests in female-led companies and has an impressive track record for their first vintage. However, what I liked most about her profile, is that she is another example of a very unconventional way of getting into venture capital. By 'unconventional', I partly mean that despite being a Draper, becoming an investor wasn't her plan until several years ago. She was one of the first people to test AIM (AOL's Instant Messenger), attended the first Skype board meeting in Estonia, and participated in the first ever Skype video conference when she was 16. All of the investing insights that she absorbed so early in life, would make any budding investor appropriately confident, but Jesse wasn't really into it. Another remarkable part of her story, is that venture investing grew on her while she was hosting a TV show.

Jesse Draper, the oldest of Tim Draper's four children, graduated from the University of California, Los Angeles, with a degree in theater. She had always wanted to be an actress like her aunt, Polly Draper, who is best known for playing Ellen on the 1980s television hit "Thirtysomething". Jesse was in demand at numerous castings and even got a part in the Nickelodeon show.

With an inherited bone for business, Jesse decided to launch her own startup, but in entertainment. She leveraged her passion and connections in the tech world to create her own show, The Valley Girl — for which she negotiated widespread distribution, received critical acclaim, and even got nominated for Emmy Awards. She had hundreds of renowned guests from the tech and startup worlds, including Steve Wozniak, Ron Conway, Eric Schmidt, Mark Cuban, Elon Musk, Sandra Day O'Connor, Jessica Alba, and Sheryl Sandberg. "The best part of what Jesse does, is forcing overly serious people to take themselves less seriously," said Kara Swisher, a long-time Silicon Valley journalist, about her show back then.

Jesse learned a lot about TV show production and distribution in the early days of digital media, and she went through all the processes herself, including booking, producing, hosting, and even selling sponsorships. The epiphany happened when Jesse noticed that out of all her guests, very few of them were women. She decided to leverage the popularity of her show to increase the visibility of female-led startups that she invited onto the show, and invest in some of them. That was how Jesse slowly and organically became an angel investor, thereby embracing her Draper DNA.

It was just a matter of time before Jesse began to realize that she could do much more good, if she raised a venture capital fund. Now, you might think that for a Draper, that would be a piece of cake, but you'd be mistaken. When Jesse was raising her first fund in 2016, she had 157 potential investors on her shortlist after eliminating all the no's and maybe's. She closed 40 of them, which is a pretty great result for a first-time fund manager, however, it wasn't as simple as it might seem.

"Some of the institutional investors I was talking to, had eagerly signed million dollar checks to a first-time male fund manager, while I had to fight for each $250,000 check. By the time I started fundraising, I had had a 25x return on my previous investment, which is a great track record on its own — especially at my age. So when I heard again and again that I was a first-time VC, hence the reason for only giving me a small check, I felt really frustrated, because as a woman I was obviously being held to a higher standard, even though my previous investments could speak for themselves," Jesse confessed.

"Fundraising is tough in general — you just have to stay at it. I tried to optimize the process by using several tricks. Firstly, I knew that if I hadn't closed an investor by the third meeting, then I probably wouldn't close them at all. You know who is interested and who isn't pretty early on, so don't waste your time on someone who hems and haws. Secondly, there is such a thing as a bad investor, so I tried to avoid taking money from such. Even if it takes you a little longer to raise it, you will be happier in the end. Finally, Leah Busque from Taskrabbit changed my perspective on fundraising by teaching me to enjoy it. I get to meet many incredible people and tell them about my passions, and then listen to their experiences and advice. I found myself having a one-on-one meeting with a huge idol of mine — Diane Von Furstenberg — and telling her about my fund, and I had to pinch myself!"

Besides the fact that Jesse was a first-time investor, Halogen Ventures' investment focus was on female-led consumer companies, which was yet another turn-off for many investors back then. "I think that attitude towards funding female entrepreneurs has changed in the last couple of years in general but it hasn't yet changed that much when it comes to writing checks. With my first fund, I had people telling me that I was limiting myself by only investing in women. I don't hear that as often anymore, but I still have to convince some men, who control the majority of the capital, that female-founded companies perform better than they might think. Now, I have some results to present to them from my own portfolio, as well as examples of many other companies founded by women, including some unicorns that can help them buy into that fact. My first investors who took a bet on me with my first fund, are pretty happy, because we've seen some impressive returns," she told me.

I wondered if Jesse had any women among her limited partners, and here is what she had to say. "I see more women investing these days, and I think that's fantastic! Finally, women who have a high net worth, are putting their money to work themselves, instead of just letting their husbands do it. However, I also noticed one interesting fact with high-net-worth individuals in general and women in particular. They would have billions of dollars sitting in a bank and have no problem writing a multi-million dollar check to a charity or non-profit, while paying no attention to my investment thesis. Funding women is still very often seen as an impact investment associated with trading off profits for a good cause. And when it is seen that way, it loses to other charitable causes.

"Nonprofits are oftentimes preferred to venture capital, because nobody expects you to make returns off the former. When you invest in venture businesses, you'll be asked about your returns very often, and due to a possible lack of such, people subconsciously try to avoid creating premises for this question at all.

"When I show that it's actually a very much for-profit investment, and I still see these high-net-worth individuals avoiding funding tech ventures founded by women, it makes very little sense to me. Giving money to nonprofits is mathematically the equivalent of backing entrepreneurs in general, but especially women: both create a significant impact, even if a venture investment doesn't make returns. That was another very frustrating discovery for me, because I knew for sure that we could do so much more and create a bigger impact if we invested in for-profit opportunities led by women.

"I'm trying to create female billionaires of the future, who will then disperse their wealth more equally between the genders. I know some brilliant women, like Cindy Eckert, who is most definitely one of the greatest role models for all of us. She sold her companies, which were responsible for the first female sex drugs, for more than $1 billion, and subsequently founded an incubator — The Pink Ceiling — which invests in companies founded by, or delivering products to, women. That's an example of what women will do!" Jesse was passionate.

"I make my founders promise me that they're going to invest part of their future wealth back into the female founders, because that's what Halogen is all about. We need more women taking risks. We need more women starting companies and having great exits, but also more women starting funds or becoming partners of VC firms, in order to level the playing field."

We spent some time trying to find the cornerstone reasons why women are reluctant to deal with venture capital. "I think it goes all the way back to when men handled the pocketbooks," Jesse started off. "Women still feel uncomfortable making or even talking about investments. It has been taboo to talk about money for years, so unless women work in finance, you really have to force this conversation onto them. I see women of my parents' generation and older, as well as women from my generation, who still avoid talking about investing their own money. I feel so lucky that I had a family that talked about how capital works, how you make investments, and how you lose money. That is a conversation that we all need to have. It is unfolding slowly, but I still get surprised once in a while when I meet people of my age who work on Wall Street and aren't actually buying stock."

Being the fourth generation in a family of venture capital investors, Jesse Draper could definitely share some valuable advice. "Take risks and think big. My dad always kept saying, 'Think bigger, think bigger, think bigger!' That was almost like a mantra. Today it helps me a lot, and I try to pass this lesson along to female entrepreneurs. Many women bring me ideas for a $15 million market, and I say, 'Cool! Now, go and figure out how you can multiply that market by an infinite amount. How big can your idea get, if you find another customer base, if you add a subscription, or a B2B service? Come back when you find your billion dollar market'. And they often realize that they haven't thought big enough and come back with a bunch of new revenue streams that make their ideas much more attractive for any venture capital investors. It always makes my day!

Beyond her focus on female founders, Draper has another unique practice that's a bit unorthodox for Silicon Valley. "I do believe in education, but I don't always bet on the MBA," she revealed. "I love the people who have a chip on their shoulder, who are trying to prove something, or who have come up with some new ideas out of necessity. They're solving a problem that they've experienced. That's something I'm passionate about investing in."

"I think general and limited partners have to stop investing in the same thing over and over, and finally put their money where their mouths are. Diversity is not just about women, it's about gender, as well as ethnicities and backgrounds. Diversity at large can break these investing cycles, and we'll see more women naturally getting more funding.

On a personal note, Jesse said that she finds inspiration in her parents and her two children. "I think that right now, I am incredibly inspired by women out there doing it all. I just had my second child and I am the oldest of four.

My mom is a huge hero in my eyes, because she raised four children, as did people like Meryl Streep and Maya Rudolph. I find it fascinating, and women who have children and somehow make it all work, inspire me — second to my mom. I hope that my sons will know what women are capable of by my own example. I will definitely tell them about the successes of our portfolio companies!"

Chance Du

Founding Partner, Coefficient Ventures, United States

Chance Du was a new name for me, but several entrepreneurs had mentioned her to me a number of times. She launched Coefficient Ventures at the end of 2017, and in just eight months returned more than 100x the fund's initial $200,000 worth of crypto assets at the peak price. Coefficient Ventures then started co-investing with top-tier funds, such as Andreessen Horowitz and Polychain Capital, and even after the crypto winter started, the firm's ROI didn't suffer, although most of the other crypto funds were losing money.

"I knew that Andreessen Horowitz or any other major venture capital firm were not going to hire me, no matter how determined I was," she admitted. "At that point, I realized that the only way I could succeed, was to hire myself."

Du grew up in a small village in China, where an entire family earns $3,000 a year, and only one person can get into a top university every five years. She was not that person. Despite endless hours of study, the top two universities in the country she applied to, rejected her. Chance spent three years building her first business in order to make enough money to go to Silicon Valley.

She came to the United States to sleep on a bunk bed, attending free Stanford classes and endless startup events. After some time, she gathered all the savings that were left from her business, and started investing in artificial intelligence as an angel investor. "I used all my savings to invest in startups at $25,000 per deal on average, and build a track record, to prove myself in the industry," Du said. "I had very little time to convince others to believe in me, before I completely ran out of money."

Chance started investing in blockchain companies and crypto assets, found a strong mentor among Silicon Valley white male VCs, and built her network. I, of course, asked about the challenges she faced. "I do believe that each person tends to attract a certain kind of people, regardless of gender. So even if the accumulated experience of one person is not very pleasant, it shouldn't be projected onto males or females in general," Chance proclaimed. "I certainly remember the times when I had to prove myself, but I very soon discovered that once I brought real value, people immediately started recognizing me as an equal partner, and my gender didn't really matter."

Coefficient Ventures is Du's first fund built entirely with her own money. She built a team of partners, but didn't accept outside investors. The firm operates more like a family office now, and focuses on investing not only in crypto projects, but in blockchain companies as well. Chance established a rule to step away from any investment if any member of the team behaves in a way that could be detrimental to the project, the VC, or the blockchain community as a whole. She withdrew some of her investments that could seemingly have given immediate returns, to avoid associating with people or projects that were doing the things she disagreed with. "Reputation is everything in the blockchain space, and I did not walk all the way from my home, through all the challenges, just to have my reputation destroyed."

When we talked with Chance, the crypto market was in the midst of its winter mode, and I couldn't help but ask about her next steps, now that crypto fever had been reduced. "Our main strategy is to adapt to the market, because the crypto and blockchain industry is very liquid."

Chance used this crypto winter season to build the infrastructure of her fund. She called me from Latin America where she was looking for high-quality deals. "Blockchain technologies are in high demand in developing countries, because they have broken financial systems," she said. "We are planning to spend a lot of time there this year — in Turkey, Argentina, Africa... Learning from the real world gives me a lot of insights into what the industry trends will be in the near future. We're looking at the traditional financial markets and try to figure out the existing problems and then find entrepreneurs who are ready to solve them."

Chance Du is at the very beginning of her career, so I asked about her goals for the next 15 years. "I do have a goal of making a fortune, but not for the sake of money. I want to gain more resources, in order to reinvest them into helping people to serve their communities. I want to give people like me an opportunity to be ambitious and achieve their goals," Du announced her mission. "I appreciate my own capital more than borrowed, and prefer to hold a major stake in any investment vehicle I found. Working with borrowed capital is not sustainable. At the end of the day, you return most of the proceeds to your investors and retain too little money to make a real difference. So, while having outside capital is convenient, you cannot control what the returns will be spent on. My goal is to keep reinvesting my capital for as long as I can to bring changes to depressed regions and communities. That is why my 15-year goal is to grow my own assets to a billion."

Samantha Du

Founding Partner,
Quan Capital, China

Dr Du is known as the mother of biotech in China, due to her significant influence on the industry, her work with government bodies in the country, and also for being a seasoned, successful drug developer and entrepreneur. She is also a prominent venture capitalist with a handful of successful exits, however, she warned me right away, at the beginning of our conversation, that she prefers speaking of herself as an entrepreneur more than an investor.

Samantha Du received her PhD in biochemistry at the University of Cincinnati, and began her career with Pfizer in the US. She achieved her first success as an entrepreneur after founding Hutchison MediPharma, a company that became widely recognized as a leader in innovative drug R&D in China. The company made it to IPO just five years after inception, under Du's governance. She stayed with the company for ten years in total before she decided to have a break.

"I was six months into my long-awaited vacation when Sequoia Capital approached me. I had built my network in venture capital by then and had been contemplating the idea of becoming an investor myself. However, I knew that entrepreneurship would always remain my true passion, and I was upfront about that with Michael Moritz, Sequoia's partner, when we met," Samantha recalled.

Sequoia Capital asked Du to build the firm's healthcare practice, which they didn't have at that time in the United States, nor in China. Within two years with Sequoia Capital Group, Samantha made six investments, half of which had successful exits, which is a great ratio for any investor.

It was time for Dr Du to return to her passion of building companies again. "Sequoia Capital supported my decision to return to being an entrepreneur, because it was a part of our initial agreement. That helped me to save my strong relationship with the firm. The reason I wanted to go back to building companies, was because I saw plenty of opportunities in China. The country was going through a lot of changes, from state regulations to innovations and market trends in healthcare, so I thought that it was the right time to start a new company."

Not only did Samantha want to build something new, but she also decided to build it at scale. The mission of Zai Lab is to address the largest unmet medical needs and transform patients' lives around the world. The fundamental principles of the company are discovering, developing, and commercializing innovative treatment modalities by combining both in-licensed products and internal R&D, in order to achieve a rich pipeline. This means that building various products that can exist stand-alone, is at the very core of the company. Why does it matter? Because this paved Du's way back to venture capital.

Zai Lab was launched in 2014 by a three-person team, including Samantha, and went public in 2017 at a valuation of more than a billion. This success couldn't have gone unnoticed by venture capital investors. Among all the other products that Zai Lab developed, the team also incubated three biotech startups. When Du decided to take Zai Lab to the IPO, she was contemplating the fate of these startups. "We had a lot of interest from our investors to buy them as a portfolio, but some of them also suggested creating a separate fund for these and other companies that I may find interesting in the future. That was a great opportunity, and I decided to leverage it," said Du.

She quickly formed a team for the new firm — Quan Capital — and raised $150 million from institutional investors, including such leading firms as Sequoia Capital and Qiming Ventures. The word 'quan' means 'fountain' or 'spring' in Chinese, which reflects the firm's investment approach, which is to discover, incubate and grow next-generation life sciences companies. Dr Du was very humble about her role in the firm, saying that her 'only' focus is on deal-sourcing, overall strategy, and chairing the investment committee as a founding partner.

All of the managing directors of Quan Capital are females, so I couldn't help but ask how that happened. "I didn't do that on purpose," Samantha smiled. "I just invited people that I had previously worked with, and whom I trust.

"Although venture capital in China is still dominated by men, overall, I think more and more women in the industry are becoming influential, and I am pretty satisfied with how we are advancing on this matter. I, personally, was lucky to have only positive experiences of working with men in my career, whether at the very start or later when I proved myself. However, what I have noticed, is that there are very few female entrepreneurs in China. Sometimes I even wonder whether there is a higher proportion of women in venture capital compared to women in the startup world.

"Although people in China are used to saying, 'Women hold up half the sky' [part of a proclamation made by Mao Zedong], for most women, family still comes first. I think that our traditional view on male/female role distribution holds women back. If only we could start being more accepting of stay-at-home dads, as is seen in the United States — that would change the dynamics a lot! In China, a working mom is not even a widely accepted norm yet.

"Every time I speak at events or coach female scientists and younger generations of female entrepreneurs, I encourage them to go and build something of their own. I know that it cannot be forced onto any person — male or female. There is no glass ceiling in entrepreneurship to break. Entrepreneurship is founded on one's own will. If you don't have your own will to be an entrepreneur, if you don't have a very strong mindset, commitment, and discipline, and if you haven't developed your leadership skills yet, it will be very hard."

Anu Duggal

Founding Partner,
Female Founders Fund, United States

Entrepreneur turned investor Anu Duggal launched Female Founders Fund to invest in seed-stage female-led technology companies in 2014. It took her 700 investor meetings and two years to raise just shy of $6 million for something no one had ever done before. Over the years, she invested in companies like Thrive Global, Zola, and Maven Clinic, and had her first big moment at the end of 2018, when one of her first investments, a company called Eloquii, was acquired by Walmart for a reported $100 million. "Returning capital to your investors for the first time is incredibly powerful. We want to be able to prove to the investment community that they can generate great returns with a portfolio that is 100 percent female-founded. For those male investors who still have a hard time believing that, the results will be something they can't argue with," she said. Anu and her partner, Sutian Dong, raised $27 million for the second fund with a roster of limited partners including Melinda Gates and Katrina Lake, which still keeps them in the micro VC category by Silicon Valley standards. Female Founders Fund is more evidence of the fact that even sub-$10 million funds can make impressive returns. That is why we set it as a rule at Women.VC to never ever exclude small VC funds from our studies, which is something that all the other organizations conducting similar research on women in venture capital do. Raising just a few million dollars is oftentimes harder than raising hundreds of millions.

"There were definitely days where I was wondering, 'Is this actually going to go anywhere, given how long the journey has been to even just raise capital?'" Anu admitted. "Raising a fund, as a first-time fund manager, is incredibly difficult for anyone, and that challenge wasn't unique, but the additional challenge was to convince investors that I could provide them with strong returns by investing in 100% female-founded companies — something they had never done before. Female-run companies didn't have national awareness back then, there hadn't been the Stitch Fix IPO or Eventbrite IPO yet. I heard many no's, but I would ask anyone who decided against backing the Female Founders Fund to introduce me to one additional person who might be interested. That resulted in a ton of introductions, which eventually got me to people who really understood the concept and were excited about it."

Duggal didn't attribute the challenging fundraising to her gender, but she agreed with the notion that institutional investors still prefer making safe bets and aren't active enough when it comes to diverse emerging managers. "To increase the number of female general partners starting their own funds, we should keep showing them more and more success stories and role models, so they'd know it's possible. As for the hiring of women by established VC firms, I think they need to be more aggressive in their recruiting practices. There is a lot of interest in venture capital from the candidates, but VC firms have a lot of room to grow in how actively they are looking for female investment professionals. I think this issue needs to be addressed in a more structured manner." This is exactly the problem that our niche recruiting platform for the venture capital industry is addressing.

Anu came back to New York after living in India from 2009 to 2011, where she co-founded the first wine tasting room and bar in the country and an e-commerce company called Exclusively.in. "I thought about the millions of Indians who lived outside of India and didn't have access to Indian retail or designer products. Looking at the Gilt model, there was an opportunity to build something that was really different. It was the first flash-sale online marketplace in India, and male investors, who obviously dominated the community, couldn't understand the business model. They had to go home and ask their wives, girlfriends, and daughters, whether it was something that they would use. Nevertheless, we raised about $20 million for it and eventually sold the company," Anu recounted.

In New York, Duggal started doing some angel investing and noticed that female entrepreneurs were struggling to find capital, build community, and get support. "It didn't really make sense to me, although I understood that many other investors, historically, had never seen many large technology companies built by women, so female founders in 2013 were sort of a novelty. But a lot of macro factors had changed. More women worked at large technology companies like Google and Facebook. The entry cost for tech startups had come down, there was a difference in the basic structural hardware that was in place and the platforms that were accessible. These factors made it much easier to build a brand or consumer product than 10-20 years ago. I felt like we were at that point in time when more and more companies started by women were about to rise. And that was really the genesis for Female Founders Fund: to build a brand that offered not just access to capital but also to a base of other operators and founders who could really help women starting companies."

Like some other investors featured in this book and a true New Yorker, Anu prefers high fashion to fleece vests, and always finds time for being a woman, along with working long hours on making female entrepreneurs successful. "From the outside, a VC job looks relatively cushy — you're sitting there making investments and dictating where that capital flows. But at the end of the day, venture capital investors are also entrepreneurs. We're hustling in a very similar way in terms of always raising money and building our brands."

Elodie Dupuy

Founding Partner, Full In Venture Partners, United States

The internet knows that Elodie Dupuy started her career at Insight Venture Partners as an analyst. What the internet doesn't know is that she actually started there as a receptionist. I've heard many various career stories when interviewing for this book, but this one definitely stood out.

"I had really different skill set and perspective, which I would never have guessed could have been applicable to venture investing. It turned out to be very applicable though. The other reason why I made it in venture capital is that I worked harder than anyone else I knew," Elodie started telling her story. "I grew up in Ohio. Unlike most of the people that I work with, who went to a handful of Ivy League schools, I went to a public state school, which means I had very different teachers, studied very different topics, and basically just didn't have anything in common with the people who typically end up in venture capital.

"At school, I studied languages, which had nothing to do with economics or finance, except for the fact that I studied eight of them. The way I was learning languages was much more around abstracting the pattern of grammar and word construction. Once I understood those patterns, I could rebuild a language from all the different components without actually having to memorize the words or grammar. When you think about what makes somebody good at investing, it's really an ability to abstract business patterns and understand and manipulate those components to get a sense of where the business is going."

After Elodie started working at the front desk of Insight Venture Partners back in 2008, she soon approached the partners and asked if she could move to the investment team. "My only value proposition was that I spoke other languages, whereas most people on the team at the time spoke only English.

So I pitched that I could help them to get into other markets," she recalled. They gave her a shot and put her on identifying potential leads in Europe. Two weeks after she joined the investment team, the entire banking infrastructure in the US collapsed. While most of her peers struggled to generate attractive investment opportunities in a paralyzed market in the US, Elodie was stuffing her pipeline with proprietary deals from Europe. What was an international drama, became a lucky pivotal moment in Elodie's life. She then replicated that good luck by moving into the Brazilian market in 2009-2010, two years before it started getting a lot of international attention for its growth dynamics. Her work with other countries added to her unique perspective, as she was looking at investment opportunities across 35 countries. "Being able to see the same problem getting solved in 15 different ways created a lot of my personal value in terms of the broader view on what could happen across the portfolio and across borders," Elodie explained.

The last component of her success was her competitiveness. "I did competitive gymnastics for 26 years. I love competition more than I love my family. Every time I was faced with a win or lose situation at work, it was just a matter of doubling down, working three times as hard, pulling all-nighters if I had to, until I could figure it out and keep going. Every time I faced a setback, instead of giving up, I just got up and fought back twice as hard, and not because I was a woman in a man's world. Venture capital is tough for anyone, regardless of gender, but if you have grit and perseverance, it doesn't have to be something that gets in the way."

Elodie didn't focus on the gender issues existing in the industry like many other women I've interviewed. She decided not to internalize or feel victimized by them, or put any energy into giving them more of her time and energy. So we skipped that part and I asked what her other biggest challenge had been.

"Paranoia!" she replied with a lopsided smile. "Like I said, I went to the wrong school, I studied the wrong subjects, I came in through the wrong channel, and I didn't have an MBA. I just felt like I fell so far short of most of my peers that I always had sort of this operating fear that I just wasn't good enough. This paranoia extended to not really trusting people, who, in fact, had my best interests in mind, and I sold myself short of what would have been really beneficial if I had just trusted the people around me a little more. Now that I have 10 years of wisdom behind me, one of the biggest things that I've worked to change in myself over this last year, is my ability to ask for help and then trust that people will have the best intentions. I wish I would have done that a lot sooner," Elodie confessed. "I have been plagued by impostor syndrome and I couldn't change the past. Even when I achieved impressive results, it still haunted me, and it still does occasionally. It sometimes feels like this industry is so laser focused on the irrelevant criteria like titles, pedigree, or certificates, that it can be blind to outcomes staring it in the face," she added.

Dupuy has worked for two very powerful venture capital firms — Insight Venture Partners, established in 1995 and currently managing over $23 billion, and ICONIQ Capital, known as an exclusive members-only Silicon Valley billionaire's club that operates as a cross between a family office and a venture capital fund, and manages the money of the founders of Facebook, Napster, Twitter, and LinkedIn, etc. Elodie could easily have gone on to work at any other top tier VC firm, but she didn't, so I couldn't help but ask why.

"The first reason is that the current VC model doesn't intuitively make sense to me. I'm obsessed with efficiency: if I see something that's not being done in the most optimized and efficient way possible, I can't sleep. I'd like to bring the empathy back to the industry and recognize that founders have a lot going on, and they shouldn't spend most of their days taking calls from 100 analysts of 100 different firms. I think technology should be a part of VC practices, beyond just using CRMs and reporting software. For years, I never wanted to be an entrepreneur. Then, all of a sudden, I got the itch to do operations, and this deep desire to really push myself on a product and build a VC firm on our own vision.

"Another reason why I wasn't looking to work for another VC firm, is because Insight got me young. By divine intervention of some sort, I ended up with the firm whose values basically exemplified my tool to the maximum. Insight Venture Partners is an incredibly competitive firm, and competition is my single greatest source of fuel in life. So I fit in really well in terms of the respect that I earned for the level of aggression and competition that I brought to the table.

"However, at ICONIQ, I realized that I was actually a terrible employee, because I had strong opinions. I'm not shy about sharing those, and I tend to think I'm right 99% of the time. This combination doesn't work well if you're trying to fit into someone else's mold, and I'm so out there, that I don't even bother trying to fit it anymore. So I was hesitant about taking a job anywhere else, because when I did the math on where I was more likely to fail — my own venture or fitting a mold — I concluded it would be riskier to try to fit into someone else's vision.

"Finally, I had a pivotal moment when I was speaking with an extraordinarily talented woman that I've known for a while and I asked her why she had never started a VC firm. She immediately came back at me with 100 different excuses. It was so surprising to me, because I felt like, of all people, she was so insanely qualified and absolutely would have nailed it. I interpreted her response as a fear of going out and doing something herself, and after that meeting, I told my husband that I didn't want to be that scared person, 20 years from now, when a young woman asks me why I didn't do something. That really pushed me to start seriously exploring the idea of establishing my own fund."

Elodie then remembered another reason. "By the way, the most serious job prospect I had been entertaining where I'd had dozens of meetings, accidentally convinced me not to join that firm. I agreed to meet with a partner there, just two weeks after giving birth. When we met, this person asked me if I was going to come back to work after having the baby... That was my 15th interview with the firm. I was meeting him right after giving birth, and he seriously asked me whether I was coming back to work after maternity leave. So I thought that I just couldn't do that anymore. It was one of those moments when I realized that it didn't matter how good people's intentions were — a lot of our biases are just so deeply rooted in us that we really can't escape them. I wasn't willing to live under those conditions anymore. I want to change the rules of engagement.

"When I started talking about raising my fund, almost everyone I met was like: 'You're five months pregnant — is this really the right time? What if you just waited three more years, and then you could do it...'. The more I was told that, the more it made me angry, because I didn't understand why other people were deciding what I could and couldn't do, just because I was pregnant.

"I needed to show the world that there is no limitation when a woman is pregnant or has kids. It just means we need to reconfigure the construct of how we do things. Two weeks after my daughter's birth, I was back working. I would basically put her in the little kangaroo carrier in the front and my laptop in her diaper bag on my back. And so we went around Manhattan pitching potential investors, and meeting with entrepreneurs and lawyers.

"All these people talk about a work/life balance, like it's some type of trade-off: you have to have one or the other — you can't be working to enjoy life, and you can't be enjoying life if you're working. That doesn't make any sense to me. One, I love working. If I have any spare time, I usually spend it working because I just enjoy what I do. Two, if I can integrate my life and work, then I get to do both at the same time — have my cake and eat it too.

"The culture that we want to build at Full In, is that we're not going to prescribe to you what your life should be like, we're just going to set objectives and let you figure out how you want to hit those. We want to try to be a platform that has avenues and opportunities for people who may have fallen through the cracks in a traditional system, and yet have all the makings of greatness. Maybe with a different rule set, they'd be playing a different game, and they might actually be phenomenal winners."

I couldn't help but think that while Elodie would be recognized as a white person, her untraditional background was the foundation for her diverse views.

Beth Engel

Partner, Dundee Venture Capital, United States

When Women.VC first studied the backgrounds of female VCs in 2015, many of them didn't fall into any commonly recognized category, so we had to call them 'other' for the sake of universal terminology. Back then, I was dreaming of finding a way to tell people about the many different paths into venture capital that I had observed. This book made my dream come true.

Before venture capital, Beth Engel worked at the Federal Bureau of Investigation (FBI). She wasn't a spy, but she was doing a really important job — the learnings from which she now applies today as an investor. "I saw many people who were very well-trained in the technical parts of their job, but were less trained in managing and leading others. We were set on creating a leadership development program, which we implemented over time, and I think we managed to really address the issue. It felt very much like a startup, because we were building it from scratch — working internally, as well as inviting external experts," Beth shared as much as she could, given the nature of the organization.

"Working at the FBI debunked every myth I had about what a federal employee is. It was so heartening to see every single person driven towards the same mission, which is to keep our country safe and our civil liberties protected. It was just absolutely imbued in the entire organization. I observed the culture, the community, the character of these people, and their competences directed at creating something genuinely great.

"Based on that experience, as an investor, I always try to see what entrepreneurs are centered around, what is their crystal, what is their mission. Is it keeping your country safe? Or delighting your customers? Or bringing efficiency to the workplace? Or is it a drug that cures a dangerous disease? And then I want to know how they are delivering that each and every day — from their email newsletters to post-sale services. I think having a mission that you can work towards is really important. You hire people who agree with your mission and find investors who believe in it."

Engel graduated in biochemistry and became a teaching fellow at the University of Portland right after college. "I don't think I really knew what the job of a doctor was, other than personal care and being in school for 12 years, so I decided to pursue something different instead, and that was a service teaching program in Catholic school, where I got a master's degree in teaching. I think when you are 22, you rarely build a solid career plan and rather follow new interesting opportunities. A desire to do something that I could enjoy and where I could add value, defined my first few career choices."

Beth worked for several startups, including Hayneedle, a B2C e-commerce brand launched by Mark Hasebroock from Omaha, Nebraska. "I was an early employee and really enjoyed that things were always changing in every startup I worked for. I was wearing so many hats that no job description could ever fit what I was doing at those companies, and no MBA could cover the whole spectrum."

After four years at Hayneedle, she moved to Washington DC with her husband, who was getting a PhD there. Engel didn't waste her time either and got an MBA at Georgetown University. After finishing her tenure at the FBI, the couple returned home to Omaha, and Engel was open to new challenges.

Mark Hasebroock, who had stayed in touch with her all that time, was raising a venture capital fund to address the funding needs of entrepreneurs in the central and midwest states of America. "Mark could not get regional investors to back Hayneedle when he started, so he had to fundraise on the East and West Coasts. He ended up getting money from Insight Venture Partners and Sequoia, but he never could accept the fact that entrepreneurs have little to no funding opportunities between the coasts, and he decided to become one."

Hasebroock had always been a visionary, but he needed an operator and integrator type of partner to glue the parts together and set the processes in place to deliver on his vision. "Mark asked me to join Dundee Venture Capital, because he knew that if he laid out 50 things he thought we should do in front of me, I would be able to pick the one that was the most important, and help him figure it out. We are very much like the ham and egg kind of partners."

With the focus on early-stage startups, 25% of the portfolio companies of Dundee Venture Capital are founded by women. "It's not our mandate to invest through a gender lens, but we are proud to back so many female founders. Mark would always say, 'Most things should be run by women,'" she laughed. "He knows first-hand that women get things done — he is surrounded by his wife and four daughters, and others like me, who help him run his home and business. This genuine women-friendly attitude attracts more women to our fund.

"We should start showing successful women to our children early. For the first 12-18 years of their lives, when many dreams and perceptions of the world are being formed, kids are rarely surrounded by role models. Girls don't pay attention to female founders, female funders, female presidential candidates — all of those who can make girls think, 'Yep, that's something that I can do too!' Boys aren't exposed to many female leaders either. We need to give them examples of female achievers, so that it would be a norm for them later on. I think it probably starts with the media, which is why work like what you are doing is very important, because it shines a spotlight on female role models," Beth reflected on the issue.

Beth Ferreira

General Partner, FirstMark Capital, United States

My conversation with Beth Ferreira reminded me of a proper brainstorming session: our whole discussion was focused on diversity, and she had a lot to share. Beth had been a founder of the corporate venture arm of WME IMG — WME Ventures — where half of her portfolio companies had at least one female founder, and is now a partner at New York's FirstMark Capital, with a slightly more modest portfolio diversity ratio. "Some VCs say that the lack of diversity is a pipeline issue, but I don't really buy that," she said.

"We all understand one side of the story very well: venture capitalists have to triage thousands of deals a year, but they only have a certain amount of time in which to invest, so the deals that come in from trusted sources will generally get more attention. The trusted sources typically look like them, and they consequently recommend people who also look like them. Venture capital is the type of business where you have to take a leap of faith on an individual, so it's easier to get your head around someone who's like you, versus someone who isn't.

"But there is also the other side of it: when we say that a VC partnership is like a marriage, we are usually talking about the general partners, but we rarely think about it from the entrepreneurs' perspective — accepting a venture investor as a part of their business is the same kind of marriage too. If you don't see yourself reflected in a VC partnership, you may not send your pitch deck there in the first place. That is a missed opportunity for an investor. So the more people we have in these roles, across all minority sectors — not just women — the more likely we will see more diverse founders in the pipeline," Beth broke it down.

"At WME Ventures, we had a very diverse team: two women and an underrepresented male minority. We organically got more deal flow from underrepresented groups. Consequently, as representatives of

underrepresented groups, we were able to evaluate those companies differently than many of my white male colleagues in the industry would do. Venture investors are able to construct their teams in a way that allows them to provide a sufficient pipeline of diverse entrepreneurs — it's just that very few of them actually think about that.

"While we're having this conversation, I also think that it shouldn't be a social issue, but rather a matter of business — to make sure that you're in a position to create positive returns. Venture capital is a small cottage industry, and that's how it has perpetuated itself. It's no one's fault. If we do want to change this, we need to see to it that more women get into tech to start companies, and this is a huge opportunity to make a lot of money, which is what our business is all about."

Beth had a lot to say, and I was making a lot of notes to ensure that her most explicit ideas would make it to the book. "Historically, venture capital has always been an apprenticeship business. There's not a lot out there that's written or taught, or that can be learned in other places — it's more about seeing and doing. While there's a lot of value in spending some time within an established firm as an associate or principal, waiting until there are more open seats for women in venture capital to get to gender parity, may take decades. In order to really change the ratio, not only do we need women starting funds, but we need them to start funds across the entire spectrum of investing — not just the seed stage, but the growth and expansion stages as well.

"My expectation is that VC firms will continue to hire women after their first female hires. I hope they won't be like: 'Oh, we got one — we're done". I want to hear more: 'Let's make sure that every time we're looking for a partner, we're really opening that funnel to all of the candidates that could be great for this role", Beth was optimistic.

Sophie Forest

Managing Partner, Brightspark Ventures, Canada

Sophie Forest is democratizing venture capital in Canada by building a platform where accredited investors can co-invest in deals pre-vetted by Brightspark Capital, alongside the firm, on a deal-by-deal basis. You'll learn about similar models from investors featured in this book several more times, all of whom, however, employed them only prior to institutionalizing their investing practices. After more than 20 years in the venture capital industry, Forest sees great potential in this model in the long term.

"We've built a network of more than 5,000 accredited investors (individuals, family offices, and small institutions) that invest in Canadian early-stage companies through us. Every investment that we present to our network first goes through a deep due diligence, so investors only see the deals that we have screened and ultimately decided to invest in. Our VC expertise in vetting companies is really what differentiates our model from crowdfunding, and we also save investors a lot of time on deal-sourcing by giving them access to our high-quality deal-flow," Sophie explained.

Forest is one of those people who are on a mission to eliminate inefficiencies, of which there are plenty in venture capital. She has been in traditional venture capital and corporate venturing, and received the Canadian Angel of the Year award in 2017. Brightspark's blended annual return over 14 years from the most recent fund and the investments made under the new model is close to 30% net of all fees, which is quite an outstanding result in venture capital, so Forest definitely knows what she's doing.

Sophie started out as a financial analyst at a large investment company, and soon followed her colleague to start one of the first private VC funds in Canada. "It was the beginning of the 90s, when nobody was talking about venture capital in Canada. I had absolutely no idea what I was getting into. Even for the founder of the fund it was a foray, so we had to learn as we went along and had to invent some things, because there were no models to replicate," she recollected.

She then joined the Caisse de dépôt et placement du Québec — a large pension fund that was starting a group to do direct investments in tech companies, and Sophie grew their investment practice from focusing on Québec only, to the rest of Canada, the US, Europe, and beyond. After seven years with the Caisse, she realized that she needed something different. "I had always been entrepreneurial, and I knew that I wanted to work in venture capital. I wanted to help startups and entrepreneurs create value and grow, but I also wanted to have a certain freedom for my own entrepreneurial spirit."

I heard Sophie speaking in a friendly, soft voice, which didn't give away how resilient she is until she started telling me her more personal stories.

At her first job, she didn't hesitate to join a typical boys' club to play pool or golf, and have beers with her male colleagues after hours. "I knew that they talked about deals after work, and that the only way to keep up-to-date was to be there. I really wanted to learn everything and become an experienced investor, so I persisted until they got used to me being part of that club."

Sophie also admits that she is very competitive, and she experienced a great boost in motivation when she heard her male friends bragging about raising their own funds. Some of those boasters never closed their imaginary funds, while Sophie did — multiple times.

Earlier in her career, a former boss warned Forest to not get pregnant after she'd been promoted. "At the time, I was actually planning to have a child with my husband, so I couldn't believe my ears and went home to rant. After thinking about it, I decided to carry on and take the promotion instead of creating a conflict. I thought that I'd cross that bridge when I got there, if I got pregnant."

The next morning, her boss admitted that he had said the wrong thing, and he believed that Sophie would become even more efficient when she had a child, because she would be a happier person. "He realized that his mistake was merely rooted in his traditional family background: his wife stayed at home raising kids, so he never knew any different," she justified his words.

"I must admit that although I have this type A personality and think of myself as a very confident person, I ignored a lot of questionable behavior instead of speaking up. I have three daughters who are young adults now, and I'm sometimes torn about what advice to give them. On one side, I want to teach them to not accept disparities. But on the other, I know that if they get frustrated with everything happening around them, it'll be very hard for them to build their networks. It's sad that women still have to bend to be successful.

"I see many VC firms and tech companies hiring women in executive positions today, without changing their real attitudes towards them at the table. You cannot fake a corporate culture — if you have never believed that women are as good at work as men, you won't be able to change your attitude overnight.

"My partner at Brightspark didn't need a #MeToo movement to invite me to work with him. That is the type of person you want to work with — a man or a woman who genuinely appreciates the opposite gender. It bugs me to see people pretending to get rid of their biases, luring women into their PR campaigns using executive titles, but not giving them any actual power", Sophie condemned such actions.

Constance Freedman

Founding Partner, Moderne Ventures, United States

Constance has never let the gender issue get in her way. She thinks it is important that we pay attention to it from the diversity standpoint, but gender alone doesn't give anyone a pass. "While we may have to try harder (as women), I don't focus on the gender thing too much," confessed Freedman during our conversation. "I think about doing my best to try and be as successful as I possibly can with the goal that the results show themselves."

Freedman started her career in real estate when she was earning money as a realtor in Boston, while also being an undergrad student. After graduation, she worked in two tech startups in an operational capacity, but real estate at large, and purchasing and selling 'fixer-uppers' in particular, remained her hobby.

She first got into venture capital as a senior associate at the VC firm Cueball, which was looking at the real estate tech company she was trying to buy and develop herself. They both lost that deal, and Constance decided to meet the partner of Cueball. "I just called him up and said, 'You know, we should meet.' It was right before I graduated from business school and wanted to start my own business by buying that company, so I hadn't been looking for a job at the time. However, we met and got to know each other, and it seemed like I was a good fit for the firm," Constance recalled.

In 2008, Constance moved to Chicago, Illinois, and launched and managed the National Association of Realtors' $20 million investment arm, Second Century Ventures (SCV). Later in 2013, she also founded its accelerator program, REach, to begin a systematic process of bringing together technology companies and the real estate industry.

After fully investing the SCV fund and building an impressive record with investment wins like DocuSign, Updater and August, she decided to spin off from SCV to start her own venture capital firm, Moderne Ventures. "I think the career path I took gave me depth and breadth in the industry, as well as foresight as to how I could best create value in a portfolio: joining a traditional VC firm first, then working in corporate venture capital, and finally starting my own firm.

"Both firms I worked for prior to Moderne Ventures were stepping stones for me to build a great track record, which enabled me to raise my own fund. I believe that no matter which career path in venture capital you take, you should prove yourself as an investor, build that track record and earn a spot in the industry. I am often asked whether angel investing is a good lead into starting one's own VC firm, and I believe it can help, but I also sense that institutional investors appreciate one's prior experience in managing outside capital as well.

"I never had a five-year plan until I started with Second Century Ventures," Freedman said. "By that time, I knew that venture was what I wanted to do and I set out to build a track record with top tier returns — if I did that right, I would have options at the end of the fund. By the time the capital was fully vested, my returns exceeded those of most top tier funds and I was in a great position to launch Moderne Ventures."

I pointed out that Constance also had operating experience and asked if she finds that to be critical for becoming an investment partner of a VC firm.

"There is no right or wrong way to get into venture capital, but if you asked me for advice on starting in VC by joining an existing firm, I'd say: find a VC firm that is most like you. If you are an operator, find a VC firm that has partners who were operators too. If you are a consultant or a banker, find a firm where partners came from that background. Be mindful that some firms approach it from the opposite perspective. When I hire, I actually like to hire people who are not like me. I think that helps to diversify the deal flow."

Freedman takes hiring matters seriously. Her interviews run in rounds, and candidates fill out a questionnaire, with one of the questions being about a candidate's personality type according to the Myers Briggs test. "I just want to understand whether people know about this test and their personality types — how much they are self-aware.

"I think that knowing one's personality type makes people better team members and negotiators, especially if you know or try to understand the personality types of people you talk to. For example, I'm an extreme extrovert. I focus on the big picture. I realize that when I talk to someone who's an introvert, a sensing and very detail-oriented person, I need to adjust my perspective to how that person thinks about the topics we discuss. I will also take that person's answers a little bit differently than the answers of someone who's extroverted. I think this helps me eliminate any bias I might have, in a very efficient manner."

Freedman is very conscious of everything she says. Throughout our conversation, Constance explained things in almost an educational manner — she had it all figured out and was ready to share her thought-through conclusions. However, I also wanted more emotional stories that described the environment that shaped her and many others of us, for that matter.

"I think it's tough for people who don't have a thick skin to work in venture capital, because you have to ignore some of the BS while trying to show your worth, prove that you're serious, and show that you can do it despite the biases," she opened up to tell me her behind-the-curtain stories.

"The number of investors that I approached when I was raising Modern Ventures, who actually just wanted to waste my time, was incredible! I ran into guys who just wanted to ask me for a date or make some other kind of pass at me, and it was really frustrating. As women, we end up getting used to this behavior, even in the workplace, but at this level in my career I expected something different. The thing I was most upset about, was the amount of time I wasted on those people who were never serious about investing in my fund in the first place.

"But at the end of the day, you've got to just push that aside and move on. You need to be confident in having the ability to do this as well as, or better than, your male counterparts. Do women have to prove themselves a bit more in venture capital? Yes, but so do women in most other fields.

"Do I think there is a gender bias? Yes, studies and personal experience prove it exists — in almost every profession — and it needs to be addressed. However, to really fix the problem, I think it needs to go all the way back to kindergarten and be considered on the micro level. For example, there are studies that show that girls are not getting called on as much as boys in math or science classes and things like that. Hence, we need to start changing that paradigm much earlier in people's lives than when they are already doing business."

When I asked Constance to give any advice to female investment professionals and aspiring venture investors, she said, "I'd advise them to be confident — make sure you have a seat at the table, your voice is heard and most importantly, build your brand by building your success.

"But on the micro level, the number one thing women should do is show up. Women often tend to self-select out from many challenges, competitions, even just meet-ups. It is so important — you gotta network, as this industry is all about relationships. You never know where your next deal will come from and you never know where the next LP will get introduced to you because of a connection you may have made years earlier." On fundraising, she said that it is also important to have a thick skin. "Just like our entrepreneurs, you sometimes have to take 100 no's before you get to one yes."

Moderne Ventures is looking proactively for female founders. Nevertheless, it has been quite a challenge to find companies founded by women for their portfolio. "When I send out our newsletters to recruit for a new Passport [accelerator] group, or even in a cocktail conversation, I constantly remind people, 'Think about the female entrepreneurs in your network.' I actively try to get more women in, not because it's just a chick thing, but because I truly believe in diversity and the value that people of all genders and ethnicities bring. But I often feel that I just don't find enough of them. We go through 4,500 companies in a given year. We interact on a deeper level with 500 or so of them, and bring fewer than 20 of them into the fund each year. We need more women at the top of the funnel in the first place.

"I also think that women tend to focus on industries that aren't traditionally very popular among VC investors. I don't have enough data on that to confirm this perception, but we see many women in consumer goods, retail, and beauty sectors, while male investors are often more tech-oriented. This fact alone may limit the number of funded female entrepreneurs, because VCs at large are traditionally interested in tech-enabled products and solutions."

Constance said that she has been happy to see some changes in the industry over the last several years. While there doesn't seem to be any mandates for institutional investors to back diverse general partners, there is definitely a higher level of interest today than there was even just three years ago for them to look for a broader array of fund managers. Women's board roles are starting to expand as well. Freedman joined her first public board last year, Equity Lifestyles [NYSE:ELS] where there are three other women serving as Directors, and she received several new inquiries from other public companies. She has started to notice that she is not the only woman at the table of many of the private boards that she serves on as well. "We have a long way to go," she commented, "but we are seeing progress!".

Darcy Frisch

Managing Director, Hearst Ventures, United States

Darcy Frisch thinks that women have a special job to do: "It's our responsibility, as women, to walk into a room with confidence, and to show the other people there, that our contribution matters," and I entirely agree with that. Each win by one woman is also a contribution to the success of other women.

"I see that many women still need to constantly remind themselves that they deserve to be in that room, that at times we need to act with more confidence than we actually experience. It doesn't always come naturally to us, but confidence is table stakes when trying to be heard and add value," Darcy said.

"We need to remember that, as humans, men and women can become lazy when they are not challenged — we'll keep doing what we've been doing. If we want to change the status quo, we need to do something we've never done before. And if we need to stand up for ourselves in order to do that, and make our voices louder so that they matter, we should do that."

Frisch decided that she wanted to work with entrepreneurs when she was graduating from business school. She moved to New York from Washington DC to join a newly created startup incubator. Her job was to help set up the incubator and assist its companies with raising future venture funding. The incubator didn't have enough money to last very long, and in a matter of months after starting, Darcy was out looking for a new job.

Although her first working experience in venture capital turned out to be somewhat of a disappointment, she stuck to her goal of working with entrepreneurs. She went to the only other VC firm she had managed to work with during her short employment at the startup incubator — the Hearst Corporation.

"I just asked them to keep me in mind if they saw any opportunities where I might be a good fit," Darcy recalled. "And right there they offered me an open position in their venture group. It has been 19 years since I joined Hearst, and now, looking backwards, I can say that yes, it was luck — I found myself in the right place at the right time, and yes — the industry was also less competitive. But most of all, I think I got the job because I never doubted my decision to work with startups. Sometimes, you make your luck by being committed to what you're doing."

Frisch came into venture capital with almost zero experience and learned everything, simply by doing it. "I certainly had some skills and smarts after business school, but no relevant training or experience, other than a couple of years of work with entrepreneurs. Back in 1995, venture capital had fewer dollars, fewer corporate venture investors, and fewer startups — I was learning on the job. But isn't it true that everyone has to start their career somewhere, knowing little to nothing about it? At that stage, you take a new job, and you have to quickly learn everything about it, so that you can make a difference.

"My co-workers at Hearst helped me a lot — they taught me the ropes in many ways. It's worth mentioning that the company and our fund's focus was also morphing overtime, because the business transitioned from traditional media into digital media. Venture capital is an industry where you have to learn constantly — it's not something that can be written in a book once and forever."

Darcy also agreed that corporate venture is a good place for women to be in. "I don't have any statistics to prove it, but I do think that large corporations, for whatever reason, have done a better job at embracing women in executive roles. When you contrast them with smaller partnerships, such as traditional venture capital firms that may be called 'tightly knit' or 'fraternity', nobody ever really questioned their hiring or investment decisions with regards to diversity, until very recently. So they didn't really have to think about it and never struggled over the question: 'Is diversity important?' I would argue that large corporations have been asking these questions for a longer time, and have been incrementally moving towards the goal. I don't want to say that corporations have nothing to improve on anymore, but I do think that they are a couple of steps ahead. This alone might be the main reason for the larger number of women in corporate venture capital, than in traditional smaller partnerships.

"I do think that today, we are doing much more for diversity than what we were doing five years ago. I have actually just fired off an email to introduce one of the women I know, to an independent director position. There was a bullet point in the job description that said, 'We're looking for diverse points of view', and I took that as an invitation for all my candidate recommendations to be diverse candidates — either women or people of color. That wouldn't have happened in 2000 — the ask wouldn't have been there.

"The change is happening, but not as quickly as everyone would like it to happen. Whenever I think about it, I just keep my head down and ask: what can I do, what are those little changes I can personally make that will eventually add up to a bigger change? As an investor who looks at hundreds of deals a year, I had to find the framework to narrow the choice down and pick one company to invest in out of all of them. Diversity of the management team is top of mind for me. If every investor makes this pointer a priority, we will see the change much sooner," Darcy challenged the community.

Shuly Galili

Founding Partner, UpWest Labs, United States

An immigrant from Israel, Shuly started her career in international relations, working on global issues for international non-governmental organizations. She was identifying programs with social and commercial impact and worked on getting them funded by global investors. Through that work, she was meeting with leading tech executives who were interested in some of the programs in Israel where tech and social entrepreneurship is thriving side by side. Israel has always been a hotbed of innovation producing top tech talent and highly sought after products and technologies, so it is no wonder that there was a whole spectrum of interests — whether they wanted to invest in, or directly acquire, Israeli companies, or build R&D departments there. It became obvious that there was no organization that could bridge the two ecosystems, and that's when Galili became a Co-founder and Executive Director of the California Israel Chamber of Commerce (CICC) based in Silicon Valley.

"We established the organization in 2000 and started identifying issues, sectors, and people that would be most helpful in building it," Shuly explained. "I spent about 11 years building the CICC, which eventually became the gateway for every Israeli entrepreneur or investor that was looking to access Silicon Valley or the US market — and the other way around. This experience allowed me to see the ecosystem from a macro level, and also to understand the challenges that both ecosystems have on a global scale.

"One challenge was clear: while Israel is rich in innovation and even in venture capital, its distance from the US market was a tremendous handicap for Israeli entrepreneurs. We simply had to level the playing field and provide these talented founders with better market access. In 2011, I started UpWest Labs, a pre-seed fund based in Silicon Valley to address that challenge. My co-founder Gil Ben Artzy, an ex-Yahoo executive who I have known for a while, shared my vision and partnered with me to launch it. Seven years later, UpWest, with $30 million under management, invests primarily in Israeli founders who are looking to break into the US market, and help them scale through that process."

Shuly Galili doesn't shy away from challenges. As with other Israeli women featured in this book, she served two years in the military, where she was an artillery instructor to other soldiers when she was only 18. This trained her to feel comfortable among men and to see them as allies instead of competitors.

"We, women in this industry do not proactively take a place at the table, even though we are super qualified to lead and build. Sometimes we are waiting for permission. Oftentimes, for way too long." I agreed with Shuly, that many women think that we need men to make space at the table for us, instead of claiming our seat because we deserve it.

"It has only recently happened that we started seeing more awareness among traditional venture capital firms that women deserve promotions to executive and partner roles. But there is still a question that remains unanswered: are these women equals in the partnerships? Are they really able to make clear investment decisions? Do these appointments really bring women into the forefront of the firm, or is this just window dressing?" Shuly articulated questions that many people are afraid to ask. Someone has to do this though, because otherwise we are just getting stalled and missing momentum.

"Even when promotions happen within VC firms, it takes a long time to climb the traditional career ladder. I am super thrilled to see women who start at larger VC firms, then go out and say, 'I am going to start my own fund, where I am an equal partner and a decision-maker, where I make investments as I see fit, in order to make the most impact.'"

For the purpose of this book, I am seeking advice as to how women can excel in entrepreneurship and venture capital, and Shuly highlighted the most critical issues. "Firstly, we tend to scrutinize ourselves even more than we are being scrutinized by others. Women think that they have to have everything perfect, while I see plenty of male entrepreneurs who have no problem in self-promotion ahead of the execution. Women are more concerned about the execution before they actually go out there to talk about their vision and aspirations. I think that is, obviously, something that requires a proper adjustment.

"Secondly, this is not women/us vs. men/them battle and it should not be — that is not going to work, if we want to make a difference. I've witnessed many men in our industry who are very mindful and very much looking to change the status quo by inclusion, mentorship, and promotion of female VCs or entrepreneurs. I actually think that the new generation of male founders are a lot more sophisticated in regards to inclusion and diversity. Maybe I sound a little bit more optimistic than most people who have talked to you..."

...And the opposite being the case, is the reason why I am so in love with this book. Keep reading to hear that all the investors I have interviewed, are very optimistic about the future of women in venture capital and entrepreneurship.

Jan Garfinkle

Founding Partner, Arboretum Ventures, United States

Timing is one of the most important factors that must be taken into consideration in venture capital. When I reached out to Jan Garfinkle to feature her in this book, I didn't know that she would be starting her tenure as the newly elected Chair of the National Venture Capital Association (NVCA) in the US, soon after the book is published. "It has been a wild journey for me in venture capital, because 16 years ago, I had no clue what I was doing, and today, here I am, the Chair of NVCA, which I'm a little nervous about," Jan shared with me. I am happy to witness this moment and have NVCA represented in the book this way as well.

Garfinkle told me a lot about her windy path into venture capital. Born and raised in San Francisco, she was one of the first people who studied bioengineering at the University of California. At the time, Berkeley had only just started offering a major in that sector, and it was very difficult to get a job in bioengineering and medical devices, because the industry didn't quite exist then. With a rather unique education, Jan ended up working at Procter & Gamble in manufacturing disposable diapers, aka 'Pampers'. It wasn't exactly her dream job, but the choice was no better: it was either that or mining petroleum down in Houston, Texas. "My years at Procter & Gamble were actually pretty fantastic and I loved it! I learned a lot about managing people and really grew up at that particular job," Jan recalled.

She then went to Wharton Business School to get an MBA, and got a summer internship at Eli Lilly, a global pharmaceutical company. She joined their M&A group, where the goal was to acquire medical technology companies.

"I was the fifth employee in that very small group and was doing the due diligence on different medtech companies, one of which became my favorite. It was an angioplasty company from San Francisco, called Advanced Cardiovascular Systems (ACS), founded by a wonderful physician — John Simpson, MD — who has become a very famous serial entrepreneurial physician in the Bay Area," Jan went down memory lane.

"During the week I worked in the catheterization lab with him, learning about his company for a potential acquisition, I also learned everything about angioplasty, which was fascinating. They could put a little balloon into the coronary arteries to stop a heart attack, instead of using one of only two existing alternative solutions. Up until that point, cardiologists could only prescribe a drug that would relax the coronary arteries a little bit, but the patients would still have the underlying blockage. The second option was having a major cardiovascular surgery — a bypass procedure, which is very invasive. In heart attack prevention, it was the first alternative to major cardiovascular surgery and a prescription drug that didn't cure the underlying reason. After watching what John was doing, I was in awe of the magnificence of his solution, which could instantly prevent a heart attack and preserve the heart muscle.

"I went back to Eli Lilly and told them about ACS. They decided to do a closer due diligence on the company, but I had to leave the process to go back to Wharton and finish my MBA. Nine months later, I decided not to return to Eli Lilly, but to work at a startup instead. I called John Simpson to tell him that, and he connected me with the CEO of ACS. I was thrilled to get a marketing position there as an early employee! Within a year after I joined them, Eli Lilly acquired the company and I continued doing its marketing and sales."

At ACS, Garfinkle launched about 20 different technologies and worked hand in hand with John Simpson for six years. When he was getting ready to start his next company called Devices for Vascular Intervention (DVI), he asked Jan to write a business plan and then invited her to join the company as the director of clinical research and marketing for the cardiovascular product. She was helping to get the premarket approval (PMA) trials to get approval from The Food and Drug Administration (FDA), and then launching the products worldwide once they were approved. Eli Lilly acquired that company too.

In 1994, Eli Lilly decided to spin out the cardiovascular device companies in an IPO that was the founding of Guidant, Inc. They, of course, invited Jan to stick with the company through that IPO.

Jan's personal life, however, wasn't delayed by her career. In the meantime, she had gotten married, and luckily, her cardiologist fiancé moved to California to marry her, when she had just started working for DVI. After a few years, Jan's husband decided that California wasn't a good match for them and suggested that it was her turn to move to another place for him. Jan agreed to move to "anywhere in the Bay Area or Seattle", but her husband found a job in Ann Arbor, Michigan. Jan reluctantly moved there, while continuing to work for DVI remotely. The Guidant IPO occurred at about the same time, but then Jan and her husband had three daughters in 18 months (a single and then twins). Her twins were born 9 weeks early and that was the moment when Jan decided to finally take a break to take care of her daughters, and quit Guidant.

However, Guidant called her right back and asked her to work as a consultant for them. "I said, 'Sure, I can do, like, 10 hours a week...'" Jan laughed. "So I started my consulting business, with Guidant as my main client. I was helping them with clinical marketing, which was my area of expertise, but also advised their venture group on a whole variety of other things over the next eight years."

Aside from Guidant, Garfinkle worked with other healthcare startups, helping them with their business needs, and assisted Michigan-based healthcare-focused venture capital funds in doing due diligence on potential investments.

After some time, Jan realized that she'd really love to work for a VC firm, but she couldn't go back to the Bay Area, and there were only two of them in Michigan. She approached them both and asked to consider hiring her. "Both said no, for reasons that were unrelated to me. A partner of one fund decided to start a political career and stopped investing, and the other fund didn't know what they were going to do next. Although I understood the reasons for their no's, I was totally frustrated and just couldn't believe that I couldn't work for either of them with all my experience. I walked home from the last meeting, went onto the IRS website, filed a tax ID number, and started Arboretum Ventures," Jan smiled proudly. "Arboretum was founded with the mission of investing in healthcare companies that would drive cost out of the health system, while still providing great clinical care, a mission important back in 2002 when the firm was founded, but even more critical today.

"It was so crazy and very naive, because I knew nothing about how to run a VC firm. I did, however, have a mentor from one of the two funds that had rejected me, who was really wonderful, and he said that I needed a partner. 'Great, how do I do that?' I asked. I put an ad in 'VentureWire', and even got a lot of replies. Candidates had good operating experience, but didn't really have any venture capital background, which I needed, in order to complement my competencies back then.

"Luckily, I ended up partnering with Tim Peterson, who had been a Managing Director of Wolverine Venture Fund, which had been established on the platform of the University of Michigan business school. He had run it for about five years and had made about ten investments in healthcare and some more advanced manufacturing technology during that time. He joined me very shortly after I started and is still my partner at Arboretum after 16 years."

I asked Jan if she would advise aspiring venture investors to follow a similar career path or choose a different one, and she replied, "It's really hard to get a job in venture capital. You do have to be really lucky timing-wise. I think it's very difficult to raise your own fund as well, but this may be the best way for women and minorities, in particular, to get into venture capital. Finding room to grow into a decision-making position in small partnerships, is oftentimes just not an option. Then, doing it yourself with the right team around you, is as good as it gets.

"On the other hand, I think venture investors have to really commit to their profession and take some risks — not only when they back startups, but also when they hire people. The same goes for limited partners — if they decide to take risks by investing in venture capital as an asset class, they should also take those risks when investing in diverse general partners. I, personally, didn't have exactly the right background: I had really good operating experience, but I didn't have any investing experience, yet, I found investors who believed in me. I am now managing the fourth fund, and we have had several significant exits, so that bet worked out very well for my limited partners.

"Institutional investors do have to go outside of their norm and comfort zone and be more experimental with who they fund. It's already a well-documented fact that teams with diverse backgrounds and experiences, create a lot of value, and perform as well as traditional all-white-male teams."

When I asked Jan about the main skills necessary for achieving success in venture investing, she named just two of them: pattern recognition and operational experience.

"All our daily activities revolve around these two things, and they are quite different skill sets, in my opinion," Garfinkle stated.

"The pattern recognition ability can only be developed over time. One needs to know what makes a good team, what makes a good business model, what makes a good product, and how much capital is going to be needed for the company. Unless you are exposed to a lot of startups and can compare dozens or hundreds of them to learn how to identify the winners, the other way of approaching that is to build a very solid foundation of different life and professional experiences.

"The second skill set comes from being an operator and preferably working in different startups. These startups don't have to be successful, but the person has to learn how to wear many different hats within those companies. Every single company hits a road bump at some point, for some reason. They always do — it's just life. I think it's really important to have empathy and patience at the board level to help founders and management teams overcome those hurdles. Because how can you help and advise a company if you haven't gone through the same troubles?"

With all that experience up her sleeve, I wondered what the one or two main lessons were that Jan had learned over the years in venture capital.

"Firstly, I realized that there are three main things that venture capitalists do: we raise a new fund every three to four years, we look for new companies all the time, and when we find those companies, we help them be successful. I always say that we can only do two of the three things well at a time. So, at least for me, if I am raising a fund, I don't think I'm doing nearly as good a job at searching for new potential investments, because I just don't dedicate enough time to it. You need to be realistic of who will be doing what in your VC firm and when.

"But the most important thing that I learned in venture capital is that you're only as good as your last exit," Jan said with satisfaction.

Jocelyn Goldfein

Managing Director, Zetta Venture Partners, United States

Jocelyn Goldfein spent her career building software in the formative years of companies like VMware and Facebook. During her seven years at VMware, when the company was skyrocketing and doubling their headcount and revenue, Jocelyn was also precipitously rising from lead to senior manager, to director, and then, senior director, to vice president and general manager — all in about six years. When she joined Facebook in 2010, she had to learn a lot — not just about the technology, but also the life cycle of the consumer product and its business model, because everything was different.

"After four years with Facebook, I started to notice that I was applying all the skills that I had built, but I wasn't developing new skills anymore. I took some time to really think about that, and came to the conclusion that I had been in technical leadership roles for so long, that the new learnings had become more incremental. I don't mean to say that I was perfect at my job, or had nothing else to learn. But I had gotten used to a vertical learning curve, where I felt that I was doubling my capacity to work every day, so that incremental growth was not enough for me. I felt certain that I had at least one more career arc in me, where I would learn a ton every day. I knew that if I stuck with the same job function that I'd been doing for 15 years, I wasn't going to find that," Jocelyn shared.

Her first impulse was to start a company and become a CEO. However, she recalled that she had co-founded a startup in her 20s with co-workers, largely for the sake of becoming founders. "In hindsight, I have to admit that we started Datify because we just wanted to be entrepreneurs, rather than having a mission and solving a problem. That's not a good enough reason to start a company, and not the motivation that will see you through the tough times and ultimately lead to an outsized success. This time, I decided not to start a company, for the sake of learning the CEO job. The company had to be an end in itself".

Goldfein needed to figure out what mission in life was calling her. She wanted to meet other founders, and be exposed to many ideas, hoping it would spark her creativity. "That sounded a lot like an entrepreneur-in-residence role at a VC firm to me, but I also wanted to stay independent at that point. I decided to become a DIY [do-it-yourself] entrepreneur-in-residence and hang out my shingle as an angel investor to have the same advantages," she laughed cheerfully.

Jocelyn wrote a goodbye letter to Facebook, changed her status to 'angel investor' on all social media platforms, started a blog, did public speaking at tech events, attended accelerator meetups and demo days, and proactively and deliberately reached out to entrepreneurs and venture capital investors in her network. "I made up my mind to write small $20,000 checks, so I pretty quickly started investing and was making roughly one investment a month. The startups in my portfolio ranged from those that loved me right up until the minute they closed their funding round, and then I never heard from them

again, to CEOs who met with me every week, so I could coach and help them. In one case, I even joined the board.

"At some point, I realized that I was working closely with a dozen different companies, leveraging all the skills I had, and applying them across all of those companies — not just one — and, by the way, I was also learning a lot! It was probably at around the one-year mark, when I had an epiphany... 'Wait a second, I shouldn't become a CEO — I should become an investor!'"

It was clear to Goldfein that she needed more capital, which she didn't have personally. She was also not ready to jump into an existing institutional fund. So she started off with an angel syndicate that allowed her to write substantial checks. "I was having lots of coffees with VCs for networking purposes — to make introductions and see deal flow. Those conversations also shed a lot of light on how venture capital firms function, so it became less of a black box to me along the way. I knew that I wanted to be a pre-seed or seed stage investor. I wanted to be the invention capital — the capital that comes in before product market fit, not after. I knew I wanted to work with very technical teams solving hard problems, because that was what I knew best. I knew that I wanted to play a significant role and write big enough checks to be material to startups.

"That all directed my interest towards small seed VC firms, rather than multi-stage or later-stage firms. I actually had interviews with a couple of larger firms, just to confirm for myself that it was not what I was looking for. I started networking with as many smaller VC firms as I could meet, and I learned that the trick to joining a seed-stage VC firm is: you basically can't.

"Although big firms rarely admit that they're hiring, they're always hiring, because they are large enough to accommodate new partners, and they're always thinking about succession and coverage of different domains and networks," Jocelyn went on. "Whereas small VC firms have anywhere from $20 to $200 million in assets under management, which is exactly matched to the number of partners they have. The only way they can absorb more partners is to either lose a partner that they need to replace (which is oftentimes a terrible red flag for a firm), or they would have to be able to raise a larger new fund and increase the partnership size, which gives a tiny window of opportunity that I'd need to catch them in. And let's be honest, that firm probably has dozens of great candidates they've already known for a long time," Jocelyn explained thoroughly.

"It became clear to me that it's really hard to join one of those firms. I suspect that's one reason why so many micro VCs have appeared in the last few years: if you cannot join a fund, you have to raise one. I started 'partner dating', seeking a co-founder to complement me and raise a fund together. I spent six months doing that and didn't find my perfect match. Meanwhile, my impatience to get going kept rising, and my fear of failure kept falling. Originally, I didn't think that I could raise a fund on my own without a venture track record. However, midway through my second year of angel investing, I had 15 investments in my portfolio that were doing well. I was getting more and more confident that I knew the lay of the land, and I wasn't a total stranger to venture capital investing anymore.

"At the end of the second year of my journey, I came to the conclusion that a perfect partner was not coming along, and although I am very collaborative by nature, I didn't want to keep waiting. So I started raising my own fund. I got several anchor commitments, and a few more folks who were interested. When I pitched Diane Greene, the former CEO of VMware, she introduced me to her friend, Mark Gorenberg, who had just started a fund of his own and could take me under his wing and mentor me as emerging manager.

"I scheduled coffee with Mark near the train station, so that I could catch a train right after our meeting. He brought his fundraising deck, shared the story of founding Zetta, and just showed me everything he had done. It was so generous of him to give me his time and help, and it was one of those meetings where you instantly feel a kinship with the other person. We hit it off so thoroughly, we just kept talking, and I missed my train. I missed the next train, too!" she belly-laughed.

Mark Gorenberg was managing his first fund of $60 million with his partner Ash Fontana. When he met Jocelyn, they were raising a second, $125 million, fund and actively looking for a third partner. Shortly after that first meeting, Mark told Goldfein, 'You should really consider joining forces with us!'

"My first thought was, 'No, I can't possibly join you, because I'm raising a fund myself and my anchor investors are committed!' But then I thought, 'Wait a second, my own fund was always Plan B — I'm only doing this because I didn't find the opportunity to join a seed VC firm before! I realized that it was only after I gave up and stopped looking for the perfect job, that it fell into my lap!'

"I still decided to take my time and be very sure of fit. I see partnership as almost a marriage — certainly a decade-long, or more, commitment. I wanted to make sure that I could really go all in with these partners, and a normal interview process just wasn't enough. We started spending more time together trying things out. I came to Zetta's Monday meetings, joined a number of pitch sessions, and got an upfront view of the decision-making and teamwork. I even attended their annual meeting and met portfolio founders and limited partners. Ultimately, through the time we spent together, I became confident in how comfortable I was with Mark and Ash. I could definitely see myself spending years of my life with them! I didn't have to compromise anything with Zetta — it was the perfect match for my personal and professional goals."

Jocelyn made her first investment with Zetta Venture Partners in January 2017 and was closing her fifth deal the week we talked, in the spring of 2019. Her approach to all her learnings was so thorough, that I assumed she could vividly describe the differences between being an angel investor and a partner at a VC firm.

"When people ask if angel investing can really prepare you for becoming a venture capitalist, the best metaphor I can think of is this: angel investing is like cooking for your family, while being a venture capitalist is like being a restaurant chef. They both look like cooking, and maybe you can apply a few of your knife skills, but in fact, they are totally different jobs. There's so much more to the job of a partner at a VC firm," Goldfein exceeded my expectations.

"A big part of that is the responsibility for investing other people's money. As an angel investor, I had a strategy to invest thousands in perhaps a dozen companies a year. As a partner, I make multimillion dollar decisions and make 2-3 investments a year.

"As an angel investor, I felt free to write a check out of patronage — because I wanted that product to exist, or I really liked the founder. At Zetta, I'm looking for more ingredients. I'm certainly looking for amazing founders, but I'm also mindful of a large enough market, long-term defensibility against competitors, an achievable financing path, and an exit strategy that could yield venture scale returns. I also have more power than an angel investor, because I'm offering to lead the round. I can ask for more information about the company, I can ask them to do more thinking through how they'll put that money to work, and perhaps most importantly, I can ask to meet customers.

"I also realized that deal-sourcing is a big part of the job, which I didn't appreciate enough as an angel investor. I worked hard to source back then, but for an institutional investor, deal-sourcing is absolutely fundamental to success, and a surprisingly overlooked part of our job. It doesn't matter how good a decision-maker you are, if you never meet the best companies, you never had an opportunity to make the right investment decision."

Jocelyn definitely comes across as a confident, and maybe even at times intimidating, woman. I asked for advice for other women who are building careers in venture capital. "I don't want to say that women are less confident than men, but I think that it is easy for us to feel like we don't belong in a male-dominated environment. All of us, men and women, are at our best when we feel comfortable at work to be ourselves. That's intrinsically a lot easier for men than for women when the numbers are so lopsided; only a few women (and I'm fortunate to be one of them) can feel at home when they are the only ones in the room. But I don't really think my path represents the solution — women shouldn't have to twist themselves into knots to conform to an environment that isn't inclusive. Ultimately, if we want to draw on all the talent that should be available to our industry, and not just the talent that happens to coincide with a thick skin, the environment needs to become more inclusive of all kinds of people."

Theresia Gouw

Founding Partner, Aspect Ventures, United States

Aspect Ventures' office in Palo Alto was once the original headquarters of Facebook. Theresia Gouw is used to saying that it has 'good karma': in 2005 she was one of the investors from Accel to deliver the first term sheet to Facebook.

Prior to Aspect, Theresia was the first female investor at one of the top-tier VC firms — Accel Partners. She then became the firm's first female partner and first female managing partner. In February 2014, Theresia co-founded Aspect Ventures, one of the first and currently the largest female-led venture capital firms, backed by such renowned investors as Melinda Gates' Pivotal Ventures and Cisco. Theresia is a well-known investor, having been recognized eight times on the Forbes' Midas List as one of the "worlds smartest tech investors".

Summarizing all her wins, some media called Theresia an overachiever, but she doesn't think that way about herself. "I was trained by my parents to certainly be a hard-working perfectionist, which is what I would call myself."

Gouw came with her parents to the US at the age of three, from Jakarta, Indonesia, where she was born. For a family of ethnic Chinese, there was a lot of political turmoil going on at the time and a lot of backlash against their people. "My parents are true believers in the American Dream and they felt very strongly that if you do well in school and work really hard, then America is the place where you can achieve whatever you dream of. They are true believers in the American dream, and that was the reason why they chose to come here in the first place. This belief impacted me the most, but another lesson that I learned from my parents, is that you can always start over and create opportunities," she summarized her early learnings.

Theresia's father had been a dentist in Indonesia, and her mother had been a nurse. They came to the United States, and as many other immigrants did, had to literally start over. Her parents worked at a Chinese restaurant: her father as a dishwasher, and mother as a hostess. But along with that, her father was also studying at a medical school to get his American certification in dentistry.

After getting her MBA, Gouw joined a startup called Release Software, launched by some of her Stanford classmates, just after they had raised their first million dollars for the seed round. She then helped them raise more than $30 million of venture capital over the following rounds, all the way to pre-IPO. But when they started getting the company ready to go public, she realized that they had once again changed the CEO, which meant that they had had three CEOs in 12 months. "I felt that it wasn't the greatest sign for my stock options, so I went to one of our venture capital investors, and asked him to introduce me to some of his other portfolio companies that I could possibly join. He did so, but he also introduced me to three venture capital firms, because he knew my background and experience and thought that I would be interested in that as well," she described how she mitigated career risks in her pre-venture times.

"I realized that working in venture capital would allow me to still be involved with startups, but with multiple companies at the same time, and it seemed like a really exciting opportunity to me. It was certainly a career risk to move from something that I had known, which was being an entrepreneur and executive at a venture-backed startup, but I took the chance, because my parents had always said that I should try what I am drawn to.

"When I was choosing between VC firms, I followed the advice I was given by the investor who had introduced me to them. He said, 'The most important thing is to find a place where you feel like you're going to get good mentorship. Don't be so focused on what your title is. Find a place where you're going to learn from some great people who will be willing to invest in your development.' Accel Partners seemed like the right place. I started out as an associate, and in just one year I became a partner, and then a general partner, and a managing partner later on. It all happened in less than five years, so it obviously ended up being a great opportunity for me. Looking back now, I could have definitely chosen another firm that would have offered me a better title to start with, but I remembered the advice I was given and was more focused on what I could learn".

When I asked Theresia what the most important skill was that she had obtained prior to getting into venture capital, which helped her in investing, she told me, "Fearlessness. I had done a lot of jobs at the startup, from product marketing, to customer support and beyond, but I was really good at business development. I was not afraid to do cold calling and cold emailing. I landed big tech companies like Symantec, Macromedia, and Netscape as our customers. I had to start doing the same at Accel, with the only difference being that I was looking for investment opportunities. I had to identify the startups that would be a good match for Accel, go out there and get in front of their people, get connected, and convince them that we were the right partner to have."

Despite having a skyrocketing career in venture capital at one of the top international VC firms, Theresia then decided to become an entrepreneur again. She chose to launch her own VC firm. I wondered why.

"Why do people leave Google and start their own companies? It is because they saw a market segment while working at Google and wanted to do something in that area on their own. It was very much the same for me when I decided to leave Accel. I had worked with startups from many different sectors, we had invested in all the stages — from seed to pre-IPO — but at some point I wanted to be laser-focused on Series A investments in sectors that I enjoyed the most and had the most success in. I wanted my firm to be small enough to provide flexibility and close collaboration with entrepreneurs and co-investors."

As with many other investors interviewed for this book, Theresia was very involved in sports growing up. She was a figure skater, played field hockey, volleyball, and ran track. She still loves football, which she used to watch with her dad every Sunday. "My dad was an avid sports fan and he had always wanted a son. When he had two daughters, he instilled the love of sports in us and we were season ticket holders for the Buffalo Bills. It would be 5 degrees below zero and snowing and we would still be sitting in the stadium, huddled under blankets and cheering on our team," she remembered.

Theresia gives some credit to sports for building her character. "I grew up being a very competitive team player. I'm a big believer in team sports, where I not only learned how to be competitive, but I also learned how to play in a team, in order to achieve my goals.

"I also have to admit that being a sports fan has helped me to build relationships with my colleagues in the venture capital and tech worlds. These are male-dominated industries, and many men are sports fans as well, so I can always find common ground. But aside from that, many sports terms have populated business language at large: we all talk about home runs, and hitting a Grand Slam. Even just knowing the lingo can help you to strike up a conversation and connect with people.

"Nevertheless, earlier on in my career I definitely felt more like I needed to play by the boys' rules. Chatting about sports was just one thing. What was funnier is that there was a kind of a dress code when I started in the venture capital business, in the late 90s — blue button downs and khaki pants, (just like now it's jeans and a fleece vest now). I was dressing like that for quite a while. As I became more secure in my career, however, I started dressing the way I like to — dresses and skirts more often than pants, and high heels instead of flats.

"Earlier in our careers, we often find that we need to play by the boys' rules, because it helps us feel that we belong here. But what we are looking for is commonality, and that could be anything! For example, could I still talk about sports in a dress and pumps? Of course I could! And that would be enough for me to be regarded as one of them. So to all the younger investment professionals, especially women, I'd like to say that you just need to find what unites you with other VCs without changing yourself.

"Most likely, you will have at least a couple of other things in common, which are your love for startups and passion for technology. And they are the foundation of our business. You can always talk and bond with your male colleagues, whether they are other VCs or entrepreneurs, about the things that you mutually care for. The best part of it — you don't need to change anything about yourself!"

However, on a different note, Gouw pointed me to a study conducted by the BoardList that suggested differences in Midas List members. "If you take a look at the Midas listers, you'll see that about 80% of women have technical degrees, while only approximately half of the men on the list have them. What it says is that if you don't belong to the majority, you'll absolutely need to have all the credential boxes checked."

Despite all her titles and speaking the same language with male colleagues, Gouw has, from time to time, found herself in uncomfortable circumstances. "I always find that humor is a great way to defuse an awkward situation. It has been my tendency, especially in a group setting. And then if I still felt like there was something I would want to say to the individual who created the awkwardness, I would do that at a different time, in a one-on-one setting. I'd tell them very calmly something like, 'You know, what you said (or did) made me feel uncomfortable.' In my experience, people are more open to a different point of view when they aren't publicly exposed at the moment.

"Way too often, people don't necessarily understand how others perceive what they are saying. I've heard so many times, 'I didn't mean it that way', which only confirms my tactic of bringing humor in and changing the topic in awkward situations. It helps to avoid a lot of drama — so that you don't get upset, but also that you don't embarrass that person in front of others."

I would like to highlight that this advice is very common among the top women-investors in this book.

Kirsten Green

Founding Partner, Forerunner Ventures, United States

You'll notice Kirsten Green's name in the book several more times beyond just this chapter for a good reason: she became one of the most respected venture capitalists in the world, despite her very different profile, that would have very little odds of making it in venture capital back when she started — and also today. Fellow investors just love mentioning her name as proof that there is no rule book in venture capital. She didn't go to business school and never worked for a powerful VC firm. She has never built a tech company, and never even worked for one. She isn't an engineer, and had never been on the board of tech giants before becoming a VC. She was a solo general partner when she was raising her first fund, and a woman, who also had a toddler at home during the fundraising process.

Green started with a modest $40 million and grew her firm to a platform in less than ten years, recently closing her fourth fund at $350 million. She invested early in big hits and avoided disasters. Kirsten has built one of the most recognizable portfolios in the tech world and become one of the most prominent players in this male-dominated industry. She is a true unicorn among venture investors, who also says, "I do not want Forerunner to be about me. I love coming into the office and there are other people who also care about the firm. That is my proudest moment." Oh, and when I asked Kirsten to connect me with her assistant to make some arrangements, she replied that she doesn't currently have an assistant.

Green studied business economics at the University of California in Los Angeles, and went straight to Deloitte as a retail auditor, skipping an MBA, for which she never found time anyway. She doesn't regret not getting an MBA, instead, saying that if she were to start over, she'd opt to take a year off after college and explore the world. "In retrospect, I think I should've done that, because I think there's so much good to be found in embracing experiences — be open-minded about what your path and your journey might look like," Kirsten said.

She then became a retail stock analyst at the investment bank, Montgomery Securities (now Banc of America Securities), before industry consolidation left her displaced. While she was offered the opportunity to move into another area of sector coverage, she chose to move to a buy-side investment role. "I thought, 'Geez, no matter how good I'm at a job, it can be taken away from me for one reason or another. I'm not going to put myself in that situation again,' and I think that really unearthed the entrepreneurial side of me, which was taking things into my own hands," she spoke about taking ownership of her career.

Kirsten founded a hedge fund specializing in consumer stocks, but a year into it, she felt that it wasn't the right choice. "I sat in an investor meeting, and

thought, 'I can't do this...trading in and out of companies following short-term trends.' It's not enough about a thesis and not enough about people; it's about next month's sales prediction." Within days of this realization, she returned her investors' money and began learning about venture capital, where she felt she could use her almost decade-long experience in brick-and-mortar retail and foot traffic in malls, to guide and support entrepreneurs.

The obvious step for a person with her background would be to join an established VC firm, at least for the sake of getting experience fast, but Green decided to start learning the art of venture investing herself. "Starting my own VC firm wasn't my original intention. In fact, I was probably open to the idea of joining another VC firm along the way, but as time went on, I got more and more ideas about how I might approach the opportunity, which ultimately became the impetus for starting Forerunner. I developed a certain vision around the kinds of companies I wanted to invest in, and the kinds of people I wanted to work with, and the sort of team dynamic I wanted to have. I found myself, organically, getting excited about tackling that from the ground up."

Kirsten spent the next six years proactively taking on a variety of opportunities and experiences that enabled her to learn and develop her skills. It was not only the era of the internet, but also the fact that another economic downturn happened that boosted the change in the retail industry. She realized that her public market and brick-and-mortar experience didn't quite qualify her for investing in tech-enabled companies in the consumer space, and so she took every chance to be as close to entrepreneurs as possible, in order to understand how an idea turns into an operation. She engaged in brainstorming conversations at every opportunity, offered to build financial models and write business plans. Aside from that, not only did she work on consulting projects and helped different investment firms, but she also enjoyed writing, photography, and painting classes for her own personal growth.

As her network in the startup community grew, she got a deal flow, and soon identified founders and dreams that resonated with her developing investment thesis. She'd scout a startup, raise the money from other investors to back it, and then manage the back-end of dozens of mini-funds. But she was also trying to add value to companies, to build credibility in the sector. "I wanted to show entrepreneurs that I had some hard skills to help them, and to show investors that I had some tangible, real examples under my belt. By raising money on a deal-by-deal basis, they were investing in the deal, not me," she explained the way she approached it due to her lack of personal investing experience. While investing this way for three years, she got acquainted with institutional investors, and collected a ton of references.

As important as proving herself to founders, was demonstrating a process and discipline to prospective investors. Kirsten highlights the responsibility, even weight, of managing people's money as a serious consideration as she contemplated a path forward, "As a general partner you are at once responsible to founders and your funders."

As she contemplated raising a fund of her own, there were plenty of people who told her along the way that she couldn't start her own VC firm if she hadn't been in venture. "It was a good thing that I didn't listen to them," she smiled. "I have approached Forerunner like a startup, in thinking about what the big picture is, what the main goal is, what the big idea is, and what is the North Star where we want to go. Then I kind of dialed back to ground zero and thought about the things I need to do, brick by brick, to lay the foundation on which to really prepare myself to take the opportunity. Ultimately, I developed the idea of Forerunner being a helpful, best-in-class, early-stage venture investor."

When I asked her how soon she managed to close the fund, she said that while it technically took five months, she could easily count those six years of self-study in. "I put a lot of upfront effort into my first fundraising, which I think helped set Forerunner up for success. Before I started talking to LPs, specifically about the fund, I took as many opportunities as I could to learn about how other people had done it, and what LPs were looking for, particularly in a first-time manager. By the time I started to fundraise, I had a shortlist of investors I wanted, a strategy around how to approach them, and a mindset that was geared towards that. When I did officially show up for raising capital, I was presenting what I thought of as the best version of myself and the best opportunity for investors.

"I had a data room and written memos for every investment I had made, and my point in doing that was to demonstrate that I was really serious about the process, the data-driven approach, about setting up an infrastructure, and institutionalizing what I had been doing.

"I think that venture capital is a decade-long journey, before you can really see whether people are successful, and success in venture capital is defined as returning a handsome amount of cash. So along the way, from when I started learning about venture capital until my first pitch to limited partners, I tried to identify the things that I could do to build confidence for myself, my team, and my LPs — how we're setting ourselves up to ultimately be successful in driving returns. I thought of where we would want to be a couple of years from now, in terms of the process we have, the data we use, and the transparency we build. I was going to do as much of that as I could, up front, to demonstrate that."

Despite years of preparation and experience, Kirsten Green heard her share of no's from institutional investors along the way. "When we went to market, we had a thesis-driven approach, which people didn't fully appreciate. By saying 'commerce', we thought about it as a lens for addressing the market in general and advancing the evolution thereof. In that context, there were a lot of companies that fit in that space: anything that inspires or facilitates a transaction, which covers B2B companies, service companies, product companies, and retail platforms. However many people, back then, saw the word 'commerce' differently. They thought we were talking about some narrow slice of the market."

Green proved everyone who doubted her wrong with just one of her very first investments made by Forerunner. "I met Michael Dubin, the co-founder of Dollar Shave Club, while I was just starting to raise the first fund. He immediately captured my imagination as a truly special founder. While I didn't yet have any financial commitments to the fund, I knew that I needed to get my stake in the company as soon as possible. I borrowed money to lead his seed investment round and rolled it into the close of the fund four months later." Just four years later, in 2016, Dollar Shave Club, was acquired by Unilever for a billion US dollars.

All this experience could have come with some disappointment, where Kirsten might have felt herself being underappreciated or undervalued, so I asked how she had responded to that. "My operating agenda has been to show up every day, to be the best version of myself, and to do a good job. There will always be people who will doubt you along the way. But I hang on to the idea that I will win them over some day, because I am good at what I do. I believed in and trusted that approach, and it has served me well.

"However, that doesn't mean that this approach will work for everyone. I think that we should all do what we're comfortable with. At the end of the day, success is about getting to the truth of our own capabilities, and ultimately demonstrating that. I think you've got to live with yourself along the way and feel proud of how you're showing up."

This approach seems to be traditionally feminine, and Kirsten was not always comfortable with it. "I'd like to think my strengths are in connecting with people and the relationship aspect of this business," she said. "There were times when I felt uncomfortable with putting them forward as my differentiation, because it seemed to be too soft for Silicon Valley in venture capital, however, my approach eventually helped me to get into the best deals. It's the entrepreneurs who have to give you permission to do your job. That's it."

Christine Guo

Vice President,
Wells Fargo Strategic Capital,
United States

When Guo's name appeared on the list of nominees, I was quite surprised, because Wells Fargo's venture capital arm was a pretty new formation, and it doesn't happen often that the investment and entrepreneurial communities recognize new corporate players that soon. I am pleased to have a chance to introduce both Wells Fargo Strategic Capital and Christine Guo to my readers.

"During my entire life, healthcare and business has always been intertwined. My family immigrated from China, so we are first generation immigrants. My parents were physicians back there, and they decided to go through the whole training again to become licensed doctors in the US as well. They then opened two primary care clinics as a family business, and I basically grew up in these clinics in Chinatown, New York City. When I went to college, I always thought that I was going to be a doctor and end up taking care of my parents' clinics. That is why I got a dual degree in both biology and finance at Penn."

After graduation, Christine worked for the private equity group at Goldman Sachs, on private equity strategies, doing secondary transactions and learning about the full spectrum of investing, from venture to turnaround. "I really loved the investment component of the job, but I felt like I was too far from the real action — where the innovations were happening. I interviewed with a bunch of different VC firms, but I didn't quite realize that they differed a lot in terms of the stage of investing. It was my mentor, Julia Feldman, a managing director at Goldman Sachs, who knew me better than I did myself, when she advised me to look into early-stage investing. She knew that I loved working with people and thinking about ideas, and that my interest was in transforming ideas to growth companies versus optimizing the financial structure of a business. I was lucky to have a chance to work with New Enterprise Associates (NEA) and be introduced to the best practices of venture capital investing."

The more I talked to Christine, the more I realized why entrepreneurs had nominated her for the book: she's an extremely down to earth investor with a deep appreciation for their hustle.

"When I started in venture capital, I was amazed by the breadth and depth of knowledge that operators had when they engaged in discussions with entrepreneurs. I couldn't truly empathize with the entrepreneurial struggle that the founders experienced. I think, to fully appreciate their day-to-day roller coasters and be an effective advisor, you need to have first-hand entrepreneurial experience. So I felt a little bit like an imposter in the boardroom, working with entrepreneurs who had so much more experience than me," she smiled — clearly possessing a great deal of self-awareness. "That was part of the reason why I decided to go into the operating world for some time, and that was what prompted me to join Collected Health, a company that I had invested in when I was at NEA.

"The number one thing I learned from my operational experience, is empathy. I think sometimes investors expect to invest in a company that has very polished and experienced founders and executives, who have all the answers. But the reality of building something completely new, is that you don't have all the answers, and partnering with the right investment partner who is able to help you navigate some of that roller coaster together, is part of the journey. This journey comes with ups and downs, and I haven't seen many companies that go straight up — it's never a smooth journey. My main goal is to build a strong partnership with entrepreneurs, so that we are able to work through this journey together.

"At some point, however, I started to really miss venture capital and wanted to get back into investing. I also really liked that feeling that comes when you build something, but I was unsure of how I could combine the two. It was the same time that Wells Fargo Strategic Capital, a new direct investing arm of Wells Fargo, was getting formalized, and the healthcare division was just getting launched. I couldn't resist the opportunity to build this healthcare investing platform. It was the best of both worlds — an opportunity to build a brand new team, define our investment strategy, and build our own portfolio. I was also drawn to the patient nature of balance sheet capital, which is well-suited to healthcare, since everything in healthcare just takes longer. Not to mention that I didn't have to pitch 600 institutional investors to raise money for the fund!" Christine laughed.

"Venture capital is a mentorship and apprenticeship business. In some ways, it is harder for women, because there aren't as many senior female VCs who are natural mentors for younger female investors. That being said, I've been very fortunate to have Annie Lamont as my mentor, who is an incredible role model, and I see her as someone I want to be when I grow up. I also had incredible male mentors, who helped me tremendously to get to where I am now — Mohamad Makhzoumi, who is the head of the healthcare investment group at NEA, as well as my current manager at Wells Fargo Strategic Capital, John Ryan."

When Christine revealed that she had felt that entrepreneurial itch, I couldn't help but ask whether she had ever thought of launching her own startup. "I feel like I am doing something very entrepreneurial right now at Wells Fargo Strategic Capital. My husband also started a cleantech company about seven years ago, and having two founders in one family does not make a marriage easy. So I tried to find a balance that would keep my personal life intact," Christine spelled it out for me and all married entrepreneurs to consider.

Arlan Hamilton

Founding Partner,
Backstage Capital, United States

No other venture capital investor has received as much publicity as Arlan Hamilton, it may seem. She took Silicon Valley by storm and everybody knows about her VC firm, Backstage Capital, and its mission. She is an African-American gay woman who had no prior investing experience nor connections, before breaking into venture capital, and who also slept on the floor at an airport while fundraising for her fund.

Hamilton's mission sounds pretty common in the context of this book — invest in underrepresented founders, which includes women, ethnic minority groups, and LGBT people. "Investing money, time, resources, access, belief — all of that — into black people, Latinx people, all people of color, and women is not something that should be looked at as 'doing us a favor,'" she said. "It is doing *you* a favor if you are a white male, because we are the future." Although venture capital is very vocal about supporting all of these entrepreneurs, Backstage Capital's bank account doesn't really believe it.

Hamilton had worked as a production coordinator and tour manager for several celebrities like Toni Braxton, Kirk Franklin, and Jason Derulo. She had every opportunity to make a career in Hollywood, but was instead inspired by Ashton Kutcher, Troy Carter and Ellen DeGeneres, who started making investments in Silicon Valley, and left the job that paid well, to find her place in venture capital.

Arlan spent countless hours online, learning as much as possible about the startup and venture capital worlds. She tried to get in touch with every person on the web who she found interesting. She reached out to Brad Feld, Chris Sacca, and Sam Altman, through his brother. In her opinion, "everything you need is on the internet if you have the willpower to find it". At the time, Arlan was broke, but she figured that $39.99 a month for the Premium LinkedIn profile was a worthy investment. For every yes, she had hundreds of rejections, which she had gotten used to since childhood when she was going door-to-door as a Jehovah's Witness — an activity that can best be described as a constant rejection.

Hamilton was looking for a job or mentorship from investors, and she didn't set out to become an investor herself until she noticed that there were people who were not getting access to the same rooms as others, and they looked like her.

After quitting her Hollywood job, her savings didn't last long, so when she arrived in San Francisco, California from Austin, Texas in 2015, she slept on the floor of the airport at night and pitched investors by day. She had a dream: to change the face of venture capital by creating a VC firm that invests in 'underestimated' founders. Hamilton very soon realized that Silicon Valley was very far from being a meritocracy, contrary to what she heard from white male investors on the web. Nevertheless, her grit paid off and Backstage Capital raised capital from such investors as Chris Sacca, Marc Andreessen, Susan Kimberlain, Slack CEO Stewart Butterfield, and Box CEO Aaron Levie. She does admit, however, that most of the checks were much smaller than these people were used to writing.

Typically, media outlets that have ever covered Arlan's story, like telling the pleasant side of it: she has backed more than 100 companies, all of which have at least one founder who is a woman, a person of color, or an LGBTQ person, from the $5 million venture fund. However, it's rarely mentioned that even this, insignificant by Silicon Valley measure, amount was terribly hard to raise. Arlan has had dozens of deals fall through and promises not delivered. She has run out of money in her firm's bank account so many times, while waiting for a new influx of capital, because something didn't work out. Not only could she not invest in startups, but she wasn't even able to pay salaries to her loyal team of 30 people. Every time that happened, she said to herself: "I'll figure it out."

She figured it out by selling pieces of her carried interest in the fund, which she hopes to buy back eventually. She believes that it would be unfair to have the smallest share in what she'd been building for years, let alone to not have it at all.

During a large tech conference in May 2018, Arlan unexpectedly announced that she was raising a new $36 million fund to invest exclusively in black female founders — she called it the 'it's about damn time' fund. However, the same story repeated itself, and earlier this year, she admitted that it was taking longer to raise than she had planned. She shared that the firm had 'lost out on a $5 million 'operations deal' with the Renault-Nissan-Mitsubishi Alliance after CEO Carlos Ghosn was arrested in Japan', and also that 'two separate anchor investors fell through'. She added that other prospective LPs had decided to wait until Backstage Capital gets more traction. Some of these investors confirmed to reporters that they had reservations that Hamilton and Backstage Capital might have spread themselves too thin. Bottom line — the fundraising was indefinitely suspended but not ended, as she said. How was she going to figure it out again?

Hamilton decided to transition Backstage entirely to an accelerator model, and to cut costs in the process, which may also mean team layoffs. Although, she did say that the Studio had generated around $3 million over 2018-2019 via corporate sponsorships and an online resource portal for founders. However, this vehicle sets Arlan up for a longer run in achieving her dream.

I'll leave it to the reader to decide what is missing in Arlan's story that couldn't convince all those people who advocate for backing diverse entrepreneurs to write her a check. Or maybe all of these people have missed out on something instead.

Meirav Har-Noy

Founding Partner, Moneta VC, Israel

"We don't have any female-led startups in our portfolio and it's super upsetting!" Meirav exclaimed before I had a chance to ask her about it. "I've met with every single female founder who asked me to meet, and I am proactively searching for a good match for our portfolio, but it hasn't happened yet. I care a lot about funding women, but there is not much we can do if for every 50 companies I meet, only one is led by a woman. The pipeline problem, that entrepreneurs don't like hearing about, exists in Israel, especially in some sectors and investment verticals," she concluded and mentioned that they are still, and always, looking.

"I think it's actually better for families if women become entrepreneurs, but hear out my explanation before you label it politically incorrect. As the situation is that most men earn more than women — which is still the case per various studies — it's less risky for a family, as a unit, if a woman puts on an entrepreneur's hat and a man remains a provider for the family. If a husband bootstraps a company and doesn't bring a salary home, and his family exists on the wife's income, that mathematically makes the household income lower, because women's salaries are lower than men's. But even if *her* startup goes belly up, which happens to most startups and is the norm, the household is losing only her unearned income, which is typically less than the husband's. Simple math and risk management in the current social realities!" she shared emotionally, being an example of doing just that. Throughout her career, her father, and then her husband, were very supportive of all her ventures, and encouraged Meirav to make risky decisions.

Her father worked at Applied Materials in California, one of the most innovative companies at the time, and she was exposed to all the beauty of

Silicon Valley innovations in the 80s early 90s. She returned to Israel at the age of 18 to join the Israeli army. When she graduated from school after that, she decided to go back to the US. "I thought that I should find a job at a big international company here in Israel that everyone in America would know about," she presented her only rationale that led her to joining Intel in an administrative role.

However, it took her only three months to find an opportunity that changed her life. Intel was setting up a venture capital group in their Israeli office, and she went up to the manager of this group and asked to give her a chance. "It was Intel where I took the advice of one of the senior managers, who told me, 'You need to know what you want to do. You need to be great at what you're doing. And you need everyone to know how great you are at it'. These three keys to success worked out really well for me."

Har-Noy started with Intel Capital as a part-time investment associate at the age of 23, and became the most experienced team member a year later, when the founding team left the company. As the only watchdog left, she was promoted by the new director, whom Meirav had helped to build a new team. "He hired really amazing people, but all of them were paid about four times higher salaries than me, because I had started at Intel very low and very young," she lamented. "So I told him at some point that I deserved a raise and wanted to be equal to everyone else on the team, because I was doing the same job and had been working for the company the longest. Unfortunately, I was only offered a 15% raise at the time, which quite upset me, and I started looking for another job. I got an offer from another venture capital fund, which was 30% higher than what Intel Capital was paying to any of the new team members. I went back and showed that to my boss, and all he had to do was match it! I had a lot of balls to do that! Not only was it very bold, but I was also the only woman on the team, so I am still surprised by that stunt of mine," she giggled.

She stayed with Intel Capital for seven years after that, investing in Israeli and European companies, and managing all the acquisitions of the company, before she finally decided to leave the Intel family and join a growth equity firm called Apax Partners. "I wasn't looking for a job when they approached me, but my father told me that it's okay to give good things up in order to get something better, so it gave me a much needed push, as if I was jumping into cold water. He had a lot of faith in me and encouraged me to take a risk."

Meirav said that Apax Partners really brought up her financial skills, and opened a whole new world of the growth equity asset class for her. She then joined a single family office based in London, where she managed many of their high tech investments.

"Investing from a family office was very different to everything I had known up until that point. It was the third asset class I had worked with. When you work in corporate venturing, you invest off the balance sheet, which is typically so big that you have little sense of loss. When you work for several limited partners, you are judged by your portfolio, so all the results — good or bad — are remote, and there is always a chance to improve them. But when you invest just one investor's money, and are being judged on a deal-by-deal basis, it truly changes your attitude towards the money you invest, and this makes you much more responsible for their assets. You take their losses as your own, which fills you up with a very deep sense of responsibility in terms of how to look at things and how to consider everything that can go wrong. There is no corporate team or other partners behind you if things go south at the family office. It was thanks to that experience, that I truly developed my gut feeling and became very aware of all the possible risks. Being too 'risk alert' is not always good, by the way, because it makes you prone to looking at all the possible negative things that can occur, while reducing the odds of good things taking place, among other scenarios."

It so happened that each of Meirav's kids was born while she was working for one of these three companies, which marked her life by three very distinctive periods. "Every kid symbolized some new learnings in my life. It was like when you are used to seeing the world blurry because you've never worn glasses, so you thought that the world was like that. When you eventually put a pair of glasses on, you say, 'Oh, this is so clear! My God, why didn't I wear glasses before?' Each of my kids was like a stronger magnifying power in my glasses, to see the reality," she described.

"After my youngest was born, I left the family office and said to myself, 'Okay, I need to figure out what I am going to do next, so I won't have to work for someone else when I turn 50'. It was very important for me to find that right thing, but I also knew that I needed a partner, and I didn't have anyone who I could go with. I decided to take time off and to not rush things, working on some projects from time to time. I have an amazing husband, who was as supportive as my father, who also encouraged me to make all those jumps between the different companies that I had worked for."

"I think you need to have at least one parent who can teach you to take risks, and give you the understanding that it's okay to fail. Otherwise, if you only play it safe, then you might never use your full potential, because the fear of failure is too strong. When I look at my daughters, I know that the best I can do is to teach them by my own example."

Meirav is one of the many women I interviewed for the book, who believes that having a supportive life partner is important. "It's also important to have an honest relationship and open discussion at home with your significant other, because you need to place yourself in the center of that relationship alongside your partner. Traditionally, it's the man's career that comes first, so it's difficult to change that, unless you both agree on the equal importance of both of your careers. I have plenty of brilliant female friends who are Harvard, Yale — you name it — graduates with PhDs and whatever, but they spend their lives at home, raising their kids and debating at PTA meetings over the choice of juices served to children. What a waste of their accomplishments!

"I think I have the right to say that, because I have three children myself — two daughters and a son. But I managed to have them along with my career. I didn't feel that I had to give up something for that. Nor did I think that I was a bad mother due to having a career. I spent as much time with my kids as was critical, but not too much to become their Mary Poppins. I believe that we shouldn't overmanage our kids, the same way we don't do that to our portfolio companies. We have limited rights to interfere in the business of the latter, so we should limit our interference in the lives of our children as well.

"I try to spread the message that women can have it all in their lives. It is very important for me to pass this on to younger women and to show them my own example. Yes, you can have it all without giving up on anything. Don't wait until you're 40 to have kids. Make your board meetings start at 2pm instead of 5pm. If you're at the level that you are invited to attend them, you may as well affect the scheduling — just ask. The same can be done with many other things," Meirav stated with passion.

When I asked her what else she does to advance women in the industry, while looking for the first female-founded company for her portfolio, she said: "Becoming an entrepreneur is a self-driving thing — we cannot force anyone to start their own business. What we can do, is encourage founding teams to have more women among their executives and board members. Whenever my portfolio companies are looking to hire someone, I try to bring in female candidates. I know that I can definitely affect that, and these women may become founders later, after gaining all that experience. I may not have found an amazing female founder for my portfolio yet, but most of the senior positions in my portfolio companies are actually filled by women."

Meirav eventually found a partner she could trust, and raised a small seed fund — first in 2015, and then she closed the second fund of $80 million last year. She named the fund Moneta Ventures — after the Goddess of Treasure, Juno Moneta.

Heather Hartnett

Founding Partner, Human Ventures, United States

Heather Hartnett appeared in the tech press out of nowhere with the flare of a big win. When I learned her story, I realized why I got that impression.

"I have a very unconventional background for venture capital," she started explaining. "I came from a line of entrepreneurs, starting from my grandfather. Hence, there was never a traditional path of what we were supposed to do in our family. Our mentality can be described as the following: when you see a challenge, you go and find a solution for it.

"When I graduated from college, my parents didn't ask me where I wanted to work or what I wanted to do. They asked me what company I was going to build. My parents were adamant that I should find my true strengths and find what brings me joy in the first place. They didn't set me up for any traditional business or career path — like becoming an investment banker, or a lawyer. It has always been emphasized that I should place my well-being ahead of everything else and derive joy out of what I do.

"I've tried quite a few different businesses in my life, starting when I was in sixth grade," Heather told me. "I was always selling something. My first business was probably buying a special type of candy in the Netherlands (when I was studying there in high school) and reselling them in the United States, because there was nothing similar to those candies here. I would take orders from my classmates, buy the candies in bulk, and bring them to the US to sell. I made a good amount of money for a sixth grader! It was then that I learned about demand, knowing your market, and setting the right price!

"After high school, it was a no-brainer for me to go and study business and management as an undergrad, because I had always been attracted to business, and had already learned some of its components. For example, I had watched my father negotiating at GemTrade and with big telecom companies, and I learned as much as I could from him."

Heather was influenced by her father from her early childhood. Dr Chris Hartnett is known as the sole owner of approximately 12,000 domain names, and a part owner of around 20,000 more back in the 80s. He was also a gemologist who scored a 169-carat pink emerald — the world's largest heart-shaped pink emerald — for his private gemstone collection. Finally, he was known as the "Father of Internet Telephony and VOIP technologies" after being dubbed that by the Financial Times. The latter was possibly his greatest success.

"As a gemologist and a jeweler, my father would travel to find precious colored stones, and he would take me to gem shows all over the world. When we were traveling, he would call my mom at home and ask her to call him right back, because the outgoing long-distance call fees in the US were much cheaper than international calls on the US number. The industry was obviously monopolized,

so my dad started a company called USA Global Link — the first enabler of global phone-to-phone calling via the internet. This innovation launched a massive trend toward the deregulation of the telecommunications industry and opening up of lines, in order to make international calls much more affordable. It was definitely a revolutionary time for that industry, and I got to see how telco really merged into the internet, at a very young age.

"I also remember very clearly how my father was buying domain names. It's a funny comparison, but he followed my grandfather's advice who was in the real estate business and would always say, 'Location is everything!' For the next generation of businesses in the internet era, that location was a domain name. When I got older, I also started buying and selling domain names. I then became a day trader at a stock exchange, and learned all about market dynamics at a pretty young age."

Heather started looking into a venture capital career back in 2005. "I was truly enamored with what investing in companies could do for the world, and that was my main drive. At that point, my job search wasn't successful, but I don't think being a woman affected it in any way. I wanted to be a part of the investment decision-making process, and one obviously needs to have a strong, relevant track record for that. My background didn't exactly match a typical profile and I had little to offer to VC firms. I decided not to waste my time and instead, started helping different startups do their job, getting some domain expertise in different areas for myself, and building out my network. It wasn't until about six years later that I started thinking about venture capital again," she guided me through her career.

"Looking back, I can now advise anyone who wants to work in venture capital to start with breaking down the components of venture investing, so as to really understand why this is the place for you. It's an industry that gets glorified more than it should. I see people who go into venture capital and then get disappointed because it turns out to not be what they thought it was. There are so many jobs in venture capital that depend on the stage of investing, or the investment focus. You don't have to come from a top school or a top company to work in VC — really smart people will find you if you're standing out, but you need to examine your background and understand how it translates to venture capital, and what value you can add to the ecosystem.

"Speaking of women in the industry, I think there is a slight misconception that more female investors will proportionally affect the amount of funding allocated for female founders. I believe that a different metric should be used. Female investors are definitely able to spot the opportunities that male investors simply cannot see, and those opportunities could be pretty significant. It's still about investing in promising businesses and large markets — and not just gender. I think that is a better angle from which to approach the diversity subject, because limited and general partners are both interested in making returns on their investments, and we should speak their language and use the metrics that they do, instead of just talking about gender. Drawing the link between female funders to the capital invested in female founders oversimplifies the actual roles that both are playing. Limited partners who invest in Human Ventures aren't investing just because I'm a female fund manager, they invest because Human Ventures is positioned uniquely as a fund franchise. We're being thoughtful about our strategy, and we're here for the long haul," Hartnett declared.

Today, as the startup building process is becoming more sophisticated, early-stage investors — even angel investors — are looking for significant traction prior to writing a check. Having traction brings a startup to a certain stage that requires more funding than just a couple of dozen thousand dollars, which is why the average check gets bigger and bigger, and early-stage VC firms are raising larger and larger funds. On the one hand, this is a really good trend, because we should be funding products and services that are proven by the demand in the market, and not just because there's a good salesperson on the other side of the table.

But on the other hand, it creates a big gap, where founders at the idea stage have no one to turn to for support. This is where Human Ventures steps in. Heather built what the industry calls a venture studio — a platform for founders who identify their stage as pre-concept, where they can find the support of a business design team to co-build their product or service and help them get their first check. When the team proves that there's traction and conviction, then Human Ventures invests cash as a traditional VC firm.

Heather's debut fund is backed by sophisticated industry titans and investors such as Beth Comstock (the former vice chair of General Electric), Chris Sacca, and First Round Capital's Howard Morgan. She is a good example of a generalist investor, but she is also a people's person. "I do think that early-stage investing requires very specific skills and a broad range of knowledge and experience, which helps you see things coming out of nothing and identify non-existent trends. But I built Human Ventures on the premise of people. I think that an idea can only be successful if there is a founder behind it who is able to be a catalyst for change. The biggest opportunities come with changing market trajectories. I believe that having a strong sense of people, understanding what they're good at, and knowing their true zones of genius and skill sets, are all critically important abilities in early-stage venture investing. We then need to access the risk tolerance, the drive, and the ability to execute that.

"We look for founders beyond the typical investment patterns that venture capitalists normally have (for example, the 'repeat founders', who are more likely to be men — we back them too), but we are also interested in those who have a 'PhD in life' — folks with a non-traditional background; the 'person behind the person' — people who were previously the 'number two' in organizations; or an 'entrepreneur in corporate clothing' — those who we often call intrapreneurs. If Human Ventures could be known for anything, 10 years from now, it should be for redefining that pattern recognition for the venture capital industry."

I asked Heather if she learned anything new after three years of running Human Ventures, and she replied, "I named the company after our mission to focus on people, but I didn't realize how much team dynamics affects a business, and how often founders and investors underestimate this — it's absolutely phenomenal. One really needs to have a high emotional quotient across the executive team to be able to execute their job in an efficient way. We've placed a lot of importance on data, and rigor on the metrics of execution. We brought in a coach-in-residence early on, so that each of our founders would have access to him. We hired a head of diversity and inclusion to scout for a wider array of founders, but also to help them attract pools of untapped talent."

Talking to Heather, one cannot mistake her for someone who is an entrepreneur first. Being one myself, I know how difficult it is to switch to the investor mentality and not interfere in portfolio companies' operations. I asked her how she feels about that. "There's no doubt that starting your own VC firm is absolutely being an entrepreneur. You build something from scratch — your brand, your reputation, your network. You have to know how to fundraise and communicate your vision clearly, and you have to get early buy in all these things. What raising this fund taught me was just how many times you have to go through the pattern of: no, test, reiterate, go back out there. It was very much learning by rejection, which I think is the fastest and best way to learn.

"However, when it comes to relationships with portfolio companies, no matter how much an investor would want to micromanage them, it would be impossible to do that in an efficient way once you have many companies in your portfolio. That path leads to nowhere. For me, it's really important that the founders or executives of the business have full autonomy, but also that we can rely on them. That is why we pay so much attention to the human factor in the first place — for us it's part of our scalability model.

"At Human, we have what we call "the myth of the big idea" — a notion that any first idea will iterate 100 times before it finds that product/market fit. So we need a leader who knows how to pivot when it's time, how to react to a change in the market, and how to be resilient to the forces and dynamics that come their way. As you can see, that initial stage of all the ideas that go through Human Ventures, is more than enough for me to satisfy the entrepreneur in me."

Mar Hershenson

Founding Partner, Pear Ventures, United States

When Mar Hershenson was a little girl back in Spain, she was a pretty geeky, nerdy, somewhat strange kid, who loved long car rides with her family because she could do math with all the numbers on the road. She would add numbers on license plates and try to divide them, and would be ecstatic to find license plates with multiple factors. At school, she always managed to escape from whatever her class was doing, and hide in a corner to play with numbers, being fascinated by arithmetic puzzles and infinity. Teachers gave her a nickname — Pythagorean — for being really good at math.

Mar was excellent at numbers, but she said she was not good at anything else. "Art — no talent. Sports — clumsy. Cooking — dangerous. Dressing up — hopeless. For many years, I let that math label define me. I would sit on the benches watching my friends playing soccer and not daring to join them. I failed the third-grade art class, and my parents had to actually go and meet the teacher to figure out how I was going to make it through the year. I didn't even try any non-academic things, because I thought I couldn't," Hershenson remembered.

Something magical happened when Mar came to the United States in 1995. "It was just me — no family, no friends, no second-grade teacher. Nobody here knew me and I somehow felt the freedom to try all the things that I was terrible at. I peeled off all the labels, and the more labels I peeled off the freer I felt.

"This trying new things turned into somewhat of an obsession that has defined the rest of my life," she shared. "I'm constantly on a quest for the new. I've changed my career twice — from a chip designer to a software engineer, to a venture capitalist. And I'm not done with changes. My husband is scared of my long list for retirement! That's what's beautiful about life — it's just so full of possibilities, which are completely under our control."

In her commencement speech at Menlo College, California, in 2018, she said: "To everyone here, but especially to the women and minorities — don't let the labels, or other people's prejudices and biases, determine what you can or cannot do. Don't let anybody tell you what you can or cannot try. Don't let your past limit

your future, and whatever you do, do not wait until tomorrow. As my graduate school office mate used to say, 'The best way to finish is to start'. Get out there and start today on your biggest, most important, impossible dream."

Mar did exactly that after her graduation. She started a company called 'Barcelona Design' based on her research. "I had done really well by any standard. I was a straight A student. I had finished my PhD and master's at Stanford in a record four years. I thought I was pretty much invincible, and that I could do anything," she added.

Her company started off well enough. She hired a number of the smartest PhD students from her class, raised $40 million in funding, built what was possibly the most sophisticated circuit design software at the time, and had paying customers across the world. The company got a lot of press coverage and she even became somewhat of a mini-celebrity. However, the business wasn't growing so much, and the board decided to hire a new CEO.

"It turned out that the CEO and I couldn't figure out how to work together, and eventually I had to leave the company that I had started. It was a big blow. I felt like my whole identity had been stolen from me. It wasn't just emotionally painful, it was physically painful. I spent a couple of months inside my head, replaying every possible scenario: what I could have done, what I should have done, how I could have made it turn out differently," Mar vividly described her emotions as if she had just recently gone through it.

When I asked why she left the company, and if her being a female with a new male CEO played any role in that, she replied, "There is always a male/female dynamic in the boardroom, but I don't think it was the problem. Honestly, I think it was me more than anything else. I had just finished my PhD and didn't have work experience. If I had been in that situation, knowing what I know now, I could have done a much better job. I know now that it's really important to trust your gut and to raise your hand and speak up when it's necessary. I should have done that."

Luckily, Mar was able to hit reset, turn off the emotions, and think logically. She decided to take everything that she had learned about running a business, and start a new company. "At that point, I wasn't a flashy, recent PhD graduate, but a failed founder who was hard to work with. It felt impossible for us to raise money, to hire people, and even to get customers to talk to us. There was so much rejection every single day, but eventually, we found a true angel investor, made some great hires, and customers started using our product. There was a lot of hard work with little money, long hours and countless faraway trips to visit customers. But eventually we built a thriving business and we successfully sold it to a public company. It turns out that it was good to have failed so big, that the only answer I had was to try again. I am so grateful that I did not give up," Mar summarized.

"Today, I sit on the other side of the table as a venture capitalist, often surrounded by moments of failure — by founders who cannot raise money, startups that cannot pay payroll or whose customers cancel contracts, and companies that are being shut down. Despite all of this, I also get to witness many success stories up close — stories of overcoming failure despite dismal odds. It is by far the best part of my job — seeing people persist, meeting people who have worked really hard to overcome a near-death situation. The companies that make it are not the best companies, but those companies whose founders refuse to give up, are," she proclaimed. I have to quote her commencement speech at Menlo College again, as it is one of the best speeches I've heard: "We all fail. You will fail and it'll be painful. It will be agony. When that happens, you look that failure directly in the eyes and say, 'I will beat you. You're just this life's test. I have to get through."

At that point, I couldn't help but ask Mar about the challenges that she had probably faced when she was fundraising for her venture capital firm 'Pear' and she shared some lessons learned from that too.

"I received my first experience in venture capital at Foundation Capital — one of the investors in my very first company that I had left. Even though the first company wasn't successful, they let me join their firm. I worked there for a short time, but I learned to evaluate companies. I understood how a VC firm works, etc.

"I was most fortunate to have one of the co-founders of Foundation Capital, Kathryn Gould, as my mentor. She was one of the first female venture capitalists but has unfortunately passed away. She guided me through my first fundraising experience and was always very positive about the entire male/female relationship thing. I learned that venture capital is very heavily a people business, whether it's fundraising for a fund, supporting founders, or working in a team. Everything that is a soft skill is actually really important in this industry.

"My partner at 'Pear', who had been one of my investors before, was really going after me for years, trying to convince me to start a VC firm together. I kept telling him that I wasn't really an investor, and was actually an operator, but he didn't take 'no' for an answer. He said that investors needed to be operators as well, so they could help companies to build their businesses... and so I surrendered. I realized that I wasn't truly a venture person until I started my own firm. My partner was an experienced investor already by then, and I complemented him well with my operational experience.

"Institutional investors are very performance-driven. They saw our prior track records and were willing to work with our team. Today, I see that they stay the course of backing the best performers, however, they have also started paying attention to diversity on investment teams. There's sufficient data that shows the better performance of diverse teams in the corporate world, but we are still here to provide more data on the same for venture capital firms," she continued.

"For emerging managers, whether men or women, it's always harder to raise the first fund, especially if you don't come from the venture capital world. The advice I give people, is to start investing as an angel to build your own portfolio, which can make one an attractive candidate. If you show up to a firm or an institutional investor and say, 'I've been angel investing for the last two years. Here is my portfolio. I helped these companies to achieve these results.' Not only would this help you to get a job in venture capital, but it would also help an institutional investor understand how you fit into the ecosystem.

"If you ask me about women in venture capital, specifically, I have noticed that it's harder for us to self-promote. We have to accept that fundraising — whether you are a venture investor or an entrepreneur — is basically selling yourself. Therefore, we can't be afraid of that. I think, it's something easy to work on for women, although it needs a little bit of help and mentorship, if it doesn't come naturally to you.

"Finally, venture investing is not for everyone. It's a very extreme job — you have to work extremely hard, but it is extremely rewarding."

When I asked Mar what she looks for in a founder, she was utterly decisive: "There are many things that matter, but at the very first meeting, I'm only checking for one thing — the character of the founder. Even in a 30-minute meeting, I can learn a lot about their characters. For example, I learn from the interactions within their team in the room. Do they let others in the team speak up? Do they correct them? Do they finish their sentences? Do they recognize their efforts? I learn how they talk about their career experience. Do they say good things about their previous employers, previous bosses, and previous colleagues, or negative things? Do they take responsibility for their failures or do they blame them on others. I learn how they think about the future and what type of company culture they want to build — what are their values? These things matter. We know that the character of the founder will ultimately determine their ability to lead a company, to stay calm in moments of distress, and to build and retain a team.

"It is the same with all of us. Our character is not only the greatest indicator of our external success, but it is, more importantly, the true source of our own internal happiness. Being generous, empathetic to others, and putting others first, is not easy, but these may be your greatest investments in life."

Eva Ho

Founding Partner, Fika Ventures, United States

It took Eva Ho 600 conversations to raise $40 million for Fika Ventures. Although this happened in just six months, unlike the normal 12-18 month fundraising cycle, it wasn't as easy as it might seem. "We certainly pounded the pavement every day and sold like salesmen to convert just a handful of the hundreds of conversations that we had," Eva painted in words. "And I've never played the female card during fundraising. I really believe you have to compete and win based on merit and not gender.

"I know that a lot of people feel like they want to say, 'Hey, I know that you might be interested in backing diversity – I'm a female... choose me because I will fit the quota.' There are some investors who are looking for that too, but I would never say it, because I think that doesn't make anybody feel good.

"You can't let the fact that you're a female be the schtick of your fund. That is not differentiation. The differentiation is that you are competent, and you bring unique skills to the table. Institutional investors want to see that you have access to an uncommon network, which will yield strong deal flow that they cannot access through their other funds. They want to see why founders would want to work with you and have you as a partner to build and scale companies, because there's a ton of capital out there today, so money alone isn't enough anymore. You can no longer sit in your office with a checkbook and wait for people to come to you. You have to fight for the best deals," Ho asserted.

Eva has been familiar with the need to fight for a better outcome from early childhood. She was born in China, moved to Mozambique to escape communism, and then left the country during the civil war. She was seven when her family moved to Boston and opened a small Chinese restaurant, where Eva worked seven days a week after school till 11pm. By age 11, she started doing the restaurant's taxes, because her parents didn't speak any English. "My parents couldn't help me much with my studies or career, but they gave me a big gift nevertheless. They taught me to work as hard as I can, build internal drive, and educate myself'," Ho noted.

Eva's efforts paid off when she received a full scholarship from Harvard. However, it wasn't Harvard that helped her build her way into venture capital. "The truth is, I absolutely didn't take advantage of the university's network at the time. I literally came from across the tracks in some of the most hardcore housing projects in Boston, and I never felt that I deserved to be at Harvard. I see that a lot in women these days, and multiple studies confirm that if a guy and a girl get into an Ivy League school, the guy feels as if he always belonged there, while the girl often feels like she doesn't deserve to get in. I fell into that category, where I felt lucky to get in, but I also felt that I shouldn't be there.

"Most of my classmates had come from lives that were very different from mine: they traveled overseas in the summers, had really rich cultural experiences, their parents held PhDs — and I didn't have any of that. So it was pretty difficult for me to connect with my classmates on a deeper level. That doesn't mean that I didn't come away with a handful of close friends, but I certainly was not popular at Harvard. It kept me from taking on leadership positions within clubs and even from just speaking up in classes," she admitted.

"Over the years, as I was able to accomplish more, my voice started growing stronger. But it wasn't until my 30s when I would really feel confident. I fall into the category of people who develop confidence over time through various things that happen to them, as opposed to being born that way. Later, I came to the realization that I was quite competent in the things that I set out to do during my time at Google and other companies I worked for. All those experiences helped me realize that I'm actually valuable, and can truly contribute significantly to the world and help other people.

"Even now, when I sit in a big room, I'm still quite nervous to speak up. But at some point, I felt that if I didn't speak up, then I was, honestly, losing a gift that was given to me. I achieved success in life pretty early, and if I had just remained silent, then I wouldn't be able to help a lot of folks who were coming up through the same journey that I had come up from. Today I feel more open about sharing those experiences for others to learn that anybody can actually do it, but often it just takes a lot of time, persistence and commitment," Eva recounted how she found her voice.

I am actively involved in the online groups of female founders, where I see many female founders in their 30s and beyond, who still haven't quite found their voices. I sought advice from Eva about what these women could do to accelerate that search.

"I think it really depends where one gets started, Renata," Eva said. "If one starts behind first base, it will take longer. One has to be very fortunate to be able to psychologically overcome one's demons. I find that people who blossom later tend to come from disadvantaged backgrounds, so it's really hard to give advice in this regard, because each situation may be quite unique.

"I hate to generalize, but for those who come from more traditional backgrounds — middle income families, college educated parents, etc. — and yet, feel disadvantaged because of their gender or race, my main advice would be to find champions and personal advocates as early as possible. Whether those advocates are teachers, or neighbours, or co-workers — try to get yourself into a place where you're surrounded by people who are invested in your success.

"It's very hard for younger people to do so, because when you're looking for your first job, you rarely have many choices. But if you are choosing and thinking about what to optimize for, I would suggest optimizing for a team or a group that will be invested in you. For that, I would sacrifice some of the compensation and other perks that many people choose to have."

Eva had plenty of challenges to deal with, so being an immigrant woman in the US was just one challenge among the rest of them. She dedicates her time to supporting women in the startup and venture capital communities, but doesn't allow popular agendas to define her business.

"I think that I've never actually believed in having a mandate to back female founders. I don't think that is necessarily the best strategy," she framed the next part of our conversation. "I want to make bets on the most promising companies and most talented people to support them, regardless of gender, race, socio-economic background, etc. By default, I think that having an XX pair of chromosomes in a fund is helpful for attracting different people. We see more diverse founders coming through the pipeline, and as a result, exactly 33% of our 22 companies right now have diverse founders, whether it's an African-American male, LGBT founder, female, or Hispanic person. Even though we invest in only 1% of the thousands of companies we see in any given year, this 1% ends up having many diverse founders, and we're really proud of that."

For a venture capital fund with a gender-agnostic investment thesis, having a third of the portfolio founders representing diverse groups, is a true achievement. Among other wins, this ratio also doesn't create a reverse discrimination. I shared with Eva a point of view that focusing just on female founders is one way to undermine diversity as the ultimate goal. It works the other way too, and having one specific group being dominant in one's portfolio — whether it's women or a certain ethnicity — means a lack of diversity in regards to other groups. It is also a big financial responsibility, because we all pitch institutional investors that diversity can provide better returns, but focusing solely on one group contradicts this thesis in the first place.

"That is a good point, Renata," Eva agreed. "There are many different perspectives here, besides what you've mentioned. In addition to what you said, I wish we didn't need to create female-only communities to let women feel safe and truly express themselves. It's not only about reverse discrimination, but also about solving a different problem: we should make the environment we all live and work in more accepting of women and other underrepresented groups, instead of creating fences that keep setting us all apart.

"I also agree that having a gender-narrow investment focus might be challenging from pure math and risk management perspectives. Let's look at the list of unicorns and count how many of them were founded by females. It's still too small to rely on when it comes to a fund's returns. I might as well shoot myself in the foot if I say I will only look for companies that could be unicorns and are 100% female-founded. It may just hurt my ability to hit the returns and raise a larger fund, if I can even raise any, which is eventually a lose-lose situation. Some good intentions can be inversely detrimental.

"I also don't believe that having a portfolio community that's 100% female is healthy for the world. Male founders in our portfolio like that we have a lot of female founders and CEOs in our community — they actually use them as advisors for increasing diversity in their management teams. This is just a healthy representation of the world," she said with conviction.

"I think building funds with diverse investment teams and a commitment to investing more in diverse founders is a good model. If we absolutely stick to that, it will cause a greater change in the long term."

When I asked Eva about her own team at Fika Ventures, she was consistent in her dedication to true diversity. "You need so many different types of skills to actually run a successful VC firm, that looking for partners who have complementary skills, must be the main priority. My partners are a little bit younger than me, but do some things better than me, and I always recognize their contributions and why I chose them.

"Besides the actual fund management, if you support portfolio companies, you need a multi-skilled team — people who can be rotated to work with founders in various moments, across the many aspects of building and scaling a company. This is when you can feel a real need for diversity, especially in terms of backgrounds, skills, and knowledge," Eva shared her secret sauce.

"I'm a huge proponent of interdisciplinary skills. There are many prominent investors with backgrounds in fields other than finance or tech. As we move forward, my prediction is that there's going to be more doctors, lawyers, journalists and other folks who have the core fundamental skills to actually succeed as venture capitalists. It's the cumulative effect of all of your life and career experiences that makes you who you are today, and allows you to be great in what you do." I entirely agree with Eva, which is why I believe that recruiting in venture capital should be skill-based.

Veronique Hördemann

Investment Partner, innogy Ventures, Germany

As I pointed out in the introduction, this book is the result of research that we regularly conduct at Women.VC. One of my goals, as an author, was to make each personal story unique. However, as a researcher, I included similar opinions as well, to amplify the overall results of the research. Veronique Hördemann is another VC from Europe who introduces us to the challenges their market faces.

"Investing and founding a company are both very risky, and women haven't been truly welcome to do one or the other for decades. Eliminating that natural fear of taking risks is the most valuable thing we can do for both the startup and venture capital industries, if we want to increase the number of women in them," she summarized the problem with unmistakable German precision.

"Europeans can definitely learn from the United States how to be more tolerant to failure, in order to make working through trial and error a norm. It's a very different mentality that probably didn't exist in the United States initially either, but at least the venture capital industry has had decades to work it out, and today, the western investment community takes risks more willingly. Europe as a whole, and each of its countries separately, still need to learn the art of venture."

We were talking about the tech ecosystem in Europe in general, and in Germany in particular, and Veronique was giving me very forthright answers. "If you think that the venture capital community in the United States is difficult to break into, in Germany, I'd say it's even more so. The venture capital industry is very narrowly located here and almost sealed from outsiders. It's naturally difficult for women to join the ranks.

"Ten years ago, most VCs in Europe would only hire partners from their closest networks and never develop talents within the firms. Many European VC firms still have definitive non-partner track positions, and only hire middle and principal level investment professionals for a 2-3-year stint, with no promotion.

This approach is especially detrimental for women, not only because they see no further career opportunities, but also because they remain the minority voice with no powers when hired. I know some cases where women quit principal positions because all the partners were men and there was no room to grow or sometimes even breathe. Some younger European investors call it an old-school approach to hiring and can't wait for first- and second-generation VCs to retire, together with this redundant attitude.

"I believe that VCs in the United States have become more receptive to diversity due to the generational shift, among other factors. When older VC firms hire a new generation of partners, they naturally change the narrative. In Europe, this shift is yet to come," Véronique concluded.

Hördemann worked for energy trading companies straight after she graduated from university, and is now an investment partner at the corporate venture arm of innogy SE — one of the largest utility companies in Europe. She started at its strategy department as a portfolio manager, and became a part of the founding team for the corporate €130 million VC firm, investing in tech companies in Germany, Israel, and the United States.

When I assumed that the corporate venturing in Europe is friendly towards women as it is in the US, Véronique was sceptical. "I would say that it may be sometimes even more difficult for women in Europe. We are still talking quotas for women in executive positions. And although the trend of having more women represented on top levels across organizations and companies of all kinds is coming, it's still too weak to make a real change. And I'm not sure that getting there through quotas is a good development at all..." she dropped a bomb.

"Ideally, there should be no barriers for women to overcome, so we wouldn't need to create all these laws and quotas marginalizing women in the first place. But since we're facing this reality, we should think about the consequences of this policy. Will women get these positions because they are women, or because they are actually qualified for them? I see more risks in forcing companies to do so, than if we get there naturally."

Hördemann is not the only female investor who is not a fan of such developments. You'll read about this phenomenon in Europe — as well as about an attempt to implement similar quotas in California, USA — again and again in this book. Véronique's position can be explained by a pretty common trend among European companies, which sees female hires as a token more than an actual source of competencies. Despite the fact that women represent almost 80% of product purchasing power, the majority of European startups don't even have one woman on the team. When you ask them why, they will tell you that they're going to hire women once they get funded.

"I think we need to start solving this problem at a really early stage, at least at universities. Women are as well educated as men, but they are less connected, they don't even know about existing job opportunities, and they don't pursue them actively enough, because they don't feel welcome. Large corporations, startups, and VC firms need to communicate better to female candidates. Some companies say that they are proactively hiring women, however, either they aren't that active, or this message doesn't reach the women."

Jalak Jobanputra

Founding Partner, FuturePerfect Ventures, United States

"I've broken a lot of rules in my career," Jalak Jobanputra confessed when we started talking. Born in Nairobi, Kenya, to parents of Indian origin, she immigrated to the United States at a young age. Since then, she has built an impressive resume, listing several top private equity and venture capital firms as previous employers, having been recognized with numerous awards, and having taken over several positions in nonprofits and New York City initiatives. Aside from all that, she also founded a VC firm called FuturePerfect Ventures, which was built around the thesis of decentralization and smart data — one that was global in its thinking, and diverse by its very DNA.

"When I was raising a fund back in 2013-2014, a number of things were working against me. I was an immigrant, a female, a solo general partner, and I was going to invest in blockchain — a concept that was very unpopular then. Many people advised me against focusing on blockchain when pitching limited partners. However, I was a very strong believer in this sector, with a lot of conviction. There were only three other firms at the time, worldwide, that focused on blockchain, and most people just couldn't wrap their heads around it — all their attention was drawn to Bitcoin, which was the main and only example of blockchain technology for them," she said. "Starting a venture capital fund is a huge leap of faith — one can't be risk-averse when doing it. It is all or nothing."

Jalak had never been exposed to business early in her life. She went to a very basic public school, was a gifted ballet dancer, enjoyed writing, and thought she would end up doing something creative later in life. Jalak wanted to turn her love for writing and global travel into a career in international journalism, so she ended up going to the University of Pennsylvania as an English major. But when she took an economics class there during her freshman year, everything changed. "I loved it!" she exclaimed. "I didn't even know what that was, but I started learning more about economics and other business-related topics. At that point, I decided to also get a degree in finance.

"Back then, I was very interested in the diffusion of information in society — it was 1990, pre-commercial internet — and I wanted to study communications theory. I got a degree in communications from the Annenberg School as well. I studied social cybernetics and political communication. From there, I went into investment banking with the focus on media and telecommunications, working in New York and London. I would say that my whole career has been about combining my interest in business, market dynamics, and human interactions."

Jalak had a chance to continue her banking career in London, but having watched first tech IPOs from an investment banker perspective, she decided to join a startup back in New York. "People were telling me that I shouldn't do that, because nobody in their right mind would leave a prestigious job for a startup," she remarked. "A company called Horsesmouth was distributing financial information online and I became part of the founding team. That was the moment when I became interested in the personalization capabilities of the internet. I helped build software that allowed us to send personalized content to our subscribers, but I felt that there was greater potential to it."

Jalak loved operational experience, but she was missing portfolio management. "When you're an operator at a company, you are very heads down on that one company. I wanted to think more strategically about the sector. I concluded that venture investing would be kind of the best of both worlds, where I could apply my skill set of working with new ideas and startups, and helping to shape them, but also building a portfolio in an asset class. I went to the Kellogg School of Management, thinking that it would be very challenging to get into venture capital, and I needed to find my way into it. I ended up sitting next to a senior director of Intel Capital at a conference that I helped organize at Kellogg. He appreciated my background and mixture of experiences and offered me a job."

After Intel Capital, Jalak tested herself in a handful of executive roles at different VC firms. She worked with New Venture Partners on tech spin-offs from Fortune 100 companies. She then joined the New York City Investment Fund and helped create the Fintech Innovation Lab. She invested at Omidyar Ventures and helped establish RTP Ventures. But that wasn't enough. When I asked Jalak why she decided to start her own VC firm instead of continuing with any other established one, she said, "Blockchain tech, as an industry, was in a very nascent stage akin to the internet in 1994. I wanted to thematically look at what was happening in the world, and back entrepreneurs who wanted to create a better world, utilizing this new technological shift. I needed the freedom to invest in what I deeply believed in, which became one of the reasons why I started my own fund.

"I also saw how the micro VC asset class emerged. One doesn't need a large fund to create good returns, since tech companies need less money to start and scale. With many opportunities for exits at smaller amounts through acquisitions, you can still create returns for your limited partners and have more flexibility in the stage you invest," Jalak explained.

Her gift to go against the flow and win, brought her to the White House, when she was asked by the Obama administration to speak on entrepreneurship and innovation ecosystems. The next time someone tells you not to break the rules, remember the go-to person in New York — Jalak Jobanputra.

Rebecca Kaden

General Partner, Union Square Ventures, United States

Rebecca Kaden got into venture capital thanks to Bill Campbell (passed away in 2016), a legendary business executive and coach, who played an instrumental role in the growth of several prominent companies, such as Google, Apple, and Intuit, and helped such Silicon Valley visionaries as Steve Jobs, Larry Page, and Eric Schmidt, to achieve their greatest potential. Campbell mentored not only the top leaders, entrepreneurs, investors, educators, and football players, but also young professionals and MBA students who were trying to figure out their future careers.

Kaden was one of such students at Stanford Business School, where she was contemplating going to work for Google or Facebook after getting her MBA, because she wanted to join a big platform and learn about tech and operations from within. Bill Campbell knew many tech giants first-hand, but instead of supporting Rebecca's idea, he said, 'I think you should join a venture capital firm instead. With your people skills and curiosity, you would fit well and learn a lot about many different things relatively quickly. A stint in venture would give you a way to discover different business models and product categories, and understand the evolution of different industries and landscapes quickly. Then you can decide what you want to do from there, but you might like venture.'

"When I came to California from the East Coast after college, I don't think I even knew what venture capital was, but I trusted Bill and his instincts a lot. One thing I've learned about great mentors is that they can see something in you that you don't see in yourself, or put pieces together in ways you can't," Kaden said.

Campbell was an advisor to Maveron, a San Francisco and Seattle-based VC firm, and introduced Rebecca to its partners. She first joined as a summer intern during her MBA years, and when she graduated from business school, built her way all the way up to a general partner of the firm.

"Looking back, Bill was right in the reasons he thought venture capital would be a good fit for me. A lot of the fundamental parts of the job resonates with my interests and curiosities."

Rebecca studied English during her years at college, and specifically enjoyed Russian literature. She loved writing and telling stories and saw herself pursuing a job in journalism. She started writing for different fantastic publications, including The Economist, and learned a lot from doing so. Kaden then joined an early-stage online magazine called Narrative as a member of the editorial team. "I was interested in how technology was going to intersect with the future of writing, the future of journalism, and the future of readers. I was happy to be on the editorial side, which had always been my passion, however, I pretty quickly realized that where the company really needed help was in developing the revenue side of the business — how can content make money online. I got involved in designing ways to generate revenue from different channels, experimenting with ad platforms, and testing subscriptions. I became truly fascinated by that job and eventually went to business school to continue to think about how technology intersected with existing industries such as publishing."

There are several investors featured in this book, including myself, who also have a journalism background, whether professional or as a hobby. Adding Michael Moritz, a legendary partner of Sequoia Capital, to the mix, it's fair to say that journalism develops a skill set valuable for a venture capital investor. I asked Rebecca to give her opinion on this matter.

"First of all, both are really people-centric jobs, particularly early-stage investing. You interview people and try to understand their motivations, inspirations, their goals and approaches. Both professions imply that you need to be able to recognize what people really mean behind the words they say. Both jobs depend significantly on your ability to quickly develop a relationship in which your counterparts divulge things that they may not be telling other people.

"Another skill that is fundamental for both professions, is an ability to piece together stories out of less information than you would like, but probably more than you would need. Although the output of these things is wildly different — venture has a different risk tolerance and decision set required — this is something you start with in both jobs," she decoded.

When Kaden joined Union Square Ventures (USV) as a general partner in 2017, not only was she only the fourth new partner that this close-knit firm had added in their fourteen-year history, but she was also the first female partner. When we spoke with her, she mentioned, "I don't think that the diversity problem can be solved by adding just one diverse person to the table. It should be more than one woman, more than one person with a different background." I made a note in the back of my head that Rebecca was the only female partner at USV at the time, so I was curious what would happen next. Rebecca's opinion didn't remain unnoticed. Right before the book went live, USV added another female partner.

"I think a hallmark of venture capital is that people with lots of different perspectives, backgrounds, and personalities, can succeed in it, because it's about their personal ability to spot a talent, to recognize an opportunity early, and to make the right investment decision. There is no prerequisite necessary to become a successful venture investor — not gender, nor race, nor background. Even when the numbers show a different story today, I am confident that they are moving in the right direction to confirm my opinion."

Gerri Kahnweiler

Founding Partner, InvestHER Ventures, United States

Gerri Kahnweiler was appalled when she first heard that female tech entrepreneurs have trouble raising money. "It seemed ridiculous to me, because in my mind it was clear that gender shouldn't make any difference when someone brings in new ideas and disruptive technologies," she told me at the very start of our dialogue. This epiphany took place when she was finishing up as the Chair of the Jewish Women Foundation in Chicago. Kahnweiler had spent nearly two decades in philanthropy, being heavily involved in giving grants to women. Before she even left the foundation, she was already thinking of how she would be promoting social change further and in what capacity.

Together with her then new acquaintance, Cayla Weisberg, a sales startup executive, they started exploring the Chicago venture capital and startup arena in order to understand the state of things. "We met a lot of people — entrepreneurs, investors and operators — and we saw some contradictions," Gerri unfolded. "Although VCs kept saying that neither the color, nor the gender of entrepreneurs mattered, as long as they had an idea, when we checked on their portfolios, we saw no companies with female founders. It felt great to them to say it, but it didn't always come through.

"That was the point where we could have kept talking, but both Cayla and I finally sat down and said: 'We have to stop talking. We know that we don't know a lot. We know we both have a great deal to learn. We know that we're really fresh in this investment market. But we need to put a stake in the ground'. So that was when we started."

InvestHER Ventures was born three years ago. At that time, Gerri attempted to do some fundraising for the fund, but it was really difficult, because neither she, nor her partner had any prior venture investing track record. Instead of giving up when facing this roadblock, Gerri decided that if she wanted other investors to invest in female entrepreneurs, she needed to let her money show the way. Her family had been investing in real estate for years, so she decided it

was time to diversify her family's portfolio, and she put some of her assets into venture capital.

At the time of our interview, InvestHER had made 14 investments and only one of them had gone under. All of the other companies are still in business and have either raised another round, or are in the process of doing so, at increased valuations. "I feel like I'm proving my thesis that these companies are really solid, viable businesses that are gaining traction, revenue and cash flow, and increasing their headcount — doing all the things that any investor would hope they do," said Gerri in a very pleased manner.

It's a good track record, and I wondered if InvestHER is going to fundraise the next fund. "I now feel much more confident and able to tell a great story around investing in women, however, I'd probably try to use a syndication model instead," Kahnweiler surprised me. "Having real estate investing experience, I think I can borrow something from there and bring in people who are interested in joining me, as opposed to running a VC firm marathon. If a person wants to become an investor, he or she doesn't necessarily need to become a general partner of a traditional VC firm. There are different ways of becoming a venture capital investor and they are as satisfying as building a VC franchise."

Gerri Kahnweiler is an experienced philanthropist as well, so she has seen investing from another side, and can definitely marry different models. I asked her if she brings that investment approach to InvestHER.

"Unlike in philanthropy, I do not need to sacrifice returns to make an impact. Investing in women makes great business sense, so you don't really need to think about what you are ready to give up, to get results. By investing in women, you can actually get not only financial but social returns as well, since women tend to hire a diverse workforce. As more women take the entrepreneurial leap and succeed, the norms around what success looks like, will change, and other women will gain more confidence in their own ideas."

Freada Kapor Klein

Founding Partner, Kapor Capital, United States

Being a contrarian is broadly acceptable and even celebrated among men in venture capital, but it still raises an eyebrow when it is associated with a woman. Freada Kapor Klein has a contrarian public image because she doesn't allow popular agendas to define her standpoints. Whether you are a man or a woman, an entrepreneur or an investor, she will not sugarcoat it for you, so think before choosing an appropriate reaction to any of her candid opinions. She is as bold in her opinions as she is in her looks, being one of only a few women in Silicon Valley venture capital arena, who prefers heels and stylish jackets, vogue accessories and brightly polished nails, to casual jeans and vests. The truth is, Freada is a very optimistic and positive person, and even if her point of view is exactly opposite to yours, it's impossible to take her in a negative way, because all she wants is to help you make a real change, backing her words up with action.

"We have to once and for all take a deep hard look at the BS notion of meritocracy. This society has been moving farther and farther away from being meritocratic, for many decades. As one venture capitalist put it recently — in the last 50 years, there has been a bull market in inequality. I think we have to look at all of the forces involved in this trend, including the ways in which tech has made things worse," Kapor Klein said in one of her most recent interviews.

Freada has been on a mission to fight discrimination in tech since the mid-'80s, and is known for a handful of achievements and discoveries. She and her husband, Mitch Kapor, are also most broadly known for their open letter to Uber, where they publicly condemned their portfolio company when it was exposed for a culture of harassment by one of its female employees. The whole scandal led to Uber's founder and chief executive, Travis Kalanick, stepping down.

It isn't common among venture capitalists to publicly challenge their portfolio companies for wrongdoings, and the couple took a lot of heat from other investors. However, people did not know that she and her husband knew the company way too well, since they backed it yet at a seed stage, and had badgered Uber's leadership and board members to pay attention to their toxic culture for a couple of years prior to the exposure. "When we could not get the company to take things seriously, we had no qualms about speaking up," Freada explained their decision.

She started working on diversity and inclusion issues decades before it became a popular platform for publicity. Freada co-founded the first group dealing with sexual harassment in the US, in 1976 in Cambridge, Massachusetts, and has been an activist of some sort or another her whole life. "The group was named 'The Alliance Against Sexual Coercion', which I actually think is a more apt descriptor. Today we think of harassment in the workplace as street harassment, while coercion has the implicit dimension of a power imbalance, and speaks to the situation better. I think this concept of coercion in the workplace is the part that most people don't understand," she pointed out the important nuance.

Having a degree in social policy with a focus on employment policy, she wrote a dissertation on sexual harassment based on 20,000 research subjects — 10,000 men and 10,000 women. Freada was then aggressively recruited by Lotus Development Corporation for a job that was described as: 'Make Lotus the most progressive employer in the US'.

When she left Lotus years later, she continued doing her work on bias, harassment, and discrimination internationally. As she worked with tech startups and investors, she became increasingly proficient in investing practices. In 1996 she reconnected with Mitch Kapor, the founder of Lotus, whom she first met in 1984 when she worked for the company. Not only did they have common goals, but this time, as both were single, they also clicked as a couple. As Mitch was doing angel investing, they were working together on philanthropy and nonprofits, and their collaboration became more fused. "I would help him with due diligence on various investments, and increasingly suggested that we should be focusing on impact. It's really through the merger of the work that we were both doing separately, as it became more intertwined, that Kapor Capital was started," Freada recollected.

Kapor Capital was born in 2011, and Freada thinks that they have somewhat rigorous criteria for investment opportunities, which should be tech-driven seed-stage companies committed to closing gaps of access, opportunity or outcome for low-income communities and/or communities of color in the United States.

I remember when we first met with Freada a couple of years ago, we were discussing the then freshly released movie 'Ghost in the Shell', based on a Japanese manga, with a white actress — Scarlett Johansson — as the main character. Asian women were very upset with this fact, because they expected Hollywood to find a more ethnically appropriate actress for this role. I asked Freada if bringing more female characters and giving women more roles in Hollywood wasn't enough.

"Diversity became a dirty word, and inclusion is following suit, because most of the people who use them, don't really appreciate the underlying concepts, which is about growing the pie — not about competing for crumbs. A mere increase in the number of female characters, who are always portrayed by the same white actresses, doesn't change the situation much — it's leveling the playing field for women of different ethnicities that does. I think that white women have been very slow in understanding the inclusion of women of other ethnicities and recognizing where our experiences are similar and where they are different," she said back then. Today she repeated the same notion, but for the venture capital industry.

"The aim of increasing diversity in venture capital shouldn't just focus on women. It should be intersectional, whether it's women, or women of color, or men of color, or minorities as well. If all that we do is count the number of female investment partners, and if those women are just white and Asian, who went to the same schools, grew up in the same zip codes, and now live in the same zip codes as their male partners, that doesn't get me very far on diversity. All it does is merely replicate, again, the same zip codes of decision-makers, but among women," Kapor Klein again proved that the devil is in the details. "That is why I am not so much interested in the raw numbers of female investors, as I am interested in the goals that a VC firm pursues. The goals, for me, are about building an investment firm that has a nuanced eye for building a portfolio of companies that close gaps of opportunity, rather than continuing to advance inequality.

"Some startups are gap-widening and some are gap-closing. The former can be founded by both males and females. I pass on investing in companies targeting affluent customers, regardless of their founders' gender. I am interested in helping to improve the venture capital industry by being selective about who gets funded to build what kinds of companies. I care about that and who benefits from those companies, more than counting the number of female players."

Our conversation this time was also honest and intense. Freada possibly didn't realize that she was giving me a compliment when she said, "One of my reservations about participating in your book was that I don't think that just adding a random woman (like white or Asian women who are already well represented) to an existing VC firm, is going to change anything. It's not the goal I have." I was very pleased to hear that, because we also had a different goal, and it became yet another proof that Women.VC has been doing something right.

"Just focusing on increasing the number of females in venture capital isn't the answer. It must be much broader than just hiring new people, most of which, by the way, still fit the typical mold and don't change the culture of older firms.

"There are many organizations aiming to increase diversity in venture capital and entrepreneurship, and All Raise as one of them, is an incredibly well-intended initiative, but I think its founders didn't dig in and do their due diligence as VCs ought to do. One of the things that matter, is who's around your founding table, and whose voices are there when you design your organization and its purposes. I think if they had a different group of women involved, they would have a different set of goals and their organization would look different.

"Doubling the percentage of female partners in tech VC firms seems to be a good goal, but if all they were seeking to do is to increase the number of privileged women who become partners at VC firms, as VC currently exists, then that's an incredibly low bar. Why add yet another body that is trying to hold tech and VC accountable for increasing the number of women among decision-makers.

Don't you want to think about VC 2.0? How can we help venture capital live up to its potential? Don't you want to think about making the industry better in all dimensions of diversity? A different composition of the founding team could have tackled the bigger issue of what the venture capital industry has not done that it could have.

"Women should come into the industry with a new approach. Venture capital has yet to grapple with its contribution to income inequality, with racial gaps in wealth. Until venture capital becomes a responsible citizen, we're going to continue to have big problems. I'd like to see more women who have an explicit focus on some kind of gap closing, as opposed to just greed. I would encourage everyone to think about the impact they create. If you are doing investing for financial returns only, you are widening the gaps of income, wealth, access to opportunities, and outcomes. There needs to be a reckoning. I'd like to see more people get involved in venture capital that changes the profile, not just of entrepreneurs that they invest in, but also the profile of consumers of their businesses," Freada continued.

"I think our aim should be to build a team that reflects your customer base. It can be applied to investor/entrepreneur relationships, but it can also go further than that: who are the people who actually interact with the products? If you think about it, there's nothing radical in that at all, and it even sounds like a pretty good business strategy. For example, women are half of the world's customer base and they make more than half of all purchasing decisions in households. The question is... why haven't we adopted this aim more broadly in venture capital among both investment partners and portfolio companies?

"That said, we shouldn't just blindly homogenize all women together, because we face different challenges. We need to be working together, not just as women across generations, but also across groups that are excluded or underrepresented in the industry. If we just focus on sexual harassment as experienced and defined by white women, we are not going to be respectful of the experiences of black women and Latinx women who are the recipients of almost 10 times more inappropriate touching from investors as are white and Asian women. And if you're a white woman mentoring a black or brown female entrepreneur, and you don't know that, you can't possibly be a good mentor to her."

Indeed, I've heard many stories from women of different ethnicities about job search and interviewing, experiences in the workplace and outside of the office, reaching out to investors and pitching them, and I could see Freada's point.

"Speaking of investing in diverse founders, I think that venture investors have much more power than they pretend to have, when they say, 'Oh, I can't do it because of my LPs.' Well, if you are a desirable VC firm, and your fund is oversubscribed, you can define your investment focus and investment approach yourself — you don't have to blindly follow your LPs' leads," she added.

"We also still have this notion of a 'warm intro' in venture capital, which is often a public statement from both male and female investors. Don't we see how that would limit the pool of entrepreneurs? It's yet another bias: your zip code isn't close enough to mine," Kapor Klein had a collection of good intentions gone bad.

Now you know who to talk to for a reality check, although admittedly, you'd need to have a skin thick enough to benefit from what she has to say.

Karin Klein

Founding Partner, Bloomberg Beta, United States

Before co-founding the venture capital firm — Bloomberg Beta — Karin Klein led SoftBank's investment team, achieving some of the most successful exits in New York City at the time, such as Buddy Media, The Huffington Post, and Associated Content. You won't find much about Klein on the web, so I felt really fortunate when she shared her personal stories with me.

"From the early years, our parents always wanted my younger sister and me to appreciate the good things that happen in life, and they wanted us to work for them, so they instilled in us a tremendous work ethic. For example, when we were in elementary school and decided to sell lemonade in front of our house, our parents saw the opportunity to offer a teaching moment, and they charged us for the lemons, the other ingredients, and the real estate. We still ended up a few dollars ahead after deducting the money we 'owed' them.

"When we were in middle school, we started dreaming of driving our own car, like most other kids did. Of course our parents had a similar idea about that too! They said that if we wanted to buy a car, we would have to pay for it, and that would include the insurance, the gas, and the parking costs..." Karin laughed. "While we might not have appreciated those lessons at the time, it was a pivotal moment that shaped my entire future."

"We started brainstorming after school about what kind of businesses we could start to pay for the car. The lemonade stand would obviously not earn enough, so we considered babysitting, pet watching, and many other things. At some point, we realized that we had unique skills that we could employ. My sister and I competed nationally in baton twirling, which required a lot of practice every day. We would often be in front of our house practicing, and passers-by would ask us if we could teach their kids what we were doing. It finally occurred to us that there was a demand for something we knew well!

"We set up an after-school training program for other kids and started out with baton twirling. We grew this to include a whole host of activities and a team of instructors at multiple locations. And the business was successful enough to help fund undergraduate and business school for both my sister and me. I must say that I credit my parents (and grandparents!) with who I am today."

Karin is yet another professional athlete featured in this book, so I asked her whether sports helped her become competitive to navigate the venture capital industry. "Again, my parents were brilliant, because they created a healthy way to learn about competition. We were super competitive, but not against each other nor with other teams. We were driven by the perspective of how we were doing relative to our previous attempts.

"Venture capital is indeed a competitive business, but it is also a very collaborative business, and my athletic childhood helps bring out the best. My

sister and I worked as a duo, but also as a team, and then as part of a larger, national team. So it was more about leadership and collaboration, which is relevant to my job today: we need to work as a VC partnership, and also be partners to our founders and other investors."

When I asked Karin about other important lessons that she has learned during the two decades of her investing career, she said, "I believe that being a great partner to founders is what makes someone an extraordinary venture capital investor. And for that, two things are critical.

"The first thing is trust — an ability to establish trust with other people and to be a trustworthy person yourself. Sometimes a founder's job feels similar to that Discovery Channel show, Naked and Afraid. Two people must survive 21 days in a remote location, like the Amazon rainforest or the Australian outback. They have no clothing and can only bring one item along with them. Founders can often feel alone, with no one to help. Building trust and developing effective communication over a short period of time is critical. Our founders are navigating psychological and environmental challenges, and we want to be the people they can turn to for help when they feel like they are on a remote island," Klein drew a picture.

"For our team at Bloomberg Beta, that trust often starts with something as simple as our website — we created it on GitHub, and open-sourced our operating manual, which introduces us and our approach, as well as our investment documents. We share openly how we work, because we believe it shouldn't be a mystery as to what we invest in, and how we think about investing.

"The second thing that makes a great difference for an investor, is working through several market cycles. We've been in a bull market for almost 10 years now, but I'd navigated tough markets as well. When you have experienced multiple cycles, it provides a unique perspective on building companies, financing them, and helping teams through challenging times."

Miriam Kröger

Managing Partner,
Next Logistics Accelerator, Germany

Miriam Kröger broke into venture capital straight after the official failure of a company that she had co-headed. "That was the greatest lesson for me, which I always teach my portfolio companies and corporate partners now: 'Failing is not a problem. You learn most things if you fail,'" she shared.

Kröger started her career at the world's largest freight forwarding company — Kuehne + Nagel — as one of their selected management trainees, which was a great honor. She loved logistics, but after six years, she realized that she could do much more than what the company had to offer. She observed that the online e-commerce business was growing very fast, and started reflecting on what could be changed in logistics, to adapt to the new reality. "I realized that the logistics function would be a crucial part of the online retail business, so I decided to switch to the retail industry to employ my experience in a fast-growing environment."

She went to work for one of the world's top five biggest and most successful retail companies — Otto Group — a German group of retail companies and retail-related service providers working worldwide. The pressure of pure online retailers, especially forced by the upcoming Amazon business, got very high in the market, so Otto Group decided to invest heavily in digitizing its business. Miriam met a team of intrapreneurs who had an idea of how to disrupt the wholesale business in the apparel and household categories. The team was keen on creating a marketplace and service provider for all retail companies across the globe, which would eliminate agents and distributors and reduce the transaction costs. Miriam was responsible for planning the logistics and financial supply chain operations between the parties, and the team built the software for the platform.

The newly created e-commerce B2B platform showed a great initial traction. Otto Group saw this project as being of high potential and was totally convinced that it should be spun off. The team agreed to create an independent company to raise more financing from other parties. "When we started this fundraising journey, we turned to other large retailers who, in our opinion, might have been interested in the platform, and we very soon decided to develop our business together with JD.com, a leading Chinese e-commerce company. We formed a joint venture by giving JD.com 50% of the equity. However, with no force to balance the equal shareholders, it turned out to be very complicated. After more than two years in suspension, we had to close the company."

After the company's break up, a German VC veteran reached out to Miriam and said that he had an idea for running a logistics-focused accelerator. He had talked to many people, but had never met anyone who had both logistics and venture capital expertise. Kröger had them both, and after a 30-minute meeting, they agreed that she was the right person to co-build and co-run the accelerator.

The NLA had been incorporated during summer of 2017. "A few weeks after we started fundraising, the fund was closed. We got so much interest that we had to subscribe investors on a first come, first served basis, and apologize to those investors who came in with checks later," she proudly stated.

As with any other accelerator, NLA provides expertise, mentoring, access to network, and, of course, cash. However, there are no other multi-corporate accelerators in the world that focus on the logistics sector exclusively, which is expected to grow to $12,256 billion globally by 2022. If you think that it's a dull industry and there can't be that many startups, you'd be dead wrong. NLA has had no shortage of applications from around the world. "Even governmental institutions from the Asian region have reached out to us and asked if we could open a branch of NLA there," Miriam added. What started as a small accelerator, turned out to be a substantial venture capital firm with strong interest and support from institutional investors, corporations, and high network individuals.

I assumed that the logistics sector is as far from being female-friendly as venture capital is, and Miriam confirmed that. "Those guys in the logistics and shipping industry think that they own the world! I have known that from the beginning of my career, but I had no problems with it. At first, I was very naive in a way, because I had been raised by parents who were successful serial entrepreneurs, and they planted it in my head that everything is possible. I didn't think that there were any differences between men and women in business, and maybe I started behaving 'like men do' because I didn't see another way around.

"But later, when I learned that there *is* a difference in how women are treated and promoted, and that there *is* a pay gap and a glass ceiling, I started noticing that I was the only woman sitting at the table. Luckily, I had already showed what I was capable of and earned enough respect from the men. So when I started in the venture capital industry, it was all the same for me. I think growing as a professional in a male-dominated environment is an advantage.

"Many problems that we face with men can be resolved, because they are a result of miscommunication way too often. Their way of talking to each other is substantially rougher than how women communicate. When I realized that, I stopped being shy of talking with my male colleagues in the way they did. That said, I noticed that women also have different styles of communicating with each other. So ultimately, it's not about gender — it's about attuning to another personality, establishing healthy grounds for working together, and building an appropriate dynamic. We could wait until other people figure us out, but I prefer to control the situation and start building rapport myself."

Elaine Kunda

Founding Partner,
Disruption Ventures, Canada

Female-focused venture capital firms exist not only in the United States. While this book was in the making, Elaine Kunda announced that the third largest bank in Canada — Scotia Bank — had committed $10 million to her Toronto-based VC firm — Disruption Ventures — which she had launched back in 2018. Along with other investors, Kunda has come much closer to her target CAD$30 million fund.

"There is a large and growing ecosystem for female entrepreneurs in Canada, for sure, and we see all the same problems as the United States does when it comes to women in a startup world. Female-focused products and services, which are more often than not founded by women, are an untapped market. Female entrepreneurs are so underfunded that they are seen almost as a different asset class today. It's upsetting, on the one hand, however, for investors who recognize this opportunity, it's a whole new market to work in."

Elaine credits her father's inclusiveness for her growing up a confident woman. "I always had a natural curiosity as a child, and asked a lot of questions on a regular basis. I would come home from school and say, 'Oh, I want to be this or that when I grow up', and my father, who was an entrepreneur in the lumber and real estate industries, would grab me and take to people who could tell me about my aspirations. I wanted to become a lawyer — he took me to his attorney. I wanted to become an accountant — he took me to his banker. That was his way of providing me with information and educating me, because that was pre-internet days, so getting any kind of information was a lot more difficult than today.

"More often than not, people who he introduced me to, were men, so for a young girl it became the norm that men who were professionals and held senior positions, were eager to help and support me. I saw them as humans, rather than the opposite gender, and never knew that I could be intimidated by them. My father made me think that anything was possible, and that there were no restrictions for me as far as gender was concerned. He supported me in everything I was doing and really believed that I could do anything that I put my mind to. No one ever told me, 'Hey, little girl, you can't be a lawyer', so the world was an open oyster for me.

"My brother was a hockey player, so I was also exposed to all-male teams from that perspective as well. I think growing up in a male-dominated environment was an advantage for me. Not everybody has that exposure and access to it before career competition starts," Elaine echoed Miriam Kröger's opinion.

"I do believe that we need to start building an inclusive society early. We need to proactively show our children the paths that they can take. For example, we traditionally introduce children to a lot of different sports, but we hardly ever explain to them that being an engineer is not only about building bridges, but it's also about developing a heart valve, or solving social or environmental problems. There is a study that found that most women who are in engineering, had a parent that was an engineer as well. If this is not our case, we should at least expose our children to things we didn't study and don't do, because they might."

Elaine excelled in math and had an interest in investing, even at a young age, but growing up alongside the development of the internet, she got attracted to online businesses early. She started her career in advertising and joined Canada's top online regional portal — Toronto.com. She later became the CEO of Ziplocal, an advertising company that developed advertising innovations for mobile devices, the internet and traditional print media, and sold it to a business listing company. Her biggest challenge, however, was the rescue mission of a 3-year-old online women's network — b5media — sold after revitalizing in 2012. Her goal was to restructure the company as a business and media with a focus on intelligent, honest content for women. Elaine came in as CEO and had to make some difficult decisions, from cutting staff to changing the editorial direction.

"People who think that serious company reorganization doesn't cause sleepless nights, are wrong. It needed drastic measures and the faster you cut what's not working, the better. You have to take that window of opportunity for a change. Picking away at it only hinders morale. When there is no certainty or direction, it's hard for anyone to stay invested. I have come to realize that you can cut back a lot deeper than you think.

"The greatest challenge in a startup is staying focused when things aren't working. Keep your eye on the goal. You can't stay emotionally tied to something that is not working... and there will be a lot of things that don't work. You constantly have to step up. You can either cave or make it happen.

"Firing staff is awful, but the alternative is that everybody loses. Recognizing the right fit in a company that has existed for several years, is a challenge. One person can break a startup. It's not what they are doing; it's what they are *not* doing. Not everyone is cut out for it, even if they think they are. It's very different from the corporate world. It's not a job... it's a disruption."

Leveraging her experience and passion for working with women, she spent several years advising entrepreneurs, helping them build products, and raising venture funding. The idea for Disruption Ventures started about seven years ago, but only came to the attention of potential investors recently.

Kunda recognizes that early-stage investing is only one part of the solution. Successful companies will need more funding and support at later stages. This is where institutional investors like ScotiaBank come in handy to provide access to capital and banking services to sustain startups' growth and long-term success.

Rachel Lam

Founding Partner, Imagination Capital, United States

Rachel Lam's career in venture capital may seem somewhat like it has happened in reverse, which makes it an interesting case. She started in investment banking and then joined a private equity firm to invest in companies at the expansion and pre-IPO stages. She then joined corporate venturing to invest in less mature companies at later stages. With all that experience, she recently decided to start her own fund to invest in early-stage companies.

"I thought that I was finally experienced enough to become an early-stage investor," she laughed softly. "Early-stage investing is based not on financial calculations, which I was schooled in, but rather it's more of a judgement call. It's pretty fascinating how different the skills are, that are needed for investing at the different stages.

"When I started my career, I never wanted to be quantitatively challenged in any room, ever," Rachel started telling her story. "I knew that women's quantitative abilities were sometimes doubted, so I wanted to be the quant jock in the room, to not let anyone doubt my use of finance and financial theory in my approach to evaluating investments or risks. I made it my objective, and, in addition to my undergraduate engineering degree, I accumulated a lot of academic knowledge and practical experience in finance, accounting, and even derivatives, by the time I could make and affect investment decisions."

Lam leveraged her investment banking and private equity background in the telecom and media industry to rejoin Time Warner in 2001 to work on strategic investments. "Initially, corporate venture capital funds were mainly interested in later-stage companies. Why? Because at the time, the main KPIs for corporate investments were the number of partnerships or acquisitions between the portfolio companies and the corporate VCs' operating divisions. These relationships could be best built with portfolio companies advanced enough to have a strong product and management team able to negotiate and deliver on a partnership with the operating divisions of the corporation, in order to have any impact on the corporate parent's strategic objectives. Financial returns plus the number of strategic partnerships that were struck each year between my portfolio companies and Time Warner's operating divisions, were the two key performance metrics for my group. I was mainly focused on companies at the Series A+/B stage and beyond, albeit way before a private equity firm would become interested in an investment round.

"Typically, corporate venture investors try to protect the downside risk, because losing a ton of money on venture capital bets is a good way to not be in the corporate venturing business for long. People don't usually buy the corporate stock of a public company, thinking that this stock will be affected by a lot of venture capital risk. The best reason for a large corporation to make venture capital investments is to do it for strategic reasons, particularly if your industry is shifting a lot, which is what was happening in the media business in 2003. If an industry is in a healthy, steady state that isn't shifting markedly, it's hard to justify taking on that kind of risk," Rachel explained her view on strategic corporate venture capital.

Although, today we see that more and more corporate VCs are interested in getting financial returns first, and may not be targeting mergers and acquisitions at all, we can still observe that corporate venture capital is the most vulnerable department when internal capital becomes scarce — they are the first in line for reorganization or dissolution.

As with many other investors in this book, Rachel and I agreed that corporate venture capital seems to be friendlier to women. However, with intrinsic thoughtfulness, Rachel came up with a unique explanation.

"Aside from everything else, I think that corporate venture capital welcomes women because it also takes the fundraising element out of the job. The selection process in corporate venture is different — it doesn't have that chicken and egg problem, i.e. needing established investment track records to raise money. The money is on the balance sheet and track records are measured by different parameters.

"Another reason is that corporate venturing may be much more focused than traditional venture capital. Thus, corporate VC and women are a good match, because many of us prefer having a strategic investment lens to specialize in a specific area and bring real industry expertise, versus being generalists and fighting for the amorphous, big winners of the day where you are constantly battling FOMO [fear of missing out]. Since you are investing in sectors where you bring strategic value, you can often approach interesting companies directly and can map out an entire space, so your ability to generate quality deal flow is advantaged. This gives you more structure to how you develop your deal pipeline and thus control over your time and schedule, so that time management becomes a reality, which was really important to me as I was able to build my track record at the same time as building my family."

However, when we talked about Rachel's new fund, I heard her modest self. "I launched Imagination Capital together with one of my mentors from Time Warner without raising outside capital. This may be a typical female way of thinking, but after having invested $330 million in 54 companies in the 14 years that I was head of the strategic investment group at Time Warner, having generated top quintile returns, and having found a lot of strategic partners, I decided to first invest independently and raise money from institutional investors later.

"Like the early days when I wanted to be the quant jock in the room, it's probably the same now — I want to make sure that I am going to be good at investing independently and hit certain benchmarks, before I go to institutional investors. It goes back to my quantitative kind of mindset and old-school training, that I want to have data behind me if I'm going to go out and market myself. I think a lot of the limited partners want to see the data too, and because I will inevitably be rejected a lot, I want to show people that I am highly qualified to do this before asking them to back me. First-time funds can be very difficult to raise, but it's possible if you're willing to really go all in. If I raise external capital, I want it to be very obvious why my fund is going to be a good vehicle to invest in.

"Nevertheless, I'm seeing the younger generation of women who don't feel as compelled to establish an investment track record first. They have a bit more of the swagger that the guys have, and they're more willing to take on the risk of just putting it out there, looking someone in the eye and saying, 'Don't you believe that I can do it?!' And I definitely know a lot of guys who would probably have taken their track record from Time Warner and gone off to raise outside money immediately — just not my style," Lam outlined her fundraising strategy.

When I asked Rachel why she didn't join any other established VC firm, she replied, "I was asked by a couple of headhunters if I would consider talking to different firms to be their first female partner. All I could say was, 'I don't want to do that, because I don't understand how a 20-year-old firm has 15 partners, and has never hired a woman!' I think that would be a hard decision to make for any woman who already has a track record. My interest in dealing with the politics at a VC firm that has never hired a female partner, is just not very high."

Rachel worked in several male-dominated industries (investment banking, private equity, and entertainment), and learned some lessons you want to file carefully. "Firstly, I've always wanted to work with people who value smart, who value your work product, for whom work results come first over being buddies and enjoying hanging out with you. With such people, you have to work hard and consistently deliver great analysis and work product, but you know there is a clarity of priorities and values between you.

"I had two mentors in my career who both happened to be African-American men, and were both also my bosses. It might just be a coincidence that they looked through a different lens in their businesses, but they definitely weren't necessarily searching for someone who looked just like them. When a hiring decision for the new head of investments at Time Warner was in the making, I was one of several internal candidates, who were all guys aside from me. They chose to go with me, a female leader, which was absolutely not the norm in 2003.

"Having a mentor-mentee relationship with your boss is tricky, because people may think you're their favorite. However, when the values are clear and performance goals are well defined, it doesn't become a problem. Evaluating your performance as an investor is one of those things that is pretty straightforward:

no one gets away with murky, just qualitative results. In venture capital, you are supposed to make money. So having clear financial benchmarks like that can really help women stand out when they make successful investments.

"Working for and with people of that kind, who can mentor you, must be a clear goal early on in the career of any person, especially women. However, another lesson I learned, was probably the most important in my life: as long as you're really smart and you make other people around you and senior to you look smart too, your gender won't matter!"

Lam credits Ellen Pao and Susan Fowler for kickstarting the dialogue about diversity and inclusion in venture capital and the tech world. "It took these women, who were willing to really stick their necks out and say, 'Here is what's happening...' And then all of a sudden, you feel a groundswell. They empowered a lot of other women to point out what happened to them too. But someone had to be willing to take the risk of being the first to speak out. This really takes an inordinate amount of self-sacrifice, because for the majority of people, it's a lot easier to lay low. I admire these women greatly and think that they are very brave.

"Although there were a number of negative aspects to these stories, they also helped people realize that there is a huge talent pool that is not being tapped into. More data was gathered that demonstrated that diverse teams perform better. It really was a movement that needed to happen and we needed leaders to get it started."

Among other things that venture capitalists can do immediately to bring more women and diverse people into the industry, Lam named extending their networks. "Networking has a whole new meaning these days, because today, it's investors who have to expand their networks, do it deliberately, and do it sooner rather than later. We need to build more awareness around the fact that there are many more female investors than those who appear in the media most often or are listed on The Midas List. Yes, they are extraordinary investors, ultimate heroes, and that's great, but it's like saying that the venture capital industry consists only of Mike Moritz, Andreessen and Horowitz. It's not. The venture capital industry is much larger than that — there has to be more women to recognize, as well as to invest alongside.

"We need to push ourselves to look a little harder, to make that extra call. I was asked by two funds to keep an eye out for them and help them find a partner. I've also been asked for public board suggestions. And here is where female VCs step in: we have a much larger network of women than most men do. We need to not be too busy to tap into our networks. We should be the first to pay it forward and recommend other younger women to our peers for investing positions.

"The industry needs to have more touch points for connecting with diverse candidates. I think there should be more products built to make them more discoverable. I see it to be a combination of online and offline communities for women to really tap into the industry and expand the pool. Books like yours, which show not only seasoned female investors but also introduce new names, are critically important. I'm sure many of my colleagues will want to talk to some of the amazing women from your book, some of whom they haven't yet heard of or met." At that point, Rachel didn't know about our recruiting platform just yet.

Annie Lamont

Founding Partner, Oak HC/FT, United States

"If you're writing a book that says that the opportunities for women in venture capital are limited, I don't want to be part of it. The sky's the limit for us!" That's what Annie Lamont, co-founder and managing partner of Oak HC/FT, said during our conversation. Strong reactions like hers make for an engaging conversation, so I felt energized when she passionately disagreed with the widely held perception. Annie was one of the first women in venture capital, and is perhaps one of the most successful investors in healthcare and financial technology services who has been a Forbes Midas lister for several years.

Annie started her career in two other male-dominated industries: law and investment banking. After deciding that law school wasn't for her, she joined a boutique investment bank where she also worked with the in-house venture capital group. Annie recalls one time she had to carry Steve Jobs' bags when her bank took Apple on its IPO roadshow. Somewhere around that time, she realized that she wanted to be a venture capitalist. "I didn't think that I'd be an entrepreneur, but I knew I could be a really good partner to an entrepreneur. I decided that this was going to be my life's work, and it was all incredibly fortuitous."

Starting out, she admitted that she never really thought gender would be an issue. "I had a lot of male friends and I never thought I'd be treated differently. In fact, I thought that being one of the few women in the industry was beneficial, because people would remember me as the only woman in the room. I also felt that entrepreneurs could be more open with me."

At the time, Annie frequently talked about wanting to become a venture investor. One particular conversation brought about a decisive change in her fate. Waiting for an elevator, Annie began chatting with Mike Levinthal, an acquaintance she knew from Stanford who was working at New Enterprise Associates (NEA).The next day, Levinthal happened to mention Annie's name to Ed Glassmeyer, the founder of one of the top VC firms, Oak Investment Partners.

They were discussing an investment opportunity which Glassmeyer didn't express much interest in (Victoria's Secret, ironically) but made a remark that he was looking for an analyst. Oak Investment Partners missed out on that particular deal, but they acquired another valuable asset in the form of Annie Lamont.

"Ed is someone who always championed the underdog, and I think he had a lot of respect for women, in part because of his strong wife. I think he liked the idea of bringing women into the industry," Annie gave credit to Levinthal.

"The hardest thing about the venture capital industry is getting in — seemingly harder than Stanford's admissions. I knew I had to take the opportunity," she added. "If you had said to me 30 years ago that there would be as few women in the industry as there are today, I wouldn't have believed you."

In the late 90s, we observed a great influx of investors of Indian and Asian descent. It happened because they followed the traditional career path of becoming venture capitalists after being entrepreneurs. There were a lot of tech and telecom entrepreneurs, engineers, and developers in the 'post-dot-com' era, so we ended up having a lot of Indians and Asians in venture capital. On the other hand, we barely had any female entrepreneurs during those years. This is one of many reasons we now have fewer female VCs.

"Very few women really knew enough about venture capital, and it wasn't an industry that was targeted by women. If you add all of this to the fact that people tend to hire other people who look like them, and that partnerships are naturally small, it just wasn't top of mind to hire women," she explained. "There is no doubt that tech culture and machismo in the tech industry didn't help, but women possess many of the great qualities needed, to be exceptional investors."

At that point in our conversation, we talked about the lack of women, not just in venture capital, but in entrepreneurship too. After all, if there is a clear path from being an entrepreneur to becoming a venture capitalist, then fewer female-founded startups is the problem.

"A Harvard Business School professor invited me to speak to his class last year and said, 'I don't understand why women in my class are more likely to want to be COOs rather than CEOs.' I've thought a lot about it. What I noticed is that when women get into an industry, and they're confidently moving up the ladder, at some point, they look around and say, 'Wait a minute, I am the most competent person in the room. I now deserve to be the CEO of the company.' They may not have meant to become CEO, but they grew into it. Whereas men — whether it's innate or societal — feel that being CEOs is what they should aspire to.

"I see more and more limited partners who are focusing on diversity in their own teams. There are very powerful women now among them, and they are pressing the topic with general partners. According to an analysis by one of my friends who manages institutional capital, women and minority group representatives deliver better performance on average as general partners than white men. They're more risk-averse, in a way, yet consistent in performance, because they know that if they fail they may not have the same shot at it again.

"Lastly, this new generation of women make us all think more about diversity and how we can become more proactive. It is now a priority to hire more women, while women are also realizing that venture investing is a great job to pursue."

Brittany Laughlin

Founding Partner,
Lattice Ventures, United States

We've had a lot of discussions in this book about what is holding female entrepreneurs back. Some investors agree that women tend to ask for too little money, that they prefer focusing on non-scalable businesses, and that they are generally more risk-averse. Brittany Laughlin, however, argues that some of these stereotypes have little to do with gender. "I've seen women who match those descriptions, but it's not limited to gender. It can be attributed to any person who is outside the information bubble — that means anyone who isn't a white male, Ivy League graduate, or who doesn't have access to a network of experienced entrepreneurs. Given the entrepreneurs who were funded over the last 20 years, there are fewer women, people of color, and non-Ivy league individuals inside of those core circles of successful people," she explained.

"Long before we launched Lattice Ventures, I noticed that there were a lot of women who were falling in a gap between raising seed and Series A rounds, even though they had the traction to get them there. Their mentality was, 'I'll just raise another seed round, because I'm not ready to pitch next-stage investors'. I saw that as a solvable problem by building a network of people supporting them on the journey, which many men already had. My business partner and I called this group the Gladiator Club — because they were tough and wore skirts!"

Gladiator Club was a professional group of women who have raised seed rounds and were ready to take their business to the next level. The goal of this group was to provide peer feedback, introductions, and advice. Peer support from people who are in the same boat, or already ahead, can be the most impactful. Accelerators like YCombinator have turned this into a huge business.

"Looking at the metrics, the 65 women who participated in Gladiator Club, raised over $100 million in venture capital combined, across seed, Series A and even Series B rounds," Brittany said. "We found that this network effect was a big differentiator. People who had really strong networks of successful peers were more likely to think big, but people who didn't — whether they were women, men, or minorities — were more likely to be stuck at their current level."

Brittany had been building her peer network for a long time. She sold her first travel startup to Groupon, and then founded InclineHQ, a company that was providing military veterans with access to training, mentorship and employment, to support the transition from service into the technology industry. Through the growth of InclineHQ and it's merge into VetsinTech, she built a large network of startup companies interested in hiring veterans for their open tech jobs.

When Union Square Ventures (USV) started asking around about the right person who could build a network among their portfolio companies, Laughlin was the top of mind community builder. She got a lot of portfolio management experience during these three years, however, USV was one of those firms back then with no room to grow to a partner level. "I knew that I wanted to write checks, so I was looking for opportunities to join another VC firm, or start my own. Unfortunately, there weren't many early-stage investors in New York that had a vacant seat at the table. I realized that if I wanted to invest at the seed stage, then going on my own was a more realistic option. I learned from USV that an investor should have a very explicit thesis about where they want to invest and why — and why they're good at it. I had a clear vision of what I wanted to do, and I knew that I could execute it."

It took Lattice Ventures only six months to raise the fund, but the firm remained low key for quite a long time. "Our goal was to back a number of high-quality startups before we started promoting the Lattice brand. In venture capital, it takes years before you know if you're good at investing, since the returns can take 5-10 years, so the best way to announce yourself at the beginning, is by letting your portfolio companies speak for you and tell the story," she advised.

While fundraising, the team learned from established VCs that it takes about 20 meetings to get one 'yes' or 'maybe', so Brittany's other advice is to have a really long list of potential limited partners, in order to get to the finish with a win.

Lattice Ventures is a female-led VC firm, and it also faced a stereotypical challenge. There were too few VC firms led by women, and potential limited partners automatically believed that female investors would only invest in female entrepreneurs. That wasn't Lattice's case, but Brittany had to spend a lot of time clarifying that to investors upfront. "I also remember one limited partner asking us, 'How do you plan to negotiate, being two women?' which was pretty shocking to hear, but we decided to address it, instead of getting angry about it. We took it in our stride, used it as a chance to educate the investor on the explicit bias, and to explain why our negotiation strategies and tactics had nothing to do with our gender. In the end, the investor appreciated us being direct and asked to invest."

Although Laughlin learned a lot about venture investing at USV, she said that nothing can replace one's own experience. "When I started my own VC firm, the learning curve was still incredibly steep. All sorts of things that we didn't anticipate came up — from new deal terms to new industries like cryptocurrencies. We had to figure every new challenge out as we went along. So you can learn all the typical stuff in books and blogs, but until you actually start making real deals, these lessons will remain in theory. I think everyone in venture capital does something they've never done before. That's the moment when you really need a network to lean on."

Aileen Lee

Founding Partner, Cowboy Ventures, United States

When I first approached Aileen Lee regarding a book about female venture capitalists, in spring 2017, she said that it was too early for her to be featured in a book like that. "I need to focus on making sure that Cowboy Ventures is successful!" Her firm had already exited almost a dozen portfolio companies, including unicorn Dollar Shave Club. So I waited. A year later, on the exact anniversary of her own startup, a non-profit called All Raise, which is dedicated to accelerating the success of female funders and founders, we finally talked.

Although Aileen Lee is one of the most well-known and respected investors in the US, she says that her VC career happened by accident. Lee was the first-born child of a Chinese immigrant family, and grew up on the East Coast. Her father was a dentist, and her mom managed his office. Aileen wasn't surrounded by technology, and all her parents dreamt of was a good education for her. She did indeed go to MIT, but for a different reason. "When I was growing up, I had lots of smart classmates who were girls, but none of us were really pushed into math or computers or anything like that. Girls took history and language classes, while boys studied calculus and physics. I remember reading an article in the late '80s, about scientific illiteracy, and how the stats were showing that girls were not pursuing careers or majors in quantitative or STEM fields. That pissed me off. So I decided to apply to MIT," she explained her decision. Lee said that she was completely underprepared, but passed the test to get in.

After college, Lee joined Morgan Stanley as an M&A analyst — at the time when legendary Mary Meeker was still there. Aileen heard about venture capital in the hallways, and it sounded like the coolest job ever to her, although she didn't

quite understand the full meaning of it. A lot of other analysts around her would take a third-year job in venture capital, but it happened that all of them were mostly white guys. When Aileen went to the library to look up some of the VC firms out of curiosity (back then, people actually had to go to the library for that) all of the VC partners were men as well. "I just figured that I would never fit into this world," she recalled.

Lee was drawn to high-quality retail brands that gained consumer love organically with moderate marketing, and worked for such brands as North Face and Odwalla. After business school, Lee joined the business development team of GAP, which was a really hot company back then. She was doing plenty of strategic work, but she also worked hands-on with merchants on pricing, store strategy, and business plans, etc. After working in an 'intrapreneur' capacity, she was selected to be chief of staff for Mickey Drexler [CEO of Gap Inc.].

The dot-com boom was happening, and some of her friends from business school went on to work for such startups as Amazon or Netscape. "I was like, 'Good luck with that internet book thing!'" Aileen laughed. GAP also attempted to create an online store, but wasn't agile enough to run as quickly as pure-play internet companies at the time. Lee was fascinated by the internet and decided to join a startup too. "I basically interviewed with anyone who would talk to me."

At some point, Aileen was approached by a recruiting firm that was doing a search for one of the most renowned VC firms in the world — Kleiner Perkins Caufield & Byers (KPCB). The recruiter said that John Doerr was interested in hiring a woman, and her experience was a good match. Lee was very skeptical about the job, because she wanted to continue being an operator, and the recruiter had to literally sell it to her. It wasn't a partner-track job, so Aileen agreed that she would do it for a couple of years, learn more about startups, and make a better-informed decision on where to go next.

As an associate at Kleiner Perkins, she reviewed thousands of companies a year and worked mostly with John Doerr. "Venture capital firms had a lot of network and chip people, but didn't have many consumer people at the time, so my experience was pretty unique. We saw almost every single startup out there: we didn't have to look for them, because everyone called us, and my job was mainly evaluating. Back then, we would print out business plans, put them in folders, and every night I would take home 20 folders or so to read."

She stuck with Kleiner Perkins for more than two years, and when the firm had grown a lot bigger, Aileen was promoted to a senior partner. She found herself in a lot of partner meetings on very different subjects. "I started wondering whether that was what I would be doing for the next 15-20 years." Suddenly, at a home dinner, her friends, who were entrepreneurs, asked her if she was considering leaving Kleiner Perkins and starting her own firm.

Lee admitted that it had not crossed her mind before. She started thinking about it, drafting financial models, and working on a pitch deck, and the more she thought about it, the more it seemed like an amazing opportunity.

"Kleiner Perkins was a very service-oriented VC firm — for them, venture capital was to be in service to entrepreneurs. It was all about sitting shoulder to shoulder with founders and figuring out the plan, the priorities, who we needed to hire, and to which customers we needed to reach out... I learned to basically walk through the walls for the teams that we were working with. I really loved helping portfolio companies.

"But when a VC firm grows bigger, things get complicated. Meanwhile, seed stage was an emerging category back then, where you wouldn't need a large firm and a big fund. There may be a lot of money in seed stage investing, but there's never enough really experienced, helpful investors who are going to work really closely with those teams after writing the check to help them stay on the right path and get to the next round. I was really into product, road-mapping and prioritization, and the idea of launching a seed-stage firm grew on me."

Lee has seen it all in her 20 years in the industry, and I asked what her own experience as a woman in venture capital was. "I had personal experiences with what we could categorize as being 'inappropriately approached' by men in my profession, which put me in awkward situations. It was very unnerving, because it made me question all of my prior and future interactions with men, and wonder whether they were nice to me because they saw me as a human being with a brain, or whether they saw me in a different way and were just waiting for the right moment to drunk-call me later. This experience was very unsettling.

"The other dimension was like the slow boil of being an outsider — I saw small glimpses, but there were no specific events that could be addressed. For example, many of my male peers in venture capital were spending a lot of time together outside of the office: they were attending games, having barbecues, and going for drinks — you name it. Women would generally never be invited to these gatherings. We were constantly missing out on a lot of shoptalk, comparing notes on deals and companies, and follow-on financings, etc. Men in the industry shared a lot of learning with each other, and I was never a part of it. As a result, I'd come to partner meetings to see that everyone was talking about companies that I had no information on, because they were trading information with each other, but not with the women. So I felt like I had little to bring to the table, compared to my peers, who often did. That was a constant running thread for years in the industry.

"To be fair, some of the senior partners behaved differently. I remember in meetings where we had people with big personalities, who are awesome debaters, John Doerr would suddenly say, 'Aileen, what do you think?' And after I replied something, he'd say, 'I think that's a really great point.' Those kinds of small things that men and women can do for each other, or people who are different from them, can make a huge step forward towards equity in the industry. I don't think we do it enough," she concluded.

One of the biggest lessons Aileen learned in her venture capital career, is to not succumb to the fear of missing out. "In situations when we don't have enough time to do the correct due diligence, but have to make a decision fast, investors are used to relying on other firms that are participating in the round. I've gone through this myself, when I was given a term sheet and the founders were pushing to make a decision within a week. That's not enough time to really get to know the team and the business, and meet with them multiple times to ask all the questions we have, etc. It is very tempting to think that other VCs who have or are investing in this company have done their due diligence, especially when they are well-respected firms. But that's just not good enough. In my dream world we have adequate time to get to know the team and make an independent decision. As a general partner at a VC firm, you meet with hundreds of companies all year long, to make one or two investments, and you're married to them for the next eight or ten years. And if we liked the company, we would make the investment, even if everyone else passed. You have to have conviction, and you have to be willing to be a contrarian. To overcome that, you just have to put your blinders on and not listen to anyone, better yet, not even ask who else is in the round — just make your own decision."

Aileen was very reluctant to speak about her successes, so when I asked about the results she achieved with All Raise after a year, she was mainly speaking about the iterations and improvements the team still has to do, as in any other startup.

"The venture capital industry has basically dug itself into a hole after many decades. Crawling out of it is not going to be easy. It's going to take a combined effort by a lot of people, to get us back on the ground level, and it's going to take many years. I'm really encouraged by how many founders, investors and operators are currently paying attention to diversity, and actually making an effort to change the way they hire, to change the way they evaluate, to change the flow of conversations, to listen more and include other people in decision-making discussions. Today, I advise both men and women to invite both genders into conversations. Women are not going to solve this problem by themselves."

Jess Lee

Partner, Sequoia Capital, United States

I first met Jess Lee soon after my meeting with Michael Moritz in 2016, where we discussed the findings of our first study on the performance of female VCs' portfolio companies. The media had just announced that Sequoia Capital had hired Jess who would be the firm's first female tech investing partner in the US. When I asked her for an interview, she said humbly, "I first need to become a good investor." Seeing the companies she has backed and how much she works with female founders after hours, we can definitely say that Jess is on the right path.

Jess Lee planted her future success by trying to improve her favorite startup, Polyvore, which was a little-known fashion website back then, that allowed users to create shareable collages of clothing and interior designs. At the time, she was working as a product manager at Google and liked spending her free time playing around the website with everything she loved: objects of art, technology, and fashion.

One day, she sent the founder of Polyvore an email with unsolicited, extensive feedback about the website. The email was pretty blunt, instructing the addressee on what she wanted to see changed on the website: "loading images in search results is slow", "I want image rotation", "Could you add a lightweight way of bookmarking items for future use," and the "'Fgnd' and 'Bgnd' prompts are confusing... "'Send to Front' or 'Send to Back' would be more user-friendly".

The founder of Polyvore was so impressed by her advice that he invited Jess for a coffee, and offered her a job. Jess joined the company, and after a couple of years, its founding team decided to recognize her as a co-founder, due to the significance of her contribution. She later became CEO of Polyvore.

During the time when she was raising Polyvore's Series C, she attended a Goldman Sachs conference in Las Vegas, and met Roelof Botha and Alfred Lin, two partners at Sequoia. She shared a cab to the airport with Alfred and promised to send her notes from the conference, which she later did. Soon afterwards, Roelof asked her to meet him for lunch. "When he reached out to me, I thought maybe he wanted to invest in Polyvore," she told me. "That turned out to not be the case. He asked me instead, 'Have you ever thought about becoming an investor?' Because I was running Polyvore and was not planning to leave the company, I said no."

Polyvore was acquired by Yahoo! for ~$200 million, 3 years later, in 2015. Around the same time, the Silicon Valley community was shocked when Michael Moritz said on TV, 'We'll hire women, we just don't want to lower our standards'. All the while, Sequoia was still looking to hire bright new investors and had kept Jess in mind. But the community rushed into judgment. As usual.

Following the acquisition, Jess felt that it was time to leave her life at a big company and pay it forward to the next generation of founders. She reignited the conversations with Sequoia, who went on to hire her. In Sequoia's books, her achievements qualified her for the high standards of one of the most successful VC firms. Although anyone would accept an offer from Sequoia Capital, Jess made sure that she and the firm would be a good fit before doing so. "I always make career decisions based on three criteria. One is the team and culture. Do I like the people? Are they talented and good people? Will I learn a lot from them? Is it a culture where people are empowered? When I met Sequoia's partners, I was really wowed by their accomplishments and appreciated that many of the partners were former operators. Roelof Botha was CFO at PayPal, Alfred Lin was the COO of Zappos, Mike Vernal ran a huge chunk of Facebook.

"The second thing I look for is learning. Am I going to be doing something that pushes me to grow personally, to learn things that I haven't done before? The feeling that I am growing is a part of what makes me happy. That was definitely the case, because I had never done a single investment before.

"The third thing I look for is impact. How can I make a dent in the universe? That was probably the strongest drive. I knew from personal experience as a female founder working on a product targeted at women, that it wasn't always easy for women to raise money. I felt that if I was on the other side of the table, maybe I would have a shot at funding some of those interesting opportunities that had traditionally been underfunded. Maybe I could make a difference and level the playing field for female entrepreneurs. On top of that, maybe I could take the nine years of painful lessons that I had learned running a company, and help the next generation of founders by paying it forward a little."

We talked about the fact that we see more female entrepreneurs in such sectors as retail or social, but not that much when it comes to tech-heavy companies. "It is true that many female-led companies are currently in sectors targeted at women, but I think that will slowly shift over time. We just need more women starting companies, period. They will then gravitate to the different sectors that they are most excited about. What we can do till then, is to make sure that the playing field is even.

"Part of the problem at large, is that you can't be what you can't see. We are just now seeing more examples of triumphant female founders like Katrina Lake of Stitch Fix, Jen Hyman of Rent the Runway, or CEO Jennifer Tejada who just took PagerDuty public — all of these companies are unicorns. We are witnessing possibly the greatest change in the industry since its inception!"

Millie Liu

Founding Partner, First Star, United States

Millie Liu calls herself a nerd. She always thought that she would become a trader on Wall Street, because she graduated in mathematics and studied finance at the Massachusetts Institute of Technology (MIT). However, while at MIT, she fell in love with math from a purely technological perspective.

"I was pretty tired of seeing a lot of super talented and rigorously trained PhDs or researchers who were coding mobile applications to get your laundry done," Millie shared her frustration. "Instead, I wanted to bring all those talents, trained at places like MIT or Harvard, and other universities, together, so that they could focus on solving real problems that are so difficult that not many people can ever solve them. My main argument in support of that was, 'You guys are trained to do exactly that!'"

Millie was diligently telling me about the artificial intelligence lab at MIT, and the first startups that took off there as academic papers, which ended up being the most life-changing companies, used by the majority of the American population, and beyond — and going public at valuations of a billion and above. She looked up to her math professors and soon after starting her studies at Sloan School of Management, she launched an on-campus incubation program.

"I started that incubator as a student organization under the umbrella of MIT. I was basically recruiting students and researchers to work on really challenging, non-trivial problems. I started building the startup ecosystem while I was still on campus, making sure that the incubator was not exclusive to MIT students, but was very much open to the entire country, and even internationally. Let me give you an example of how it worked.

"There would be 2-3 computer scientists working together, who could be developing, let's say, an event detection algorithm using machine learning. It wouldn't even be a fully formed team, let alone a company — just a couple of super nerdy folks like me, or even more so, who were working on some interesting academic research and thinking, 'Okay, we have a really interesting data set. How can we turn that into a startup, or a product, or anything at all?' At this point, I would step in and help those technical founders to connect with the right people — potential customers, investors, or partners, who could help them push their findings to the next step towards creating a business. I worked with the crew of 20-something teams at every batch."

Liu joined one of the participating teams that fell under this description and turned it into a successful business. She worked so well with this particular company after they joined the incubator, that when the team realized that they needed a business person among them, they invited her to join them as the CEO/co-founder of the company named TwiThinks.

"Back in 2012, machine learning or deep learning weren't buzzwords as they are now. Even those who studied computer science, but didn't specialize in these areas, would have wondered what those words meant. It was very much a novel approach," Millie recalled. "Therefore, finding a business development person who could understand the product and technology behind it, was somewhat impossible.

"Experienced entrepreneurs wouldn't be able to speak sophisticatedly about the product, when interacting with customers, and vice versa — very technical people wouldn't be able to develop the business. It was very hard to find that balance. So my math education, coupled with business school in finance management, came in handy. I was still a technical nerd with a pure math background, understanding algorithms, but also knowledgeable enough about business development and finance, to be a business co-founder. I found myself at a startup as a result of running the incubator."

When Liu graduated from Sloan, she had to find a company that would sponsor her visa in the US. She went to work for Applied Predictive Technologies, based in Washington, DC. The company was still a startup, but had grown to a decent size. Millie's function was half data scientist and half customer relationship manager, in order to help the company with product development and some marketing. Not only was she exposed to the data analysis solution for enterprises, but also to such giants as Walmart or Procter & Gamble, which were the biggest clients of the company. She was in charge of some of their largest clients from the retail, banking, and insurance sectors, as well as any other business you can think of in the CPG [consumer packaged goods] sector. The company was acquired by MasterCard for $600 million and Liu was ready to jump back to the very early-stage startup world.

All of that was happening while she was still a co-founder at TwiThinks. In 2013, after multiple pivots, the company developed an initial product. "We were trying to figure out how we could make an algorithm into an actual product. Where could we find a product market fit? How would we define the right angle or the right vertical? How would we find our first customers?

"When we finally figured it out, I was the one who was the face of the company, handling all the investor and customer relationships, marketing, hiring — pretty much everything, aside from coding itself," Liu described.

But an entrepreneur's life is never simple. One of Liu's co-founders couldn't extend his US work visa and had to move back to China. The team were planning to have dual headquarters in China and the US and to build two teams. Millie faced a new challenge: how to grow the company both in China and the US — the two largest markets, which are very different and may have different needs. "It was hard to operate in both markets at the same time, especially at that early stage," she said.

The team had to make a decision and choose one market to grow in. That was China. The entire team moved back there except for Liu — she made the decision to stay in the US. When this separation happened, Millie was at a crossroads. She didn't have a plan B, except for her good relationships with the early US investors of TwiThinks, who said: 'If you want to move back to China, that's fine — we'll support you. But if you want to stay in the US, we'll also support whatever you're going to do next.'

"Now that you know a little bit about me, Renata, you can understand what I really aspired to do. I think you can also agree that the US was a better fit for me," Millie made sure that I understood the reasoning behind her decision to leave the company. TwiThinks pivoted to become Infervision today and is doing very well in China: it is now backed by Sequoia China and has raised hundreds of millions of US dollars at their growth stage.

What happened next was truly a matter of luck, but also the result of the hard work that Liu had done. It was 2014, when Millie Liu became the founder and managing partner of First Star [fka Procyon Ventures]. What she had up her sleeve was the incubator she had started at MIT, a company she had joined as a co-founder, and a part in the successful exit of Applied Predictive Technologies. She had startup experience, both on the investor and operations side, as well as being an entrepreneur herself.

Those investors, who promised to support her, decided to put their money in the type of fund that would invest in startups or other young entrepreneurs like Millie, who were working on cutting edge technology at a very early stage without revenue or even a product. They recognized that it was critical for machine learning and artificial intelligence, and that there was definitely a big knowledge gap between seasoned investors, who might not necessarily be familiar with the concept, and young scientists, who were showing where the future was headed.

"We're investing from our Fund II today, and have made 26 investments in total since 2014. We are moving pretty steadily, making about 5-6 investments every year. If you look at our portfolio companies, you'll see that I stayed loyal to my initial passion, which became our investment thesis. We back only technical founders — about 70% of them have a PhD or a research background," Liu explained.

Millie is one of the youngest venture investors in the US. I caught her off-guard when I asked whether she would like to remain a GP with a smaller fund, or go work for a top tier VC firm. "Oh, I am usually asked whether I would choose between being a VC and an entrepreneur again," she laughed.

"I have never really thought of joining a top tier VC firm. I think managing my own fund is something I can do for the rest of my life. Being a weird early-stage investor, who backs very technical stuff, really satisfies my nerdy curiosity about the latest tech advancements. Every day I learn so many new things, that I am constantly fascinated. I think I spend much more time reading academic papers than when I was in graduate school and I love it!

"I think replacing that with being part of another startup could be the only alternative for me — one of those companies that starts from something seemingly very academic and very non-practical, that can be transformed into something that fundamentally changes people's daily lives. I still love that effort of figuring out how I can turn a piece of academic paper into a business. And then after years of navigating and pivoting, to have one of the largest encryption or data companies in the world, for example. That's just really fascinating and super fulfilling to me, and I would love to be a part of that.

"As a matter of fact, I now work with some entrepreneurs even before their companies are incorporated. As a fund, we sometimes incubate companies and play almost a co-founder role. I'm now in the right place to have access to something like that, which speaks to my original character — being a math nerd and transforming the world with math and algorithms."

Two years ago, Millie was invited by MIT to join their Computer Science and Artificial Intelligence Laboratory (CSAIL) as an advisor. The largest lab at MIT, where the tech icons and her idols have been working for decades. She shares the advisory board with some of the MIT professors she admired the most, such as Tom Leighton, founder of Akamai Technologies, one of the largest American content delivery networks and cloud service providers. Rodney Brooks, founder of iRobot, the robotics company that created Roomba. And the list goes on.

She is now the go-to person for many researchers and PhDs who would like to commercialize their research and convert an academic paper into a steady business.

Susan Lyne

Founding Partner, BBG Ventures, United States

There are quite a few well-known success stories about men who dropped out of school, and still succeeded in life. But how many women do you know of, who had the audacity to do the same and succeed? Susan Lyne is a media legend, who brought some of your favorite TV shows, such as Grey's Anatomy, The Bachelor, Lost, and Desperate Housewives to your television screens, but she's also much more than that.

She has a lot of stories to tell, but one of the notable lessons she learned, is truly applicable in any male-dominated industry. "You can't sit back, be passive, and assume that by being the good girl, you're going to succeed. Sometimes it takes a fight!" she shared.

Susan was the oldest of 5 children, and the oldest of 18 grandchildren. "There were always different expectations of the oldest children in the family. I grew up in a very conservative republican household, in a very conservative neighborhood of Boston, Massachusetts. I definitely felt like there were a lot of people who expected me to do something. If I had stayed in the Boston area, I think my life would have been radically different. There were a lot of extremely well-educated women who never had careers after they got married and started having children. I looked around and thought, 'This is not the life I want.'"

Throughout Susan's childhood, and up until she graduated from an all-girls school, nothing posed a threat to this Irish Catholic girl's quiet suburban life until she applied to Harvard. She was turned down, and after studying in DC for a year, went west to UC Berkeley. "It was a completely different world and also a completely different time — the early 70s. I always wanted to do something and create an impact on the world, and California was eye-opening and really exciting."

Lyne grew impatient to be out in the world and not be a student anymore. She was doing some freelance work for a couple of magazines while at school, but she eventually dropped out and talked her way into a job as the assistant to the editor-in-chief of City Magazine, acquired by Francis Coppola.

It didn't take her too long to develop a taste for the magazine business, and in time she even found a niche where a new magazine launch could be very successful. "Oddly enough, it was a technological development that enabled me to start Premiere Magazine. When the VCR [videocassette recorder] came to our homes, it immediately became a stimulus for a wider movie assortment, and created a much larger audience and stronger interest in films, than what the movie theaters and three networks had at the time. Our magazine was a look at the movie business as well as movie making, and at Hollywood as a small town," Lyne described.

"I started the magazine for NewsCorp and my sponsor there was a man named John Evans, who ran Rupert Murdoch's magazine group. I had never been Editor-in-Chief before and I was constantly looking around for somebody I could show my work to, because I still wanted approval. I still wanted somebody to say, 'Yes, this is good. Go.' In fact, I tried to make John Evans that final say for a period of time. I kept sending him stories and he would ignore them. I finally sent him my editor's letter, and he called me up and said, 'Susan, don't ever send me stuff. This is your magazine. I don't buy a dog and bark for it.' It was his way of saying, 'This is yours and you've got to own it.' Our relationship was definitely tough love, but it was a useful thing for me to hear. It was a turning point, as it took me the whole first year to get really comfortable with the idea that I *was* the final say," Susan recollected.

After nine years in publishing, Lyne went to work for Disney, and moved to something that seemed a better fit for her — to the ABC TV network, where she truly flourished. Susan broke the paradigm that shows made for women were too niche. "When I went to ABC, the conventional wisdom was that women would watch shows made for men, but men wouldn't watch shows for women — so everyone was chasing the next Law and Order, the next CSI. I walked into a meeting one day and heard the woman running our comedy department bemoaning the fact that Sex and the City was going off the air. She said, 'All my shows are gone,' meaning shows like Ally McBeal, Melrose Place, and SITC — shows that women gathered to watch together and talked about the next day. It was a wake-up call for me, and we decided to buck the conventional wisdom and go after the next 'girl' show."

Susan knew that women held great purchasing power, and believed that TV shows that appealed to the female population would be a great success.

She experimented a lot, and eventually greenlit shows that are still popular, more than a decade later. However, her job wasn't recognized.

"When I took the job, a well-known producer told me, 'Nobody retires from these jobs. When you run primetime, there's a big target on your chest. You will be fired at some point.' He was right: a couple of weeks before we were going to announce the schedule that had Desperate Housewives, Grey's Anatomy, and The Bachelor, I got replaced. To this day, it still feels like that was the only job I didn't finish.

"Several colleagues of mine at ABC warned me that there were people who were after my job. Their advice was to go out and line up my supporters among agents, producers, and writers, but I was convinced that I didn't need to do that. I felt that if I went in that direction, it would spiral into a dirty fight. I knew that I had real results, and I thought that they would win the day.

"Looking back, I think I was too passive. I didn't fight for my job the way that I probably should have. In the world I was brought up in, there were expectations of how women behaved versus men — being good girls liked by everyone was paramount. I still thought that what worked when I was 12 years old, would work in the executive suite."

After ABC, Lyne went to Martha Stewart Living Omnimedia, during the company's most difficult times — when Martha Stewart went to prison instead of appealing what was a surprising verdict in a stock trading case. She made that sacrifice to save her media empire, because the company's advertisers, who turned away from her due to the scandal, said they would not return until it was 'behind her'. Lyne was able to keep the company afloat during that period because, unlike the advertisers, its customers remained very loyal to Martha Stewart. She then joined Gilt.com, the first venture capital darling flash-sale site launched in 2007, right before the financial crisis. Lyne led the company as CEO during its early hyper-growth phase, and as chair during its expansion into new businesses like Gilt City, Gilt Taste and Park + Bond. In 2015, Gilt was sold to Hudson Bay for significantly less than its previous $1B valuation.

"I've never been frightened by risk, by jobs with no guarantees of success. The truth is, you can't plan a career so closely that you never make a move unless you know that it's going to work. There's always going to be risk involved in change. I'm encouraged by the fact that so many young women are leaving great jobs today to build something of their own. Eighty percent of them will probably fail or underperform, but they'll learn a ton, and either be much better when they go back into a corporate job, or they'll start a second company and they'll succeed. That's the way that we learn — by making mistakes," she concluded.

For most of her career, Susan Lyne worked for companies that delivered something unique to women. She knows first-hand that women make the final decision on 85% of all consumer purchases, and that they're increasingly the early adopters and power users of new tech platforms and services — therefore, women should spark everyone's interest.

"I came of age at a time when early feminism was a touchpoint for any young woman who was growing up in the Bay Area, so those were things that made me think, and made me read. I just knew that my generation was going to change the direction the country took. Yet, 35 years after I had started working, I was shocked to realize that women were still having a hard time convincing men that they understood how to build businesses. That's why I started BBG (Built By Girls) Ventures — to invest in female entrepreneurs.

"When you look at the way the tech industry has evolved, it's easier to understand why we have such a huge gap in female tech entrepreneurship. The original Silicon Valley startups were B2B businesses — a typical customer for the product was a big tech company. Founders came out of engineering programs to serve large corporations, government, and the military. It wasn't until the focus shifted from enterprise to consumer that women began starting companies in large numbers. When I joined Gilt.com in 2008, it was the year after the iPhone launched. We didn't realize it at the time, but that was a transformational moment for entrepreneurs, because it put a computer in everyone's pocket. Women started reimagining every aspect of home and work life to be more efficient, more productive, or just more fun.

"I also realized that, for female founders, raising money was a challenge because more than 90% of venture investors were men. Before women could get to the meat of their pitch, they had to explain how we think about our closets, or why we're always on the hunt for the next great beauty product, or why women need a different kind of financial planning product. I thought it would be a competitive advantage to back the best of these female founders, who inherently understand the end user," Susan expressed a common opinion, albeit, only among female investors.

BBG Ventures started in 2014 as a corporate venture fund backed by AOL Holdings, however, it has since spun off as an independent venture capital firm.

"One thing I learned over the course of my career, prior to venture capital, is that there are many areas where men naturally have blind spots. As a result, there are always opportunities for women to get their attention and respect by challenging them to look at what they're missing. Because I was often the only woman in the room, that was, in many cases, the role that I ended up playing.

"I think the same thing is happening in venture capital today. This has been a dramatically homogeneous industry since its inception. I don't think it's because most of these guys are bad guys discriminating against women — there are a lot of great guys, trust me — but because they operated in a bubble. Founders they knew made warm intros to other founders in their circle. Their networks were incredibly insular. Only now is that starting to change.

"Every woman I know in venture capital works twice as hard as the men around her. While there's no question that women are held to a high bar in this industry, I think women set the bar for themselves significantly higher. When women see an opportunity to demonstrate that we can be great at something, we are all in!" Lyne brought a new perspective.

"Venture capital is not for the faint of heart. But you can never show fear. You have to operate from a position of strength. My advice is that, whatever it is you do every day, make sure you go in with an attitude that you've got this — and that your opinions and your work are going to be respected. Prepare for the worst, but believe that it is going to be the best!"

Jiong Ma

Senior Partner,
Braemar Energy Ventures, United States

Jiong Ma relies on everything she has learned in life to continually make a difference in the world. She believes that everyone has the potential to be a great venture capitalist if they keep an open mind in an atmosphere that encourages everyone to contribute their very best. "Being a woman in venture capital does have its challenges, but so does being a male venture capitalist," Jiong said.

Ma has a PhD in electrical engineering and started her career with creating game-changing products. She was also a founding team member of a fiber networks startup company and worked in private equity before moving to venture capital. She considers this move to be a savvy one, where she had the ability to marry her technical background with the necessary soft skills of managing a venture capital firm and multiple portfolio investments.

"Nobody's path into the venture capital industry is straightforward. I will be eternally grateful to the Kauffman Fellowship Program and the many people who assisted me in getting to where I am now. A few of my friends, who had gone through the Program, encouraged me to apply. I was so excited when I got accepted, because it was a very selective program, with only a few people being matched with mentoring firms. It is likely that my operational experience made me stand out. I knew how to build a product, could provide a different value proposition, and used my knowledge to translate theory into practice.

"At one of the venture capital networking events, a partner at Braemar Energy Ventures asked me if I wanted to join their newly opened Boston office. I said that I would be delighted, as I really liked their investment focus and knew that I could start contributing immediately. We looked at some deals together at first, to make sure that we were a good match. It is very important for me to work with people who are collaborative, who value my input, and who will include me in the decision-making process. We had a good initial period before I formally joined them, and I've been with Braemar Energy Ventures for over ten years now. I believe that what my partners and I have accomplished during that time will someday be seen as game-changing."

Jiong started as a generalist technology investor and got exposure to different investment verticals, including consumer, internet, software, and hardware. Although she found all of these sectors interesting, she thought that she would make the biggest difference in the energy sector. "This is a sector that needs a change, and we are only at the beginning of, what I believe, will be a transformational period in how we create, consume and deliver energy," she added. "I eventually transitioned into a more deep tech vertical, which would make use of my background in engineering science. The energy sector requires an extensive knowledge base, technical expertise, and practical experience. This focus would leverage what I knew the most about and could help create a broader impact. My colleagues do the same in the internet and media sectors, which they have been investing in for some time."

Jiong also thinks that there have been fewer women in venture capital historically, because fewer women were seeking careers in the industry. "I am a good example of that, having stumbled upon it myself. When I look back now, it is clear that I had the qualifications to succeed in venture capital, but it was not readily apparent to me. I had the operational, technical and investing experience, which had not been applied in the manner that venture capitalists do on a daily basis. Many women may underestimate their abilities in the same manner, so I would encourage them to be more broad-minded about how their expertise could be relevant. I may have underestimated what I could contribute at the beginning, but I felt confident that if I joined the team, I would be able to succeed. I give my all to everything I do and this was going to be no different.

"Having great qualifications is only the beginning. Venture investing is a great responsibility, and the decisions you make impact a significant number of people. If you are not ready to shoulder that responsibility, then you should not rush into venture capital. I find mentorship to be an important component of the venture capital business. There is no education that can train you to make those investment decisions, but mentorship is definitely a part of your personal development that can help you grow to that level of decision-making," she advised.

"When you hire someone with no prior investing experience, there is no way to guarantee that the person will be any good as an investor. The best you can do is to find a person with the highest potential to become such. It would require the ability to think creatively, to learn new things quickly, and to be a reliable partner for your team and entrepreneurs. That is where all the other personality traits, such as intellectual horsepower, integrity, etc. come together.

"Regardless of your formal resume, the number one skill that I find critical for VC investors, is a very good judgment and sense of people. It's really important to stay humble all the time, and to be ready to talk less and listen more. Outsized egos never help in interpersonal relationships, and venture capital is not an exception as it's people business," Jiong started listing the necessary skills.

"Another critical skill is the ability to influence others, because venture capitalists are mostly minority investors who rarely have veto rights. You need to know how to make an entrepreneur listen to you.

"Finally, I think that high integrity is very important. In a small industry like venture capital, your reputation is your main asset," Ma finalized her list.

Jillian Manus

Managing Partner, Structure Capital, United States

I know Jillian Manus as a woman who doesn't shy away from uncomfortable topics and always comes up with a solution when voicing her unconventional opinions. She definitely has the right to have them, due to her incredible life experience, which unfortunately included domestic abuse. Jillian ended up in a hospital bed for many months. "When I came out, I was so ashamed and broken that I disappeared onto the streets. I had been successful before that, but when someone takes your sense of self away like that, you bottom out," she recalled, giving me goosebumps.

Manus lived in shelters in New York for more than a year, but even there, she employed her business background and mobilized fellow shelter dwellers to collect leftovers from local businesses to bring to the shelter's kitchen. "As I decided to create a business model of efficiency for the kitchen, I started to remember who I was and felt like I had something of value to contribute. It was no longer about my survival — I was now focused on bettering the lives of people around me. Even if there is no financial gain, if you have a mission, you can address any challenge in life. When you have your purpose, you have productivity, and when you have productivity, you have confidence."

Early in her career, Manus held positions in banking and media, serving as M&A co-director for Credit Suisse Zurich, and later as Director of Development for Universal and Warner Bros. Studios. She leveraged her experience when she moved to California and became an associate publisher of Upside, a San Francisco-based business and technology magazine for venture capitalists.

"Venture capital, to me, is a culmination of all the expertise that I've amassed over the years. I started in banking, went to the film industry, sports management, and later into publishing. I advised a cleantech fund, continued to make angel investments, and eventually crossed over to venture capital. Building, selling and failing with my own companies defined me layer upon layer, not only through my professional lens, but it also established the foundation of my values. I had seen all types of bad behavior and malpractices long before I became a venture capitalist. So when I became an investor myself, a fundamental investment thesis of our VC firm, Structure Capital, became: 'Investing in Values not just Valuations'. These values include humility, accountability, gratitude, and of course, inclusion. Through every chapter of my life, I have witnessed the power and impact of advancing and protecting women. Inclusion fuels diversity of thought and action. Without it, this world will not only lack equality and ethics, but it will also lack curiosity and creativity.

"We need to be clear about the terms 'diversity' and 'inclusion'. Diversity is a quality that means uniqueness of skills, mentality, perspective, emotion, etc. Inclusion is an action that means employing this uniqueness for better efficiency," she started the next part of our conversation. By now, you could have noticed that Jillian mentors as she speaks.

"When we bring our uniqueness to the table, it should be received with inclusion. We cannot have inclusion without having diversity. But we can have diversity without inclusion. Unfortunately, that's the way corporate America has been operating, partially due to ignorance and inertia.

"Adding a person of color or a woman to your team doesn't change anything, unless you are open to listening to them, and including them in conversations and decision-making. I see a lot of companies that say they are building a diverse team or a diverse board. But then what? Will you consider diverse perspectives? Are you going to weigh those perspectives and opinions equally?

"I am not a big fan of the new California legislation that requires companies to have at least one woman on corporate boards. It has both upsides and downsides. This female quota creates the foundation for hiring women as tokens. And I don't want anybody to hire me, or invest in me, or vote for me because I'm a woman. I might be an idealist, but I really do believe all of this should be merit-based. Hiring someone because they're of color, or they're gender diverse, won't solve the division of our society. I think we should hire the best candidates and not discount them based on gender or color, giving them an equal opportunity and the tools to succeed.

"There is another side of the coin too. If a woman is placed on a board in a gender slot, or in a company as a token, she should stick her neck out and make sure that she shows her value with strength, and then she should immediately start building a bridge for other women to march into the company. We can walk away from being categorized as tokens, or we can change the ratio with dignity.

"Unfortunately, there is no way to determine whether you are being hired just to fill a quota. People will rarely admit that they were required to do that. But it doesn't hurt to ask the hiring managers directly for the reasons why they hired you — and listen carefully. If they make a pledge to you that the diversity of experience and opinion that you bring to the table will make them a better board, a better investor, or help make better decisions, it's a good start," Jillian recommended.

Paving her way into venture capital, Manus made sure that she is an equal partner at the table. She was an angel investor when she met Mike Walsh, who was raising his first $10 million fund. She was drawn to his thesis of investing in underutilized assets and excess capacity, and doing better with what we have. She became the largest individual investor in his fund, Structure Capital, but she was also actively co-investing as an angel. After having made about 30 investments together, they decided to raise a second fund as partners, and Jillian was responsible for fundraising. "I wanted to establish my value to the future fund, both on the operations side, and as a fundraising partner," she said.

The team of Structure Capital branded themselves 'architects of a zero-waste economy'. "We want to address the waste of food, waste of water, waste of space, and the most shameful waste — the waste of human potential. Our mission, and that of our portfolio companies, is to reduce waste by creating a significant return, not only to shareholders but to society." Manus has proven to apply this approach to literally everything in her life, including her non-investment activities. She knows how to sometimes draw the lines, but she always connects the dots, which she explained is 'like hearts and like minds'.

Jillian's semi-official title at Structure Capital is 'the Connector' — she is well-known in the startup and venture capital communities not only as a networking powerhouse but also for her intent to connect with strangers in need. Several years ago, she started a hotline — a number to which anyone can text and ask for help. The SOS line was initially created for women who experienced discrimination or sexual harassment in the industry. However, among the more than two thousand calls she has received, 2% of them came from men, all in the past 12 months. "Men who text me claim that they are being extorted by women. They'd say that women blackmail them, that they would 'report bad behavior' unless these men give them money or good employee reviews. This is horrific!" she exclaimed.

"Needless to say, women throughout history have been persecuted and marginalized much more than men — that's a given. However, we need to understand that devious actions like this are not the gender problem — it's a human behavioral problem. I'm now witnessing men and women holding each other hostage and victimizing each other. There are men who capitalize on their power, but there are also women who do that, albeit much less often. In this example, we see how women utilize such an important platform as the #MeToo movement in a twisted way and undermine it, diluting its effectiveness. These women think that they only hurt men, but they, in fact, hurt other women even more so. Men are now using this as an excuse to avoid meeting with female colleagues alone at the office and in casual settings, as they don't want to 'risk anything'. I understand where it comes from, but how about you just keep your pants on, your hands to yourself, and don't say anything to a woman that you wouldn't say to your mother? Let's just start there. Let's not run to separate corners or shut women out even more than usual," Manus was not the only investor to express this concern. Others featured in this book described the same issue.

I'd known Jillian for several years by the time we talked, and I had heard many stories of how she always stood up to men's insults, whether addressed to herself or other women. When I was asking about her secret power that allows her to always do so, she interrupted me on the word 'always'. "Not really... I have to say that I had a situation this past week where I actually lost my cool. That man was pushing my buttons, and I blew up and lost my temper. Now, he is taking advantage of that, and I am deeply ashamed of myself, because that is exactly what I teach other women not to do. This is probably the first time it has happened to me since I started actively coaching women a decade or more ago. And although it disturbs me that I couldn't follow my own advice, this situation has an upside. It just confirms my lesson: the minute women lose control of their emotions, the moment we allow men to push our buttons, men win! And we lose tenfold.

"Instead of being reactive, we need to be proactive. We need to anticipate, then analyze the situation in real-time with self-control. Next, we should educate other women on behaving in similar scenarios, as well as educate men on why excluding and humiliating women reflects badly on them. Only weak men will push women down. Strong men will lift them up, as they are not threatened. Regardless of gender, I think it's important for us to understand the mindset and moral fiber of every person we do business with. No matter how much money or power they have, in the end, you're going to lose if you have any type of relationship with those who have less integrity or respect for other people than you do.

"In the XXI century, one of the pillars of sustainable business is operating with integrity. If we make that part of our model, then we will never be — personally, as a business, or even as a country — on the defense. Business that operates with integrity are better at weathering challenges, hiring and retaining talent and connecting with customers. An ethical company is not only an honorable one, it's a productive and profitable one," Jillian talked about underlying issues. "The United States as a country is very divided. We are divided by the government, we are divided by corporations, by religious and educational institutions. There's so much disintegration that it's really difficult to reveal magnets strong enough to hold us together. We need to agree to disagree and then move forward in a mutually beneficial direction. We need to start learning how to reset paths of communication and work together to elevate each other rather than to marginalize and divide. We can no longer exist in a 'he said, she said' world, nor in one in which our birthplace and the color of our skin become the ink with which dangerous battlelines are drawn. The US was once a country of pride and fame; we have become one of blame and shame. We *all* need to own this and to *fix it*!"

Tanya Marvin-Horowitz

Partner, Butterfly Ventures, Sweden

Tanya Marvin-Horowitz started her first venture capital firm in New York, but within the first year, she moved to Stockholm, Sweden, and continued investing across the Atlantic.

"In 2013 I'd just raised the CapA fund after a decade-long career as an M&A banker in New York, and here I was leaving my network and moving to an entirely unknown market to me," Tanya started telling me her story.

Tanya's husband took a job opportunity in Sweden, and she followed. If you think that it was an unfortunate development in Tanya's career, you'll be surprised how well it worked out.

"Sweden is one of the largest countries in the Nordic region, which also includes Finland, Denmark, Norway, and Iceland. I did not know what was happening in the Nordics at that time, and didn't know what to expect. I saw that there was quite an entrepreneurial startup bubble happening, particularly in Stockholm, but there were very few investors around, so we started investing out of CapA in the Nordics.

"Nobody knew who we were either — they just knew I was an American making investments in pre-seed and seed-stage companies. I was lucky to be one of the first investors in the region, at a point where the ecosystem was quite immature.

"However, the technologies that were being developed in the region were far superior to a lot of tech I'd seen in the United States. I was very impressed with the people, the educational system, and particularly the technical and business universities, such as KTH and the Stockholm School of Economics. I'll be honest with you, Renata, I didn't know all that before I moved here, and I wouldn't have thought that this part of Europe had a solid foundation for becoming a techhub. All I knew was that 'Skype' was Swedish and 'Supercell' was Finnish. The local ecosystem has really populated since I first arrived, and now, Sweden and Finland in particular, have become quite substantial hotbeds of innovations," she characterized the market.

With her partner, David Mendez, Tanya invested from CapA in 18 companies, 11 of which were US-based. Out of the four Swedish companies, two Finnish companies, and one Icelandic company that the firm invested in, every single one of them is still operational. Two of those Nordic-based companies have had quite fruitful exits, including Small Giant Games from Helsinki, Finland, that was just sold to Zynga with an enterprise value of $700 million in January 2019.

"The European venture capital community at first seemed closed: the Swedes invested in the Swedes, the Finns invested in the Finns, and so on, and so forth. But it has started to open up, compared to what we first saw when we came here," Tanya said. "For example, we invested in Small Giant Games alongside other VCs such as Creandum, which is one of the oldest and largest VCs here. We were a very small-ticket investor compared to them, however, the founders of the company let us participate because of our reputation and the US connections that we had. That was how I got introduced to this company in the first place — through my relationship with a Finnish gentleman based in New York who I had known for years. So maintaining my network across the Atlantic really helped me big time."

Coming from the United States was a big deal for Tanya's local investment practice, because a lot of European companies aimed to make it to the US market. The fact that CapA could help them with that, was a big feather in Tanya's cap, and many good companies have seemed to gravitate towards her because of this value-add, ever since. "This is one of the main things that helped us to become truly successful here in the Nordics. However, I also travel all over Europe, and always try to help companies with connections in the US — even if they don't end up in our portfolio. Whether it's a US-based investor they want to meet or a US company they need for business development purposes, I'll do whatever I can to help connect those dots for them, even if we're not backing them. I believe in paying it forward."

The exit of Small Giant Games happened later than needed, however. When Horowitz and Mendez went back to their limited partners to raise the second fund in 2015, they didn't have any outstanding stories that could help them prove cross-Atlantic investments. The US investors still did not get the Nordics, because they simply didn't see what was happening in its startup ecosystem.

Tanya had to make a pivot of her own kind and joined forces with a local VC firm called Butterfly Ventures, which is one of the most active seed investors in Finland and now the Nordics as a whole.

"In 2017 we launched a 15 million Euro fund, which may seem very small by US standards, however, in the Nordics, you can do a lot with that money at the pre-seed/seed level. The local valuations are sometimes, I would say, less than half of what I'm seeing in the United States. That happens, not because the companies are undervalued, but because they are much more capital efficient. I am still sometimes amazed by how much they manage to achieve with a couple of hundred thousand Euros, for example," Tanya shared.

At Butterfly Ventures, Tanya works with three male Finnish partners, so my next question was obvious: is there a difference in male/female dynamics between Europe and the US?

"That's a tough question, Renata," she prefaced her answer. "When I worked in New York, the bankers and a lot of private equity folks that I worked with, treated me with respect, don't get me wrong, but I definitely felt inferior to them. Like I wasn't respected deeply enough. Here, I have never felt that at all. Firstly, Sweden is all about equality. Women even pay for themselves when they go on a date, or even when they already live together with their partners. It's very different here. They definitely look at women as absolute equals, especially in Sweden, but I've seen it across the Nordics as well.

"When I first started at Butterfly Ventures, it took me a while to get used to the cultural differences, but now, almost three years later, I would say that we are a much better oiled machine! It feels really great to be a part of this team — I love working with these guys! If I have a problem or issue with anything, I can easily speak up, because I know that they won't hold it against me and are very conscientious about listening to my ideas," Tanya got really excited saying that.

"It's a big leap for me, because I've always been a solo woman, if you will, and most of the stuff that I've done, I preferred to do on my own. I had always looked for true equality with partners in anything that I've ever done, whether it's a man or a woman," she added.

This courage to do whatever it is that a woman wants to do on her own, regardless of the circumstances, is something you often find in New Yorkers and Europeans. The former possess this character trait due to their ability to live an independent life, the latter — typically, because they have strong mothers as female role models. As with my parents, Tanya's mother came from Europe after going through the whole tragedy of the Stalin era. "She is a very strong lady," Tanya said. "She really instilled a lot of this in me as well".

As many other female investors who you have (and will) read about in this book, Tanya Marvin-Horowitz has an athletic background. She was swimming competitively from age six and playing tennis competitively from age eight, which she continued through the collegiate level.

"I think, women may benefit from playing competitive sports — it helps develop confidence. I have a son now, and even though he's a boy, I already worry about him getting bullied when he gets older. I've heard that this has become a really bad thing these days, but I'm having a hard time understanding what that concept is, because I never got bullied at school. I don't know whether it was because I didn't allow myself to get bullied, or maybe it was due to the confidence that I had developed from sports. But it has definitely followed through to my adult life. Starting out as an athlete helped me tremendously with walking into a boardroom full of men, being able to handle them, and being confident in what I'm saying or doing," Tanya concluded.

That confidence would definitely have helped her pitch institutional investors, so I asked for any advice she could share with aspiring venture capitalists.

"For emerging managers, raising a first fund is very tough. Although, I'd been around tech companies and early-stage investing since 2000 as an M&A banker, and had seen it from both sides — the buy side and the sell side — I'd never really made investment decisions myself. I had a lot of experience in the due diligence process, but it just wasn't enough for institutional investors to fund me. When you have a fiduciary responsibility to the limited partners of a fund, it definitely adds extra pressure, of course, on that due diligence process.

"I'd advise first-time general partners to put all of their effort into finding an anchor ambassador who would support them with a bulk of money to start things off. Once you find somebody who has credibility and who believes in what you're doing, the rest will follow. We did exactly that with CapA. We had just one individual investor who became our largest limited partner, and after we signed him up, we raised more money from a bunch of other investors.

"Something similar happened in our last fundraising at Butterfly Ventures. The government of Finland awarded us a very substantial check, which was the first for this fund, and it became a lot easier to talk to other institutional investors. Of course, we are a 6-year-old fund, so we have gained certain recognition, which makes it easier to fundraise, but there is still competition between venture firms, so nobody can relax just yet.

"Finally, when building your networks, aside from listing *all* of the potential limited partners for your fund, you should also foster relationships with those *few* who can be your lead investors."

Susan Mason

Founding Partner, Aligned Ventures, United States

Susan Mason has a no-joke technical background. With a bachelor's degree in engineering and computer science, she worked with 32-bit microprocessor teams at Fairchild and Fujitsu. She managed system and software teams to deliver solutions to the largest corporations in the world. This experience led her to start her own company, through which she was helping large Fortune 1000 tech companies — with Apple and IBM among her clients — to identify interesting technologies in their R&D centers, develop them as stand-alone startups to prove them as products, and then to merge the newly created companies back into the parent corporations. Microelectronics and microprocessing design was a predominantly white-male-dominated industry — it was the environment in which she was trained. "It was just the way it was. Women had to adapt to that environment, and often that was a struggle.

"Having a tech background helped me a lot, because I could go toe to toe with people around a boardroom table and not be intimidated. I think that women who are less assured would be unnerved by the constant pressure to be both confident and correct. But not being intimidated is only part of the solution. At that level, one must also have gravitas — a character trait often not encouraged in women. It means having a presence of intelligence and opinion, a willingness to lead by example and to take responsibility. Being collaborative by nature, women sometimes don't want to step out and just own it. Women need to work to put themselves out there, which is not a natural inclination for us. We have to consciously think about it and make an effort to do so," Susan was candid.

Mason often refers to a study that may explain one of the reasons why men are oftentimes at least one step ahead of us. "When reading a job description, women tend to think, 'I must have these skills and master them before I can apply.' Men's attitude is different and can be described as, 'I can do/learn that, so I can apply'. This difference in attitudes relates to risk-taking, something which many women are not comfortable with, partly because of the fear of failure."

It's not often that we hear women confirming a common opinion that females are risk-averse. However, Susan knows the benefits of this character trait and doesn't find it to always be a flaw. "I believe this is deeply based in our evolution. For ages, women made sure that everybody in the cave was fed and protected, so that they would all survive through the winter. Therefore, they were conservative and made sure that the tools and safety were in hand, hence, our aversion to failure. The good thing about this, is that my female CEOs do not take undue risks. I know that if they give me a plan, they will make it happen. As an investor, I can rest easy knowing that I have great management in my portfolio companies."

As with everything in life, this quality needs to be balanced. It's good to have a co-founder or an investor who can challenge a conservative approach. After all, smart money comes with some skills that investors are good at. Coaching is one of them, so Susan continued. "I often work with my female founders and CEOs, asking them questions like: 'What's holding you back? How could we double these numbers?' You have to encourage them to remove their blinkers and go forward faster. I can see when a specific thinking process kicks in: 'If I get this and that — yes, I can double that.' This is a common exercise for me and it is very satisfying to watch CEOs grow."

When Mason started a venture capital firm with Jodi Jahic, the ladies chose a relatively conservative investment model and named the fund accordingly. Aligned Partners is all about aligning with the founders' interests, which are saving a larger share in the company for themselves and their employees. The firm invests in smaller, but sustainable companies that can be acquired for up to $250 million and still provide a good return to investors due to the unique model and smaller amount of venture capital involved.

"This strategy has been working very well for us," Susan intrigued me. "We didn't expect a high volume of such deals, so we were pleasantly surprised when it happened. When we were modeling our approach, we figured that it would be very appealing to entrepreneurs. Most entrepreneurs don't understand the risks around a 'unicorn' status, and the emotional and physical energy required to move that hamster wheel. The odds of founders making good money from growing their company to a 'unicorn' are less than 1%. When they choose to not pursue this goal, they are rewarded with the confirmation that it is possible for them and their employees to own 40-50% of the company at an exit, and that their journey to it would be shorter and less risky. That is a really good deal!

"We raised our third fund recently, and entrepreneurs from Fund I, who have already sold their companies, either became investors in our new fund, or are building new companies with us as investors in these companies again. Evidently, our investment strategy is a real win-win."

Raising three funds is definitely an indicator of success, so I asked Susan to choose one thing that she thinks can help an investor succeed. "Strong self-awareness, knowing how you as an individual operate, and how you can maximize your interactions with people. I know it sounds like a soft skill, but it's the number one skill you need throughout the whole investment process — from negotiating the first deal and coaching founders, all the way to an exit. Luckily, women have a natural proclivity to be self-aware."

Michelle McCarthy

Director,
Verizon Ventures,
United States

It wouldn't be an overstatement to say that Michelle McCarthy dedicated her entire career to Verizon, 20 years of which she spent on investments and corporate strategy and development. "I was interested in joining the venture team to make investments that could specifically bring more innovations into Verizon. This opportunity came together really nicely with my background in corporate strategy and my tech expertise," she described her transition.

It's always interesting how a woman navigates a male-dominated corporate world over the decades, so I asked Michelle to describe her experience in that regard. "My approach has always been to look past stereotypes of division between genders. I prefer to see meritocracy, and overlook what could be viewed as discriminatory instances, to focus on actions I can take in any given situation instead, to influence a better, more equitable outcome.

"I try to understand the person next to me before I start talking: what is their position, background, set of expectations and objectives...? This skill never goes out of fashion — be self-aware of your communication style and make sure the person you are talking to is able to process it right. You will find that effective communication works wonders in business and in personal lives!" she shared.

"However, I hear anecdotally that a number of men are becoming less comfortable when engaging in informal networking with female colleagues or external contacts, simply because there's a concern about whether there might be a misperception of their words or actions — one downside of the #MeToo movement. We, of course, aren't talking about malicious behaviour, which is never acceptable and shouldn't be tolerated. But when it is not, this cautiousness definitely makes networking even harder for women than it was before. Casual discussion has always been one of the ways of finding a common language and building the foundation for relationships that may grow into strong partnerships, whether within one corporation or between companies. It definitely remains such between men, so if women lose this opportunity of casual networking, it may create a business disadvantage for them," she added.

During our conversation, we tried to look at the venture capital industry as a big corporation to see if any corporate business practices could be replicated in venture capital. "Corporate innovations teach us to make deliberate efforts to change the status quo. I really do think that, as a society, we need to become more creative in bringing more diverse people in and breaking down the barriers they face, because we will all benefit from it," Michelle started a new topic.

"When speaking of diversity, we need to look beyond Silicon Valley and start with diverse problems first. Merely bringing in diverse people to solve the same problems, in the same way, is not going to cut it in the long term. We need to admit that the venture capital industry is largely imbalanced today because startups that receive the most capital, offer innovations in markets that resonate with the venture capitalists providing the funding, and because the case for investment is pitched in a way that effectively speaks to these venture capitalists. It's a networking-intensive ecosystem, with its own language, expectations and connections. A whole host of other viable business innovation opportunities remain unnoticed just because we are not inclusive enough in our thinking, composition or location of VC firm partnerships. Addressing the underserved population is not a merely philanthropic matter. There are a lot of real business opportunities that investors, and society as a whole, can benefit from.

"We should encourage diverse entrepreneurs to develop robust solutions to different problems about which they are passionate, and we need to make sure they are prepared with the tools necessary to be successful. This would foster innovation in a more holistic way and make more people tackle all sorts of challenges on the one hand and emerging opportunities on the other."

When I asked Michelle about the performance of companies founded by women or minority groups' representatives, she said, "I would say that the jury is still out on that. I've seen various reports on this topic, and our own experience doesn't show a noticeable difference. We don't have a specific mandate of investing in female or diverse founders, nevertheless, we have a substantial number of them in our portfolio. For our investment team, recognizing and funding diverse teams was quite natural."

We, of course, touched upon the topic of women in corporate venture capital. "It is indeed easier for women to get into decision-making roles in corporate venturing. I think this is because corporations have long been more aware of the need to foster diverse environments, to begin with, to capitalize on the diversity of thought and skills, and also to reflect the diversity of their own customers. Fortunately, there is a growing awareness about that among traditional VC firms, but the only way to change that is to make a deliberate effort.

"One of the angles to approaching this is to expand the networks of the VC firm hiring decision-makers in a way that they could ask their equals, partners of other VC firms, or in PE and investment banking, who are diverse themselves, to help find candidates for them. That leads us to other components of the issue which need to be addressed, such as better networking and creating talent banks of diverse candidates at the more junior levels so that they can become viable partner candidates over time — something that has been done in the corporate world long time ago." And something that we address through our VC recruiting platform.

Mary Meeker

Founding Partner, Bond, United States

I caught Mary Meeker when she was working on her annual report — a world-renowned 'bible' of insights into the tech trends that made her famous in the first place. Although her reports initially targeted institutional investors, many other people read them as if they were bestselling books — one of her reports was indeed commercially published as a book to be sold at bookstores. Meeker was undoubtedly one of the major players on Wall Street and continued being such on Sand Hill Road. For most people, she is 'Queen of the Net', as anointed by Barron's, and is equated with Alan Greenspan and Warren Buffett as a market mover. However, the tech community rarely talks about how she got there.

Mary grew up in a small town in Indiana and had a typical American childhood. She recalls that her dad was a successful lawyer and businessman in the steel industry, who volunteered to go to World War II when he was in his forties. That was his first time leaving the country — on a ship out of San Francisco to Japan. He saw the world and brought back a lot of optimism, which he implanted in Mary from an early age — she was born after he got back home. "I grew up believing that one person could make a difference. In Indiana, I saw that with basketball. The small town could beat the big town. That is one of the things that attracts me to entrepreneurs," Mary said.

She had been fascinated by Wall Street since high school, when she entered a stock-picking contest and watched her stocks promptly double. Meeker started off as a broker with Merrill Lynch and earned her MBA from Cornell after that. She had a clear goal: to be a portfolio manager, and entering the analyst training program at Salomon Brothers in 1986, one of the oldest American investment banks founded in 1910, was just a stepping stone for her. She didn't plan to stick around. "I wanted to work as a sell-side analyst for a couple of years and then go manage money. But the stock analyst phase lasted a bit longer than I thought it would."

Meeker got hooked on analyzing the computer industry and was soon approached by the legendary leader of Morgan Stanley's technology-banking team, Frank Quattrone, who had taken Cisco and Apple public. He offered Mary a job as a senior analyst at Morgan Stanley, covering personal computers and software. She turned that offer down the first time, "I didn't think I was ready to be a stand-alone analyst at a firm like Morgan Stanley," but succumbed when they approached her again later, and so her journey began.

Meeker labored in the lengthy shadow of Quattrone for a few years, and although she was involved in some IPOs under his leadership, her primary responsibility was covering such established companies as Microsoft and Compaq for Morgan Stanley's institutional clients. She issued her first massive report on ten software and computer stocks in 1991, where she rated eight of them as buys.

Although most of those companies lost in market value soon after she picked them, the report became known as more than just a technical document for sophisticated investors. Meeker offered remarkably sound advice that was dubbed the 'Ten Commandments for Investing in Technology Stocks'. She warned that "technology stocks are volatile...", that investors should "buy when no one is interested in them...sell when everyone is interested in them (or when attendance at technology conferences reaches record levels, or when your grandmother wants to buy a hot technology IPO)." She also alerted that investors should not "fall in love with tech companies" and should "remember to view them as investments." Meeker herself would disregard some of those rules in the coming years, which drew a fair share of negative attention to her when the dot-com bubble burst. But that also made her a great venture capital investor.

The IPO of a tiny software company called Netscape, in 1995, was the turning point in Meeker's career. To this day, people in Silicon Valley still mark this event as ground zero for the internet era. It was the first tech IPO of a company with an incredible buzz and no profits, which set the pattern for many of the hot dot-com IPOs to come up. In covering Netscape, Mary behaved more like a steward for the company rather than an indifferent investment banker. She privately referred to Netscape as 'her baby' and actively defended the stock, even when Microsoft took dead aim at the company with its competing browser, as well as later on, when then Deutsche Morgan Grenfell analyst, Bill Gurley downgraded Netscape from buy to accumulate. When Netscape's stock dropped almost 20% after his report, Meeker upgraded her own rating two days later to a strong buy, but even after that the shares continued to lose value and recovered only after AOL announced the acquisition of Netscape almost two years later.

She developed close relationships with venture capital investors such as John Doerr from Kleiner Perkins, who was giving her early peeks at promising tech companies, called her a 'service provider' and stated point blank, 'I don't think of Mary as an analyst.' She got acquainted with all the top startups back then, to decide which were Morgan Stanley material. She became a true internet insider, a power broker, and a dealmaker. People who read her reports wanted to try all the new tech products and services mentioned in them. Tech companies were trying to catch Mary Meeker anywhere they could, including red-eye flights, to get on her radar, because if they got Mary Meeker on their side, they would get a lot of media attention too. They knew that she was very protective of the companies she picked. "I am hard-pressed to downgrade the stock of a company I fundamentally believe in, over the long term," she said.

When Frank Quattrone and his top deputies suddenly left Morgan Stanley in 1996, Mary opted to stay, knowing that Morgan had lost their star, and she became the new Quattrone. The internet was a whole new world for investors, and there was no one more credible than Mary Meeker to explain it to them. During the dot-com craze, she was the most important voice for the internet and an advocate for the idea that companies without earnings could transform the world and bring skyrocketing returns. Ordinary investors hounded her for autographs, and Bill Gurley said about her, We talked about Mary being one of the best investment bankers on the planet.'

Back then, Institutional Investor magazine, which has been ranking Wall Street analysts for decades, created a new category: Internet Analysts, in which Mary Meeker, of course, took the top line. She deeply understood how profoundly the internet affected almost every aspect of people's lives and business. She was one of the first to praise companies that sacrificed profits for rapid growth. She came up with the new metrics to assess internet companies, such as 'discounted terminal valuation' [a novel calculation based on anticipated margins and growth rates five years down the road], 'eyeballs', and 'page views'. Mary was highly selective during the early years of the internet boom, choosing only those companies she believed could be huge winners. She turned down a lot of deals and was very tough during the due diligence of those who got in the door. She likes pointing out that Morgan Stanley did only about 8% of all internet IPOs.

Meeker became a go-to person for all major companies out there, whether they were planning to go public, needed advice on their internet strategy, or were planning strategic moves and acquisitions. Her schedule became brutal, even though she had assistants working around the clock and a team of analysts who, at some point, started preparing her famous reports for her. Meeker had always been a notorious workaholic and could work through the night and give interviews to the media at her office at 4 in the morning. A Fortune reporter said that she didn't look tired at all and overdrive appeared to be her perpetual state. She was eager to give lengthy, digressive answers that could hop from one subject to another. One of her friends said that talking to Meeker was 'like trying to catch a meteor', because that is how her mind worked.

With such great popularity comes big responsibility. Meeker refused to downgrade her stocks even when the market seemed to be against them. She was not afraid of high valuations, explaining them by the bull market and tremendous shift that the new internet economy brought into the market. It'd be fair to mention that she, nevertheless, expressed her concerns about how fast dot-com stocks were rising. She warned that only 30% of internet companies would end up being long-term winners, while the others would ultimately fall below their IPO price. But most of the companies she covered were not among the latter.

Meeker did almost every internet deal she really wanted, but did she miss any worthy bets? Of course. She passed on Yahoo when they first came in; she turned down internet grocer Webvan, because she doubted its business model; she also missed the women's content site iVillage. These companies became winners at their IPOs without her. But she bet on and remained bullish about Amazon, eBay, and Priceline, which performed very well, and whenever one of them hit a bump in the road, she kept reassuring investors that the stock would go up later anyway.

Investors trusted Mary's word entirely until the dot-coms imploded and the NASDAQ collapsed. The stocks that she never agreed to downgrade, dropped by up to 90%. She was largely criticized from all corners of the investment arena, however, she remained tenacious. She called that downturn the 'nuclear winter', and was anticipating 'the spring bloom' for her favorite companies. Indeed, within the next two to three years, the aggregate valuation of the companies she recommended, exceeded the numbers they had during the dot-com bubble.

Meeker didn't ignore the losses. "Did we do some deals we shouldn't have done? Yes. Did we recommend some stocks we shouldn't have? Yes." But she also added, "Every individual has to be accountable for how they allocate their investments."

If you are familiar with the Babe Ruth effect, looking back at her story, you may see some similarity with what Meeker was doing: she was making many big bets where she could 'hit big or miss big'. Like Babe Ruth, she missed a lot. But she also hit big plenty of times. She always believed in Intuit, eBay, Amazon, and Google. Amazon fell down to $15 from $106 during the 'nuclear winter', but last time I checked, it was worth $1,840 per share. She saw tremendous revenue growth for Google and put their stock at $500, which traded at $1,124 this morning. Indeed, she wasn't very concerned about the short-term gains — she always preached to investors to believe and wait. This strategy is very much what many venture capitalists rely on, so it was only a matter of time for Mary Meeker to remember her dream and leave Morgan Stanley for Kleiner Perkins, to manage a venture capital portfolio.

With all her titles and experience, Kleiner Perkins didn't make her a managing partner from the start of her tenure at the firm, and Meeker didn't think it had anything to do with gender. She said she was comfortable not being promoted to a decision-making position immediately, and that she had never thought of leaving Kleiner Perkins because of it. When asked about how the firm treated her as a woman, she replied, "I think Kleiner Perkins' men are softie choir boys compared to the people I worked with on Wall Street."

Meeker didn't have time to worry about gender issues, so she doesn't speak about it often. However, answering questions about the underrepresentation of women in tech, she said, "No one forced me to focus on technology. I just did it because I had a passion for it. When I started, there weren't a lot of female role models either. I think there's been a lot of progress since then, and I think that if women have a passion and really want to succeed, they can. On a relative basis, the male-female ratio is certainly skewed to men, but on an absolute basis, there are a lot of very successful women in technology."

Mary Meeker doesn't need to prove anything to anyone anymore, however, she decided to turn the last Kleiner Perkins page and start a new chapter with her own new growth fund named Bond. What is so special about it? She will be the first female founding partner of a venture capital firm with more than $1 billion under management.

Bá Minuzzi

Founding Partner, BABEL.Ventures, United States

Not only was BABEL Ventures the first venture capital firm in Silicon Valley with a Latina female founder, but she is also its sole general partner. "Every time I am about to do something big, I am afraid to do it, but instead of backing off, my first instinct is to go and do it. It's like an addiction to challenges: if something seems to be hard, I'm likely doing it," Bá laughed.

When I asked Bá to tell me more personal stories about the way she got into venture capital since all the professional ones are already out there on the web, she said, "It was very personal for me, indeed."

Bá grew up in southern Brazil, in a family of doctors. However, she didn't attempt to follow in their footsteps, and opened a fashion store instead — her dream business, which was defined by the passion for fashion design that she got at college. "That was my first experience as an entrepreneur, and it was brutal. I understood finance by doing all the planning and reporting myself in the spreadsheets, and when I saw that I needed a lot of capital to keep me afloat along the entire cycle, I realized that working capital can be very unfair," she took off with her story.

Bá didn't shy away from making a change in her career when she saw an opportunity in the Brazilian real estate market. That was the time of the first affordable living complexes there, and she started raising money for their development. When she moved to the US and settled in Miami, Florida, she continued working in real estate, started managing the finances of high-net-worth individuals, and pretty soon became financially independent. She has single-handedly raised over $250 million for real estate and high-tech companies in Latin America and the United States, and has co-managed over $200 million in assets.

"I was 24 years old, buying and selling real estate in Miami, living in a very nice apartment in Bay Harbor, which seemed pretty great according to many people.

But I didn't feel fulfilled. I started spending more time on self-development, and I finally realized that I was pretty unhappy. Unlike my first jobs — fashion design and real estate development — I wasn't really creating anything anymore, and that haunted me for quite a while. The question was: 'What could I do about it?'"

Searching for the answer, Bá moved to San Francisco to learn more about tech entrepreneurship. "At the start or end of every meeting I had in the Bay Area, people would ask me, 'How can I help you?' I had never had that in my life! That made me feel extremely comfortable and I wanted to be part of that. I was so inspired by the Silicon Valley spirit, that I immediately wanted to do the same, and help entrepreneurs like myself. The best way to do so, was to invest in them. So I started learning everything I could about venture capital," she shared emotionally.

Bá would probably have spent a couple of years doing so, if it hadn't been for President Trump — it was the election year when she moved to San Francisco. Trump's anti-Latin American immigrant rhetoric angered Minuzzi. "Many startup founders and C-level executives in the United States are immigrants. I wanted people to know that there are more capable, smart people in South America, so I started fundraising my first venture capital fund right away. I thought that the least I could do was to create more examples of female leaders in areas that are dominated by male investors or entrepreneurs."

She wasn't joking. What typically takes 12 to 18 months, she made happen in seven — she raised $30 million for BABEL Ventures, an early-stage VC firm investing in biotech startups. "When I started fundraising, I thought that I would be able to raise money from my current clients whose assets I had already been managing. However, they weren't ready to invest in venture capital, so I had to start from ground zero. Those seven months were probably the most exhausting time in my life! Living in San Francisco, I started my calls with Brazil at 3, then I called American investors, and then I was scouting startups and building my deal flow. At the beginning, I was hustling like crazy! I didn't see any sign of people committing, and that was painful. After I got the first couple of checks, however, it became pretty easy and I closed the fund very soon."

Minuzzi kept breaking the rules. She pitched biotech investment focus to institutional investors when she only had a passion for that, with no expertise. Instead, she hired some of the best experts in the sector and got what she wanted from limited partners. "I wasn't trying to break any rules. I just didn't know them — I was doing things that made sense to me, and didn't limit myself by any specific order imposed by someone else.

"I get asked a lot about what it's like being a woman in venture capital, and I always have a hard time answering this question. I have never identified myself as a woman or a man — I just worked my butt off, and stayed focused and consistent, even when I didn't have enough credibility.

"I prefer not to put Latinas in a special box either. I believe we are all the same: gender, race, and religion doesn't say anything to me — I believe in people. We need to not box ourselves in by any of these parameters, or any others that can create a barrier in our minds. So my advice to anyone who wants to thrive in business, is: lead your life, find your purpose, and go for it!"

Ann Miura-Ko

Founding Partner, Floodgate, United States

In the four months since I started working on this book in January 2019, a lot has happened to the investors featured in it. Ann Miura-Ko has had the largest exit for her firm, Floodgate, when Lyft went public in March. Floodgate was one of the very first micro VC firms in the United States that believed in backing companies at the seed stage before big checks come in. Miura-Ko invested in Lyft before it became such (initially, the startup was called Zimride), which brought a nearly 10,000% return to Floodgate on its roughly $1 million initial investment.

Her partner, Mike Maples, says that she has consistently made at least one investment in each of Floodgate's funds that have the potential to return the entire fund. He wanted Miura-Ko to become a star, teaching her all the wisdom he'd gotten by the time they launched Floodgate. 'If you are going to be successful as a VC, I think the secret is to have a fast start in your first five years,' he said. 'You have to be associated with awesome companies immediately.'

Ann sees her relationship with Lyft from a different perspective. "We both grew up in the industry — I grew up as an investor alongside them growing up as entrepreneurs. So we both kind of needed each other in that moment. You hear so often about investors making a bet on entrepreneurs, and I really believe in this case, it was just as much John and Logan [founders of Lyft] taking a real bet on me."

She thinks that Lyft is a great example of 'intelligent growth', because it was a highly disciplined company from its early days, that decided to not waste venture capital dollars until they got a product market fit. Indeed, the team worked for two and a half years as the Zimride platform, where one could find carpooling arrangements, but the company couldn't get enough drivers to show convincing traction. When they launched Lyft and gained the desired traction, they knew what they were doing and went ahead with raising a large round from Founders Fund and Andreessen Horowitz. "Hacking value before you go out and hack growth is something that I don't see often enough in Silicon Valley," Miura-Ko said. Her personal story reflects this principle as well.

Ann was so shy as a kid, that she couldn't even announce her performance when she played piano on stage — her brother was responsible for introducing her to the audience. In fifth grade, unlike all other kids, Ann picked a negotiations class during the summer school program. When her mom asked her why she had made that choice, Ann explained that the class was related to the book 'Getting to Yes' and she wanted 'to learn how to get to yes'. Ten-year-old Miura-Ko was in a group with 30- to 50-year-old adults, negotiating supply lines to create a real society on Mars during simulation. "I felt like I was taken seriously," she recalled.

Ann did really well at math and science, but speaking on a stage was not something that came naturally to her. She needed to step up her public speaking skills, and decided to dive into speech and debate in high school. Miura-Ko said she was pretty terrible at it and wasn't able to win any tournaments for quite a long time, but she loved the competition during debates. "I've always been that way. Wherever I can get points, I want more!"

Ann grew up in a traditional Japanese family, and her parents wanted her to get into a great university. Although they were incredibly supportive, when her mom saw her losing records in debates, she got worried that it would decrease Ann's chances of getting into an Ivy League college, and suggested that she take fencing classes instead. Ann got the message, but didn't even consider a change of curriculum. She doubled down on her debates, and almost lived at Stanford's Green Library during the summer, reading philosophy books and articles to prepare for the next tournament. After having had a losing record for the two previous years, she had a brilliant result in the next challenge. For Ann, this was a formative experience, because she felt that she could turn luck around and make her own. "I was very prepared to outdo every competitor who walked in through the door, and that became my habit over time." She started pursuing excellence in everything after that, which was also what her father expected from her.

He came to the United States speaking very little English, but got a PhD in mechanical and aerospace engineering, became an associate professor, and made his way out to NASA. Ann described him as a very passionate academic, who would wake up at five in the morning and continue working late into the night when he got back home from work. Since she was a small child, her dad used to ask her just one question about whatever she was doing: 'Is this world-class?' He expected her five-year-old writing to be world-class. He asked whether photocopying the documents that she was doing when she worked at the Dean of Engineering's office at Yale, was world-class as well. His message was always: 'Is this really the best that you can do?'

Ann remembered how she was standing in front of the photocopy machine with a stack of papers thinking, "What is world-class in photocopying?" She decided that she would make copies that were of such good quality, that one couldn't tell that they were photocopies. She then continued doing everything in the same top quality manner, so that the Dean or his executive assistant would experience delight. It was another lesson Miura-Ko learned: have real ownership of the things you do and create opportunities for yourself.

This effort paid off big time when the Dean of Engineering, a legendary physicist working under George Bush Sr., and who barely knew Ann's name, poked his head out of the office once and said, 'I need you to go and give this friend of mine a tour of the engineering facilities. I know you'll do a good job — Sarah [his executive assistant] has told me you're great.' Miura-Ko took the guest around and at the end of the tour, he asked if she wanted to shadow him at his office for a while. Ann didn't know at that moment that the guest was Lou Platt, the CEO of Hewlett-Packard. She felt embarrassed that she hadn't done her homework on the man, but was incredibly happy to take that opportunity. She literally followed Platt everywhere and met many Silicon Valley pioneers, including Bill Gates.

Miura-Ko believes that mentorship is critical for personal and professional development and can mean many different things. She found that experience to be an incredible example of mentorship, because Lou Platt never asked for her resume, but saw her potential instead. Reflecting on that, she said that potential is something that one has to find inside oneself, and that there are no tests or any other form of recognition for human potential. She knew what she was capable of when the test scores showed that she wasn't, as well as when her parents believed in her, but she didn't.

That happened when she had a conviction that she was going to become a doctor. She took an organic chemistry class and was planning to go to medical school, until she was about to start preparing for the Medical College Admission Test (MCAT) with her friend. Before they got to open the books, Ann looked at her and had a sudden realization that she herself hated hospitals, didn't like being around sick people, and didn't want people to always complain to her. That happened literally days before the test, when she had been constantly observing her friend who seemed to become that world-class doctor, while Ann didn't see herself becoming one.

Looking back, she admitted that she had probably known that she wasn't going to become a doctor in her gut long before that epiphany. However, medical school seemed like a bullet-proof career path, where she knew every step of the way: which classes to take, what exams to pass, what school to apply to, etc. It was a predictable future, but the actual work at the end of the day was not something she was going to love and enjoy.

At that point, Ann was uncertain of her future profession. Living in Palo Alto, she couldn't avoid hanging out with entrepreneurs, but she had never considered doing business until then, so she didn't have a plan. One of her friends mentioned venture capital as a possible career option, considering Ann's technical education. Although she knew what that was, she didn't take that idea to heart and decided to go work for McKinsey to figure out what to do next. During that time, she met Ted Dintersmith, a partner at Charles River Ventures, and rather than formally interviewing her, Dintersmith was more interested in her tastes in literature and music. They had many things in common, and after a two-hour conversation where they didn't discuss Ann's previous experience, nor technological developments, Dintersmith invited her to work for the firm. This was another turning point in Ann's life, when someone recognized her potential and put it ahead of the formal requirements for a job again.

Miura-Ko said that one of the things she learned from Dintersmith was his way of networking. For him, it was never just working a room, shaking a lot of hands, learning a few names and moving on. He networked with a deep curiosity about the human being who was sitting across the table from him at that moment.

She met her future investment partner, Mike Maples, when she was teaching a course on entrepreneurship at Stanford, where he was a mentor to a group of students in her class. She wasn't quite satisfied with the work he was doing as a mentor and challenged him on the results of this group. He bluntly promised her that the students would all get A+ at the end of the day, and he delivered.

The next time they had a serious conversation, happened when Ann was contemplating starting a company in cybersecurity. She was doing her PhD in computer security when she realized how big the issue was becoming. She wanted to talk to some investors before jumping into deep waters, and called Maples. He was nice enough to show her his deal flow and discuss some of the companies and investment strategy. Soon after that, he called Ann and suggested that she drops out of her PhD and join him at the new $35 million fund that he had just raised. He said, 'It's not the venture-backed startup that you've been thinking about, but it's a backed venture startup.'

She had a lot of reservations about doing that. She knew that she didn't have the experience to become and investor, and that should she decide to become a VC, there were a lot of large, established VC firms she could join. However, there was something in Maples that she wanted to learn from him — he had that mad genius of storytelling, positioning and strategy that Ann was missing as an engineer who focused on the product instead.

Miura-Ko accepted the offer, but decided to get her PhD as well, and that was the most intense time of her life. She was waking up at 4 o'clock in the morning to do the research until her one-year-old daughter woke up; taking her to daycare; working from 8:30am to 6:30pm at Floodgate; going home and cooking dinner; and then working on her PhD again. After half a year of this schedule, she got pregnant with her second baby and set up a date to defend her doctorate before her baby's due date. However, it didn't go as planned, and she ended up defending her doctorate weeks after giving birth to her son. The time between 2008 and 2009, when she managed to have a second child, to get her PhD, to make her first investments at Floodgate, and 'to stay married', Ann calls 'the most creative and productive period of her life'. She would probably say that she wouldn't do it the same way again if she could go back in time, if not for the outcome of all that hustle: that extreme level of chaos and multitasking made her much stronger.

Her partner, Maples, couldn't appreciate it more, as he thinks that the venture business clearly recognizes whiners from warriors. People who complain when they run up against a brutal obstacle, and those who just get it done. Women's ability to remain warriors during the hardest times, is one reason why he wanted more women at his firm.

If you think that Ann was welcome everywhere and her career was made of roses, it wouldn't be true. But she learned to tune out the naysayers, knowing that although there were things that she wouldn't be good at, there were also things that she could be great at. "My curiosity had me exploring a ton of very different paths in life, but self-awareness allowed me to close doors that weren't a fit."

Patricia Nakache

General Partner, Trinity Ventures, United States

Patricia Nakache was writing freelance for Fortune Magazine when she interviewed the partners of Trinity Ventures. They told her repeatedly how busy they were evaluating the torrent of dot-com startups, and Patricia responded, "I can help you out." After some consideration, they asked her to join them. "My move to venture wasn't premeditated, because I was literally only six months out of McKinsey, and I was having fun working at a startup. But the more I learned about venture capital, the more intriguing and exciting it became," she said.

Patricia majored in chemistry, at Harvard and was going to get her PhD, when she decided against it. "Suddenly, I had this epiphany: I love learning, but I don't love research. My experience of working in labs was fairly isolating. I'm more of a people person, and I have a broad range of interests. Once I accepted that, it was like a load of bricks tumbled off my shoulders."

Nakache opted to learn about business. For her, consulting seemed like a good way to get exposed to a wide range of industries and to learn about different business aspects. She joined McKinsey & Company as a jumping off point.

"I never actually intended to make consulting my long-term career. It felt like a great stepping stone, but then the dot-com revolution happened in Silicon Valley, and I started writing freelance for Fortune Magazine. I wrote columns about management best practices in some of Silicon Valley's fastest growing companies, such as Cisco and Yahoo!. I grew more and more entranced with the startup world and ultimately made the leap to join a startup myself."

Nakache went to work for Shoppinglist.com and continued writing for Fortune. She interviewed a lot of venture capitalists as part of her reporting, before she joined Trinity Ventures, initially as a contractor.

"What I learned back then is that in any career, it's important to be willing to take risks and explore exciting new avenues. There was definitely risk involved in leaving my more or less stable job at Shoppinglist.com for a gig with no guarantees, but it felt like a risk worth taking. It's always a good idea to keep your eyes open for opportunities, even when you're not actively looking. This is especially salient for people who are new to a field. When you're open to do work you've never done before, you might be surprised by how much you enjoy it.

"Two years ago, I was approached about lecturing at Stanford Business School. I hadn't thought about teaching and wasn't sure whether I'd be good at it. I saw a door open and decided that it would be worth walking through it to see what was on the other side. Today, I'm so grateful for this experience. Teaching at Stanford has been even more fulfilling than I had imagined," Patricia shared.

"We hear that women don't apply for jobs or raise their hands for promotions when they think they aren't qualified enough. My encouragement to women who are interested in exploring new jobs or new levels of responsibilities is not to worry too much about whether you're completely qualified for a job. I had no experience in teaching, but I took up that challenge, and it has worked out great! The chances are that you're more qualified than you think — and more qualified than, or at least equally as qualified as, the male candidates applying for the same job."

That was encouraging advice, but I challenged Patricia with the fact that the vast majority of VC firms still prefer hiring people with investment banking or consulting experience, and an MBA, preferably from an Ivy League school.

"I'm glad you asked that question, Renata, because there are lots of different models or profiles that can work in venture capital, and I'd like to explain how we see it from the inside.

"First of all, many business schools, consulting firms and banking programs have worked aggressively to recruit female and diverse candidates, so there is an increasing number of diverse candidates with those backgrounds now. Secondly, when we conduct a search through a recruiting firm, we have to spell out specific qualifications, so that the recruiters would know what to look for. These qualifications reflect the soft and hard skills that successful investors tend to possess, and by including them, we also provide guidance to candidates, so that they don't completely waste their time applying if they're not at all a fit.

"That said, while these are our preferences, there's room for variability. Our firm recognizes that the needed skills and qualifications can be obtained through a variety of experiences. In these cases, candidates should tell us their stories and share how they've built their skill sets. Venture capital investing requires a high level of proactiveness in seeking out and approaching investment opportunities. If a candidate gives up on the job because of its description — knowing that he or she may still, in fact, be a great fit — maybe this is not the right occupation for that person after all. It never hurts to ask, and it never hurts to put yourself out there and show what you are capable of."

Nakache believes that the more female investors we have, the more female-founded companies will be funded. We discussed why the funding needle is moving too slowly, even though we see more and more female funders. We brainstormed specific steps that every single venture capitalist can take to move the needle, and agreed on the idea that I discussed with other VCs. We encourage every investment partner to allocate some time to coach and mentor at least one diverse young investment professional within a year, even if they aren't hiring.

Cindy Padnos

Founding Partner, Illuminate Ventures, United States

Cindy Padnos became a venture capitalist because she wanted to be the type of investor she had always sought as a founder. "I am a founder at heart, and nothing about that attribute changed when I launched Illuminate Ventures. As a founder you are able to set an authentic culture, to define your market strategy and differentiation, and to build a great team with shared values," she said.

Padnos had sold her enterprise software startup to a publicly traded company shortly before 9/11, and wanted to gain exposure to all that was new in the world of high tech before deciding on her next big step. Initially, she wasn't sure whether she would launch a new company or choose a different path.

Because of the turmoil in the tech sector at the time, Cindy had the opportunity to be selective in terms of both the projects and the partners that she might choose to work with. "I had a few criteria that I applied to make it a better experience for myself and for those I would collaborate with. I wanted to learn the VC business from experienced investors in parallel with working with companies where I felt my skills could positively impact their outcomes. I was fortunate to be invited to work with some top VCs who allowed me to attend their partner meetings, involved me in due diligence for new companies, and enabled me to see all sides of their investments — both successes and failures. That was an amazing learning curve."

It was the combination of this apprenticeship in addition to her broad network in the entrepreneurial and VC ecosystems and prior operational experience, that made Cindy a strong candidate to join the Outlook Ventures investing team. "When Amazon Web Services (AWS) came into the market, I saw that entrepreneurs could suddenly build an initial prototype product on a shoestring. They could literally use a credit card to pay $1 an hour for a cloud computing resource that was of a higher quality and more scalable than what entrepreneurs had historically needed — hundreds of thousands of dollars and significant time and skill set, even before they could even begin building their own unique products. I realized there was a really interesting opportunity to build a firm that would target a new set of seed- and very early-stage investments in companies that could be much more capital-efficient in their early years than in the past."

Illuminate Ventures was among only a few dozens of micro VC firms when it was formed and one of a very few firms that focused exclusively on B2B/enterprise software. The number of micro VC funds has grown to several hundred in the US alone since then, and Cindy remains a strong supporter of investing small amounts of capital into startups to help them gain product market fit prior to adding fuel to the fire with the larger capital allocations of traditional Series A financings.

"Over the long history of venture capital investing, it has been demonstrated that the first institutional investment rounds historically outperform all of the later rounds. This fact is even truer today than in the past. The pre-money valuations and round sizes at Series A and beyond continue growing astronomically as compared to seed financings. If you don't get in early, your potential for a significant outcome is diminished," she talked venture. "Of course, you have to weigh the risk/reward balance between the higher potential for failure of early-stage investments versus more significant return multiples. In recent years we've seen some interesting structural changes that help improve this balance.

"Early-stage investing has become more attractive, in part, because many startups are already somewhat "de-risked" before they go out to raise their first institutional financing. More companies than ever are able to bootstrap at early stages or raise a small amount of capital from angels, incubators and accelerators, who support them in building initial product, and potentially even gain a few customers before they seek institutional financing. They don't need to raise $3-$5 million as their first step, as my company did in the late 90s. Across our most recent portfolio, all of the companies had already gained initial customers before we invested and only one had taken a prior priced/ institutional financing round. Perhaps these factors contribute to the reason that there are fewer seed-stage rounds being done in the US than ever before.

"As for micro VCs, one significant positive thing about them is that they tend to be much more diverse than traditional VC firms in a variety of ways. For example, many of them are being formed in non-coastal areas of the US — opening up entrepreneurship in new geographies. Micro VC firms also have twice as many female partners as traditional firms and a much higher ratio of other diverse team members. Since data shows that women VCs are twice as likely to invest in a female-founded startups, that diversity at the partner level also trickles down into the entrepreneurial ecosystem as well.

"However, not everything about micro VC firms is without tradeoffs", added Padnos. "For example, with the large proliferation of new small firms, there is some risk that some will not have the wherewithal to build a firm, versus just raise 1-or 2 funds. There is a big difference between raising capital and building a sustainable franchise that will deliver value over decades. At Illuminate we've always been focused on building a firm with a strong brand, and not just raising funds. To accomplish this, beyond the capabilities of our own direct team, we leverage an entire platform of resources," Cindy stated.

When raising her first fund, Cindy wondered if she needed to have at least one other partner in order to attract institutional investors. And if that was the case, whether it would be smart to identify an experienced male teammate. As she chatted with prospective limited partners, she heard feedback that changed her perspective. They said that if Padnos brought someone onto the team with a poorer track record than her own (which was quite strong), that would not help her with fundraising. And if she brought someone on who she hadn't worked with before, everyone would worry about the team risk. They advised that she was better off starting alone, raising money from investors who were willing to back her on her own, even if that meant raising a smaller fund. "It took a big weight off my shoulders to not have to worry about that, in addition to everything else that I needed to focus on at the time," she said.

Her fundraising strategy was also somewhat unconventional. She chose to put her own capital into a handful of investments, as a first step, and then go out and raise money from investors, allowing them to buy into those original investments at their original cost.

"I wanted to show prospective limited partners the high quality of the investment opportunities that we would have access to as a firm. In order to accomplish that, I created a warehoused portfolio of investments and then allocated them into a proof-of-concept fund that we now call our Spotlight Fund. In parallel, I was raising capital for our main Illuminate Ventures I investment vehicle. We only offered access to our already well-performing Spotlight Find to those LPs that were committing to our Fund I. By the time I closed Spotlight Fund, we'd already had some nice mark-ups on some of those investments, so it was a real win-win for us and our limited partners."

Padnos likes to base her strategic decisions on hard data. For example, when she launched Illuminate she had a strong belief that investments in companies with more diverse founders would yield high performance, but she wanted to have an empirical foundation for this strategy. Through her assessment of this hypothesis, she accidentally became one of the first venture investors to study the landscape and to collect and share significant data about the impact of team diversity on venture-type investment outcomes.

"I think my soft spot for leveraging data is shaped by my early career experience in management consulting and my learnings as a student at Carnegie Mellon. I like to know what the data can reveal, as opposed to just having an opinion about something. That said, as an early stage investor, once you have the data, there is a lot of value to add from instinct, experience, and gut feel.

"I did my first research regarding female-founded tech companies in 2010, in order to better understand the baseline — how many investment opportunities were going to come from women-led companies in the next decade? Was there any difference in a woman's ability to perform as a founder versus a man? We reviewed hundreds of white papers and other research that had been conducted by major universities and corporations about women in tech in order to inform our perspective. We learned that women were just as entrepreneurial as men, that they were gaining relevant work experience, and that once financed, they were typically more capital efficient and failed less frequently than their male counterparts. This combination of findings was unexpected and had not previously been documented.

"We were claiming things that were controversial at the time — that women founders performed as well, if not better, than men when they have received investments, and that we were on the verge of a massive influx of women who had the potential to be entrepreneurial. We knew that these claims will be challenged, so we felt the need to be very data-driven. Our goal was to illustrate what many VCs were missing out on," Cindy explained her motivation.

Eight years later Cindy's expectations for women in tech were still not playing out. As a percentage of dollars committed into venture, the ratio gained by women-led companies had actually declined to 2% in 2018. As a result, Cindy began to wonder if there might be hidden barriers to the expansion of women in founder-level roles. With help from students and interns at Carnegie Mellon's Tepper School, Illuminate conducted a survey of 1,200 VCs and entrepreneurs to better identify and understand the potential obstacles.

"The most important finding that struck me, was that virtually all of the venture investors we surveyed, male and female, perceived women as facing much higher barriers to entrepreneurial success than men," Padnos shared her discovery. "We identified 16 such barriers in general, and women were facing 80% of them more often and at a higher degree than men. It really caused me to step back and realize that this perception alone might, in itself, be a huge barrier for women founders.

"Think about this for just one moment as an investor, Renata: if you see two equally interesting investment opportunities, and you believe that one of the founders is going to face much higher barriers to success than the other, which one would you invest in? Which one would you offer a better valuation? Which one would you write a bigger check to?

"This unconscious bias has an enormous potential impact. We didn't have the wherewithal to conduct a survey that covered other minority groups, but I don't doubt that they face similar investor perception bias. While this data cannot be considered good news, the fact that we can help make people aware of the risk of this bias is the first step we can take toward eliminating it.

"At Illuminate we're really proud of our portfolio that includes women in nearly half of the founding teams and where three fourths have founder diversity overall. We've accomplished this without ever using gender or diversity as an investment criteria. Instead we go out of our way to open the door wider and offer a leveled playing field to all entrepreneurs. We offer these entrepreneurs our operating experience and networks, access to our Advisory Council, and our compassion from having been in their shoes.

"Our responsibility, like the founding teams that we serve, is to not accept the status quo — but to be always looking for ways to encourage new ideas and to create an environment where innovation can thrive."

Stephanie Palmeri

Partner, Uncork Capital, United States

Stephanie Palmeri had a dynamic career before she decided to pursue venture capital. She had worked in technology consulting, marketing for big beauty brands such as Estee Lauder and Clinique, and at a startup building applications for global sales and marketing teams. When she told me how she approached the desired career switch, I thought that it could be a manual for many other people who are trying to do the same, so here is her story.

Stephanie had decided to pursue a full-time MBA with eight years of work experience up her sleeve. "I didn't get an MBA for the sake of adding another title to my resume. It was a chance for me to step back and explore where I wanted to take my meandering career in the long term, while also growing my professional network. At the same time, if I was going to step away from working full-time to pursue a degree, I felt very strongly about staying relevant and applying what I was learning in the classroom in the real world at the same time. Going to Columbia Business School afforded me the opportunity to split my time between the classroom and working in New York's emerging startup ecosystem, in both venture and operating roles."

You can't be what you can't see. Stephanie networked a lot and researched the background of investors to learn more about the leaders in the industry. "I noticed that the vast majority of the very few senior women in venture capital, had started in junior roles and worked their way to partner level within their firms, compared to the many examples of men who had joined firms in partner roles with no prior investing experience, having been either operators or entrepreneurs. In this male-dominated industry, it seemed pretty clear to me that prior investing experience was a requirement for female partners, but not necessarily for male partners. This disparity made me more determined to give landing a post-MBA role at a VC firm a shot. I was determined to get real experience as an investor, even if I ended up spending more time again as an operator of one of the portfolio startups," Stephanie revealed her findings.

"Through a chain of introductions, I got connected to my now partner Jeff Clavier of Uncork Capital [SoftTech VC at the time]. There was no official job opening — much like in many other VC firms I had talked to, however, he wrote me a very thoughtful note with some advice about doing venture investing 'later' in my career. I wrote back to him and shared why I was interested in this job in my current stage of professional development, and mentioned that I was open to both investing and operating roles. I said, 'I'm going to be in Silicon Valley, so if you'd like to meet and talk about startups, I'd love to do that.'"

Palmeri moved to the Bay Area with two suitcases and no job leads, with the goal of putting her name out there and expanding her network node by node. "I met with Jeff, thinking that he might help me connect with some interesting startups, as I was just starting to settle in the Bay Area. Four days later, I came back to his office where he said, 'You're not going to take my advice,' which was to do venture capital later in life. 'So here's what you're gonna do. You're gonna work for me for the next eight weeks and prove that we need someone to hire and that you're the right person for this job. And maybe then I'll hire you.' I started that afternoon, and a little over a month in, I had a full-time offer to join the team.

"On the surface, it might sound like I landed a job in a matter of days. In reality, I had done an awful lot of work to get to the point where, when the opportunity was in front of me, I was able to capture it. While I met Jeff through an acquaintance, who happened to be one of Uncork's investors, we had many connections in common. Sometime between getting connected and our second meeting, Jeff reached out to several folks who could speak to my work ethic, my ambition, and my potential as an investor. Ultimately, I was in the right place at the right time, but I also capitalized on an opportunity that I'd been preparing for.

"I started my journey into venture capital a decade ago. While my path to becoming a Partner through 'growing up' in a firm was similar to many other women who came into the industry before me, I'm encouraged to see that more and more firms are opening the doors to senior women with operating backgrounds straight to partner positions. However, we are still deeply under-represented in the industry at all investment levels. I really believe there are a number of things we can do to accelerate the process of getting more women into investing roles at all levels," Palmeri went straight to offering measures to improve the industry.

"One of the first to-do's on the list is to provide more visibility for jobs in VC, particularly for partner track jobs that lead to check writing roles. Oftentimes, those jobs are shared through personal networks, to which women and underrepresented candidates have less access.

"The second thing is to shine a spotlight on the great work being done by as many female investors as possible — not just a small subset. There are plenty of smart, talented women investing from early stage through growth, in life sciences, consumer, enterprise tech, hardware, robotics — you name it. The more stories we tell, the less it will be an anomaly to see a woman in VC and the more women will be inspired to pursue investing. Your book is a great example of that work, Renata.

"Finally, the third thing is to involve more women in startups as founders, early employees, and executives. Exposure to startup operations is a great way for women to get hands-on experiences in the challenge of building and scaling companies, and to build a strong professional network of future founders to back when they transition to an investment role."

Kimmy Paluch

Founding Partner, Beta Boom, United States

If you read books diagonally for the sake of speed, you'll feel that Kimmy's opinions echo what many other women featured in this book express. However, if you read it attentively word for word, you'll see that she explains her perspective in a way that only diverse people can. We may all be pursuing the same goals, but it takes courage to see that even among women, there is a diversity of opinions and perspectives, and without people like Paluch, we may be less effective in solving diversity issues than we think we are.

"Diversity cannot be achieved when minorities and majorities are opponents, but it can be achieved by bringing them all together. Our fund is purposefully not exclusive to underrepresented founders — we invest in entrepreneurs who create impactful products or businesses that address underserved needs. That means that we willingly back Caucasian founders as well. It's by bringing different perspectives together, that we will have a transfer of thoughts and an exchange of experiences. This is what will push us all forward," Kimmy started telling me where she stands.

"Right now, I feel that only truly underestimated and underrepresented people put their money where their mouths are. The majority of investors — both male and female — are mainly focused on checking the boxes. I feel like the status quo is doing nothing behind slogans and aggressive publicity, and that's what frustrates me. There are a few allies — I don't want to say that they are non-existent — but we need more partnerships that help new people pave their way into the industry. Because promoting people who are already in there, doesn't make the change we're talking about — it's just window dressing.

"I went to a conference recently where they were trying to show first-time fund managers how the fundraising process works, because it's a black box for most of us. All the people who were on stage, were white men. I am thankful that they found time to do that at all, but how should I feel when I see that there is no one like me on the stage? If there is no diversity on their team to showcase at an event that is supposed to increase diversity, in front of a diverse audience, what are the odds that I will get funded by these guys?

"There's a lot of room for improvement. Conversation matters, but it all goes back to the core where representation matters more. I think we need to highlight people who are doing things differently. Arlan Hamilton has been at the forefront of underrepresented general partners — she is the one who's fighting for the same kinds of people. There are many more stories like this, that aren't big enough for major media outlets, so we barely know about them. But if we heard more of those stories, they'd stop being anomalies, they'd unavoidably draw the attention of institutional investors, and change the ratio. That would make a difference. Fresh, unbiased, and diverse minds among general partners, limited partners, founders, and other players are able to discern things that may not be seen otherwise.

"I think we need to approach the diversity issue in venture capital and startup worlds the same way that you're building your book: looking through all the verticals, making sure that first-time investors are involved as much as seasoned venture capitalists, considering all the geographies, ensuring that people of diverse ethnicities, backgrounds and experiences are included, and of course, inviting male counterparts to the conversation," Paluch concluded.

An undergraduate in computer science, Kimmy started her career by looking for a job in software companies in the Bay Area, only to find out that people were not as open to hiring black women as they are now. "I didn't want to admit that in the beginning," she said. Paluch nevertheless carved her path into tech and worked in a variety of roles. "User experience design was a fairly new field back then, so I threw myself into that and started building my expertise in it to start my own innovation consulting firm later. I was building innovative products with a lot of startups and corporations, trying to create them and bring them to market, and got an MBA later to add strategic consulting to the mix and help my clients grow beyond just the product line."

Her way into venture capital was quite unorthodox. In 2015-2016, she realized that women and minorities have to fight harder battles in everything, and in the venture capital world, in particular. "I began to wonder what would happen if I was a part of the change that everyone had started talking about. It was just a thought, until I stumbled upon an opportunity to become a venture fellow at a venture capital firm without having to abandon my current career. I immediately fell in love with venture investing, and wanted to do that.

"I realized that there were many more opportunities for early-stage investors outside of Silicon Valley, somewhere where we could help an ecosystem grow and provide local entrepreneurs with access to capital.

"In the beginning of 2018, my husband and I, our kids, and our dog, came to Salt Lake City," Kimmy continued. "We drove around, spoke to entrepreneurs, met with municipal economic development groups, and we loved it! There was so much happening in Salt Lake City, but the recurring theme that struck me was the same: diverse and female founders were left behind in the tech startup space, in terms of funding, partnerships, and even access to mentorship. So we realized that there was a wide gap there that we could help to close.

"We confirmed our assumption, that there was less seed capital available in Salt Lake City, as well as other rising cities like Atlanta and Chicago, which also fell into our area of interest. We wanted to be one of the most recognizable players in the field, rather than one of hundreds, like in the Bay Area. We wanted to work with city authorities and other critical actors of the ecosystem, while on the coasts, all seats at the table had been already taken.

"On that trip, late at night, my husband and I made a decision that we were going to do that — to start investing in startups, raise our own fund, and become a global player. In a matter of three months, we renovated and sold our house in California and moved to Salt Lake City. We used part of that capital to launch Beta Boom, and started investing in startups through a cohort model in June 2018.

"We're now raising our first fund, and I am very encouraged by the response we have received. Our investment thesis and what we're trying to do, resonates with the potential investors we talk to, and many of them recognize that it is important to invest in entrepreneurs, regardless of the state they live in, regardless of what they look like. It has been quite a journey, we have learned a lot, and I'm excited to start backing startups from our new fund. It's such an amazing challenge to work with so many brilliant underrepresented founders who really just need to be given a chance."

For most of this path, Kimmy has walked side-by-side with her husband, Sergio Paluch. She met him in college, they started the consulting firm together, and did that for more than 12 years. "We have both been in the startup world for quite a bit, and I don't know which of us is crazier! It might be a kind of race to the bottom on that one," she laughed. "I think we've always been very impulsive and following what we want to accomplish by any means."

Her husband is an immigrant from Communist Poland and heavily believes in power of diverse people, women, and immigrants, because he knows first-hand how to achieve more with less. Aside from physics, he also studied development economics — economics of the poor — and decided against going to academia, instead choosing to create an impact through innovation rather than research.

"Sergio has a background in physics and thinks a lot in systems. In many ways, he encouraged me to do the craziest things in my life. I remember when I had that moment of dreaming about starting investing, he was pushing me in that direction," Kimmy added.

The Paluchs don't take their diversity for granted. She says that they are proactively looking for diverse entrepreneurs, and don't rely on the possibility that they will find Beta Boom on the internet and knock on their door.

"Our office is in Lehi, Utah — one the least diverse cities in the United States — yet, we have invested in black founders there. So I think it's easy for investors to convince themselves that there are no diverse entrepreneurs in the pipeline, because they decided to opt out of raising venture capital, or that their firm is located in a very homogenous place, or whatever other excuse they feel comfortable with. However, I am sure that the core issue is none of these.

"I've heard many founders say that they feel like they are begging for an opportunity to be taken seriously and not be treated as charity cases. Diverse founders have been disenfranchised for a long time, so today, we need to actually work to attract them. We need to go out there, find them, and show that we are listening and hearing them wherever they are. It would require investors to leave their comfortable offices and work in the field, but that's the only right way to get those diverse founders they claim to be looking for, in the pipeline."

Beta Boom invests in the pre-seed stage, but Paluch is aware that tech companies stay private longer, and it may be challenging for such early-stage investors to maintain a reasonable share in portfolio companies. Although many investors like her would turn to the secondary market, she is more mindful about the issue. "I'm committing to the entrepreneurs when I invest in them, and see this as a long-term partnership. We work very closely with our founders to help them scale up their operations as they go, so I'm in it for a longer haul. I think it's kind of short-sighted to try and get out earlier, and although I know that some limited partners would prefer to get liquidity sooner, that's not what we're focused on.

"We aren't the only ones who don't want to play classic rules. There are some new models that are coming out in venture investing, where investors are looking at revenue share and other ways, rather than just playing a zero sum game. But a very large part of venture capital is going to continue to rely on the traditional large exits. So I don't think that the venture capital model will change entirely — more than likely, we'll see a blend of the two."

Shelly Porges

Founder,
The Billion Dollar Fund for Women,
United States

Although this book features, by design, only those women who make investment decisions at their VC firms, I made a couple of exceptions due to a critical role that some other women play in the industry. Shelly Porges is one of such exceptions for her initiative, The Billion Dollar Fund for Women, which organizes venture capitalists into another powerful group worldwide. Since one of the goals I set for this book is networking, I thought that many women who venture will benefit from learning about this initiative from it.

Shelly Porges started her first business at the age of 37, after she had dedicated more than a decade to a corporate career. She then sold her company and went on to found or co-found and exit five others. Porges then got involved in Hillary Clinton's Presidential campaign, launching a fundraising effort called Entrepreneurs for Hillary, which mobilized tens of thousands of entrepreneurs all over the country. Shelly has a lot of stories to tell, but for this book, we only focused on The Billion Dollar Fund for Women, a pledge initiative, which aims to mobilize capital to fund female entrepreneurs and general partners.

"When I dug into the different statistics showing the distribution of venture capital funding among male and female entrepreneurs, I was shocked! I was caught up by the lack of fundraising progress that women were making, even when they were innovating across every sector, had their PhDs and MDs, were getting traction, and so on and so forth. I realized that we had to change the way things work. Women end up with the crumbs at the bottom of the pyramid, when there are trillions of dollars out there in both institutional and private capital markets," Shelly was very expressive talking about the numbers.

"I started conceiving of a model that would create a flow of capital from institutional investors who are interested in gender diversity, into the VC firms that would invest in female entrepreneurs. I couldn't wrap my mind around the fact that investors entirely disregard the compelling statistics on the consumption of female-focused products, on women's purchasing power, and finally, on the amount of wealth being handed to the next generation, of which women are expected to be the primary beneficiaries in years to come.

"Then, I learned that the World Bank was looking for a partner initiative that would address one of the 17 Sustainable Development Goals — gender equality. I immediately started thinking if I knew anyone who I could invite to become this partner. But the more I thought about it, the more I felt that presenting at the World Bank meeting would be a great opportunity to promote venture funds who would pledge to invest more into female-founded companies.

"I knew that to match the scale at which The Bank operates, we needed to speak in large numbers, so I called the initiative The Billion Dollar Fund for Women. In August 2018, I presented the idea to the host of the Finance Forum where it would be announced, and she loved it! We said that we would come with the first $100 million pledged by October, when the Forum was scheduled. At least, that was what we hoped for. We had no idea if that was even possible, and I began wondering whether we could really do even that," Porges divulged.

"By the due date, we ended up having mobilized over $460 million in pledges! Believe me, no one was more amazed by this number than I was," she laughed. "When I started going out there and asking venture capital firms for pledges, everyone was so receptive to the idea, that I couldn't have been happier!

"Since that initial amount of pledges of $460 million, we're now at over $700 million, and we have quite a lot of VC firms in the pipeline — funds of all sizes, from micro VCs to billion-dollar funds. So we do certainly expect to get to our goal amount by our one-year anniversary.

"Our intention is to create positive momentum and inspire concrete action among both general and limited partners. We want to catalyze the change and get out of this place where I felt we were stuck without seeing much forward movement. For that, we developed a two-part model.

"Firstly, this pledge provides an added incentive to encourage VC firms to consistently build a deal flow of female-founded companies. Although the pledges aren't legally binding, they are a benchmark that we, as a community, agreed upon. Secondly, we connect the general partners of the VC firms that pledged, with institutional investors. By bringing limited partners to the table, we can drive more capital into these funds, and this is how we are going to advance this cycle and keep the wheel turning," she continued describing their model.

"We connect general partners with institutional investors who are looking to gender diversify their portfolios, at our regular event — The Billion Dollar Breakfast. We have been fortunate in having attracted notable high-net-worth individuals, investment banks, and family offices, who express a lot of interest in what we are doing. I am very encouraged by the response that we're getting from both sides of the table! And we're just getting started — we're only 6 months old.

"I cannot stress enough that we reach out to VC firms, regardless of whether they have female investment partners or a gender lens investment focus. For a catalytic effect to happen, we cannot wait until we have enough female VCs to materially change the amount of funding for female entrepreneurs — it'll take too long, unfortunately. We work with both female and male investors, who understand that when you invest in women, you're in good company!"

Archana Priyadarshini

Partner, Unicorn India Ventures, India

Archana Priyadarshini is a very rare kind of person. Not only is she a female venture capitalist, and an immigrant who came to work in the United States and held senior positions in the financial industry, but she also decided to move back to India and start everything all over. Being a woman in venture capital in India was the least of her concerns. What she also had to deal with, was being the wife of a very successful entrepreneur.

A computer science graduate, she worked in the US for consulting companies like Price Waterhouse and Capgemini, and joined Wells Fargo as a Vice President later on. She moved back to India when her husband launched a startup there, and started working in corporate business. When she decided to take the plunge into entrepreneurship herself, she built a chain of fitness centers that became hugely successful. She grew the network by reinvesting the profits, but something didn't feel right. She sold it after five years of growth, for two reasons.

"I didn't feel that I was growing myself. I am a tech person, and a business that doesn't involve tech becomes boring to me. I needed mental stimulation, which I couldn't find in that business," she explained. "The second reason was my incorrect approach to its growth. I was scaling in a traditional way by using my own capital. I knew that it had a greater potential, but my mindset at the time didn't allow me to take risks. This was how I realized that venture investing was something that could help me change my mindset.

"I started investing my exit money as an angel investor, but I soon realized that to be more involved with the portfolio companies and be a part of their journeys, one needs to sign larger checks. It works both ways in venture investing — you learn from unproven business models created by a new generation, while also adding value as an experienced corporate person.

"I set up a VC firm and even subscribed several investors to my fund. Although some of the investors I approached were sceptical of me as a woman, what bothered me much more, was that they saw me as 'the wife of that guy'. The startup that my husband launched, when I moved back to India, took off in a very big way. He had a big exit and became a very successful entrepreneur in the country. He then started his second company, which is also doing very well, and is almost a 'unicorn' now.

"Once people I talked to knew that I was his wife, their whole tone changed. I tried to hide it for as long as I could, but it always popped up at a certain point in conversations. I wanted them to take me for who I was, and to recognize my own qualifications and capabilities, but that was not what was happening," she confessed.

"Then, I realized that I needed to have a partner who would take some of the attention away from me. I started looking at other VC firms and proactively contacting them. I was eager to bring the capital commitments I had for my own fund to theirs. However, it wasn't easy to find VCs who appreciated me separately from my husband's achievements either. I didn't want to be invited to join a partnership just because my husband was a success story. The team of Unicorn India Ventures turned out to be much more mature than many others I encountered. I felt that I could work with them and that they wouldn't be introducing me as the wife of my husband."

Archana's story is something we don't hear often, but women are being judged by their husbands' wealth in many countries. That is a good case study I was lucky to have in my book.

If there is a new market where venture capital money can flow to, it is India. I was really curious about the local venture capital community and the entrepreneurship ecosystem, and Archana was very realistic when describing it.

"When the Indian startup trend had just started, back in 2000-2003, venture capital money was not there. Very soon, however, a few companies showed skyrocketing growth, and we saw that angel investments brought impressive returns within just 3-5 years. God, that changed the mindset! Suddenly we started seeing a lot of money going into angel investing. Everybody who had money was writing $10,000-20,000 checks just like that," said Archana.

"Women in VC is a very touchy thing in every country. Even entrepreneurs sometimes question whether women are able to understand technical details. Using the same yardstick that is applied to men, women probably need to be more qualified than men are, but once we get into venture capital, the gender bias tends to fade away. For that reason, and also because there aren't many women in venture capital in India — probably a dozen — we don't have any sort of a movement of women in VC yet. We meet and talk to each other as often as our business may require, but not more often than we would meet with male colleagues. There just isn't much that can be done now by women in venture capital. I think we'll see more women VCs and more activities in the future."

Renata Quintini

Partner, Lux Capital, United States

Aside from sharing a name with Renata Quintini, I also have a thing for the legal profession, which Renata started her career in, and I really appreciated her manner of speaking in great detail. She patiently explained each and every of her opinions — the kind of talk that lawyers do well.

Renata Quintini came to the United States from Rio de Janeiro, Brazil, with a law degree up her sleeve. She started her career in the US as a tech M&A attorney, and also had a stint at JPMorgan's Tech, Media and Telecom group, where she focused on consumer internet companies. By the time she got into Stanford Business School, she knew that she wanted to work in venture capital.

"I'm very persistent, but I wouldn't be here without a lot of luck and being in the right place, at the right time. The dots connected," Renata started our conversation. "I had a very clear idea of what I wanted to become, so I focused on how I could make that transition into venture capital happen. Then I realized that Stanford's endowment had backed many of the best venture capital firms, and I thought: 'They should know a thing or two about venture capital, and maybe there's something that I can learn there.' I found a way to get introduced to the then CEO of the Stanford endowment, John Powers.

"Serendipity struck and John became my mentor and highly influenced my career. What started as an MBA project (I worked under the supervision of two professors analyzing the endowment's liquidity profile — super timely, given it was 2007) turned into a full-time job offer. At the end of the project, the CEO said, 'Why don't you stop interviewing at other companies and just stay here with us?' And I did.

"During that time, I was trying to really understand and practice what it meant to be an early-stage VC and a later-stage VC. I knew the textbook definition of it, but I had no good, direct exposure to it. So that was the question that I was trying to answer for myself.

"It was really a one-of-a-kind experience to be in a place where every fund that was raising money came to talk to you, and you had access to these incredible people, and amazing data on their performance and their portfolios. I don't think there's a better institutional venture portfolio in the world, potentially," Renata concluded. And it was also a perfect time to be in that role, since the venture capital landscape was transitioning drastically in 2007-2010: new great franchises were emerging."

Obviously, I couldn't help but ask what Stanford's endowment looked for in a fund manager during the vetting process. "At the end of the day, it's all about delivering returns consistently," Renata replied. "Institutional investors hear a lot of stories and opportunities that make sense today, but they can't fast-forward 10 years from now and see how they'll evolve. Although, it's a common perception that LPs are locking themselves up for at least a 10-year commitment on one fund they invest in, in reality, oftentimes, it's more than a one-fund commitment. By the time the same general managers come back to raise their second fund, there hasn't been enough time for LPs to actually see the returns yet, so in most cases, they have to think about the odds of this particular team delivering over two decades, as well as whether this team is who they want to be in business with for many years to come.

"If there is no track record, limited partners don't have a lot to draw from, and are really going after the belief. An emerging manager needs to convince potential LPs that he or she really sees a differentiated opportunity, and will be able to make the right decisions as the landscape evolves. Those are never easy or simple conversations.

"Venture investors are expected to have a point of view and be ready to back ideas with capital — this is why we're in business. So I would encourage aspiring investors to really have an investment thesis or an outlook on the world around what is valuable now, or where valuable things are going to be created. You have to tell the story of why you need to exist as a firm and what your point of view is — an investment thesis that justifies why people should give you money. Very often, it stems from the GP's access to networks and people doing interesting things, which is another important differentiator for limited partners."

I was, of course, curious as to how many female general partners pitched Renata back then, and it took her a minute to answer. I thought she was counting, but she said, "I can think of one..."

Renata then continued, "Emotional quotient is equally as important as intellectual quotient for a venture investor, and I think women are naturally great on this front. Not only are we good team players, but also game leaders in a cohesive setting. I think women are very intuitive about feeling out the mood in a room, and calling out BS nonsense. We can joke all along about the sixth sense or a special nose for it, but in our business, it really matters. We can feel things, such as what exactly drives the founder, what the team dynamics are, and what might happen next. Women are just a lot more attuned to that in a natural way, and that's really valuable.

"I think we are in a great position today to increase diversity, because more and more people are aligned with it. General partners want to make money for their LPs, entrepreneurs start targeting and serving diverse groups of customers, and are genuinely interested in making their teams diverse as well. Everybody agrees that women control the purchasing power of the household and make many important decisions on behalf of the entire family. I see people finally saying, 'Listen, we're leaving money on the table by not making investment teams or decisions more diverse'. When buyers' opinions come into play, these things resonate with decision-makers. And I think it's a wonderful time to capitalize on this."

At that point, it was time to ask Renata about her own experience in fundraising, as she had been a partner with two firms so far — Felicis Ventures and Lux Capital.

"First of all, I don't think about whether my gender helps or doesn't help me to do this or that. When I was five years old, I started fighting karate. I was in one group with boys, fighting them equally as hard as with other girls, and I learned how to just roll with it. I grew up in a different country, I had a different career, and there was so much going differently for me, that if I added one more challenge when I was fundraising, I couldn't function," said the three-time Brazilian teen karate champion with a black belt.

"Raising a venture fund is always hard, and I never let it get into my head that there was an extra hurdle because of my gender. What was in my head instead, was the main message I wanted to deliver to investors: 'We're trying to build something new, and something different here. Let me explain why it matters.' At the end of the day, you want to work with people who understand your values and believe in the same things that you do, which turned out to be my case. As a general partner, you need to find investors who understand who you are as a person, as an investor, what you believe in, and what your values are. If they're happy with that and proud to back you, that is what you're going after. Otherwise, they'll find a reason to justify their 'no', whether it's your gender or anything else — the reason doesn't matter at that point.

"I think that when in doubt, people should take a step back and try to understand what their unique perspectives are, and what they bring to the table. Your gender doesn't define you, but it's a part of who you are. Use that to inform the way you think about investment, or the way that you approach things. That's, I think, a different nuance. So instead of focusing on: 'Oh my God, I am a female, Brazilian, ex-lawyer, whatnot,' I focused on: 'What do I need to succeed?'"

'What do female entrepreneurs need to succeed?' I asked.

"That is only one part of the question. Because the other part of it is: how do we get more women to start, in the first place? Those are different parts of the problem," Renata corrected the narrative and I appreciated her clarity of thought again. "I think that women are extremely scrappy, gritty, and resourceful. There are studies that show that women are more likely to bootstrap their companies or use other ways of financing, rather than venture capital. Because women are so used to bootstrapping, sometimes I see them raising small rounds or asking for the least amount that they need, in order to get by, instead of really thinking big and swinging for the fences, in a way. It's critical to think big, not being afraid to ask for what you want, instead of the minimum that you need to survive.

"The other important thing is to really understand what the other pieces are that you need to have, to be successful. I find that so many people are so focused on the near term of getting started or solving the problem that is in front of them, that they don't have the time or latitude to think about the ultimate goals and opportunities to go really big.

"And then, the third one is finding a way to actually explain why the problem you are solving is important. Especially if you're dealing with people who don't understand the problem — how do you actually make them care about what you are doing; how can you make it interesting to them? The straight way of doing it is to use numbers and metrics, be objective with revenues, and compare what you're trying to do to other businesses and other areas that have been successful. By making that proxy, you can show that you are as good as, or better than, some other company that that person who doesn't understand your business, is familiar with.

"There are many misconceptions about technology. The tech industry boasts about its ability to disrupt everything, including other industries, complex systems and processes. Many scientists and engineers build things because they can, without asking whether they should, or what the long-term effects will be. We need to ask the tough questions ahead of time, discuss them openly, and preemptively address potential impacts. Often we find that unintended consequences come down to a lack of diversity in experience, perspectives, and values. The combination of IQ and EQ is becoming more critical, and this is where more female entrepreneurs can really make a difference," Renata looked beyond our immediate challenges.

Katie Rae

Managing Partner, The Engine, United States

Katie Rae's venture capital fund, The Engine, is an independent offshoot of the Massachusetts Institute of Technology (MIT) — the university known all over the world as a hotbed for innovations — that wants to help founders make their potentially world-changing ideas a reality. She invests in 'tough tech' — startups whose products require years of research and development before they're ready; startups that many other venture capitalists avoid because they require more time to get off the ground than the typical photo app, and more time to pay off, if ever. Katie is another great example of how STEM education can make people better investors: schooled in biology, she has been successfully investing in all kinds of tech, except for life science.

"I'm a generalist, which means I use my general knowledge to understand if this is the right technology for the business we want to create," she addressed my question about the relevance of her education to venture investing. "I have to be able to dive into any technology, to understand the people and the business. When it comes to the due diligence of a suggested solution, I always find people who understand the technology behind it extraordinarily well.

"The job of venture capitalists is figuring out the trends and making the best decisions we can, with the information we have. While it may be helpful to be an expert in a field you're investing in, if your investment focus is broader than just one specific field, it's pretty difficult to catch up on all the new technologies in these fields by yourself. That is why the best VC firms have large networks of experts who can do the appropriate due diligence of a technology."

Katie was indeed correct. The best overall and industry-adjusted performance is associated with more generalist venture capital firms (albeit, only if they are mature enough). Kleiner Perkins, one of the leading venture capital firms, is a generalist firm comprised largely of generalists such as John Doerr, who has made investments in the internet (Amazon, Google), computer software (Intuit), and computer hardware (Sun Microsystems). The same goes for Sequoia Capital. Some generalist VC firms are comprised of venture capitalists who are themselves generalists, while others are comprised of a diversified group of industry specialists. Having a team of PhDs available at any time, Rae proves the findings by her own example.

From a pretty young age, Katie wanted to be a doctor. She ended up studying biology at college, and loved it and all the sciences. When she graduated, she felt very drawn to mission-focused organizations that create a change in the world. She went on a journey of doing different things, all of which were part of a big mission at heart. She applied to medical school while working part-time for an organization developing policies for better living conditions and education for kids, and the rest of the time, she worked in an emergency room (ER).

One night, when she was working in the ER, and thinking about changing the system, so that more people could live stable lives, and also planning her future at med school, a big car accident happened, and one of the victims who was brought to the ER, died. Doctors decided that it would be Katie who had to tell the family of the deceased about his death. "I realized at that moment that this wasn't my calling. I didn't want to watch people die. I didn't want to become a doctor anymore," Rae recalled.

"I started asking myself what I wanted to do. My passion for meaningful change sent me down the path of developing businesses that create jobs. I ended up going to business school, very naively thinking that I was going to figure out how to create businesses."

Yale School of Management immediately sank Katie into a whirlpool of scientists, investors, and technologies of all kinds. She started one business with two amazing PhDs in computer science, which was the launchpad for her next 15 years in product development and management. "I loved to help people start companies, which brought me to my next career turn, when I started learning how to invest in those companies," she recounted.

Katie then joined Microsoft Startup Labs to develop internal innovation. She was helping create startups inside the corporation by using the same tools and methodologies as if they were stand-alone companies. Her team proposed to the senior leadership team at Microsoft, to actually create a corporate venture fund, because that might be a more effective way of bringing innovation inside, but the proposal was turned down.

When Rae left Microsoft, she started to invest individually as an angel investor. "The only way I know how to learn something is to actually do it. I took some of the money I had and started making angel investments. I was chatting with Brad Feld, founder of the TechStars accelerator, who I had met at Microsoft when hosting TechStars' demo days, and learned that they were planning to do a leadership change at the Boston TechStars program, which was just their second program. I thought that maybe I should throw my hat in the ring for that position, and they hired me. I ran, certainly, one of the most successful programs TechStars has ever had in terms of returns, and I stayed with them for almost four years."

With quite a handful of experience and great connections, Katie Rae could join almost any established VC firm — or so I assumed. "I don't think that's true," she sighed in response. "If you look at what has happened in venture capital, very few women have been invited to actually be equal partners. The intention is definitely there, but we've been seeing changes happening only over the last couple of years. Most women who want to actually have a seat at the table, gotta go and establish their own funds.

"Besides this objective challenge, I also knew what I was doing, and wanted to run my own firm. My thesis for the first fund was that we were like TechStars, but we were planning to be even more deeply involved with portfolio companies, taking a more active role and a larger ownership share. But along the way, I also realized that I was more interested in the deep technology startups, which were pretty common here in Boston. I knew that there were a lot of very rich opportunities in this local market and wanted to stick to it, to be more efficient, working side by side with entrepreneurs. I like investing locally, and I think Boston is pretty overlooked at this stage," she said.

When we were discussing the fundraising process, Katie mentioned that, like many other investors who I have interviewed for the book, she didn't have time to think about gender bias at that point. "All I could think of was how to get to 'yes'. Fundraising is a sales process, so all you should really focus on is getting to a 'yes'. If it's an immediate 'no' or 'if' — you're done, move on. The 'maybes' can take a lot of time. So you want to hear that 'yes' as early as possible, in order to advance faster.

"Fundraising for the first fund is always hard, but I had made a bunch of returns to other people by that point of time, and had helped dozens of entrepreneurs to achieve success, so I had a really good track record. I'm sure there was bias when I was fundraising, but what could I do? I was doing what I had to, and it served me well.

"When you're raising from high-net-worth individuals and family offices, you need to figure out their network and get to the right people to convince them. It's never simple and takes a lot of commitment and a lot of sacrifices."

Katie's advice to aspiring VCs was crystal clear."Help entrepreneurs. That is the only thing that truly matters, and that is how you build your reputation to get into the best deals. Roll up your sleeves, make phone calls, and work your butt off for the founders. Whether you have a piece of the company or you don't, it doesn't matter. You start to really do the venture capital job, and the rewards will come from that."

However, what I appreciate most is that Rae is very proactive as a senior player in the field. Not only did she speak about the things that experienced investors could do to bring new names into the industry, she has also done some herself. "Earlier this year, I ran a first of its kind conference called 'Equity Summit'. I teamed up with Mar Hershenson from Pear VC, and Trae Vassallo from Defy, to gather the best LPs in the world with the best female venture capitalists, in one room. Business happens when people know each other, so it's all about relationships. And that's my approach to everything: I create formats where people meet and get to know each other, and more dollars flow between them. Whether it's a big event or just one intro, this is what venture capitalists can easily do to make a change," she affirmed.

We then talked about the numbers. Katie shared that she didn't agree with the figures of 7-11% of female VCs in the United States, which had been circulating in the media. She estimated that to be more like 5%, which I confirmed from the findings of our think tank, Women.VC. This difference is easily explained by the fact that all surveys out there only assess a limited number of venture capital firms. Whether they make their pick based on the volume of assets under management, or fund performances, or membership with certain organizations, the findings only reflect the state of things in a certain group of VC firms in the US. At Women.VC, we include all of the VC firms in the country, even the smallest micro VCs, which brings us to the significantly larger number of all the funds scanned — more than 1,600, as a matter of fact — which, in its turn, shows that there are far fewer women in investment positions than we can see among the most known VC firms.

Rae suggested a very simple and measurable approach to increasing the number of diverse investment partners in venture capital. "I think about it in this way: how do we double the current number and continue to do so? How do we get from 5% of women VCs to 10%? From 10% to 20%? From 20% to 40%? We can get from 5% to 10% pretty fast if every venture capital firm today commits to 50% of their next hires being women. But to get higher than that, we need to have more women starting shops and running them. They are going to hire other women, because it's going to be a culture that they understand," Katie shared a simple formula that we can all apply.

"I know that women simply don't apply for VC jobs, because they either don't feel welcome in the industry, or they just don't have the network to access these jobs. We hear plenty of unpleasant stories in the media, and keep seeing a lot of dudes on the news along with that, right? So many women think, 'Why would I want to deal with that?'

"That said, most of my male friends who run VC firms, are making serious efforts to hire women and other diverse candidates at the associate and principal levels, or sometimes, even at the partner level, in a way that I've never seen before. I do think we're going to make some inroads. I'm very hopeful."

Talia Rafaeli

Head of Israel, Porsche Digital, Israel

Talia Rafaeli grew up as a competitive tennis player. Being an athlete is an evident distinction of many of the investors that I've interviewed for this book, but how is sports related to venture investing from her perspective?

Talia intelligently addressed the connection between athletes and venture investors. "I don't think that competition defines me, but the whole dealmaking business is a competitive field to be in. You have to have the endurance, which is best trained by sports. You need to keep your eyes on the goal and not give up when things get hard, because things tend to always get hard. You need to be comfortable with speaking to entrepreneurs and telling them your compelling story, which makes you stand out among all other investors. Venture capital is a seller's market today — not buyer's. Most good companies have numerous term sheets being thrown at them from different VC firms, so you really have to be competitive to win the best deals on both a personal front and the firm's front.

"Growing up, I wasn't an overachiever. I never had to work really hard in school to get decent grades, but when I went to university, I actually got a little slap in the face for the first time that showed me that life was not always going to be easy. I wanted to become a doctor, but I failed genetics. That was the first time that I had failed at doing anything, and I took that really hard because I had never failed before. At that moment, I decided that I wasn't meant to be a doctor, which I sometimes still regret," Talia admitted.

"This experience set me on a path to determine who I would like to become. I started looking at different areas to study. I was good at science and math, but I had no idea what I wanted to do with it. I went from international politics to psychology, to sociology, I ended up in the financial field and graduated with a degree in computer science and economics," she added.

Born in the United States, Talia later moved to Israel with her parents after getting all her degrees in the US and Europe, and was lured to work at a local investment bank. That happened right before the dot-com bubble burst in the late '90s, and Talia stayed with the company until it dissolved as a result of the crisis. She then joined Accenture as an IT consultant, but soon had a chance to move back to the United States with her husband, who relocated there for a job. "I said, 'Okay, if I'm going to New York City, I want to go back into banking, and I want to work at the greatest bank. I want to be in the middle of Wall Street and have it all! I joined Goldman Sachs and also received an MBA in the meantime. When I finished school, I joined Barclays to work in tech banking as well, but this time in London. My husband and I were doing a little bit of back and forth, as he stayed and worked in New York at the time, but I found myself in the middle of another stock market crisis in 2008. We then decided to move back to Israel with my first newborn, where I immersed myself in the venture capital industry.

"My story of starting as an investment banker and becoming a VC may sound boring, but there were so many inconsistencies, ups and downs along the way, and even insecurities, that I sometimes felt that I had no idea about what I was doing or where I was going," Talia shared.

When she returned to Israel, nobody was hiring after the crisis, so after spending a year doing some freelance advisory and consulting work, she had to reconsider what to do. She decided to use all her banking and business experience to help startups raise capital. Everyone was having a hard time fundraising, so she contacted startups and venture capital firms to help them.

"I basically founded my own advisory firm, joined forces with two other people who were doing the same thing, and the three of us would take Israeli startups on road shows around the world to showcase them in Paris, Singapore, Chicago, New York, and wherever else we decided to go.

"It was a very interesting and enriching experience, and I built a great network, but it was not a sustainable business model for me. I then joined one of Israel's first VC funds called Gemini, which was created by the government in the early '90s and started the venture capital industry here as we know it. I learned a lot about new industries and became part of the VC network. I attended really interesting conferences all over the world and fell in love with the industry and my venture capital job. I knew at that moment that I had found my sweet spot — my true calling where I could work on a number of projects and use both my technical and financial skills. It was definitely much more interesting than investment banking!

"Later, I joined a small VC firm, where just four of us shared all responsibilities equally. I saw the other side of the venture capital business when I was also helping the partners with fundraising. So, I pretty much managed to get a 360-degree view of the venture capital business."

Over the course of her career, Talia had the privilege of working on several automotive deals in Israel, which she found compelling. This led her to the corporate venture arm of Porsche, known as Porsche Digital, which she recently joined as an investment director. Having seen it all, she shared many insights about Israel's venture capital industry.

"I'm sure you know, Renata, that the military plays a significant role in Israel, and almost everything related to technology is linked to the military in one way or another. So is networking! In the United States, you see clusters of people formed around universities or companies, such as Stanford graduates or the PayPal Mafia — in Israel, we have another layer, which involves military connections. Many entrepreneurs come straight out of the army, and investors also have close ties with the government or their military past. They stick together and raise money together. Although women also serve in the Israeli army, not too many of them are in the center of the industry here yet. Regarding really great deals, you'll see mostly men with military connections around the table. I feel that it's even more challenging for women to break into this network here than in the United States.

"An interesting anecdote was when Angela Merkel came to Israel with her entire entourage to meet the Israeli Prime Minister Benjamin Netanyahu, who then escorted her to meet the heads of Israeli tech industry including the Israel Innovation Authority Chairman, Aharon Aharon. The Prime Minister brought her into an entire room of men who were supposed to represent the leaders of the technology industry in Israel, and not a single woman was among them. Then, Angela Merkel started the conversation by saying, 'Prime Minister Netanyahu, can you please tell me, first of all, why am I the only woman in the room? I know for a fact that you have a very advanced technology industry, and I can't imagine that there is not a single woman that you could find to represent it in this room,'" Talia chuckled.

"Netanyahu had nothing much to say, as he was slightly unaware and embarrassed, but it was evident that this question had never crossed his mind. Such situations will continue happening until they're called out, because men in power here just don't have it in their subconscious to have more women represented.

"Men in the VC industry in Israel belong to two main typecasts — those of the older generation, who may be in their mid-60s today and have had longer military careers. They often speak differently to women, especially in conversations surrounding technology, trying to educate them or just doubting their intelligence, at times. These individuals can be found on both the investor and entrepreneur fronts. Just yesterday I met with an entrepreneur who was older than I am, and I couldn't help but feel that he was oversimplifying his technological solution so that I would understand.

"The younger generation of men, however, is more open to working with women. Of course there is the infamous 'boys club' that comes in various forms, whether in chat groups to discuss proprietary deal-flow or gatherings for happy hour that are often even less inclusive. It's still hard to crack that.

"I'm seeing women in business development positions as well as executive positions, but I don't see as many of them founding companies and rising to general partner positions. It's not readily apparent at the present time that the number of women in the startup and venture capital industries is growing as fast as the number of various movements and initiatives we have today.

"There is always the risk of a backlash to every movement. I see a number of my male counterparts claiming that female empowerment movements in the workforce could hurt women more than help them. Although, I do feel that they will help us after all, I also note that good intentions do not always result in positive actions.

"When I was fundraising, I noticed that many women held senior positions at institutional investors. I have been at the table when the GPs were asked why there are no women among the most senior ranks. So we do see some push coming from the limited partner community towards diversity. However, some VC firms hire women just to look good when fundraising, and not many women would want to hold that trophy position if it wasn't based completely on merit.

"Although, we have several great success stories of female entrepreneurs, academics and scientists in Israel, there are still too few. The last fund I was with invested in two female-founded companies that are doing quite well now. Many more resources, mentorship, and encouragement for women are present today. You see more women in entrepreneurship programs at universities. You feel that panels at conferences don't only consist of men anymore. Just a couple of weeks ago, the government launched a funding program specifically aimed at female entrepreneurs because you can't ignore the statistics that the percentage of venture capital dollars that go to female-led startups, are dismal. Challenged by studies from Silicon Valley that showed how little venture capital goes to women, the Israeli government conducted their own study to find even more staggering numbers. There is almost a subconscious awakening happening right now regarding gender bias, which, I think, will benefit women and eventually lead to more women establishing companies on their own. I also think, however, that it'll take time to break into the male-dominated industries due to the tremendous effect that the military has had, and continues to have, on the Israeli community today."

Amy Raimundo

Managing Director,
Kaiser Permanente Ventures,
United States

As you might remember, one of the aspirations I had for this book, was to introduce the women featured in it to each other, because I realized that the female community in venture capital is very much divided into clusters. Throughout all one hundred interviews, I confirmed that this goal was set right.

"The thing I learned at the very beginning of my venture capital career, is that it's all about who you know," said Amy Raimundo during our conversation, and we talked a lot about the networking effect in the venture capital and tech industries.

Indeed, Amy's career in venture capital started at Advanced Technology Ventures, after her friend Sam Brasch, who had just joined another VC firm himself, advised her to consider this career option. This same friend invited her to become a part of the team at Kaiser Permanente Ventures years after.

Raimundo describes herself as a failed chemist. She went to undergraduate school thinking that she would be doing chemistry, but after having worked at the Yale Medical School lab for a couple of summers, she realized that chemistry wasn't her calling. She still liked new technologies in the medical field, however. She decided to give it a try and focused on the business side of healthcare by working in management consulting for hospitals and health systems, which nicely married her education in economics and passion for medicine.

"Consulting gives a great exposure to lots of different organizations with different problems to solve, which is why consulting background is oftentimes desired in new hires in venture capital. Such a background signals that its holder is able to learn new things quickly, analyze them from a strategic perspective, ingest new information daily, and switch contexts rapidly. That said, although I had worked in management consulting for five years and a medtech company for more than four years after that, I still had a lot to learn when I first joined venture capital."

Raimundo entered the venture capital industry through a traditional VC firm, but has dedicated the last nine years to corporate venturing. She worked for two corporate VCs, Covidien Ventures and Kaiser Permanente Ventures, and shared her opinion on the role of this type of investor. "I'm probably biased here, but I think corporate investors can bring very valuable perspectives and connections to the table. I think having a healthy mixture of corporates (assuming that they're not all vying to acquire you, which would get a little awkward) and traditional financial investors in a boardroom, surrounds a company with a blend of customer, pure business and financial perspectives."

Like most of the other investors I interviewed, Amy agreed that corporate venture capital is an amiable environment for women, but she saw how women started disappearing from the venture capital arena during the financial crisis, which encouraged her to create a professional network for women in medtech.

"The healthcare industry, relative to other industries, has a greater representation of female leaders in general, and in venture capital in particular, but the numbers are still quite small. However, soon after I started in venture capital as the Great Recession was unfolding — I noticed that there were fewer and fewer women visible in the industry. I was the only woman in the room most of the time, and I stopped seeing women represented as experts on the podium... I couldn't help but feel that the trend was going in the wrong direction. Trust me, there were enough powerful women in the medtech sector back then, and I wanted to really pull them together, so that they could leverage that power — do deals, partner, access talent. By launching MedTech Women, I wanted to create a competitive advantage for female experts."

We spoke with Amy when the documentary 'The Inventor: Out for Blood in Silicon Valley' had just premiered, so I couldn't help but ask for her opinion about Theranos, now that the investor community could finally speak out.

"I think that there are two types of investors — the pragmatic investors and the visionary investors. The latter back companies like Google at an early stage, when nobody knows how the company is going to unfold, what the business model is going to be, and how much money they are going to make. There is absolutely a place in certain industries for that kind of investing, but less so in healthcare.

"With all the regulations, infrastructure, and payment mechanisms, it's more difficult to be an unconstrained visionary in healthcare, because reality catches up to you really quickly. When tech started to enter healthcare, these worlds collided. Tech brought a fresh perspective of what was *possible*, but often lacked an understanding about what was *doable*.

"Theranos is a cautionary tale for all of us. It was a big vision with few details about the product, due to all the secrecy around it, so that no one could actually look under the hood. That alone should be a red flag for any investor. I cannot imagine myself investing in a company without looking under the hood, to really understand whether or not the innovation is, in fact, real. I also see that particular case as a confirmation of this phenomenon in venture capital where investors base too much of their decisions on looking at other investors in the deal, assuming they've done their due diligence, and not doing enough homework of their own. There are definitely some positive signals that strong co-investors send, but you've got to do your own due diligence. We can all get caught up by FOMO and rely on a proxy evaluation, but in healthcare, there are very few things that even fall into the category of incredibly disruptive inventions that defy gravity, and so you should do due diligence on them yourself."

Cynthia Ringo

Senior Managing Partner, DBL Partners, United States

Cynthia Ringo moved to California, from Atlanta, Georgia, with her 11-year-old son as his only form of support. To provide their living, she decided to join a tech company she had consulted remotely from her home city. "I had no idea what I was doing. When you're the sole support of your child, you're ready to do anything, but I didn't realize back then how vulnerable it is to be in a venture-backed startup," she recalled.

After a change of management, she decided to accept another job offer she had received at the time. Madge Networks, a global leader and pioneer of high-speed networking solutions in the mid-1990s — also known for its significant contribution to technologies such as Ethernet — was going public, and its founder wanted Ringo to lead corporate development. "That was the most ideal job I had ever heard of!" Cynthia said warmly. "I was supposed to be on the senior executive team whose job was not to think about quarterly performance, but to plan the strategy for years ahead. That was something I really liked doing and I was also paid for it!"

Ringo accepted the offer and before she even started, the founder of the company called her and said, 'I just fired the VP of Marketing and need you to take over that role too'. All of a sudden, Cynthia was in charge of marketing for a global public corporation and building its strategy around the world. "Madge Networks gave me a lot of confidence in my abilities. I ran an organization of hundreds of people all over the world, had an $80 million P&L, took the company from $60 to $400 million in revenue, and did three M&A transactions. It was very humbling, but also formative experience."

Many people think that building a startup is more difficult than working for a big corporation, so I asked how it was for Cynthia. "Working for Madge Networks was harder in many ways. I was thrown in the deep end, without knowing how to swim. The company was more complex, it was instantly global — as opposed to gradually global if it were a startup — and it was growing incredibly fast. But I figured it out."

Ringo didn't have any plans when she left Madge Networks. She was approached by several venture capital firms to join them, but she chose none. It was a very unconventional move, because common wisdom in venture capital is to take any opportunity — purely for the sake of getting into the industry.

"It didn't feel right," Cynthia contemplated when I asked her why she didn't go into venture capital at that point. "Firstly, we can all have these big freaking egos, but not all general partners are created equal. Secondly, I always wanted to feel that a company I work for was going to be successful. Because if you are not sure in that, then what is the point of spending your time on it? A VC firm is a business. You can like team members individually, but if you don't feel that the firm, as a business, is going to be successful, then don't settle for less."

The next step was directed by Cynthia's mentor. He told her that it was time for her to build her own company and be a founding CEO. She wasn't quite sure what to do, and then he introduced her to the engineers he worked with to evaluate their ideas. He told Cynthia that he'd give her $750,000 as an investment, with which he wanted her to try and develop some of them. "There were 10 ideas on the table, nine of which didn't make much sense, but one had this little tiny kernel that drew my attention. I called up two people who had worked with me previously for a long time, hired those engineers that came up with the idea, and that was how CopperCom — the next-generation network switching company — was born. We eventually had to change a whole lot in the initial idea, in order to build a product and a viable business. We then drew up a business plan and went up to raise money."

Ringo took the company from pre-revenue and five employees to an industry leader in two new communications markets.

"We started in 1997 and were planning to go public at the beginning of 2000. Within six months of product availability, we had shipped $25 million worth of orders, which was a skyrocketing result. Then the market went to hell in a handbasket. It was at the time when John Chambers at Cisco just missed his first quarter in ever, and we were very much affected by the crash around telecom too. However, bankers were insisting on taking the company public. I resisted because I knew what it meant to be an officer of a public company, and didn't want to create either an illusion or delusion about an IPO. So I said no to the bankers and raised another $65 million of private financing instead, to get to the point where the company would become self-sustaining.

"The reorganization during the market downfall was incredibly painful, but I managed to consolidate everything in Florida, which was much cheaper than California, and soon after, I retired from the executive role, and the team eventually sold CopperCom in 2003."

Ringo was again highly sought after by VC firms, so I couldn't help but ask what she thought was her secret sauce. "If you want to get into this business, I think the best way to do so is to be known. By 'being known', I mean that people in the industry should not only know your name, but also know what you can do. Not like, 'Let's go to a cocktail party and I'll chat you up', but, 'Let me show you what I can do that will create an impact'.

"When people ask me how they can become general partners, I always say that by definition, a partner is someone who makes things happen. So if you can't make it happen, you can't be a partner. That thing can be anything — whether you are an entrepreneur, an operator, an angel investor, or anything else. There are many ways of getting into venture capital, and the formula that combines them all is: make things happen."

While Cynthia was interviewing with quite a few VC firms after her exit from CopperCom, she received a call from a general partner of Vantage Point Capital Partners — a $4 billion venture capital firm — and an offer to join it as an IT investor. "I thought I was going to be among people who would teach me everything about venture capital, but before I even showed up to the office, he told me that he wanted me to head the IT investment group, which would invest in all forms of hardware, middleware, software, internet — everything but semiconductors," Cynthia remembered.

"When I learned that I was supposed to be in charge of 16 investment professionals, half of whom were already general partners, I thought that he had lost his mind! I'd never worked in venture capital before, and all I had was operational experience. However, that was apparently something they were looking for. 'You are the only person in the firm who has any management experience,' he told me. It seemed pretty naive of me to step into this story, but I had already given up other offers and all I had to say to myself was: 'I'm gonna figure this out.'

"I vividly remember my first meeting with my group in a large, long conference room with a glass wall behind my back. I was explaining to my group how we were going to work daily. I was showing the framework — the rules if you wish — everything that I had learned in my past. The great thing was that they were all just so happy to have a clear path for moving forward! I kept saying that I might have had that title, but they all had way more experience in venture investing than I did, and that, regardless of the governing structure, we were all partners and were going to make it work, together.

"Needless to say, they were all men! They were amazing, accepting and never ever undermining men, throughout the years!" Cynthia was yet another female VC who really appreciated men in her life and at the table. "It's really hard for me to understand why we have all these problems in the industry between men and women today! The male partners that I have had and that I have today, have been incredibly supportive!" Ringo stated with assurance, "Maybe I'm just really lucky, but I have no bad stories to tell..."

We dug deeper into the possible foundation for this luck. "If there was one thing that they all had in common, I'd say that most of them had daughters. We can debate causation, correlation, and whatever else, but I believe that it has something to do with that. Because they look at them and think, 'How do I want my daughter to be treated?'"

Indeed, according to research conducted by Harvard Business School in 2017, VC funds with investors who have daughters, have a deal success rate — where success counts as a profitable IPO or sale of an investment — that is more than 10% better than average. Having daughters also improves the Internal Rate of Return [IRR is a measure of profitability based on existing and projected revenues] of a VC fund's portfolio by more than 20%. No wonder, these men are confident enough to advance women in the workplace.

"When I am asked what I did personally to be surrounded by supportive men, people expect me to say that I'm just such a badass, and men don't want to mess with me, but the truth is that it has always been the opposite," Cynthia continued. "Each success that I've had, was earned by me being authentic, open-minded, and vulnerable.

"I never walked into a room thinking that I'm the smartest person there. I never let this bug get into my head. If I come off like that for someone, that's because they're projecting something on me, as opposed to how I feel myself. I remember where I came from — a lower middle class person, who is the first in her family to ever go to college, and the first to have a postgraduate degree. I'm awed almost all of the time at this amazing world, where somebody who comes from a very modest background can do what I've been able to do."

When Cynthia spoke about being authentic, I asked her if she had ever had to adjust to another person's behavior, especially a man's, and whether we should expect them to adjust to us. "There's always a bit of give and take. If you can't read the other party, you can never make anything good happen, but it has little to do with gender," she replied. "What makes a good negotiator? An ability and genuine desire to truly understand and appreciate where the other side is coming from. What do they really want? Can they come together in a way that satisfies everybody? And if you can't, just stop whatever you are doing and do something else!"

It wasn't easy to catch Cynthia for an interview, and we had to replace our meeting with a call instead, which we then had to reschedule a couple more times. We finally ended up talking on a weekend, and she said, "Everyone who wants to work in venture capital has to know that there is no work/life balance in this line of work. If this is one of your requirements for a job, check it at the door! Not ready for this sacrifice? Go get another job."

Jen Gill Roberts

Founding Partner,
Grit Ventures, United States

Jennifer Gill Roberts followed the traditional path of becoming a venture capitalist, as was outlined by her father, Jack Gill Roberts, a PhD-scientist-turned-entrepreneur, and then, founder of one of Silicon Valley's first VC firms — Vanguard Venture Partners — in the early '80s. "What I learned from my father, is that venture capital is an opportunistic career choice. There is no singular path to becoming a venture investor," Jennifer said.

Although electrical engineering was not a popular major for women in the '80s, Jennifer was taking computer science, calculus, chemistry, and other classes at Berkeley High School. "I don't think I would have chosen to major in electrical engineering if my father hadn't exposed me to technology and entrepreneurship, because I was good at many subjects and was contemplating becoming a lawyer."

Jennifer's father began introducing her to tech founders when she was in college. "Every time he'd say, 'I want you to meet this Founder or CEO,' I was just dreading those meetings!" she recalled. But she did that and got exposed to entrepreneurship and tech innovations very early in her life. She also attended Vanguard's corporate parties and annual meetings with her father, and met some of Silicon Valley's very first tech pioneers.

Jack Gill developed a technology career path methodology, which he later incorporated into his entrepreneurial class at MIT, and Jennifer followed this path almost to the letter. She did her undergrad in electrical engineering at Stanford, and her master's in the same field at the University of Texas. While developing hardware at pioneering companies, HP and Sun Microsystems, she was able to see innovations in the labs before they became commercially viable products in the next decade. After business school, Jennifer was recruited by Technology Venture Investors (TVI), a wildly successful VC firm that backed Microsoft.

"What I learned through my own experience, is that one can certainly increase their chances of getting into venture capital and being successful by being deeply immersed in a disruptive technology wave. My advice to aspiring VCs is to take risks and bet on new technologies, either by joining a startup or working in a smaller group at a large tech company on innovative projects."

Jennifer stayed with TVI for a year until they broke up into August Ventures and Benchmark, which is when she moved on to Sevin Rosen Funds, the third largest optical investor in the 90s, and became a partner. "I spent 10 wonderful years at Sevin Rosen, scaling the California office from 2 to 10 partners. The firm grew to have billions of dollars under management, but I knew that I needed to leave and pursue a startup and a new technology wave," she added.

Every decade or so there is an opportunity to dive into a new technology trend, and identify and fund the leading companies who will dominate the market. After funding and helping to build out internet infrastructure, Jennifer got really excited about the early days of the mobile revolution that she saw coming. She became a strong believer that the mobile device would be the primary device for everyone. She left Sevin Rosen Funds and co-founded a mobile application company with a business school classmate, Doug Keare, in the pre-iPhone and pre-AppStore days. It was a social gaming app for wellness, RallyOn, which she launched five years too early.

"One of the most important lessons about Silicon Valley, that I learned, is that we tend to see things here first, and so we think that the adoption beyond California is going to happen at the same speed and success rate. Although it's definitely an advantage to see innovations being born right in front of you, it is also important to understand customer adoption curves and market timing."

The company pivoted to SaaS model and was selling the service to enterprise customers, enjoying success for quite a number of years. "It was really fun to be on the entrepreneurial side of the equation — to be part of a founding team and take on an operating role," she remembered. "I think it's vital for VC investors to have strong operational experience. If there was no chance of acquiring it before your time in venture capital, go back and get it!"

After RallyOn and at the beginning of the Internet-of-Things era, Jennifer decided it was time to go back to investing in hardware. "As we move into the 2020s we are experiencing a huge technology wave around artificial intelligence and robotics. My partner, Kelly Coyne, and I have launched a new pre-seed venture fund, Grit, where we are investing in PhDs out of the labs who have developed AI-powered robotics solutions that will transform older industry verticals like construction, agriculture, transportation and logistics. Robotics will disrupt these verticals that are facing extreme labor shortages, in part because these jobs are dirty, dull and dangerous." Jennifer and Kelly are leveraging their deep backgrounds in hardware and go-to-market experience to differentiate themselves from the hundreds of other micro VCs.

There are many women in the micro VC segment, so I asked Jennifer whether smaller funds are a woman's thing because it speaks to the notion of women being risk-averse.

"No," Jennifer replied sharply to my provocative question. "I don't think women can be generalized as risk-averse. Women are a large part of the emerging fund managers tribe who typically raise smaller funds first. If you are successful, you can then raise larger funds and build a franchise. Forerunner's first fund back in 2012 was only $40 million. Recently they closed their $360 million fourth fund in 2018. So it's a typical path."

Beckie Robertson

Founder and Managing Director,
Versant Ventures, United States

Rebecca Robertson thinks of herself as an underdog. She grew up in upstate New York, didn't have a fancy private high school education, and started out with people who were a lot more prepared than she was. When she studied at Cornell University, she didn't get a scholarship and had to find a job. Most of the jobs seemed pretty boring to her, until she discovered an undergraduate research position. "The hiring professor was reluctant to hire me, because my grades weren't that good. But then he told me, 'Beckie, you're persistent. You're the only student that keeps calling back. I'll give you the job.'" she recalled. That professor became her first mentor in both academics and professional career aspirations, and helped her solidify her decision to move into the biomedical field.

"I'm very appreciative of the opportunities and support that I've been given. I think that does play a big role and ultimately affects your career trajectory. When I counsel young people, I tell them that when picking your first jobs, who you work with is as important as what your job is. I didn't know that at the time, but I do understand it now.

"I was very fortunate early in my academic career, and then in my professional career, to have connected with very successful people who were also very generous with their wisdom and experience. Having mentors is a wonderful thing, but it's a two-way street. I tried really hard to learn from and engage with other people who I respected and trusted, but I also tried to be valuable to them.

"What I quickly learned, was that it's important to know what you don't know. I took that advice to heart, and I've never been afraid to go out and seek counsel, find expertise, and hire people who are smarter and more experienced than I am. You have to be willing to make yourself vulnerable, and acknowledge your weaknesses. You have to be open to being mentored. You also have to be ready to work hard, because successful people who mentor others, always have choices as to who they invest their time and wisdom in. Good mentors are looking for somebody who is willing to work hard and also adds value to their mentor's efforts, as well as their own careers."

When Robertson graduated from Cornell University, jobs in the biomedical field were scarce, so she decided to move to Berkeley, California, to try and break into the biotech field. "I did not grow up with a lot of money, so I had to find a job in California, and ended up working at a shopping mall a-la Macy's. Soon enough I found a real job at a venture-backed startup called Lifescan, which was developing a blood glucose monitor and diagnostic test strips for diabetics to use at home. I went in as an entry-level manufacturing engineer, and stayed with them for almost eight years, working my way through the ranks until the company got acquired by Johnson & Johnson.

"I wouldn't say that I was especially self-confident back then, but I was definitely naive, and that turned out to be a real gift for me. I remember going into my first job as an engineer who hadn't graduated at the top of the class, and the only work experience I had was in retail. I walked into this company and my boss said, 'I need you to design the process equipment for our disposables reagent line.' I don't know what he was thinking, giving me that job — he really should have given it to somebody with a lot more experience!" Beckie laughed. "I was too naive back then to realize that that was a job I probably shouldn't take on. But I did take it, worked really hard, and learned what I needed to learn, in order to accomplish it. It never occurred to me that I would fail, because I'd managed to succeed with everything I had worked on up to that point. It became one of my main character traits. If somebody expects me to do something, I'm going to dig in and work hard, and I'll do my best to make it happen."

Beckie recalls that her years at Lifescan were probably the best time to get an MBA, which she fully intended to do, but never did. "The company was growing very fast, and I was given opportunities to learn and do new things on a regular basis. Every time a job that I was interested in came up, I'd raise my hand and would take on a new role. I got a tremendous variety of experiences while I was there. I did take a few Executive MBA classes at Stanford, and other things to supplement that, but whenever I had to actually apply for an MBA, I'd say, 'I am going to learn a little bit more now, and then, I'll take my time off to get an MBA'. It never happened.

"I revisited this decision multiple times back then, but always gave my preference to real-life work experience. Working for a company that had a very steep growth curve and having a couple of mentors who took chances on me, put me into multiple different roles, and then made sure I was successful, was the right trade-off. But it was a tough trade-off to make. I think that in different circumstances, it might have been the wrong choice to *not* get an MBA. If I had to start all over again, I would definitely have benefited from it."

Robertson then joined another small company, which was less of a success story, but one of its investors — Institutional Venture Partners (IVP) — offered Beckie a job at the VC firm as an entrepreneur-in-residence. She did that for a while before she found another healthtech company — Chiron Diagnostics — to head one of its business units. Living in California, running a business in Boston, and traveling all over the world, Beckie decided at some point that she needed to settle for the sake of her family. She wanted to continue being a working mom, but she wanted a job that would be more compatible with that lifestyle. The opportunity didn't make her wait for long and IVP, one of the first venture capital firms on Sand Hill Road, was there to invite her back.

"When I started at IVP, I had had work experience at two startups. At my first startup, I was employee number 25. They were still at a very early stage when I joined them and I stayed all the way through its acquisition. As for my second startup, I took it from filing the articles of incorporation, all the way to signing the papers to sell the company. So I had seen the full arc of a company's life cycle and everything that it entailed in between. Having that full cycle experience, from the perspective of both technology, as well as market and financial perspectives, was extremely helpful.

"What I didn't have, was any real knowledge of doing the due diligence for a potential investment. I didn't understand what it meant to evaluate a company for venture funding. I didn't have a decision framework in my mind that would allow me to do it, but I did have mentors and teachers who could show me that. I think that venture capital is an apprenticeship business. You can certainly learn all of that on your own, but if you have a chance to work with people who have already figured that out, and are able to learn from them, then that is a much more effective way of developing those skill sets. I was fortunate to work with experienced general partners at IVP, from whom I was able to learn."

After several years at IVP, and when many VC firms started looking at new investment verticals, Robertson and several other general partners decided to spin off and start Versant Ventures, a new VC firm that would invest exclusively in traditional healthcare.

Beckie admitted that her experience as a female investor was quite positive. She shared that she had never seen gender tensions in the healthcare community. She attributes that to the fact that there has been a decent representation of women in healthcare for quite a long time. "If you look at the workforce or academic world, you'll see that there's quite a good gender balance. The incoming class for the biomedical engineering program at Cornell University this year is full of women! So our industry seems to be friendlier towards women, starting from the higher education level."

I was tirelessly looking for something specific that Robertson was doing that helped her gain respect of her peers. "When I was first asked this question, I realized that I had never thought about it. I did not view this, or any other work situation for that matter, through the gender lens. But I did think a lot about what my strengths and weaknesses were, and how I could create a positive impact for whatever I was doing. Firstly, I always prepare carefully for any meeting, to make sure that I come into situations well-informed. Secondly, I try to be cognizant of what I know and what I don't know, and I'm curious to learn from other people and their perspectives. Finally, I also think that we all have to find our own voices and be authentic, although this word seems to be overused today.

"What I noticed early on, is that in the boardroom, many people are trying to make sure their views are heard. But few people around the boardroom table are trying to understand other people's points of view. I found myself genuinely interested in what my colleagues had to say, why they were advocating for their position, and what their thoughts were. That's in part where I think I have found my voice — in facilitating an honest and complete dialogue that can help to inform everyone around the table. If I needed to step in and help articulate an idea better or advocate for an opinion, I'd lean on my analytical and speaking skills to weigh in."

At some point, Beckie decided to stop investing actively and focus more on helping the portfolio companies of Versant Ventures. I was curious as to whether it was a hard decision to stop writing checks. "The truth is that writing checks was the least exciting part of the job for me," she surprised me. "Venture capitalists have to keep score of how much money we make, which I did too. But it has never been anywhere close to my driving passion, and was more of a distraction. Today, I find it incredibly energizing to be freed from investment calculations being the most important part of my decisions.

"I love putting teams and companies together, connecting academics with engineers and entrepreneurs, and helping CEOs with their strategies. I wanted to do well by doing good — to solve real medical problems and help people feel good about what they are doing. I have worked with a company that developed a rapid response EEG for seizures in the ICU. Diabetes has always been close to my heart, so I have worked with several companies in this sector. One of them is developing an automated blood testing system for diabetics. The other is working on a really easy-to-use pump for diabetics to wear."

I couldn't miss this opportunity, and asked Beckie about what she looks for in people when she helps build companies or hires investment professionals. "An important character trait that I am looking for in young investment professionals, as well as in executives for our portfolio companies, is being a good truth seeker. By that I mean a person who needs to get to the core of any problem. That is helpful in understanding markets, technologies and the causes of unexpected problems in a business. Being relentless in seeking the truth, in fact, helps us make solid initial decisions and course corrections. If there was one skill that I would say is important to success in both venturing and managing a company, that would be it."

Whitney Rockley

Founding Partner, McRock Capital, Canada

The media says that Whitney Rickley — a founding partner of the Canadian VC firm McRock Capital and currently the Chair of the Canadian Venture Capital Association — is "refreshingly real". People with unconventional opinions and beliefs are my favorite kind, so I was looking forward to talking to Whitney.

In the middle of our conversation, I asked her what women should do when they enter a male-dominated environment — whether it's a room or an industry? "I am a tall woman, and I still put my heels on, which can easily make me at least six feet tall — right away I have a presence! So you walk into a room, roll your shoulders back, hold your head up high, and be who you are. Never try to be a pleaser, just be who you are." Believe it or not, her presence was tangible even on our call. Rockley as in "rock star", I thought.

Rockley's career started in the largely male-dominated industry — she came to venture capital from strategy and operations in the power/water and oil and gas industries, where she learned her first lesson while working as an analyst. She recalled how 20 years ago, she was complaining about her bonus for that year to her formal mentor, who had been appointed by the MBA program she was undergoing.

Said mentor was Gerry Protti, a senior North American executive and lobbyist in the oil and gas industry throughout the years, who looked at her and said, "Suck it up".

Whitney heard similar advice from a woman too, when she shared her doubts about having a second child with Nancy Floyd, a co-founder of the energytech fund Nth Power. Rockley wasn't sure she could manage a career and two children, but Nancy's response, like Gerry's, consisted of three words, "Just do it".

The advice she received was of the utmost importance when she was heading up a corporate venture capital program for a big power company back in Alberta, Canada, led by an incredibly tough and demanding boss. "Words can't describe how tough this man was," Whitney said. "Gerry and Nancy's words stuck with me. I stayed the course, gave it my all and learned how to be crisp and succinct when something was complex and difficult to understand."

When her boss was leaving the company, she wrote a kind note thanking him for pushing her. He came down to her cubicle with childlike big eyes and shed a tear, saying that no one had ever thanked him, let alone taken the time to write him a handwritten note. "Looking back on that experience, I was proud of myself for not quitting and for being able to see the human side of difficult people," Whitney added.

At the start of her venture capital tenure, Whitney was recommended for a number of jobs by Scott MacDonald, who is the other co-founder of McRock Capital today. "He staked his reputation on me three times throughout my career. I worked very hard, and I think because of that, I was lucky to have a number of mentors — predominantly men, but also several really effective female mentors — who sponsored me and championed me over the years."

We continued discussing the hours Rockley spent behind the desk and she told me a story of how others perceive hard-working people these days.

"I did a 'cross country ask me anything' tour where I visited a number of Canada's best universities to raise awareness for private capital among master's and undergrad students. At one university, a woman raised her hand and said, 'I have a daughter, she's very young, and I'm wondering how many hours you work a day.' I didn't lie — I said, 'I worked very, very hard. I spent more time at work than I did at home.' Then, a young man in the class raised his hand, looked at me, and said, 'Well, you're the problem then! You're the problem as to why we have to work such long hours. Shouldn't the fix be with you first and shouldn't you stop working these hours to set an example for us, so we can all have a better work-life balance?'"

Whitney was gobsmacked. She didn't know what to say to him and got really angry on the inside, because there was no way she could have done it differently through her career. "He just could not understand and relate to what I was saying. I had to work, and I enjoyed the work, and I had a passion for the work, which drove me to work as hard as I did," Whitney accentuated the word 'work' each time she said it. "I'm proud of what I do, and frankly, I expect that of my team. I don't have a lot of patience for people who don't respect the work ethic that goes into this industry. There are far more downs in venture capital than there are ups, and it takes a lot of effort. Venture capital is quite a demanding job. You do look to work long hours because we tend to manage a lot of capital, but we have small teams, and so bandwidth is always an issue. Yes, it gives you flexibility to work from home sometimes, but it doesn't mean you work less."

I could not help but ask if there was anything she would do differently, in hindsight, and Whitney had an immediate answer. "When I started my career, I had a view that if you just put your head down and work really hard, you'll get noticed. I don't know if it was predominantly because I was a woman, or because of my personality type, that I felt more comfortable working at my desk and crunching away at analyses instead of meeting new people. The one thing that I wish I had done differently, is the networking.

"I wasn't doing that until I was probably 35 years old. Then I noticed that all these men around me had phenomenal networks of people that they called on, and they got a lot of intelligence and deal flow from them. I realized that I had to do a better job in networking, and probably over the last 15 or so years, I've been spending a fair bit of time trying to extend the network that I have today. I wish I had started doing that earlier.

"For people who are trying to get into the venture capital industry, it's really important to just network, network, and network. Your paths will cross with people with whom you will click, and the relationships will continue growing because of that initial click. As they continue to grow, those people may advance you in your career. Be patient, relentless, keep networking, and you'll find your place eventually.

"Once you put yourself out there, it just gets easier and easier every time. When you walk into a room, you see one person you know, then you see two people you know, then you see five people you know. Then a few years later you know half of the room. That's probably the biggest piece of advice that I would give people who are trying to break into the industry."

Networking is advice that we hear way too often, but the reality is that it takes time for women to build the necessary confidence and courage to be taken seriously when entering that room. I challenged Whitney to share her understanding of navigating this environment. "We need to accept that men in our industry are mostly type A personalities, and they want to work with competent and strong women — women that they can relate to. Naturally, they like working with people they like.

"The weaker characters, whether male or female, get pushed to the sidelines, unfortunately. Those who are too aggressive have a very difficult time fitting in as well, because they're not accepted in venture capital as much as in private equity. Unlike the latter, venture capital is more of a team sport. Strong women pave their way by being likable, while aggressive women pave their way by being unlikable, and it's not quite acceptable in venture capital."

Speaking of type A personalities, Whitney shared another valuable observation. "It's difficult to achieve this likability if other people are intimidated by you. This obviously makes them feel uncomfortable around you. However, it also works the other way around: others may feel uncomfortable next to you, if you are constantly intimidated by your surroundings."

While contemplating this dualism of the feeling of intimidation in social settings, I looked into the Canadian diversity statistics in venture capital industry after our interview. At Women.VC, we haven't studied the Canadian landscape yet, but according to the existing report, as of 2018, 14% of VC investment partners in Canada are women, which is more than any of the reported number in the US. The jury is still out regarding the equity ownership of the surveyed partners, but I assume that the numbers will be higher than in the United States anyway, due to fewer VC firms in Canada in general: this particular dataset included only top 33 Canadian venture capital firms.

Other statistics showed that women hold 58% of all analyst roles, and 27% of all associate and principal roles. However, 84% of dollars committed to the country's top VC funds are controlled by teams with no women general partners. This report also took entrepreneurs-in-residence (EIR) into account for their ability to add expertise to investment committees and found that 18% of EIRs and advisors are women, however, zero percent of venture partners at Canadian VC funds are women. As for angel investors, women make up less than 15% of angel groups' membership In Canada, while in the US, this number fluctuates from 7% to 17% percent.

Jenny Rooke

Founding Partner, Genoa Ventures, United States

Jenny Rooke recently raised her first traditional VC fund for Genoa Ventures, the firm she founded to focus on life science startups. This experience, she said, has made her 'a much more empathetic investor'.

"When entrepreneurs come and pitch us, I'm now more aware of what they are going through. I understand that they would much rather be building their companies than raising money," she admitted. "It is very, very hard work to start a VC firm and raise a fund. It's hard for everyone — men or women — even people who have been in the business for a really long time, let alone those who are still at the start of their journey. As one other general partner I know phrased it, 'Raising a fund is like you have a jar full of marbles that got knocked over, and it's your job to pick them all up'. There's no leverage, no way to hack it, and no way to speed it up. So it is definitely a process that people describe as a grind."

Her tendency to break things down into component parts, in order to understand them better, comes not only from her quantitative background — Jenny's undergraduate work was in physics and computer science — but also from her love for genetics. "I took an elective biology course late in my undergrad work, and saw that the structure and elegance that I loved about math and physics was embodied in the physical system of living organisms as well. That was a very appealing combination, and I went on to study genetics."

After studying it in graduate school, Jenny was very motivated to help find solutions for generating genetic and genomic data efficiently, in large quantities. She knew that people were not going to unlock the mysteries of

the genome without the ability to easily read it. She joined a venture-backed startup developing next-generation technologies for genomic analysis, leading product development and launching new products for researchers. Along the way, she learned about venture capital and started exploring the space. Jenny got very excited about the idea of moving from the serial process of building companies one at a time, as an entrepreneur, to shifting to more of a meta process, where she would be working with many entrepreneurs in parallel as a partner, to help them get the financing they need to build their businesses. At that point, she started working for Fidelity Biosciences, a Cambridge-based healthcare VC, and training as a venture capitalist through the Kauffman Fellows Program.

Jenny learned that, in the early days of venture capital, there was a very fine line between angel and venture investing, and she heard a lot of stories about individuals who had often been entrepreneurs prior to their investment career. "It was incredibly inspiring for me to think about that complementary role to the entrepreneur, where I could support them and help them succeed in their ventures. I have since found out that that perspective was, perhaps, a little idealistic. It came as a disillusionment to me when I realized the difference between venture investing as a partner-to-entrepreneur relationship, and venture as a finance job."

She was lucky enough to deepen her understanding of early-stage capital formation when she went on to work for the Gates Foundation, managing over $250 million in funding in genetic engineering, diagnostics, and synthetic biology. "Venture capital is focused on making money, and is oftentimes tied to certain geographies and markets. In contrast, the Gates Foundation had these ambitious 30-50 year goals and a scope that was much more global in both the resources and problem sets they were trying to solve. It was very high-risk capital, because the objectives were so beyond what we could do with the current technologies, that it required taking enormous risks — risks that I felt I couldn't responsibly take with the traditional institutional capital as a venture investor.

"I was very intrigued as to what that investing approach would do to me as an investor. If I changed those parameters, how would that make me think about due diligence, technical risk, managerial risk, and capital requirements? It was a way to change some of the key elements of the game of capital formation, and to observe what that does to one's strategy. I wanted to scratch that itch. I wanted to make some 'so crazy — it just might work' science bets, in some really critical areas, and I got to do that."

Coming back to the startup world with Genoa Ventures, to invest in the seed and Series A ranges, made Jenny feel at home. "It is the right spot for me on that risk scale. I don't spend too much time thinking about what the near future looks like, but spend my time looking for entrepreneurs who are thinking about that instead.

"I also realized that, for an entrepreneur, it is a challenge to find an investor who can understand all those different parts of the companies that I am investing in, so I try to bring to the table other investors to syndicate, with whom we could get all the pieces of a complex, interdisciplinary business together. The more help we can put around the table and the more that mirrors what a company needs, the better. However, I don't want to oversell the importance of investors. Ultimately, it's the companies that are creating value. It comes down to teams who are doing the day-to-day work."

Her background defines the kind of companies that Rooke invests in, previously through a syndicate on AngelList, and now, as a general partner of a VC firm. VC firms investing in tech are usually distinct from those that invest in life sciences, however, Jenny thinks that these verticals have much more to contribute to each other than may appear. "At Genoa, we invest in companies that marry biology as the technology of a living organism, with other technologies like software and hardware. I do believe these intersectional companies define a class of their own, but I also believe that we should apply the best practices of investing and building both tech companies and biotech companies to this class as well."

Rooke has been investing at the intersection of applying life sciences technologies — like gene sequencing, protein expression, and genetic engineering — to opportunities where biology can solve problems beyond healthcare. She thinks we're way behind applying these same tools and innovations in such sectors as agriculture and industrial biotech.

"I use the term 'life sciences' to distinguish what we do at Genoa from traditional "biotech" investing. At least half of all healthcare venture capital dollars is invested in the development of new therapeutics, commonly called 'biotech'. What I mean by 'life sciences' is the broader set of biotechnology that has to do with living systems. So it's the science and technology of biology, but is not limited to drug therapies," she explained.

"The most exciting and powerful aspect of venture capital is the potential to bring about accelerated change toward a better future, faster than would otherwise happen through the normal course of business. We know this is true for technological innovation: by backing an entrepreneurial team who can bring an innovative technology or medicine to market faster, investors can drive progress and impact."

I asked Jenny for advice on how to navigate all that, along with a challenging environment in venture capital, gender-wise, and she replied in a way I'd never heard before.

"Rather advising on that, I think it is important to talk about framing women's decisions about how to navigate the situations they find themselves in. There's a very important division in the ways to approach any given situation. I think it's critical that we, as women, ask ourselves one question in any given scenario: 'Is my objective now to benefit *myself* in this situation, or to benefit the *system*?' And the answer can be quite different.

"In many cases — especially younger VCs who are just trying to establish themselves — people may have less power, may feel like they're at a disadvantage. Thus, they may have to prioritize a solution that preserves their benefit and their ability to get their work done, in order to strengthen their reputations and relationships with other players.

"In other scenarios, a person might feel empowered to do something that changes the system as a whole — like calling someone out or going against the flow. Such people can afford to do things that benefit the system more than them personally in the short term, and that would help the system to become more equitable. It's our responsibility to do that if we quantify ourselves in the latter group.

"However, realistically, we cannot expect everyone to do so, because they may not have the luxury and resources to make a systemic change. If you are at an early stage of your career and are thinking about how to respond to a challenge, it's okay, in the moment, to do what's best for yourself. It is a step toward a position where you *will* be able to make a systemic change later."

"On a more practical level, I can talk about empowering women all the time, but if I'm not funding female founders, how would I make a difference? At Genoa Ventures, being a female-founded and female-led venture fund will hopefully mean that we'll see more diverse founders choosing us. We're creating a place where we want female entrepreneurs and representatives of other minority groups, who have so many challenges ahead of them, to feel comfortable being themselves. It's a place where we're excited about who they are, and celebrate them.

"At the end of the day, money is power, so putting money in the hands of women is the best way to make change. It should happen at all levels. Institutional investors have a disproportionate share of the power in this system, so they have an outsized opportunity to make change."

Maryanna Saenko

Founding Partner, Future Ventures, United States

Maryanna Saenko, a co-founding partner of Future Ventures (a new VC firm of Steve Jurvetson), doesn't need to prove that she's a risk taker. She rides motorcycles, she kite surfs and rock climbs, along with being a venture capitalist. When defining herself during our conversation, I think she found the best explanation of what being risk-averse means for women.

"I really appreciate that adrenaline-driven edge between well-paced, safe and secure, but just before you're definitely going to break your neck," she laughed, hinting at how her brain works. Indeed, in women's language, risk-averse merely means being better at calculating the odds when taking risks.

Maryanna was one of the very few exceptions who was not nominated for this book, because she was raising the capital for Future Ventures behind the scenes, when I started working on it. However, when they finally announced the fund, I did everything I could to get her attention. The main reason for that, was the fact that Saenko is an investor of Soviet descent. Having the same roots myself and knowing how the mindset of the children of the last Soviet generation is different, I wanted to have that represented in my collection of characters. As the stories of many other women featured in this book tell, strong desire opens all doors, so I opened the one to Future Ventures.

Maryanna was born in Ukraine to a family of well-educated engineers, which was a common scenario among Soviets at the time. Her family bounced around a bit before they landed in the United States, and Maryanna finished school on American soil. "My parents are extremely intelligent people, both with graduate degrees in mechanical engineering, but when we arrived in the US, my father was delivering newspapers and working at a gas station, while my mother was an in-home caretaker for a sick patient. We lived in the in-law unit of that patient's family home, and I used to hear my parents say, 'Whatever we need to do to make it work, we'll make it work.' So I grew up in an environment where grit was regularly demonstrated," Saenko started her story. "They ended up doing very well for themselves here, and thankfully, nobody is delivering newspapers any longer, but seeing them going through that was very impactful for me."

Like many Slavic girls, Maryanna was quite a tomboy growing up. "There is a very popular saying in Russian-speaking countries, that is actually a paraphrase of a precept from the Talmud, 'Every man should build a house, plant a tree, and raise a son.' My dad had this hilarious joke that he definitely did all three," she laughed wholeheartedly. "I was my father's son more than his daughter, and we had a brilliant and close relationship. I think I always had that tiny thing in the back of my head where I identified a lot more with masculine things.

"However, as a young adult, I tried to become more feminine instead. I enjoyed the fact that I am a woman, but I couldn't hide that type A personality that I had developed, which was dominating the room. Looking back, I must say that I didn't harness it in the right way, and it has only been in the last couple of years that I have realized that it's very important to create space for cognitive diversity in a room, for better decision-making."

Maryanna went to a small prep school in Connecticut — Hopkins School — which taught her that it is not *what* you're learning that's important, but *how* you are learning. "When I realized that, I quickly dropped the presumption that there is a particular type of intelligence that's better than others, for example that being good at math means that you are smart," said Maryanna. "Instead, I learned that if you're committed, you can learn anything. But you're not going to learn anything by just beating your head against a wall. Hopkins taught me that I shouldn't optimize for the things that I am naturally good at, but should focus on figuring out how I am going to learn things that are difficult for me."

At school, this immigrant girl also experienced the caste system of American society, but it only made her stronger. "I learned that there are groups of people who are just wildly privileged and fortunate. However, I never realized that I was an outsider. This attitude stayed with me to the point that I never paid a lot of attention to gender dynamics, and how they're often deeply skewed.

"It became a marching order of my life that I would never pay too much attention to the social conditions I found myself in, because I was just motivated to surround myself with interesting people who enabled thoughtful conversations, and who were passionate about their work. I never thought about whether I did or did not fit into any of those communities. Now that I look back on my university years, and early jobs, I realize that there weren't a lot of other women in the room, but I can't say that I noticed that at the time."

Her choice of field was also somewhat life-defining. When she graduated from high school, her parents begged her to choose anything but engineering. Maryanna did exactly the opposite: she found a great engineering school, Carnegie Mellon University (CMU), and immediately signed up for Materials Science and Biomedical Engineering. Consistently doing the opposite of what she was told, is another trait that Maryanna carried through life.

When she finished her master's at CMU, she was unsure whether she wanted to continue pursuing a doctorate or leave academia and find a job. She ended up joining a startup founded by one of her mentors, a professor at MIT. "This tiny university startup was the best education for becoming a venture capitalist, because I learned all of the things one shouldn't do when starting a company. We had delusions of grandeur regarding the number of things that we thought we could accomplish with our technology," she giggled.

The company was dissolved quite soon thereafter, which Maryanna didn't expect. "It was quite heartbreaking, because I was living in Boston, in my early 20s, had just been let go from my first job, and I had to make a hard choice between going back to school and finishing that PhD I was considering, and finding something else to do with my life.

"It was then that I came to a very important realization. I remembered having an identity crisis in my late teens, when I was disappointed with myself over my athletic pursuits. I had been a very serious swimmer growing up and trained as a competitive athlete. But when I recognized that I was not going to win a gold medal in the Olympics, I started getting sick from the workload and it wasn't joyful anymore. I realized that I was doing exactly the same thing with academia — I was defining myself by my academic pursuits. I finally understood that I shouldn't define myself by any one particular choice in my life, and that doing a PhD, just because I wasn't sure what else I should do at that moment, was a terrible strategy," Maryanna said of her deep self-analysis.

With that realization, she started working at a large chemical company. "I knew that I could go to work every day and do a good job from 9 to 5, and it didn't have to become my life. However, I also quickly noticed that I wasn't fulfilled by the work. I was bored out of my mind for at least eight hours a day, even though the company was great, but I just didn't have any inspiring work to do.

"I planned to make a change and joined an amazing company called Lux Research, which provided consulting and advisory services to Fortune 500 corporations. I'll never forget what one of the senior scientists, an experienced man in his early 60s, whom I considered a mentor, told me when I shared with him that I was going to leave for this new role at Lux.

"In a very kind voice, he said, 'I looked that job up and I want to tell you that this is a terrible idea for you. You could not possibly be successful there, because you're too young and have no concept of how these corporations work. Nobody's going to take you seriously. This is a job for somebody in my position to take.' As I was listening to him, I couldn't help but think that he was actually trying to do me a favor by essentially telling me to stick my head back into the sand. I thanked him in an extremely cordial manner and went straight to Lux to start my new job!"

That wasn't the only time in her life when Saenko was told to get back in line with the rest of the worker bees and keep quiet. However, she's consistently proven that she can forge her own path.

The job at Lux became the foundation for her current career and prepared Maryanna for venture capital in a number of ways. She had to hunt down startups before anybody else heard about them, so that her clients would know that they existed. She also had to look for clients among diverse corporations most in need of a massive shake-up. In addition, she was travelling around the world giving speeches, and building connections on both sides of the table.

"I spent a lot of my time studying slightly arcane and obsolete industries that desperately needed to innovate, in order to recognize which ones were willing to move quickly. Now as a VC, I'm very motivated to invest in some of those industries, because I don't think the incumbents are going to change the status quo."

While working with corporations, she noticed a bizarre pattern. "Every time I showed up to an important meeting in a business suit, somebody asked me to make them a cup of coffee. But if I wore jeans and a simple, neat T-shirt, they cleared space for me at the main table and were very keen to hear what I had to say. I realized that if I was dressed up, people were more than willing to overlook me. But if I didn't look like they expected me to look, they noticed it and thought, 'Oh, that's different. That's a little off. There must be a very good reason why she's showed up looking like that.' Although it was entertaining, I found it deeply frustrating. I enjoyed wearing jeans and T-shirts, but the thought alone that I wouldn't do that well if my natural state of comfort were to wear five-inch heels, was very upsetting."

After Lux, her current career took shape. She received an offer from Airbus to join their corporate venturing group in Silicon Valley. "At the time, I was largely uninformed about venture capital, but I showed up and took the job. I was overwhelmed at first, but then I looked at it as an engineering problem and realized that it was hard, but not impossible."

She then joined DFJ and began to work with Steve Jurvetson. However, soon after his departure from the firm he co-founded, Saenko also left to join Khosla Ventures, which she greatly enjoyed. No changes were expected until Jurvetson decided to start a new fund, and called Maryanna asking if she'd be interested in teaming up again. "I was having an incredible time at Khosla Ventures, and I would still be there, were it not for the opportunity to work with Steve again. Partnering with Steve meant debating what a new venture fund should look like. It's a crowded field and funds already have a hard time distinguishing themselves from one another. We asked ourselves what we could do that's different and valuable, and decided to focus on investing in early-stage deep-tech companies. We wanted to do it with high conviction, by writing meaningful checks in the earliest stages of companies that are building things, unlike anything we've ever seen before — companies that are inevitabilities for building a better world. We are fortunate to have our dream team of limited partners, ones who understand the breadth of our vision and are willing to support us for the long haul; it's why our fund is focused on a 15-year lifespan, as we all recognize that our portfolio companies will require time to meaningfully impact the world.

"In the course of debating our principles at Future Ventures, I realized that I am not interested in investing in companies that play to people's vices. It's a totally reasonable investment thesis, but it's a segment I don't wish to participate in. I don't really want to put our resources towards increasing access to addictive substances, for example. Not because of my moral compass, but maybe because I believe in karma," she smiled. "Today I feel honored and privileged to have arrived here. I also feel that it's now my job to make sure the door stays open for more people to enter into roles where they may feel uncomfortable or unqualified at the outset, but are willing to put in the work to make a difference."

Rona Segev

Founding Partner,
TLV Partners, Israel

"I really cannot tell you that there's something in my background or education that prepared me to become a venture investor," Rona started with, when I called her in Tel-Aviv. Trained in philosophy and psychology, she launched her tech career by developing a 3D computer game based on Lego. "We raised $200,000 unexpectedly, but it took only about two months to realize that it was a really bad idea to take Lego and put it on a computer screen."

The team then decided to develop a real action game, and the second attempt turned out to be a great success. Rona's startup — Kidum Multimedia — became the first company in Israel to develop real hardcore gaming experience. She sold her company in her early 20s, just four years after its launch, and became quite a phenomenon in Israel back then — a female founder of a gaming company. "The only thing that qualified me for that job, was severe ADD [attention deficit disorder — the most common thing that turns people into gamers]," she laughed. "I think I had that kind of ignorance, or maybe even stupidity, to jump into deep waters without knowing how to swim."

She did that again, when she decided to go back to work after giving birth to her first twins. Segev chose a venture capital job as a temporary gig before starting another company. "I didn't know much about venture capital at the time, but venture investors seemed so relaxed to me, that I thought, 'This job would be quite convenient for a young mother!' I was planning to do that for a year or two and then go back to being an entrepreneur," she recalled.

She applied for several VC jobs, immediately got into one firm as an investment partner, and hasn't left the industry ever since. She was one of the first female VCs in Israel and possibly the youngest one. Instead of becoming an entrepreneur again, after two years of VC work, she joined one of the top tier VC firms in Israel — Evergreen Venture Partners — as a General Partner, where she was assigned enterprise software and security as her investment focus, which she knew nothing about. She took it with no objections, because by that time, Rona knew how to swim in deep waters. "These investment verticals were considered very boring, with no real exits back then, so the partners handed it over to me," she smiled.

"I started learning about that and just fell in love with the space. Very quickly afterwards, I got my first exits. I was very lucky to be a part of this really exciting and fast-growing market at the time."

Segev had several large exits with Evergreen Venture Partners — multimillion and multibillion acquisitions and IPOs. She became quite well-known as a VC and expert in the enterprise field, and was then recruited by another large fund in Israel, to repeat her success again. "I never stopped learning. I had some really amazing mentors, and I learned a great deal from entrepreneurs that I met."

It's no surprise that a decade later, Rona decided to go on her own. "It's much better to have your own VC firm, because you can bring your culture and build everything around it. I have always been a strange bird anyway. I have my own way of thinking about things and doing them. I like to invest early, in new markets, and young entrepreneurs, which is altogether considered pretty risky. At my own firm, I don't need to convince anyone as to why I am doing what I am doing. And I know what I am doing very well at this point.

"I really believe in creating a win-win — very close partnerships — which is not always easy to do at VC firms that prefer a more formal and aggressive way of doing business. I do things in a calmer, very relaxed, maybe even 'feminine' way, and the two other managing partners at TLV Partners, who are males, are fine with it," Rona explained.

"Venture capital was quite a lonely place for women until a few years ago," she moved on to the gender topic. "I think everyone is aware of diversity today and trying to hire more women. Gender is a very sensitive issue in Israel. It's becoming quite embarrassing to have a picture of only white male teams for different organizations, including VCs and startups.

"I see more female investment professionals and entrepreneurs, but still not enough. Aside from all the typical barriers that women meet in venture capital and tech, there is also this cultural stereotype that Israeli women should retire from work when they have kids. It's very common here to have kids very early, and to have a lot of them. I, personally, have two sets of twins, and four children in a family is quite the norm. The stereotype claims that a woman cannot be a perfect mom if she has a full-time job. Ironically, no one ever applies the same standard to men: nobody argues that a man has to choose between being a good father and having a career. If financially possible, women in Israel today are still under a lot of pressure to quit their jobs to become stay-at-home moms. We have a lot of extremely talented women who are leaving the workforce at the age of 24-25.

"It's a road to nowhere. We can dedicate 10-15 years to our kids, but then they grow up and leave, and their moms are left alone at home with no jobs, because they've lost a decade professionally, and oftentimes, they lose their personal identities as well.

"I am happy to see how the mindsets of young women and men, are changing on this matter. More and more women realize that they don't need to give up a huge part of their lives, just because they were born females. We have some great role models in the industry and we need more of them," Rona concluded, and I couldn't help but notice that there is a strong solidarity on this issue among the Israeli investors who I interviewed, which is also similar to those from Europe.

Darya Shaked

Founding Partner, Wonder Ventures, United States

Darya immigrated from Israel in 2015 and quickly found her calling in Silicon Valley, applying her skills, which she developed by working for a private equity firm, and serving in the Israeli government and army. She has focused on diversifying the investment industry from the top down, by providing institutional investors with a framework to increase diversity in venture capital. "I've realized that to keep pushing female founders from the bottom up is not going to make a difference any time soon, unless we diversify the layer of general partners and start the change from the top down," she started speaking passionately right after we had completed our mutual greetings. Her firm, Wonder Ventures, focuses on investing in a portfolio of diverse and emerging VC funds to enhance financial returns.

"I've been working on my investment vehicle for almost a year now, and have met a lot of institutional and private investors. I was drawing their attention to something I deem to be a market failure." Darya explained. "The fact that less than 10% of investors who are making investment decisions in venture capital are women, and even fewer African-Americans and Hispanics, is mostly viewed from a social perspective. However, there is also a significant business side to it. The disparity that we observe is part of the reason why the majority of venture capitalists do not return even 1x the capital invested. Most VCs are competing on an overlapping deal flow of startups solving similar problems, when there is so much more that they could be doing. Once we get more diversified investment teams, the returns will improve due to investing in opportunities previously unnoticed."

Indeed, Dan Levitan from Maveron, said once, 'The industry has too much money and too many smart people chasing too few great entrepreneurs.' This phrase went viral and is now somewhat of a proverb in venture capital. Maybe Darya had just explained why it had happened in the first place, and how we can potentially change that.

"It is not about the words 'man' and 'woman', but about investing our money in the funds that are best positioned to see all opportunities. It means that such funds source from different communities, evaluate things from a wide range of viewpoints while having a higher team intelligence, a wider network and access to talent, and have supportive policies that they also push forward into their portfolio companies.

"My mission is to increase diversity in the investment industry, by encouraging institutional investors to create industry-wide guidelines, according to which they will invest their money," continued Darya. "These guidelines should specify the indicators of venture capital investing teams with stronger financial potential. Habits are a great force, so having a certain standard broadly adopted by the industry, will help to break the old habits of investing in only white male general partners.

"There are also cases where women who were hired by VC firms as partners, do not get decision-making powers to really make a difference, and there are simple ways for limited partners to know if the diversity in the fund is a core value or if it is just a token. Having a female co-founding partner is an easy one, but the distribution of the carried interest between the partners, and an ownership stake in the management company, are two other ways to determine the situation in an industry where 74% of all the partners in the US are male. The important thing to remember is that limited partners have the power (some would say the responsibility) to ask those questions while doing due diligence on GP teams. The reality is that limited partners are hesitant to ask that, while it would be a crucial first step for equality."

The industry is very reluctant to discuss what it has been doing wrong, and I assume that it's rather unwilling to admit the above-mentioned flaws and accept the change challenge. I asked Darya how institutional investors treat her. "Some of them are at the forefront of thought leadership and very vocal about the importance of advancing equality. I know that every single institutional investor will sooner or later adopt these values, as the world is changing, the industry is transforming, processes have already started, and dozens of powerful entities are pushing it forward. Even in conservative industries, which venture capital is, nobody wants to be the last dinosaur," she replied.

"I think that institutional investors — who are the deepest pockets in the world — have the power to move the needle and also have the responsibility of directing the ship of innovation to where it should go. Giving promising women access to capital and making a statement on how they are going to invest their money will inevitably make all the parties involved listen. For example, Blackstone's CEO has made a huge statement and is already following up on it."

Blackstone is the largest alternative investment firm in the world that specializes in private equity, credit, and hedge fund investment strategies. They launched Blackstone's Women's Initiative back in 2011 with a two-fold goal — recruit more talented women and improve their retention and career development within the firm. Due to this effort to expand its applicant pool, in 2017, the percentage of women in Blackstone's incoming analyst classes has doubled to nearly 40 percent — up from 18 percent in 2013.

"Another LP told me that since the #MeToo movement revealed cases of sexual harassment in the investment industry, as part of their due diligence process, they have been sending anonymous emails to general partners of the VC firms they are considering for investments, about possible harassment at their firm. If they do not receive a response from them, that's a strong indicator against backing such firms. Stories like this move us all one step forward.

"I can attest to the fact that some institutional investors are really trying to figure out whether GPs are doing something to move the needle regarding harassment and discrimination issues. However, this shouldn't be deemed as some kind of achievement. It should be a must-have component of the due diligence process. A variety of opinions is one of the indicators of whether an investment team is capable of recognizing the opportunities and their potential from outside of the expertise of only white male founding partners," Darya carried on.

"If we look beyond what's on the surface, we'll see that the entertainment and tech industries are siblings in a way, because their leadership is shaping the modern life of billions of people, like no other industry. That is the reason why the conversation on harassment issues started in Silicon Valley and Hollywood almost simultaneously. We need to have more role models to learn from and more female trendsetters to be involved in the tech industry and venture investing, because male artists of all kinds are already there. It will make a strong statement on the rightful place of women in innovation."

If you are wondering where these strong convictions come from, here are the three things you should know about Darya Shaked.

She is an Israeli champion in horseback riding — show jumping. Fun fact: long after the win, she started dating and eventually married the 3rd place winner in that competition. "Practicing competitive sports is important in building persistence," said Darya.

Shaked served three years in the Israeli army, where she was appointed an officer and a commander of a dozen male and female soldiers, six months after she was admitted. "I was ambitious and confident enough to agree to become an officer. I had to deal with military challenges at the age of 18 on the border between Israel and Lebanon during the time when soldiers were dying daily, and I was responsible for each soldier, alive and dead," she recalled.

Straight from the army, she was recruited by the Israeli Prime Minister's team, to be responsible for communications on defence aspects and the northern border. "It was a very interesting and intense time, and I happened to work closely with the Prime Minister. I stayed in the government for five years, went to a law school after that, and worked in a private equity fund later."

Darya had a lot of very adult challenges in her early years, so I assumed that all that made her mature pretty early. "I matured even before the army service. Firstly, my parents had a lot of confidence in me. My father always told me that I could come to him with any problems, but he knew that I was able to make the right decisions on my own as well. Secondly, due to my horseback riding competitions, I travelled alone around the country a lot, and it made me very independent and self-sufficient.

"I heard from a Jewish woman in Silicon Valley, that Israeli women are fearless. We don't think of ourselves as any different to men — we will take any stage to speak out and disregard all attempts to make us look smaller than we are. I think this is true — especially once a woman achieves a certain realization in her life. For example, serving in the army definitely gives you a sense of accomplishment, confidence, and the right mindset to be able to succeed in anything after that. I had a dozen men under my command, so it wasn't an option to think that a woman's opinion is valued any less than that of a man. But your mindset also depends on your family and education.

"Women around the world have been oppressed in one way or another for centuries. It's impossible to change our minds overnight. Despite that, the number of female-owned businesses is growing 2.5 times faster than the average in the US. So we are making an exponential jump, nevertheless. However, it will take years to reach a point of equality with men, because they have been taught for centuries (and still are) that they are the main providers and decision-makers. It takes time to finally feel that we are entitled to making financial decisions as well — at least for ourselves," Shaked concluded.

Clara Sieg

Partner, Revolution Ventures, United States

Clara Sieg technically belongs to a younger group of people who experience a lot of challenges in venture capital. However, her story is somewhat the opposite to the picture we are used to being shown. She was only in her mid-20s when she worked for an investment bank and advisory group that was helping the co-founder of AOL — billionaire Steve Case — institutionalize Revolution and raise their first growth fund. She then realized that she'd like to be on the other side of the table. A couple of years later, seeing significant opportunity in early-stage, Case decided to raise a new fund. When his partner, David Golden, asked Sieg to join the founding investment team and help start the San Francisco office, she jumped at the chance. Revolution now manages over a billion and a half dollars, which Clara invests as a General Partner.

"I was lucky to have David, who is now my partner, as a sounding board and mentor when I started in venture capital. He encourages debate, and while we often have different points of views, he always values my opinion. That openness and encouragement enabled me to have real ownership of the decisions I was making and the portfolio companies I invested in, which gave me the confidence to grow in this role. Instead of being pushed aside, I found it advantageous to bring a different perspective to opportunities we were analyzing, and challenge our thinking. I'm a female and am significantly younger than my partners, meaning I have different life experiences and perspectives than my partners do. We find that our portfolio benefits tremendously from our diverse and complementary skill sets and networks," said Clara.

Sieg graduated from Stanford and, unsurprisingly, most of her friends ended up working in technology and venture capital. Although she could choose a similar career trajectory, Sieg's path was a bit more considered. She has always looked for the opportunities that sit at the intersection of what interests her and what she is good at. Her father is a math professor and she majored in economics. With that analytical and quantitative background, she went on to investment banking after college, honing her ability to digest business models and dig through market opportunities, and making the eventual jump to joining a VC firm a no-brainer. "In venture capital, my analytical skill sets overlap uniquely with what interests me intellectually. We are constantly diving into different business models and technologies aiming to disrupt markets and partnering with outstanding founders to make those ideas a reality," added Clara.

When speaking about the challenges of being a female in a historically male-dominated industry, Clara recalled some regular occurrences. "People often assume I'm an admin when I'm copied on emails, because I have a female name. When it comes time for the meeting and I'm asked for water, I always just grab a glass and deliver it with the surprise of sitting down at the table. If you are gracious in those moments, you've made the point. Everyone recognizes the conscious or unconscious bias, but you don't derail the meeting, and instead start with the upper hand. And by the way you've learned that the person across the table from you doesn't prepare properly for meetings or know how to use LinkedIn. If we react furiously to the small things, it often triggers an equal reaction in others, perpetuating the problem and digging deeper biases."

I couldn't agree more with Clara, because I've been in situations myself, when taking a breath instead of delivering a sharp reply to an unwelcome treatment, opened doors to me that I couldn't have dreamt of opening. I also know that not all people are like me, and some women have a really hard time dealing with uncomfortable interpersonal relationships, so I asked Sieg whether her firm is equally friendly towards female entrepreneurs.

"About a quarter of our portfolio companies are female-founded and led. It's not a conscious effort on our part, we just believe in backing the best people solving big problems, and many of those people happen to be females. That's not representative of the industry as a whole, of course, and much of that stems from a lack of diversity at the partnership level in venture capital. Data shows that, whether we like it or not, women's answers to tough questions are often perceived by males as being aggressive or reactive, while a man delivering the same message is lauded for taking a stance with a strong point of view. Having a woman on the other side of the table necessarily helps balance those quiet biases out, and is the best way to narrow the funding gap," Clara explained.

"I don't think there is a quick fix to the lack of diversity in venture capital," she continued. "We have to be realistic about the fact that real change takes time, and if you push it too quickly, you end up with more losses than gains. If we have a slew of firms that make token hires but don't give the women they bring on board a real voice at the table, both the firms and the women they hire are set up for failure. We are then left with the 'we have tried — it didn't work' excuse, and renewed resistance to encouraging diversity. Taking a longer-term view, where firms commit to investing in the mentorship of diverse professionals, embracing differences in thought as necessary to top-tier investing, and recognizing that these changes will not happen overnight, is the only way to realize lasting change."

Sue Siegel

Chief Executive Officer,
GE Ventures, United States

"I am a woman, I am Asian and of European descent, I grew up in Puerto Rico, and I'm also 4'11!" laughed Sue. "I am and always have been a bit of an anomaly wherever I go, but that helps define who I am." The spirited start of my conversation with Sue Siegel immediately set its tone, and I knew that I'd get answers to my questions, no matter how provocative they were.

Whenever Sue was feeling that she was, as she put it, '100% mutt', her mother would tell her that she was a citizen of the world. Sue's mother was from the Philippines, and her father was born in Haiti to a French mother and German father. Her parents were academics whose interests helped motivate her to graduate in biochemistry and molecular biology at Boston University Medical School. "My soon-to-be husband was completing his PhD in biophysics, and I saw how passionate he was about it. I realized that I just didn't have that same passion for becoming an academic," she admitted. When she first told her parents that, despite having an advanced degree in science, she was going to pursue a business career, they were quite surprised.

Sue climbed to the top of the career ladder by working in many capacities, including running a public company. However, she had never considered becoming a venture capitalist until she was approached by Brook Byers, a founding partner of Kleiner Perkins Caufield & Byers (KPCB). Though she had little knowledge about the inner workings of venture capital, she did her due diligence on the field and decided that her next career move would be to a venture capital firm. With almost 25 years of work experience, she joined Mohr Davidow Ventures (MDV) as a General Partner, with a focus on healthcare.

Later, Sue was recruited to GE to helm the company's healthcare innovation initiative, Healthymagination. She leveraged her experience at MDV to launch GE Ventures. "We built an entire arsenal of methods of value creation and monetization," Sue said. "We create new companies from scratch, incubate them, and either make them independent business units within GE or spin them off to be standalone startups. We have invested in over 100 entrepreneurial startups and worked to find partnerships with GE businesses to accelerate areas of mutual growth."

When I asked her how she managed to create such a massive mechanism at one of the largest corporations in the world, she shared her approach. "If you compare the skills of venture investors to the skills of corporate operators, you will find them to be pretty different. The former typically have the skills of risk management, capital allocation, and portfolio management, while corporate operators bring metrics, process rigor, and execution savvy to scale projects. When you marry these two sets of skills, you get a powerful combination that helps unleash the full potential of an enterprise. I tried to build a team that represents this successful combination in the best possible way, with key GE executives and venture capitalists. This combination is key to our success."

The team may be one of Siegel's greatest achievements: women and minorities make up about 60% of the leadership team at GE Ventures. I certainly sourced Sue's recipe for that too.

"I have always believed that diversity of perspectives and thought is really important. Diversity is not only about gender — it is also about capabilities, experiences, age, race, and culture. At GE Ventures, we value diversity. Diverse talents, ideas, and perspectives add tremendous value to our business. I feel proud to work at a place that values this. We make an effort to ensure that we have diverse candidates at the top of our hiring funnel. And if you ask me about how many diverse people are enough, let me say that if you just have one such person, you are robbing your team and company!" Sue asserted.

"Women have historically not been involved in the decision-making process in many companies, and that contributes to the confidence gap that women experience. We all know that women are very well-educated and intelligent, so it's not about women being less competent. It's about awareness and effort — starting with men consciously inviting women to the boardroom. Like any habit, it requires time. Women should always make men a part of the conversations on diversity, women's issues in the workforce, and educate them on these important topics.

"To complement this, women need to ask to be included into decision-making process or considered to be part of it constantly, the same way men do. We often wait until those with more power grant us an opportunity to validate what we know we are capable of. Being good citizens by nature, we just do. Women should recognize that we are rarely asked what *we* want. So instead of waiting to be asked or told, we should offer our own solutions or step forward and ask for what *we* want. The worst that can happen is that we hear 'no'. But, I posit, the odds are that we will hear 'yes'."

Sue recalled an instance when Scott Sandell, the Chairman of the board of the National Venture Capital Association (NVCA) and Managing General Partner of National Enterprise Associates (NEA), asked the board about what it was going to do about the underrepresentation of women in the venture capital industry. The decision was made to create a Diversity Task Force and

Sue raised her hand to join. "I didn't do it because I was one of the few minorities in the room," she said. "I did it for two other reasons. Firstly, I realized that I was at that stage of my career where I could make a difference in this area, and thought 'if not us, then who?' Secondly, I got involved because influential men were asking for help with this issue, and they were, and are, the ones who can most effect the change.

"One of the tangible results from the effort is that we asked the NVCA members to voluntarily pledge to have at least one diverse candidate in their upcoming hiring pool for an investment partner, or its track. Many of them did so. We're seeing that sort of behavior becoming more deliberate and widespread.

"Do we have enough women in venture capital? No. Are we making progress, and have an opportunity to sustain it? Yes. We need to make sure this trend won't fade away, so we must continue to bring organizations that are committed to the same level of inclusion, into the mix, and that will provide tools to those that are seeking help, and want to learn how to be more inclusive."

I was curious what Sue thought about so-called token hires that other women I have interviewed for the book mentioned.

"Sigh. I understand and agree with the sentiment. But first, let's celebrate their achievements," she began. "Next, let's not diminish the accomplishments of the women who are these alleged 'token hires'. These are key women who are earning their leadership roles amongst the senior investing partners. They will be in influential roles for other well-deserving women to join VC firms. And, I do think more and more men are genuinely making the effort to include women-leaders as part of our industry.

"Many men and women in the venture community have asked me to talk to their daughters, sisters, or their mentees about women in business, because they do care about inclusion. They want them to be successful and actively work to give them equal opportunities. I believe that if we work intently to include men in our conversations about inclusion, and actively share our perspective to help them understand it, our industry will accelerate the progress that has been made."

Days before I talked to Sue, there was much attention given in the media to an interview with a Nobel Prize winner, a woman, who said, 'I don't see myself as a 'woman in science'. I see myself as a scientist.' This hype of adding the gender prefix to any powerful occupation is understandable, but some women don't like it and feel marginalized. When I faced this dilemma with the book title, I thought I could make everyone happy by naming it Women *Who* Venture. I asked Sue how she felt about it.

"Isn't it time to uplift the fact that we are women in venture capital? We are fantastic investors, and we are also women! Let's embrace it that more and more women are being recognized for their achievements in venture investing, and we can sustain this energy by being intentional about including and highlighting more of them.

"We now have the momentum that is caused by all parties agreeing that there should be more women at the table. And yes, there is still a lot of work to do. As a way to pay-it-forward, shouldn't all of us in senior positions, men and women, commit to being part of the diversity equation? One of the surest ways to sustain progress is for each of us to be inclusive and bring others along with us."

I decided to challenge Sue and asked if she had ever felt mistreated by men and what her advice would be to other women on dealing with such treatment. "I can't recall any situation where I was treated badly because I was a woman," she replied, but what Sue said next is one of the major lessons I am honored to include in this book. "We should assume noble intent when it comes to how we interact with each other. I have been on the receiving end of bad behavior, and I have a few guidelines that I personally use in these situations.

"My experience has been that rude people will find reasons to diminish or insult you, so I ignore their attempts — not because I'm rude in return, but because I know that they are entitled to their opinions. I don't validate their behavior by paying attention to them, and move on. There are going to be men or women who act badly towards each other, so regardless of gender, my guideline is: depersonalize and diffuse such situations. Cut out the noise, and continue on your path.

"Another important lesson I learned growing up, was how to understand and adapt to different perspectives, including those you don't agree with, and consider them without letting them undermine who you are. Only you can control who you are. It is also important to not impose your perspective on others, but to share it with the purpose of educating, as opposed to forcing agreement. I think it comes from my multicultural background, having to adapt to different surroundings, and being flexible enough to find a way to provide my point of view while respecting someone else's.

"That said, I fundamentally believe that everyone needs to have a position and be willing to defend it. I taught my sons the same as they were growing up. When they shared unpleasant experiences that were caused by others, I asked, 'Why let others determine what you think?' So my next guideline is: figure out who you want to be. When you're comfortable with who you are, you'll convey that to the world.

"Finally, how many times have you labored on a project, and known the materials cold, but didn't put in the time to crystallize which key points you wanted to impart, nor practiced what you were going to say and/or how you would say it? That brings me to another guideline: determine the message you want to deliver. Put in that last mile of preparation. Then communicate it clearly.

"Oftentimes, I find people of both genders work so darn hard, yet when they need to present their views, they don't drive home the key messages they set out to make or aren't clear on the ask. They know the intricate details of their work and, as importantly, need to be able to explain it clearly and succinctly. It happens to all of us. That last mile of preparation is crucial and can make the difference. I advise entrepreneurs to know what they want to achieve in a specific meeting, and before the meeting, know the three things they want to communicate. Give yourself the time to crystallize your message, or your ask. Prepare for how you're going to communicate it. You owe it to yourself."

Bonny Simi

President, JetBlue Technology Ventures, United States

"The airplane doesn't know you're a female," Bonny Simi said during the interview. I can see how reflecting on this fact could change the lives of many women out there. You don't even need to become a pilot for that — Bonny was directed by this principle from her school years. She has always done what she wanted to do, regardless of what role gender played in it.

It all started from a list of 100 things to accomplish in life, that she and her classmates were challenged to write in high school. "I was 14 and couldn't think of that many things. The first five things that came to my mind were: to go to a good college; to become an athlete — because it was an Olympics year; to work for a TV channel as a sportscaster — because I was passionately watching the Olympic games on TV; to become a pilot — because my mom often took me to visit the local airport; and to build a log cabin — just because I still find it cool. I never thought about any of this as being specifically male or female dreams — they were just what seemed interesting to me". Bonny did become a standout field hockey player and earned a scholarship to play the sport at a good college, which was Stanford.

Simi said that she didn't like to be told what she could not, or should not, do, so when she discovered bobsledding for herself and wanted to try the sport out, she learned that women were not allowed to bobsled. That didn't stop her, and she went on to attend a month-long local luge camp — bobsledding's spiritual sibling. Within four years, she earned a spot on the Olympic team, eventually suiting up for Team USA in three Winter Games.

When she was interviewed about the Olympics by the local ABC TV channel, the reporter asked what she wanted to do after graduation: "I'd love to come work for you," she replied without hesitation. Bonny was really passionate about sports, so it was only natural that she got hired to run a few stories from the Olympic games. The stories turned out to be so good that the broadcaster offered her a job. She took on the job, checking off another of her childhood goals, and covered sports for the evening news during the off-season from luge. "I majored in broadcast journalism in college, so that worked out really well. I was one of the only women doing local TV sports, but it never crossed my mind that I was in a mainly male territory," she stressed, making sure that I won't miss this detail.

Bonny knew that TV journalism wouldn't be her lifelong profession, so she used the money she earned on TV to become a pilot. She fell in love with flying and soon enough became a flight instructor while continuing working for the broadcaster. She went on to work for United Airlines and stayed with the company for 13 years, flying Boeing 727s, 737s and 777s around the world. "I thoroughly loved flying and still do, though I also wanted to expand my wings outside of the cockpit and take on new challenges."

Simi joined JetBlue Airways, where she took on new responsibilities. She spent the next 12 years working in a lot of different departments, managing large teams, and controlling a budget of $400 million. Bonny was a director of Airport and People Planning, a director of Customer Service, and Customer Experience, vice president of Talent, and of course, a pilot. She still sometimes calls up a captain and says, "Hey, would you like to have the weekend off?" and then flies up and down the east coast as a regular JetBlue captain.

Throughout her entire story, I could see how artfully she used each opportunity to build upon her experience and expand into new fields, and then find and fund another one. Even today at JetBlue Technology Ventures, she employs all her previous experience to the fullest, but also brings other people to the table whose skills and backgrounds complement hers. "In corporate venture capital, there are always two sides to the story — corporate and venture. Based on my experience, I can judge both the idea that a startup has, as well as the talent of the people behind it, and make sure that the corporation will benefit from our investments two years from now, and also far into the future. But we also have an awesome team that brings in travel, hospitality, technology, and venture investment expertise, to determine the investability of a startup."

I asked Bonny if she thinks it's easier for women to become corporate venture investors too. "I don't think gender makes any difference. I consider myself a venture capitalist, a pilot, a TV reporter — there is no room for specifying a gender here," she echoed the notion of the Nobel Prize winner I mentioned in the previous chapter. "I just do a great job and hope to inspire other women by my example. Certainly, there's a great opportunity for women in venture capital, but I don't think it's something that needs to be carved out separately. It's very difficult for a man to get into the industry too.

"Regardless of whether you are a man or a woman, you need to think about the brand of you," Simi added. "Whatever you think you want to be, challenge yourself to see what your heart says you are. If you love what you do, people will notice you, and you'll never work another day in your life."

Reshma Sohoni

Founding Partner, Seedcamp, United Kingdom

Reshma Sohoni is another example of why calling women risk-averse is just plain wrong. "Taking risks in my life is one of my greatest achievements to date," she said. "Studying two degrees simultaneously was a risk. I didn't perform as well as I could have during the first couple of years, because it was extremely challenging to take on both degrees. Moving to Europe was a big risk for the MBA, as opposed to the safer bet of one of the top MBA programs in the US. Taking a job at Vodafone in Japan, where I didn't know anyone, and didn't even speak the language, was a risk. So I have taken a lot of career and personal risks in my life, but I think they were all calculated. I was prepared to not win, but I tried to make sure that I wouldn't lose either. I believe that engineering is a way of life. It provides the infrastructure for how you think and how you process things. I always prefer to have a fundamental basis for any decision, whether it's based on numbers or is just highly structured."

At the age of 17, Reshma decided what she'd like to do in life, and after high school, she chose to do a dual degree program at UPenn — one in engineering and one in business. "While at university, I was heavily engaged in activities on campus and being a productive 'university citizen'. Whatever I did, was always somehow connected with entrepreneurship."

She then ended up in a tech investment bank, but didn't appreciate the experience. "Being in investment banking, especially as an analyst at the bottom of a hierarchy, is very similar to being at the bottom of a military hierarchy. It wasn't the most comfortable experience for me, but it really helped me learn what my limits are," she reflected.

Sohoni was born in India and moved to the US with her family when she was 10. Although she had a return ticket to the US when she went to Europe for her MBA, she fell in love with it and decided to stay. "I fell in love with Europe because of its diversity. The US may be ethnically diverse, but it is also very homogeneously 'American'," she said, smiling.

"I don't know about Europe being friendlier towards women compared to the US, but I can attest to the fact that it is less aggressive, for sure. The bro culture and sometimes even frat culture that one might face in the United States, starts in college and is fed by a high tolerance for aggression. We don't really have anything like that in Europe. There may be a stronger boys' club attitude towards women in snobbish circles, but it's far from what we observe in the US."

I assumed that Reshma also had a different cultural sense. "I have one sister, and we were always treated equally and weren't ever compared against each other or against boys. We were told that we could accomplish anything, and our parents tried to open every opportunity available, so that we could do that. I am used to joking that when I stepped into my young adult life, I started projecting myself as a tall, good-looking white man, and that conviction stayed with me since then," she laughed joyously.

"On a serious note, I think we should just focus on the things we are good at, and where we can build our excellence. That way, you're equal to anybody — man or woman — because it's not gender that you are opposing. You are trying to find your place on the bell curve of a specific occupation.

"I think the lack of diversity in venture capital has much deeper consequences than we typically read about. Old venture capital runs counter to where the demographic is going, at large, and therefore, counter to what needs society will have, and who will be serving them. Hence we are seeing so many new venture capital funds being established in the last few years, because people have realized that it is the right moment to build something of your own with the right culture and investment approach, rather than trying to fix something that may not be fixable at all."

In Europe, Sohoni launched Seedcamp in 2007, helping to kick-start the nascent European digital revolution by introducing one of the first accelerators outside of the US. The media calls her the 'queen of seed funding' who 'has Europe under her feet, America in her veins, and India in her soul'. Today, Seedcamp is known as the European Y Combinator, with hundreds of companies from more than 40 countries in its portfolio. It has been a decade-long journey, but Reshma stays true to seed- and early-stage funding.

"Maybe because I was always a foreigner to America, having come from India, and to Europe from America, I've always been kind of new and different. So there's a little bit of that underdog in my story, and I think I've seen the same in a lot of European founders. They're underdogs in a very US-dominated scene, and I want to help them fight with the same tools and play the same game."

Speaking of underdogs, I assumed that, as an engineer at heart, Reshma would appreciate entrepreneurs with technical backgrounds, more. "I look at it as a spectrum of skills. You can be a non-technical founder, but then you have to over-index on something else, whether it's leadership, marketing, or sales. There are definitely some deeptech sectors where it's very difficult to start a company without a good understanding of hardware or software. However, there are also many investment verticals today where non-tech founders are doing just fine."

Valerie Sorbie

Partner, Managing Director,
Gibraltar&Company, Canada

The conversation we had with Valerie Sorbie about gender issues was very educational. "Scientists have found that there are seven areas of the brain where women and men are different. These differences affect everything from decision-making, communicating, memory, providing, receiving and processing information, and types of risks taken, etc. If we can recognize and embrace these strong tendencies in each of the genders, it's very powerful. Once we're aware of how and why — on average — men and women think and act in certain circumstances, we can work together more effectively. The gender intelligence concept advocates that neither gender is to be blamed or 'fixed'. Gender differences are not weaknesses, but rather strengths that are often misunderstood and undervalued."

Valerie's parents were both doctors, and she assumed that she and her two sisters would continue the family occupational line. While her sisters indeed studied medicine, Valerie decided to reroute her destiny and became a 'physician for companies'. "When it was time for me, I realized that while I loved sciences and helping people, medicine wasn't the path I'd choose. I recall my father saying, 'When you go to university, you're learning to study something that fascinates you.' Since human dynamics and behavior, as well as biosciences, fascinated me, combining anthropology and biology fit the bill for undergrad. I was planning to get an MBA, but who was going to let an anthropologist into business school in the late '80s?! That was where my business journey began," Sorbie prefaced her story.

Valerie started exploring different opportunities, in order to become familiar with business. After further studies in France, she landed an analyst job at a strategy consulting boutique in London, which helped her get accepted into business school where she did her MBA and then decided to continue consulting.

"I absolutely loved it! I used to explain to my parents, who didn't quite understand what I did, that it's like being a physician for companies — dealing with 'organizational health' issues and helping them grow (or shrink...)."

Valerie eventually left consulting solely for personal reasons after she gave birth to her second of three children, and started her first business operations job, and then another one and another one. "With combined strategy and operational experience, I naturally look for gaps in different organizations, and can see where my skill set could help fill those gaps and serve a need. For instance, when I was running strategy and implementation for a bank, I worked on a project with the CEO of capital markets and noted to him, 'You've actually got no COO who's pulling everything together for you — strategy, marketing, compliance, business risk, real estate, etc.' Shortly thereafter, the bank created that role for me."

After several years of that work, it was time for Valerie to do something else. "I felt I'd had 30 years of phenomenal varied experiences, holding senior roles that fit my skill set and interests, as well as each organization's needs, but then it was time for new learnings and challenges. I recall a friend from the PE/VC world saying something that stuck with me, 'You've worked in traditional organizational settings for your career so far. At this point, why not leverage that experience to create value by making a greater impact across a broad spectrum of businesses?'"

Valerie got into venture capital through a startup board she chaired that was seeking financing. One of the VC firms that was considering backing it, was looking for someone to help them run one of their new portfolio companies. "I had lunch with one of the two founding partners of the firm, and very quickly we realized it was a great match — they had a need, which I, fortunately, had a specific skill set for. So we jumped in, and I haven't looked back since!"

Sorbie is a Partner and Managing Director at Gibraltar & Company, where she takes on board seats to help portfolio companies. Independently, she also serves as a Director on the boards of for-profit companies and not-for-profit organizations. "I have come to appreciate that paying attention to elements that are not intrinsically financial in nature can drive significant financial results."

Valerie is actively advising women on navigating relationships and behavior in professional settings, and she shared her concerns with me. "While I think exceptional progress has been made in bringing more women to the table, I worry that the current approach can lead to defensive behaviour or avoidance, which doesn't help anyone. To prevent it, I recommend that women stick to the facts when standing up for themselves. For instance, if somebody thinks they are underappreciated or underpaid, they will get a better outcome if they have done their research and have a fact-based and measured approach to the conversation.

"Another thing I recommend is always to be authentic, stay true to your values, while still catering to your audience. For instance, if we are speaking to students, we need to speak their language. If a woman is speaking to a boardroom dominated by men, she needs to approach the situation in a manner that resonates with the makeup of the room and topic being discussed. She will get further in a conversation if she recognizes the context, understands who her audience is and determines how best to communicate to it."

When I asked Valerie how she personally reacts to biased behavior towards herself, she said, "I am an optimistic person. I don't judge and am fortunate to be able to see the humour in most situations. I always treat people with dignity and never close a door."

Laela Sturdy

General Partner,
CapitalG, United States

"Any VC firm that is willing to make bets on individuals who haven't done investing before, will naturally attract a more diverse employee base," Laela Sturdy started sharing her perspective on diversity in venture capital. "One of the historical issues with the industry is that venture capitalists have been recruiting people with a relatively narrow skill set and range of experiences, and women and underrepresented groups were very rare in that group. If a VC firm truly wants to add diversity to the team today, I'd advise them to find some other criteria and use different signals when hiring people, beyond what the industry has been looking for during the last five decades. We should look for talented and capable people who display a high potential for being great investors, and give them a chance to prove our assumptions right.

"My partners made a bet on me when I was transitioning from Google to Capital G, because I hadn't done investing before. But I had a lot of different kinds of success and accomplishments in my career, so they gave me a chance to show myself in investing."

Laela studied biochemistry because she thought she wanted to be a doctor. During her junior year of college, she was doing a short internship with a doctor and witnessed a real surgery. "I then realized that I was terrified of blood!" she laughed. "I was just a bystander during the surgery, and said to myself, 'Okay, I love science and medical innovation, but I'm going to find another career to pursue.'" We then laughed together, because I, personally, had transferred from the third year of the general medicine to a financial faculty for a very similar reason: listening to the heartbeat of my group mate with a stethoscope, felt to me to be too intrusive in my personal space.

After that epiphany, Laela found her passion for human rights, social causes, business, and entrepreneurship, and applied to Stanford Business School to learn more about all that. She happened to be one of the few people in the class who hadn't worked in business at all, so she decided to find an internship that would be sort of a crash course about business. Her choice fell on consulting, of course.

"One of the great things about consulting firms is that they really are open to people coming from different backgrounds. They don't judge your experiences, but really try to evaluate what they think your potential could be instead, and then they're willing to train you to help you reach that potential. But I realized that I didn't want to stay in consulting forever, because I had more of an operator's mentality. I like to own things — I like to help create and start things."

With that realization, she was lucky to join Alphabet (formerly Google) and led different projects within the corporation, which satisfied her entrepreneurial spirit. She then joined Capital G — a VC firm entirely funded by Alphabet, but remaining an independent investment vehicle. Venture investing is pretty much the opposite of owning things, so I asked Laela how that transition went.

"It was indeed a transition, but there were certain things that smoothed it out for me. Firstly, I have been with Capital G from the ground level and helped to build the team and culture. Unlike working for an already well-established firm, it was very rewarding to me from the creation and entrepreneurial perspective.

"Secondly, what is amazing about venture capital is that I am constantly surrounded by intellectually curious people. The thing I loved about consulting is that you get to work on lots of different problems, so your pace of learning is very accelerated. It is fair to say the same about venture capital investing."

Having mentioned this commonality, Laela said that other than that, venture capital is very different from consulting from many perspectives. I wondered how she'd explain the fact that many VC firms prefer hiring people with consulting backgrounds. "Consulting firms are great at giving you a toolkit and framework for thinking about different business challenges. I still rely on the many things I learned about business analysis, strategy and decision-making, and how to answer many other questions in a systematic way. However, I think that consulting backgrounds may be only sufficient for junior level positions. I haven't seen many people in senior VC investment positions coming directly from consulting, and I think that you'd need more than that if you aim to become a principal or a partner."

When I asked her about her career experience as a woman, she replied. "For better or worse, I don't have any stories to tell, but I do think that gender bias probably had a deeper effect on me than I realize. I haven't tended to attribute any negative interactions with somebody to my gender, because I always try to block out as much negativity as I can on a personal level, in order to get up every morning and do the work.

"I'm very committed to increasing the representation of women and other underrepresented groups in venture capital. If I see or hear any bias around the table, anything that I consider to be blatant, I always call that out. However, what I see more often is that there is a more subtle and therefore more toxic bias that is a lot harder to call out. Issues around inclusion are challenging for any minority group, and I see that with women in venture capital. It is hard to be in an underrepresented group, or a woman in a male-dominated field like venture capital. As a minority, you have to compete much harder for jobs, deals, and everything, so tenacity and resilience are critical qualities of character that will help you overcome these challenges. Building a community to get support for yourself, and to give support to others, is critical to the journey."

Lisa Suennen

Venture Group Leader, Manatt Ventures, United States

I first learned about Lisa Suennen from her blog, when she was in between her venture capital jobs. She was one of very few female investors who was actively blogging at the time and I appreciated it a lot. It was absolutely obvious to me that she was diligently building her online presence and I was very excited to learn more about her career and share her experience in the book.

"Along the way, I decided that I needed to take my personal brand into my own hands, and not rely on the kindness of strangers to make me successful," Lisa Suennen defined the topic of our conversation. "There are three aspects to building your brand: mentorship, networking, and getting your voice out there. Firstly, I sought out mentors — other women in the field, but also men who I thought could help me move ahead. Secondly, I spent a lot of time on networking, which I really hated at first, but I forced myself to get out there and meet as many people as I could, in order to create opportunities.

"Finally, I started to write online and put my thoughts out there. I was amazed by how differently I was treated after I started my blog 12 years ago! It almost seemed like people didn't realize that I had thoughts before!" Lisa let out a loud and inspiring belly laugh. "The more I wrote, the more seriously I was taken. So I really made a point of keeping that up - sometimes to my own detriment, because writing takes a lot of time and energy, but it's worth doing.

"All three of the key personal branding elements — mentorship, networking, and public speaking — require a deliberate investment of time, but it pays off later, and when it does, it pays off big! It's very important to market ourselves. Make self-marketing a part of your job. Saying that venture investing leaves no time for that isn't a good enough excuse. It is definitely a trade-off of time for something else, and sometimes it's hard to make that trade-off with family, or personal time, or whatever it is, but I think you need to decide how much you want it, and which parts of your life you're going to invest in," she stated candidly.

When Suennen was brainstorming her blog name, she was looking for a word that would define her, along with the keyword "venture". She ended up marrying it with the mythical creature "Valkyrie" — one of the fierce women in Norse mythology (and, later, in Marvel Comics) who chooses those who may die in battles and those who may live. "I thought that was a pretty hilarious metaphor for venture capital," Suennen smiled. Long after she came up with this idea, she became well-known for deflating doomed business models and calling out BS.

Lisa doesn't take herself too seriously and doesn't hesitate to make light of those who do. What started as a joke, became her alter ego, and I could definitely feel it being fully embraced. Suennen stamps her personal brand on business cards and the nameplate outside her office. She keeps buying Valkyrie-themed memorabilia, like a phone case or a hand-knitted horned helmet for her chihuahua.

One doesn't need to spend much time with Lisa to see her authentic character. Suennen challenges sugar coating in venture capital, asks provocative questions, always adds humor to the mix, and keeps people accountable. She has had many investment successes and also watched would-be promising companies fail.

Her colleagues characterize Lisa as an incisive thinker who can negotiate in difficult situations and come up with creative solutions to many investment and entrepreneurial challenges. But she is also known to drop the occasional F-bomb in a conference-room. I learned it first-hand, when she replied to one of my questions with, "Some people are just assholes." When I mentioned that I would strike that from the transcript, she smiled, but I knew she was serious. "You don't have to!" People may find her intimidating, but her energy will definitely kick you forward.

Suennen studied journalism and political science as an undergraduate at U.C. Berkeley, planning to become a political journalist. She earned a master's and most of a PhD in political science, but got consumed by the tech and business world due to being in close proximity to it. After a short stint in the tech world, Lisa joined a pioneering company in managed care for behavioral health, which she helped turn from an early-stage startup into a publicly traded corporation that was acquired for just shy of a billion, back in 1998.

Having worked in marketing, sales, and operations, she then co-founded a venture capital fund with the focus on improving the quality of healthcare, along with reducing costs thereof. After 15 years at one firm, she decided that it was time for her to go. She went out on her own and was consulting largely on venture fund formation and venture strategy. She was quickly noticed by one of her clients — GE Ventures — and they invited her to lead their healthcare group. Lisa most recently joined an integrated professional services firm — Manatt, Phelps & Phillips, LLP, which does both strategic consulting and provides legal services; she leads the Digital & Technology group and runs their venture practice. She is also an advisor to several other venture funds.

A break in a venture capital career can be a killer — if you lose your seat at the table, it's oftentimes as hard to get back to it as it is for the newbies to enter. I asked Lisa for her advice on preserving one's position if a break happens for any reason. "You have to stay engaged in the community, have to nurture your network and stay connected — you can't disappear." That's why building your own social platform can help tremendously during a comeback.

Pocket Sun

Founding Partner,
SoGal Ventures, Singapore

SoGal, like Women.VC, started 5 years ago, in 2014. I remember when Pocket Sun and her partner, Elizabeth Galbut, first appeared on the news with their venture capital fund for millennials — we set up Google Alerts so as not to miss when they started making deals, in order to include them in our study.

Pocket Sun started fundraising when female-led VC firms were still an anomaly. "It took me some time to fully believe that I could do this, because there weren't many role models to replicate and no one had actually implemented a similar concept to what I had in mind. We were one of very few young fund managers out there, with a cross-continental team, while most of the other investors were two or three decades older than us, and only invested within a 30-miles radius. There wasn't much talk about women in venture capital whatsoever, so it was pretty lonely and really nerve-racking to be on this path.

"I remember having a meeting with a well-known male VC, who kept asking me why the hell I thought that I could start a VC firm, and I almost cried. I remember an institutional investor who doubted whether we had come to the meeting prepared at all, even though we had invested in a bunch of good startups by that time and obviously were serious about investing. But the strongest bias came from myself. It's a process to fully believe in one's capabilities and competitive advantage in this male-dominated, reluctant-to-change field, and many women have to go through this in one way or another."

Yiqing "Pocket" Sun will only turn 28 years old shortly after this book goes live, but she is very aware of herself and her surroundings. Pocket, as an only child, was raised amongst mostly male childhood friends, which she feels has made her adventurous. According to Pocket, male entrepreneurs tend to state world-changing ambitions upfront, whereas many women start businesses to solve a real problem, and changing the world is an unintended by-product.

Sun, a Chinese national, arrived in the United States in 2009 to earn a bachelor's degree in business administration from The College of William and Mary in Virginia. In college, she was intimidated by her US school friends and was not confident about her academic or professional abilities. "I told my dad that I couldn't even get an internship, and how defeated I felt, but he said, 'Don't worry about getting a job. You're going to provide jobs for others in the future.' I didn't understand what he really meant until I started SoGal," she recalled.

After working hard to get a job that would also sponsor her visa, she found out that she hadn't passed a computer-generated lottery, which meant that her work visa application wouldn't even be processed. When her visa was about to expire, she decided to go to graduate school to obtain a master degree in entrepreneurship and innovation at the Marshall School of Business. During the first few months of the program, she realized that entrepreneurship was the only way to make a real impact on the world, and she was determined to start something on her own. However, a problem became obvious very quickly. She saw the lack of support for female entrepreneurs, as well as there being a distinct lack of success stories about women who were role models. She was frustrated to see all-male speaker panels, judges and pitch teams everywhere, and all of the investors she met back then, were men.

Motivated to solve the problem, she challenged herself to start something on her own to help young, aspiring female entrepreneurs, but also to foster a culture where women uplift one another instead of tearing each other down. "I wanted to show that you don't have to be a certain way to be an entrepreneur. You don't have to be over a certain age or be the most experienced person in the room to start a successful business. I wanted to pass that idea on to more young women before they even step out of college."

Two months into her entrepreneurship master's course, she established the global female entrepreneurs community, SoGal, which soon began to organize events, summits and startup competitions. Six months later, she applied for a venture capital executive program at Stanford University, where she was able to validate that she actually had enough knowledge on venture investing, despite being the youngest and most inexperienced person in the group. She was inspired by Jason Calacanis, a well-known angel investor, to start a fund on her own, because the firm she wanted to work for did not exist. During the program, she met Elizabeth Galbut, and they partnered up for the first female-led millennial venture capital firm — SoGal Ventures — which quickly started investing in the US and Asia (Sun is mostly based in Singapore). "SoGal Ventures started out with the goal of only investing in female founders, but over time, we realised that we would create a problem in reverse, so we decided to focus on diversity instead," Pocket explained, and I couldn't help but notice that we talked about this with some other experienced investors on the pages of this book, theoretically, while the managers of SoGal had come to the same conclusion by actually doing it.

You might have noticed that one of my favorite interview questions for this book is how the entrepreneurial and investment communities in the United States are different from those in other countries. I especially enjoy comparing the US to Asia, because I know first-hand how different these cultures are, and it fascinates me. Pocket added more colors to what has been said by other Asian investors.

"Gender bias exists everywhere, but in different forms. In Asia, there is definitely a higher percentage of women in senior management in general, and in the venture capital industry in particular. But ironically enough, women in Asia sometimes face much more blatantly sexist comments and are objectified much more than what we see in the United States. It's not illegal here to ask women questions about their age, marital status, or plans for having kids, during a job interview. So there *is* a gender bias in Asia and it's much more straightforward than in western countries. It's a sad truth, but at the same time, it clears the air.

"For example, there is one Chinese male investor who became infamous for saying that one of his top ten investing rules is to not invest in female founders. On the one hand, it's ridiculous that this guy thinks that way and that he has no idea what he is missing out on. But on the other hand, it saves so much time for female founders on pitching him and exposing themselves to yet another rejection. Whereas in the United States, a lot of people try to be politically correct and there's a lot of talking, but very few people are actually doing something."

Indeed, I think that a lot of time wasted by female entrepreneurs on pitching Silicon Valley VCs, who have already decided that they are not going to invest in them before they knocked on their doors. But with such a strong spotlight on the industry, everybody is now looking over their shoulders to avoid bad publicity.

"Most western people say something neutral when they disagree, like, 'interesting'. In Asia, a lot of men are eager to argue openly about whether investing in women is a valid thesis. They throw around arguments like, 'Women are more distracted,' or 'Women don't work as hard,' or 'Women have to take care of babies,' and even, 'Women aren't fit to lead a big team'. However, it opens the door to educating them on the issue. Whereas when people just pretend to agree with you or they appear neutral, there is no way to start a conversation and try to change their opinion, so the issue remains."

Pocket coincidentally mentioned a study already discussed with other women in this book, that showed a better investment performance of investors who have daughters, but added an interesting personal observation to it. "I think that men with daughters do have a different approach to women in business, but this statistic applies mainly to English-speaking countries. In my opinion, it is not quite true in Asian countries. I don't see Asian fathers changing their perspectives on women after having daughters the same way as American men do."

We then focused on the status of women in the VC industry in Asia. "There are more young women in venture capital in Asia than in the United States. I think that is because venture capital, as an industry, is young here as well. When it started in Asia, women were already well represented in the workforce. Whereas, in Silicon Valley, the venture capital industry was established when women were rarely in the technology or business, so it stayed as a boys club over the years.

"There aren't enough opportunities for people with no prior investing experience to step into venture capital in the US — the industry is still only open to the chosen few. Whereas in China, I've seen a lot of people who don't have Ivy League degrees or relevant experience, but still end up being successful in venture capital. It may also be explained by the fact that Chinese VC firms probably hire more people in general, and that's why the doors are more open and there are more opportunities for career changes. In China, people are more willing to take a chance on you, while in the US, that's only true if you are in the inner circle.

"That said, this concept that diversity is great for business and society is not yet popular in Asia. Asians are practical: if you work hard and can stand the blatant sexism, you have a higher chance of success than you would have in the West."

Before starting to talk about SoGal's portfolio, I asked Pocket how her fundraising process went. "I think the limited partner community is not doing enough for diversity yet. I still find it very old-fashioned, because they prefer making safe bets on brand names. Many institutional investors say that they are open to first-time fund managers, but the truth is that they are very reluctant to build new relationships. When untraditional funders, such as state organizations and different initiatives, invite you to pitch, emerging managers usually have to jump through many hoops for a tiny allocation that comes with predatory terms. Similar to female entrepreneurs raising a small fraction of venture capital, female fund managers raise much less money for their own funds than male counterparts with a similar or worse calibre," Sun concluded.

SoGal invests in early-stage startups that have at least one female founder. When I asked Pocket whether she feels that women need to level up their game, she said that female entrepreneurs still need more training. "Women tend to underpromise and overdeliver. They are usually good at executing and are highly responsible for what they're doing." But she thinks that there is work that venture investors need to do too. "As more women become investors, the communication gap will narrow down, so that female founders won't need to try extra hard to pitch in a way that men would get it. I also wish that investors of both genders would pay more attention to whether they judge female founders based on past achievements or future potential. I think we still need to learn how to do the latter."

Pocket believes that SoGal is fishing in uncrowded waters, investing in high-quality diverse entrepreneurs at better valuations, and has a huge advantage over traditional VC firms in catching the next billion dollar companies early. She said that SoGal Ventures' fund performance so far has been proving their thesis correct.

Pocket mentioned two observations we've never discussed with other investors in the book, which are great closing topics you could contemplate. Firstly, she noticed the performance difference between female- and male-led companies in one's portfolio. "Some statistics have been collected about the share of support that female CEOs get from investors in a male-dominated portfolio. It made me wonder whether male CEOs in our portfolio — which is female-dominated — are getting the same level of support from us. I think that it's a fair concern and VCs should pay attention to this issue."

Secondly, she wanted to bring to the attention of all investors who read this book the mental health of founders and CEOs. "We don't talk enough about the emotional well-being of our founders, which is quite an oversight, because it's not just a matter of human empathy, but is also a risk factor that affects a fund's performance. This has not really been addressed in the venture capital ecosystem, but we have recently had a case with our portfolio company, where we realised that it's a serious issue. To address it, we launched a 6-month program called 'Build Without Burnout', which is fully sponsored by the SoGal Foundation for selected founders. I think for long-term success, venture investors need to focus on their founders' holistic wellness from day one."

Sarah Tavel

General Partner,
Benchmark, United States

Sarah Tavel broke into venture capital almost immediately after college, thanks to her experience in... sales. She first worked for a New York non-profit, going from door to door, trying to convince people to donate money. When she started at Harvard, she was selling ads for local publications. Having confirmed her selling skills with pretty good earnings, Sarah decided it was time to level up, so she launched a residential house painting company that became a general subcontractor, while still studying in college. "That was the most random thing, especially for a kid growing up in Manhattan, but I just knew I could sell," she said. I was prepared to hear that Sarah was actually putting up drywall herself, but she was much wiser than that. As a business manager, she was finding leads, making estimates on renovation work, closing deals, hiring crews to execute the projects, and supervising them. How does one become a venture investor after that?

"I was always interested in investing, and I had always been entrepreneurial, so venture capital sounded like the nexus of my two passions," Sarah started explaining. "When I heard about an analyst job at a venture capital firm, I knew that I could do that job well. The skills I had acquired seemed like strangely shaped puzzle pieces that would be a perfect fit for that role."

A VC analyst is an entry-level job, which is almost exclusively focused on sourcing new opportunities for the firm. And what that means, is cold calling, cold emailing, hunting down companies, and... getting rejected. You are almost like a sales representative — calling companies to learn more about them, and ultimately, in a way, selling the money that your VC firm has.

"This job rewards persistent, fast learners who have the right kind of sales experience. I can't tell you how many emails and phone calls it would take me before I would get connected to the CEOs of the companies. You can't be dissuaded when the first or 15th email goes unanswered," Sarah advised.

It brought our conversation to the point that venture capital is a service business. "Yes, absolutely," Tavel agreed. "I think the most successful partnerships that happen with our entrepreneurs are when the entrepreneurs use us as an extension of their team. We work hard on behalf of our companies at Benchmark, and I want to do anything I can to make them successful. As a matter of fact, I was recently reflecting with one of my partners on how some people have commoditized venture capital in their minds, by thinking that venture investors are interchangeable. There's a big gap between the value that really great investors can bring to a company, and the damage that really bad ones can do to it."

In just six years, Sarah rose from an entry-level analyst to a vice president of Bessemer Partners. Growing within one firm from a junior position to a senior one is not a common scenario, and I wanted to hear her advice to all aspiring VCs on building their careers without raising their own funds.

"Think about yourself as a little seed. First, you want to find and plant yourself in the richest soil that will let you grow and flourish. So my advice to young investment professionals is to make sure that they are placing themselves in a firm that will let them blossom.

"I was very lucky to land at Bessemer, because it is an incredible firm that focuses on growing people from within. At many other firms, there is no path for starting in a junior position and growing into a partner. You can get great experience as an associate, but after a couple of years, you would have to move to another firm to advance into a partner role. For example, my current firm, Benchmark, is a small team consisting of only general partners. Our philosophy is that every partner is equal, which is why we don't have junior partners.

"Secondly, in order to grow, it's important to have a great gardener who will water you and make sure the sun is shining above you. I was lucky at Bessemer, because I was hired by their partner, Jeremy Levine, who mentored me for all of my six years at the firm. That was an extraordinary stroke of luck for me and I learned so much during my time there," Sarah recalled.

This is a classic example of the apprenticeship that venture capital is known for. Is it really, though, since most of the firms are too small to let staff grow? "Apprenticeship happens not only when you are junior to the person who is mentoring you, but it also happens in a partnership. If you start as a partner, you're still leaning on your partners and learning from each other, but without the hierarchy," Sarah clarified.

Despite the rich soil and dedicated gardener at Bessemer, she left the firm for a promising startup that she had invested in when it only had five employees. That was then new social network called Pinterest. I asked her a question, which many people were probably asking her too: why would a person with a great career in venture capital leave for a startup?

"I had invested in Pinterest while still working at Bessemer and was helping them as much as I could from the outside. While I was doing that, there was always this voice in the back of my mind asking, 'What would it feel like to actually be in a startup and to be part of the team?'" Tavel said warmly.

"I loved leading teams when I was in school — whether it was sports or other groups — and I started to wonder if I would be best in an operator role. As I spent more time with Pinterest, that voice was just getting louder. Remember that video, where Jeff Bezos talks about his 'regret minimization framework', which is what made him quit his high-paying job and start Amazon? He talks about making decisions today that minimize the regret that you might have in the future. It's what gave him the courage to start Amazon. I knew that I was going to have a future in venture capital, but a big part of me couldn't help but wonder: When I am an old lady looking back at my career, would I always regret that I hadn't tried to be on the other side of the table?

"It felt like a big career risk at the time because, like you said, Renata. I knew that I could keep growing in the venture capital industry and I didn't have any clue what was required to be great at operating, and there was a chance that I could be fired from Pinterest three months later. And then where would I be? But I decided I had to take that leap, otherwise I'd regret it."

Tavel had such a strong conviction that she decided to join Pinterest as a product manager and helped the company scale for more than three years. While at Pinterest, she was approached by another VC firm, Greylock, and she asked herself whether she wanted to go back to Bessemer or not. "I loved my time at Bessemer, but going back would have been the safe and easy thing to do. I wanted to challenge myself in my next role and go somewhere where I was coming in as a general partner," she said. When I asked whether she'd go back to a startup again, Sarah replied, "I feel so lucky to be doing what I'm doing. Never say never, but I hope that this will be my job for as long as possible."

A little later after our conversation, Sarah posted her advice for aspiring venture investors who come from operational roles, on social media. I couldn't ignore it. "Going from operations to venture capital is a big transition. I spent six years in VC before joining Pinterest. When I left Pinterest to join Greylock, I thought it would be like getting back on a bike. Instead, it felt like getting a train back on the tracks one wheel at a time, for three main reasons.

"Firstly, operators — particularly in a product function — always make tangible progress from point A to point B. For example, when releasing a new feature, you make progress towards that goal daily. Sometimes, there are setbacks and frustrations, but you are always moving towards that tangible point B. When you get there, you have the satisfaction of 'shipping'. In venture capital, point B is: 'I want to make a great investment', and it is intangible. You don't know how you'll find it, you don't know if you'll know it when you see it, and it will take years to really confirm it ('ship'). That will be one of the wheels to get on the track. You need to shift your focus from outcomes to the process. It feels more like the unpredictability of gardening than building a house brick by brick.

"Many ex-operators make too many investments during their first year, because they are (A) not calibrated, and (B) used to achieving results, and therefore focus on making investments. It takes a while to internalize that the true outcome for venture capitalists is the return of capital to limited partners. This is the part of what makes VC seemingly easy to do (as in 'making investments'), and really freaking hard to be great at (as in 'generate great returns'). First-time investors should mentally prepare themselves for months of activity with no tangible results, and a long feedback cycle.

"Secondly, in venture capital, you make about ten big decisions a year: ~8 companies that you really dig in on and ultimately pass or lose, and ~2 that you say 'yes' to and invest in. These are big one-way door decisions: once you say 'yay' or 'nay', there is no going back. Of course, the feedback cycle on those decisions take years! With plenty of ups and downs in between. In operations, you're making dozens of two-way door decisions every day. The one-way door decisions in operations are rare. At Pinterest, I'd ship an experiment, and three days later, have a good sense of whether it was going to be good or bad.

"Lastly, as an operator, you feel the stress of execution. As a venture capitalist, you trade that stress for the anxiety of making one-way door decisions and the anxiety of influencing, but not controlling, the outcome after you invest. Too many operators think they'll transition to venture capital and 'scratch their operating itch' by participating in the operations of their portfolio companies. NO! That's a delusion and unhealthy for companies. You'll need to find other outlets for that.

"Again, it's a big transition, but once you get that train on the tracks, if you're someone who loves to learn, is endlessly curious, gets energized by working with founders, is inclined to be an investor, loves to sell, and is competitive — I can't imagine a better job."

Getting back to our interview, I thought that our conversation was over, because Sarah didn't sound like she had stories to tell about her being a woman in venture capital, but when I assumed that out loud, she objected. "We all face subconscious bias. Early in my career, I didn't have a word for it, and when you can't name it, you don't really understand it. Today people have a language for it and I think that this kind of awareness and acceptance is the first step toward progress.

"I talk to people who deny their own subconscious bias all the time. Those are usually the ones who have it the most," Tavel was absolutely right about that, and it's not just a coincidence, but it has been empirically proven. A lot has been said about denialism as deception and self-deception. The most racist, sexist and ageist people are the ones who are most insistent on their lack of a bias for that. Growing up among prominent psychiatrists, I am familiar with these studies, as well as the notion that for a patient, admitting that they have an addiction is the first step on the path to eliminating it.

"The acceptance of one's bias is the first step in making progress — without being aware that there is a problem, one can never resolve it. So, as a community, we have already made this important step and admitted that gender, race, and age biases exist," Tavel concluded.

Nevertheless, female VCs and entrepreneurs continue to face situations in which men omit them or ignore their contributions, such as when asked about naming notable investors or entrepreneurs. The daring women call them out on that, however, it doesn't seem to work and we see no admission of bias by such men. I referred to a real situation that had happened days before I talked to Sarah, and she replied, "I don't know the right answer for solving this, but I think you need someone who is in this person's inner circle to get through to them. Someone who is trusted by that person and can say in a friendly manner, 'I think you were in the wrong here. Here's where you might have a blind spot.' It is very human to be biased. I noticed that for myself as well, and it drives me crazy. But the only way that I can correct it is to be aware of it. Because if we are not aware of it, it doesn't mean it's not happening — it just means we're blind to it."

Laurel Touby

Managing Director,
Supernode Ventures, United States

Laurel Touby founded Mediabistro.com in 1994, the platform became a trusted resource — providing job listings, online classes, content and community — for professionals who worked in the media, marketing, advertising and publishing industries. It was sold for $23 million right before the crisis of 2008.

Today, Touby is an investor in early-stage startups, but she still has a passion for bringing people together and made it a foundation of her VC fund, Supernode Ventures. "Our investment thesis is built on leveraging our massive network to create lots of touch points between the network members and our portfolio companies, in order to maximize deal flow and help our founders. I know first-hand that without constant maintenance and grooming, your network is like an aging spiderweb: it looks strong until you test it — then it disintegrates."

Throughout our conversation, Touby was diligently describing the challenges she faced during her investing career, in the clear and precise manner typical of business journalists. "Being an angel investor has its downsides, because we write smaller checks, and some entrepreneurs don't take angel investors seriously enough. They may rush us into writing a check within days, not provide us with enough time to evaluate the deal, give us very little information about the company, and generally, behave very unprofessionally. I realized that I would be more efficient as an institutional fund and went on a fundraising journey.

"I see many people who want to be founders, because it's fashionable today. What I am looking for is a founder who puts themselves at risk to prove that their idea is a real business opportunity before pitching me. I want someone who's taking a risk, because I'm taking a risk."

Laurel Touby is a successful entrepreneur and has a strong portfolio of companies as an angel investor. "I think women have to do everything doubly well, in order to get half of the attention and respect that men do. You have to get double the returns, double the exits, double everything, in order to get people to give you a chance. It is true when they say that funders invest in a man's potential, but when it comes to women, they invest in the results and those results must be way above average to seem worthy for them," she shared. "I took my own capital and put it at risk, in order to show that I could do this, and got a fantastic 29% IRR for my angel fund, but that didn't seem good enough for limited partners when I went fundraising for an institutional fund. Investors who would normally put in a million dollar check in other proof-of-concept funds were writing only $100,000 checks to my fund. I don't think raising a fund was harder for me than it was for other first-time managers, however, it definitely felt that way."

But here's the good news: all of Supernode's limited partners are men and couples, where the men were advocates for Laurel. "Women's relationship with money is different from that of men. Women of a certain generation only learned how to spend their money or donate it — not invest it. Other women, when asked to invest in a fund, treat you as if you were asking for a favor. Well, I am just offering them an opportunity to earn returns! Finding female limited partners *can* be difficult.

"When it comes to institutional investors, I think we need more of those who can write small checks and possibly even associations of such who would bundle together to invest in emerging managers. Because the most common response that we hear from them is, 'You're not raising enough money. Come back with a bigger fund'. And there is not much that you can reply to that, for several reasons. Firstly, first-time funds, especially those managed by women or minorities, rarely raise large amounts. They are called emerging for a reason. Secondly, such funds typically invest in early-stage companies — pre-seed, seed, pre-Series A. This investment focus defines the fund size.

"That said, the industry also knows cases where institutional investors had no problems with investing in male-led, small, first-time funds. For example, Chris Sacca, who backed us, raised just $8 million for his first fund, and look what he achieved with that. I doubt that his limited partners told him back then that an $8 million fund is too small to move the needle for them.

"I think that institutional investors should become more open to emerging managers and be adventurous enough to take a leap of faith and believe in first-time managers. They should create a special bucket for us. After all, it's often the small emerging managers who are seeding the future," Laurel concluded.

We talked a little more about limited partners and that diversity for them, oftentimes, means investing in the same male-run established venture capital firms, which, by a lucky coincidence, might have added a female to their investment team. We talked about the fact that a sub-$10 million VC fund doesn't cover even average salaries for its managers, but people rarely talk about it publicly not to undermine their status. It's discussions like this that show that although it's fashionable to be a venture capitalist, the reality of the job is not that glossy is at may seem.

Trae Vassallo

Founding Partner, Defy, United States

Trae's story started when she worked as a product engineer on consumer electronics devices, one of which, PalmV, was hugely popular in former times. The then CEO of Palm Inc., Donna Dubinsky, served as an inspiration to a young engineer. "I realized that the work she was doing around building companies, was basically the work I was doing around building products, taken to the next level," Vassallo said. "It seemed like a really amazing thing to be able to build and manage companies, so at the time, I thought the easiest way for me to get from being an engineer to becoming a company builder, was business school."

Trae got into Stanford and met legendary John Doerr, a partner of Kleiner Perkins, who was a guest speaker at one of the classes she attended. "The hardest part for me was to start talking to him. I didn't like making new connections. I had to work on my networking skills for quite a long time."

Nevertheless, Vassallo approached Doerr and introduced herself. She said, 'I'm a big admirer of yours. I've just launched the PalmV that I worked on at IDEO, and I'm looking for a startup opportunity that would allow me to build on that experience. I know everyone is excited about the internet, and I'd like to bring hardware to the next level. What are you seeing that I could help start and get involved in?' "That conversation changed my life," Trae recalled. This situation alone taught Vassallo a couple of lessons: networking really matters, and when asking for help, be specific enough so that people could actually help you.

John Doerr knew exactly who would benefit from a talent like Vassallo. He introduced her to the team of Good Technology that was working on something relevant, she joined them as a co-founder and stayed for three years to grow the company to three hundred employees. When Good Technology decided to change their strategy, the hardware part of the business became redundant, and Trae was open to new opportunities again. "John reached out to me as we were going through the reorganization, and asked if I knew what I was going to do next. Soon enough, I became an entrepreneur-in-residence at Kleiner Perkins. It was really exciting to become an insider at the firm and to see all the companies flowing through their office, and working with entrepreneurs." Unfortunately, however, that situation didn't seem sustainable for Trae, who was raising a one-year-old child at the time. Her husband was studying at a business school, and they decided that it was time for Trae to get a real job. She got a job offer from Apple to work on the iPod and notified Kleiner Perkins about that. However, the conversation with them unexpectedly turned into another job interview. Vassallo knew that job opportunities in the venture capital industry didn't happen often, and decided to stay with the firm. "I was not necessarily planning to work in venture capital, but I was in the right place at the right time, so I became an associate in 2003 and stayed with Kleiner Perkins for 11 years, slowly working my way up to the partner level."

Vassallo needed to learn a lot when she started working, but she believes that success in venture capital depends on human skills. "Doing due diligence, negotiating terms, making deals — that's just a small piece of what we do. When I hire people, I don't necessarily expect them to be able to do this right away. The most important part of our job is deal-sourcing, and it's all built around leveraging your connections and tapping into what's going on in your networks. I like to hire people who are good at reaching out to others, staying connected, and making sure that they are top of their minds. Most importantly, you need to build a really solid reputation as someone who people want to work with."

Trae said that she was able to make a career at a firm like Kleiner Perkins because she was focused on nurturing relationships within the firm, and building a knowledge base to be able to do the job with little to no hand holding and guidance. "It is critical to develop a really strong rapport internally, to gain the trust of your colleagues, and to prove that you've got good judgment," she summarized.

Trae believes that the main value that she brought to the table at the firm was her passion for design thinking as a product engineer. "Fundamentally, technology is just a means to solving an important problem for somebody, and design thinking is all about creative problem solving. Very often, I see that investors and entrepreneurs get caught up by a new technology, but forget about how they're using it to address the challenge. I think that the best entrepreneurs and investors are always looking for that elegant way of solving a big problem."

When Kleiner Perkins grew quite large and started leaning more towards investing in growth-stage companies, Vassallo decided that it was time for her to leave and continue investing at the early stages that she was passionate about. She decided to partner with Neil Sequeira, who had been a General Partner at Catalyst Partners and observed the same thing happening at his firm. "I'm naturally a collaborative person, so I wanted to practice venture collaboratively. Venture investing is never black and white — it's a process of discussion and debate that makes you a better investor," Trae shared.

Vassallo has seen enough nasty things happening in venture capital and learned an important lesson. "When you are feeling that you're not being treated equally by someone, instead of ignoring it, I think, you should understand what's going on and address it. Looking back at my own career, I had a tendency to put my head down and keep chugging when something wasn't working quite right. I thought that the problem would go away. But the reality is, if something is not working right systematically, it'll never just magically go away," she advised.

Ann Winblad

Founding Partner,
Hummer Winblad Venture Partners, United States

When I read the transcript of my conversation with Ann Winblad — one of the first female investors in Silicon Valley, and a living legend in the tech startup ecosystem — I couldn't help but notice that all her answers sounded as if I was reading a book of quotes by famous people. That is not the style of this book, but I tried to save as much of the authenticity of Ann's answers as I could, so you can enjoy it for yourself.

"Venture capital is not necessarily for everyone," said Winblad. "When John Hummer offered me the opportunity to start a VC firm, it was a really hard decision for me. I was in my 30s at that point in time and was choosing whether I wanted to be a venture capitalist, or if I should go on and start another software company. John ultimately convinced me by using two reasonings: the fact that we'd be the first VC firm to invest exclusively in software, and that it was also an opportunity for me to continue to be a pioneer in the software sector after the exit from my company.

"I'm an outlier in the venture capital industry. I didn't graduate from an Ivy League school, I do not have an MBA, and I didn't set my sights on becoming a venture capitalist. But I did intend to work in the software industry, and I am still doing that as an investor who focuses solely on software.

"Investing in companies and operating a company are mutually exclusive choices in venture capital. Many women do great as founders and operators within large companies, and that's good news! Great entrepreneurs are much harder to find than good venture capitalists. It's an amazing opportunity to be an entrepreneur, and you should never forsake that if you still have it in yourself.

"You should only get into venture capital if you've decided that you're done with all your operating goals and entrepreneurial challenges, because you will have to move from being a player to being a coach. You will be an opportunist — not a visionary. So if you still think of yourself as a great visionary, you should stay on as an operator. Venture capital is not an ultimate career choice and not the only measure of success," she shared her wisdom.

Ann Winblad founded her startup Open Systems Inc. at the age of 25. The company focused entirely on software development, which was a new thing back then. No one believed that people could make money from selling software, but she was one of the first, in the 70s, to see that it was the future. Six years later, Winblad sold her company for 15 million dollars — one of the largest sales of those times.

One of the big lessons she learned during that period, happened when she was pitching to a large group of hardware resellers. She struggled to look in the eyes of top managers who had 20 years on her, and began her pitch quietly in a polite tone. The managing director then asked for a break, took her aside and said, 'Ann, if you're gonna run with the big dogs, you gotta learn how to lift your leg.' She has never forgotten that phrase.

"Careers in both tech and venture capital, demand a certain level of assertiveness, which must not become arrogance. My father taught me that there is a very fine line between confidence and arrogance. Sometimes people with thick skins can cross into that arrogance area. Others might have too much swagger, which also makes them arrogant rather than confident. Confidence is often confused with arrogance in this space these days."

Ann's father was a basketball coach and raised her, her four sisters and her brother as a team. "I remember when I became a teenager and asked my dad what rules we had as to the time I should be back home, he replied, 'We don't have any rules. You trust your own good judgment,'" she recited her father's biggest advice.

"This implied that I also had to take responsibility for my own actions and I had to take them seriously. I had to make my own decisions, even if they were unpopular with others. You can always find people who disagree with your point of view. I learned that life is not a popularity contest — you will never have 100% of the votes. That was what shaped me throughout my life.

"Applying my father's advice to venture investing, I always say that you have to be confident but not arrogant about your own value system and beliefs from which your thinking evolved and led you to certain decisions. This is really important for venture capitalists — not only from the people's skills perspective, but also in early-stage investing, when there is a lot of uncertainty about the risks as well as all the opportunities," Ann continued about her investment approach.

"On the one hand, you have to get very excited about the deals, in order to get them done. You have to see the opportunities, but also recognize the challenges. It's much easier to see a glass as being three quarters full, than half empty. Venture investors need to have a certain amount of confidence to make investment decisions, but we can't have arrogance, which would make us ignore the risks."

Winblad has been in the industry from its early days, so I, of course, was very interested in her view on the gender issue in venture capital. "I grew up in a male-dominated environment. There were no women's basketball teams yet, so my father only coached boys, and when I was of school age, I'd go with him to games and watch how they communicated with each other. When I went to university, I was a math major and a business major, and I also took all the computer science classes (because we did not have a computer science major at the time). I was the only woman standing at the graduation from the math group, I was the only woman taking computer science classes, and I had one or two female group mates in the business group. So when I started a software company and then became a venture investor, nothing really changed for me in terms of the gender dynamics.

"Venture capital has, until recently, been a very small sector with a very small number of people involved. Even now, fewer people work in the entire venture capital industry than there are employees in corporations like Microsoft, Google, or Amazon. We effectively put a microscope on a very small industry and project the picture way beyond its true boundaries, which is also happening because social media gives a powerful platform to everyone today.

"Anyone who feels that they need an axe to grind, or to stand in front of a room full of people to say something to them, can now leverage the power of social media to amplify their message. The opportunity to aggregate opinions towards extreme issues, or any issues, for that matter, is now allowed to happen on a much larger scale than at any time in the past. But the people who make headlines are not necessarily indicative of the whole industry," Ann pointed out.

"I recently spoke to a group of women in Minneapolis who had graduated from college, and one of them raised her hand and said, 'Why would anyone ever work for a tech company on the West Coast? The cultures of those companies sound terrible!' I said that the media likes writing about bad cultures, and people are eager to discuss villains rather than really nice, kind and just normal folks.

"When I was raising our fund with John Hummer we had many turndowns, but not once was it because I am a woman. Today I am happy to see more female founding partners who were first-time fund managers like I was, and today they run large VC firms and funds of multiple vintages.

"Certainly, there are firms that have been around for 40 years or so, and never had a female investment partner. I don't think I'd ever join any of such firms, because at this point it becomes a part of the culture. At the end of the day, when you accept any job offer, you join a culture, which is very hard to change if it was formed over decades. So you really need to understand the values of the company you're considering joining before signing up.

"When people start pounding on the table that we need more women in venture capital, they should point out that there *are* opportunities for women in the industry. Also, the fact that my job requires certain skills and credentials that don't depend on gender is often disregarded in debates. This includes the ability to raise money for your VC firm, to build a team, to source deals and evaluate startups, and to be a coach to your portfolio companies," Winblad highlighted. "Probably the fastest way to develop these skills, is to be an entrepreneur, and there haven't been enough female entrepreneurs in the past.

"It's very challenging to start companies, but it's also not an easy job to write checks to fund them — this is something we quickly forget during debates. Most of the venture-funded startups exist in very competitive sectors, so you are competing all the time for the best deals to fund. To help these great companies succeed, you'll need to raise further financing round after round, and have really functional corporate boards, you have to be able to work with the rest of your colleagues, men and women, and it's a very diverse group of people.

"Aside from that, you are always looking forward. If you want to be in the tech or venture capital industries, you have to love learning. I'm auditioning the future every day, which involves a lot of listening, contemplation, and additional research, once you feel that you're detecting a pattern for the future. You have to be a constant learner — you can't be a 'know it all'."

Ann didn't think for a second when I asked her for advice for women who have been mistreated by male colleagues. "If you are being devalued or treated poorly, you should leave the room. I don't know anyone who would be locked in a room and not permitted to leave. If you don't belong there, you will probably never be truly welcome. When talented people leave the room, that's detrimental for the venture capital and tech industries, because they are about people — not money. When talent starts walking out the door, many companies crumble. Have the guts to be that talent leaving the room, where you are constantly not heard or treated well.

"If we are talking about occasional situations it is still good to speak up. You need to keep your own persona intact and find your own type of kindness and clarity to tell someone that their behavior is inappropriate. You can't mirror bad people — it leads to rage. I'm from Minnesota, so I was trained to reach people's minds by kindness. Kindness is a powerful weapon that seems to startle the bad actors," Ann wrapped up our conversation with another quote-worthy answer.

Roseanne Wincek

Principal, Institutional Venture Partners, United States

"We don't always think about our own influence as a tool for elevating others and amplifying their voices. If there is one thing I learned — and continue to learn in my career — is how important it is to have an advocate and to be advocates for people who might not have a voice in an organization, regardless of whether they are junior or senior to you. You can help amplify anyone's voice," Wincek shared the number one lesson she's learned.

"I was really lucky to work with Maha Ibrahim of Canaan Partners, and John Sakoda of New Enterprise Associates, early in my career, who helped me tremendously with finding and using my voice as an investor. Now, as I become more senior, I try to do that for others, because it's really powerful. It's a small, easy thing to do at the moment, which can add up a lot in the long term. Sometimes new or young people in the room have the best ideas, because they look at things differently, so making sure that those views get heard can affect their careers, the work dynamics in your firm, as well as help with making good investment decisions, which the entire industry and society can benefit from."

Roseanne was an undergrad chemistry major and went to graduate school for biophysics. "Soon enough, I realized that I like thinking about science and talking about it, but I don't necessarily love doing science." Living in San Francisco at the time when Facebook was giving way to hundreds of new products and services, Roseanne felt like the most interesting things were passing her by. "I wanted to work on something that I could see in my everyday life, that would affect the people around me on a daily basis. That drew me out of the lab and into tech."

Wincek started a company that made apps on the Facebook platform. She then joined an enterprise software company called NextBio that provided bioinformatics analytics. As in some other stories you have likely read in this book, one of the investors of the company she worked for, challenged Roseanne to consider working in venture capital. "That was the time when there weren't that many female VC associates, let alone partners, so I didn't know any venture capitalists that looked like me. I started reading everything I could about the industry, and realized that it was the job for me. Venture capital felt like the academia of tech and used a lot of the same analytical thinking I was trained to do as a scientist. I could build mental models about how I thought products and services could impact industries and peoples' lives, but instead of pipetting, I would be talking to people, which was a lot more fun!" Wincek recalled.

After graduating from Stanford Business School, she joined an early-stage venture capital firm called Canaan Partners. "It was a phenomenal experience in my life. I thought that early-stage investing matched my background in both technical and early-stage company roles, perfectly. However, at some point, I realized that I missed the data and the numbers.

"Early-stage investors are often driven by specific ownership threshold as a way to mitigate risk and be rewarded for it. That felt like a constraint to me. I wanted flexibility to invest when I felt the time was right. When IVP approached me, I was hesitant at first, because I didn't have a typical growth investing background. The more I thought about it, the more I realized that it would allow me to be more metrics-driven and flexible than I could be at the early stage.

"Growth stage investing allows you to be more opportunistic and invest at any point from Series B rounds to pre-IPO or even in the public market, and I loved that. At the early stage, you make money from picking. At the growth stage, you make money from pricing. It is true that there are great growth-stage companies that don't necessarily make great investments because of pricing dynamics. However, we also sometimes get it wrong in growth investing when planning for the upside — we cap what we think could happen, based on the numbers we have. Unlike working with a dream at an early-stage, at the growth stage we work with the performance of the current business. I wish more growth investors could sit next to early-stage investors and share their excitement of seeing a bigger picture. In growth capital, we need to do a better job of keeping that curiosity and a beginner's mind, while at the same time staying very disciplined."

Roseanne's father put much effort into teaching her discipline and confidence. "My dad was always telling me that I could do anything that I wanted to do. It was ad nauseam, and I would ask him, 'Dad, why do you keep saying this?' But he knew back then that someday people would tell me otherwise. I didn't quite understand it at the time, but now I feel really lucky that I had it jammed into my brain early that I could do whatever I wanted, and being a woman didn't matter.

"I sometimes see women who are too shy to introduce themselves to a senior person and ask for help. Or when they aim for a COO position instead of the CEO role. I would say that waiting for someone to give us permission to do something is a mental block. First, my parents fed that 'just do it' attitude into me, later, I was lucky that I got the same message early in my investing career at Canaan Partners. Now, I try to help people by lending them some of my visibility, if they don't have enough of their own. I feel like every successful woman I know has gotten to where she is now because someone suggested or implored that she could do something she never assumed was possible. I think it's on all of us to remind each other how much we really can achieve."

Nichole Yembra

Founding Partner,

The Chrysalis Capital, Nigeria

The story of a successful Nigerian-American female consultant who moved from the US to Nigeria, Africa, to invest in local startups, was very intriguing. "It was the best decision that I could ever have made!" said Nichole Yembra when I reached out to her. She had just announced her new venture — Chrysalis Co. — a new $15 million Africa and Diaspora early-stage tech fund, and a strategy and investment advisory firm, that aims to solve problems with a pan-African lens and help establish African institutions.

"I've been fortunate to have travelled to over 20 countries for work, and about 20 more countries for pleasure. I learned a lot of new things that no degree can give. When I'm solving a problem, I am not doing it just for Nigeria — I also want to solve it for the other countries in Sub-Saharan Africa (SSA) and on a global scale as well, because I've seen that similar problems exist in other parts of the world too. As an investor, I understand that African companies can build things that will work outside of the continent. With limited infrastructure and government support, you learn that if you can make it here, you can definitely make it anywhere!"

Nichole was born in Wisconsin, United States, but lived in Nigeria for nine years as a kid. She then moved back to America and stayed there for 20 years. "I'm this weird person who doesn't plan my life like a lot of other people do. I don't have long-term goals, and I only outline my next moves for three- to five-year spurts, because I allow myself room to grow, and my vision and values to evolve, as I learn new things. I am a generalist, so I am naturally open to opportunities — I just don't know what my interests are going to be in the long term. I know for sure that I love solving problems, and I love numbers, and every day of my life has been pretty consistent in terms of applying these skills. So the only question is what company I will be doing it for."

Yembra started her career at Ernst & Young (EY) in risk advisory. After brief stints in Brazil and Thailand, she knew it was time to move to the African continent to apply those skills, and contemplated moving to South Africa, because 80% of EY's advisory revenue was coming from there. However, when she learned that a Nigerian fintech company — Venture Garden Group (VGG) — had just raised private capital for pan-African expansion, she decided to join them as CFO to structure that growth. She and the VGG founders also launched GreenHouse Capital, its investment arm that would identify and invest in African entrepreneurs focused primarily on fintech. In 2017, Forbes Africa listed Nichole Onome Yembra as one of the 30 Most Promising Young Entrepreneurs on the continent.

"Indigenous companies often struggle to raise funding at an early stage in developing countries, whether it's Nigeria or India," Yembra said. "At Venture Garden Group, we knew this well, so we decided to launch GreenHouse Capital as an independent investment fund, in order to identify, incubate, and invest in startups with high-growth potential. We saw a need to be hands-on in all aspects of scaling a business, from fundraising to advisory and even business development, which would lead investors to exits. Once we close this life cycle — from first investment to exit — the whole ecosystem will change," Nicole repeated the notion expressed by Andrea Bohmert about South Africa earlier in the book.

"Aside from being comfortable with finances, I'm an experienced problem solver and risk manager. I always try to figure out what could go wrong, to quantify it, and come up with a solution or possible development scenarios. In a super risky place like Africa, from the exchange rates to political issues, mitigating these risks is critical, so it was really exciting for me to take up this challenge.

"We don't have a lot of enduring African institutions, aside from the original founding families. When it comes to technology, there are lots of missing parts in the value chain, because the infrastructure across different countries is pretty weak. While it may be good on the one hand, because you get to set the rules, it also creates additional barriers, because you have to focus on solving several problems for your business, instead of just the problem that your business was actually created to solve," she described local realities.

"African markets are generally very fluid and still developing, which is why I always try to align my values with those of the founders. Shared vision is another key thing for me when working with startups. Things will inevitably gradually change, and team members may change, but if we started building the company on common values and shared vision, there will at least be a compass to direct all the parties involved when things get really tough."

We then talked about her new venture. "From an investment standpoint, Chrysalis Capital looks at pretty much all the same sectors that you look at in the United States, although some of them are obviously more critical than others. For example, fintech has been getting a lot of attention over the last couple of years, because more than half of the continent's population is literally financially excluded. It's hard to believe that it is possible in 2019, but it's a fact. By opening a bank account for a local person, we aren't just allowing them to pay for their groceries, but it also opens a whole world of different things that we can offer them. This investment vertical attracts a lot of money, because regulations are very different across the countries in Africa, so many fintech companies try to build platforms that simplify the transactions between individuals and companies.

"Another critical sector in Africa is energytech. The 48 countries in Sub-Saharan Africa generate the same amount of power as Spain alone. There's literally not enough power on the continent that has the world's best coverage for solar radiation. The lack of electricity has a wide range of implications, ranging from the ridiculous cost of energy, to small businesses shutting down. For example, in my house, I spend no less than $100 every week to power my diesel generator. Obviously, many companies and individual investors are eager to fund all kinds of energy generation and preservation solutions.

"Finally, the education systems in most African countries are hopelessly broken. For example, a million students pass their school admission tests every year, but cannot gain tertiary institution admission, because there's physically no space to serve all of them. So they try again the next year, and then the year after that... At some point, people give up, and then the best occupations they can find are blue collar jobs. There is an archaic law in some parts of Africa, that dictates that if you don't have an accredited degree, you cannot do your youth service. And if you don't do youth service, you can't get hired for a job. As a consequence, Nigeria and SSA as a whole, have the highest number of 'out of school' kids in the world, but the governments don't make it easier for edtech companies to solve this problem," she explained.

"This is how we get to millions of uneducated people, who have little to no opportunities to work legally in their motherland. Does it slow down the social and technological development of the region? You bet! Would it be different if the circumstances were not that damning? When you take Nigerians out of Nigeria and put us, let's say, in the US, we become talented doctors, teachers, or social workers, etc. Plenty of African people do really well in a well-developed system, which we could also harvest here on the African continent.

"When we looked at the data, we saw that over 90% of the founders who have received venture funding in Africa had ties to the US or Europe — they had either gone to school there, or were born there, or both. They indeed have better results in business, because they have been exposed to different views and social and commercial models in other countries — they are more open to changing the status quo. My own example confirms that our malleability is best used when we are shaped by seeing the world."

I must admit that I learned a lot about Africa from Nichole during our conversation, and I was really looking forward to hearing about her experience of being a female investor in the region.

"When I lived in the United States, I felt like I was black first. Here in Africa, I'm a woman first. I must say that I actually prefer America's racism to Nigeria's sexism," she dropped a bomb. "Continental Africa has a long way to go in terms of accepting women. You will barely find strong women who have real depth or substance here — not because they don't exist, but because society has set the rules for them to do well in the workplace, that are largely based on managing the egos of their male colleagues. At VGG, I worked with men who were foreign trained, so we had similar backgrounds and were more compatible. But when I work with, or hire, native Nigerians, there is always a raised eyebrow, 'Oh, she's 10 years younger than me — how can she be where she is?'

"In Nigeria, there are tables that they just don't want you to be at. You can push your way through and show your value all you want, but you will never be accepted. There's a physical manifestation of that in Nigeria, because there are literally still some venues that won't allow a woman to come in unescorted in 2019. You have to deal with that stuff here every day.

"When I was at Greenhouse, I launched an accelerator focused on female and gender-diverse founders and we hosted an implicit bias training session, where we tried to work with local investors to help them understand how they could be judging men or women unfairly. We tried to educate the men, but I also dedicated time to educating the women on staying strong, and finding support to keep pursuing their dreams, no matter what was happening. I know that you are doing the same in the United States, but trust me, here, it's on a whole different level! When the Nigerian president, sitting next to Angela Merkel and the entire house's representatives, says that his wife's place is in the kitchen, you know that there's a lot of work to be done in the country!

"From an investor perspective, I see that business people are becoming a lot more conscious about gender bias and letting data drive their decisions. There is robust discussion about female-led businesses doing more with less, and investors ending up with higher returns on their investments, so more and more people are opening up to it.

"The bias situation in the United States is not as bad as in Africa, after all, although the US has its own unique set of issues. Here, I constantly find myself in situations where men overstep business boundaries. I usually match their unwelcome behavior with sarcasm to defuse the situation, and if I'm lucky, maybe to enjoy seeing them feel silly. Unfortunately some people see my sarcasm as being aggressive, but that is as far as I can go here. If I lived in the US, I'd be a lot bolder, because there are institutions and structures in place for people to report problems. There are no repercussions for anything that men do here — sexism, ageism, and the patriarchy are still part of the culture, so we have to be more creative in how we handle that in Nigeria.

"In forming Chrysalis Capital, I want to take the further step in pushing the boundaries of what a woman in finance, tech, and investment can look like. I know plenty of dope women here, who are coming up and doing really great things, but we still need more of them for a critical mass, in order to make a change. One of the newspapers here recently featured 50 women in tech who are changing the space — we are already in dozens! So it is slowly happening — the narrative is shifting, and some male opinion leaders are being asked about their efforts to bring more women into business. I wanted to create safer spaces for more founders to have an opportunity to thrive if just given a small chance. I hope that my link between Africa and the US can create more opportunities for the world to see the brilliance we are creating on the African continent."

Elizabeth Yin

Founding Partner, Hustle Fund, United States

When I was preparing for the interview with Elizabeth Yin, I read her mission statement that says that she is going to 'change how we fund startups in Silicon Valley' in the next 20-30 years. Coincidentally, Elizabeth's interview is one of the last ones in this book, and it will definitely give you some food for thought after you close it. "Many investors say that the venture capital industry is a meritocracy, but that cannot be farther from the truth. As long as an Ivy League graduate has better chances of raising money for a startup or getting hired by a VC firm, we should stop pretending that the venture capital industry is a meritocracy," Elizabeth stated.

An electrical engineer by training, she had worked in marketing and product development before launching her own startup, which she successfully sold in 2014. She then joined one of her early backers, 500 Startups, as an entrepreneur-in-residence, and became a partner and helped almost two hundred startups go through their acceleration program. She saw it from both sides of the table and is now running her own micro VC fund.

"One of the big problems that I have with the current startup ecosystem, is that I think there are a lot of founders who don't get a fair shot at demonstrating their merit when it comes to fundraising. That's a priority issue that needs to be solved," she started unfolding the reason behind that mission statement. "Unconscious biases in how investors assess founders can be tied to gender or race, but it extends much further than that. For example, there are investors who have unconscious biases against introverts or people who have a certain kind of foreign accent. It's just hard to know to what extent there's a lack of meritocracy. If a female founder gets dinged, is it because she didn't get a fair shake? In this country, in the venture capital industry, frankly speaking, most founders are not going to be able to raise money. The odds of raising are against all founders who don't fit the stereotypical mold. Period. So, if you get dinged, you can't simply say, 'Oh it's because I'm a woman that I wasn't able to raise'.

"Assessing founders is highly subjective, and this industry has never had any objective framework to the process of assessment. We are just taking our life experiences and trying to superimpose what we've learned about other people we've met in the past who seemed similar, and applying them to the founder at hand," Elizabeth referred to that famous pattern recognition phenomenon, which we have discussed in this book many times already.

Elizabeth's point of view sounds sobering: the patterns of VCs' success have been built over decades, and keep our unconscious biases alive. How can we change the rules of this game?

"The reason why I started Hustle Fund is actually less about me being a VC, and more about me being an entrepreneur trying to solve the problems in the venture capital industry. Throughout my experience as an entrepreneur and a partner of 500 Startups, I've noticed that the best teams are the ones that can execute with high velocity. When I am evaluating teams, aside from other human qualities, I pay attention to these three traits of founders: speed of accomplishing things, learnability, and tenacity," she added.

Yin's firm operates by investing $25,000 in pre-seed startups and then undertakes a four- to six-week growth period with each company. The idea is to work alongside the team and then determine if the fund will follow on with additional monetary investment. However, Elizabeth also sees the same problem on the general partners level. "It is believed that a pedigree or startup experience makes one a good investor. I liken the investor/startup relationship to a coach/player relationship. Just because you were great at playing basketball doesn't mean you are great at coaching. You may have great access to recruiting great players because of your past startup background or connections, but there are so many other things that are also important for being a great investor. So, there isn't a great correlation between being a great founder or having an Ivy League degree and being a great investor," she concluded.

Indeed, during our research of more than 1,200 VC firms in the United States, we noticed that many of them understand diversity in a very narrow way. We can see them hiring people of color and women, however, their backgrounds would still be very traditional — Ivy League graduates, MBA degree, etc. This profile has been shaped by generations of white males, so applying the same mold to diverse candidates may limit the number of them at the top of the funnel. Many people who have accumulated very different and valuable experiences, which would be critical for growing the value of a VC portfolio, may not even get to the first job interview because they will be sorted out by such traditional parameters. We talked about it with Patricia Nakache half a book earlier, and I also asked Elizabeth how that mold needs to change. "There are four main jobs that a venture investor does: sourcing lots of deals, doing good due diligence, coaching founders to grow the value of portfolio companies, and helping them to exit. I think a better way to search for new talents is to perhaps teach these skills and then test them to see how good people are at finding high-quality deals, at evaluating companies, at methodical thinking. These are the skills and knowledge that matter." This again proved that skill-based education and recruiting is something much needed in venture capital.

Darshana Zaveri

Managing Partner, Catalyst Health Ventures, United States

A scientist by training (in cell and molecular biology), Darshana Zaveri came to the United States from India to attend graduate school. After graduation, she worked as a bench scientist in pharma and biotech companies in Cambridge, including one of the first human genome sequencing companies, but sticking to that bench didn't feel quite right to her.

Darshana went back to Harvard to get a master's degree in public policy, because she wanted to do some work at the intersection of science and policy. However, through the coursework, she got really interested in finance, and was taking a lot of corporate finance classes at the business school, except she still didn't know which career to pursue.

At one of the Harvard Business School classes, she was sitting next to a woman she'd never met before. After the class, they talked for four hours, and Darshana told her about the struggle she was experiencing in choosing her career. "I told her about the kinds of things that interested me, and she said that if I like healthcare and finance, then maybe I could marry those two things by making investments in the sector. At that time, I didn't know what venture capital was, but she put this idea in my head and I started learning everything that I could about it. After some time, she introduced me to some people in the industry, and that's how I got a job at Catalyst back in 2007," Darshana told me about her path into venture capital.

Zaveri networked her way into the industry as an immigrant, so I was really curious as to whether she felt rejection often. "When I first came to the US from India for graduate studies at Boston University, there were mostly men in my cohort. I noticed that, but I never experienced any isolation of any type as an immigrant, or a woman, or a minority. Or maybe it happened to me, but I just was not aware of it.

"At the end of the day, you have to work with people — you have to work with men, just the way you have to work with women. You have to work with everyone to get the job done. Once you're in your everyday get-things-done mode, you put some of those issues on the back burner, because there's too much going on, on a daily basis, to focus on them," she carefully explained.

As Susan Choe said in our conversation, ignorance is a blessing. I often notice that type of attitude in immigrants, due to their different cultural roots. "There is something about that type of stoic simplicity and work ethic that I saw in women back in India, that has taught me so much about self-reliance and just getting things done," added Darshana.

Zaveri said that she works with a lot more men than women in her field, however, she observes a strong networking effect once a woman gets involved. "I've sat on six boards of directors through my career, and on every board, there were women, and some boards were all women.

"That probably starts at an early deal-making stage: you get one woman involved, and she shows deals to other women in the network, and those women get interested in those same deals, and maybe they invest and come onto boards. I believe there might be an amplifying effect of adding the first woman into the equation and you'll get more for the sector in the whole. I believe it might work for any minority group too."

After we had assumed the formula, I kept asking Darshana about how we could do that at scale. "We need to increase the ways that women and men interact with each other. We need to show that the boys' club is not cool anymore.

"Venture capital is almost a cottage industry: it's small and you don't even really know who's doing what, unless you're deeply involved in it. You don't know which VC funds are investing, and which are idle or dissolved. You don't know which of them have money to hire and which don't. You need to be a part of the industry to get a job in it, which is ridiculous in the first place. The whole aspect of knowing where to look and for what, is hard.

"Secondly, I do believe that if a male investor sees a really good opportunity to finance a woman or to co-invest with a woman, they will do it, because, at the end of the day, they want to make money for their firm and limited partners. I don't think that, fundamentally, anyone would eliminate a good opportunity, simply because it came from a woman or any minority group representative. The holistic approach is to increase the interaction between all of these groups of people — men, women, and minorities."

Lu Zhang

Founding Partner, Fusion Fund, United States

I wasn't surprised to see Lu Zhang's name on the list of female VCs nominated for this book, because she's become a very well-known character in Silicon Valley due to her boldness and convictions, in just a few years. Right before this book was published, one of the portfolio companies of this unstoppable young female immigrant from China had an exit that made a 10x return on the investment for her VC firm.

"My goal is to establish a top-tier venture capital firm in Silicon Valley, with tech innovation playing a leading role for its success," she said in the interview. This bold goal has drawn a lot of attention from the media to her persona, and Lu Zhang definitely gives us all an opportunity to embrace the optimism, inventiveness, and boldness of youth.

After graduating in materials science in 2010 at Tianjin University in China, Lu moved on to earn a master's degree at Stanford. She built a new medical device for testing for Type II diabetes that uses nano-thin biosensors, as part of her entrepreneurship class, and later sold the company that emerged from that project for more than $10 million, in her early 20s. After becoming a successful entrepreneur, she joined Fenox Venture Capital as a venture partner, and quickly became established as an expert in the US tech and the innovation market.

"I didn't have a goal of becoming a VC investor, however, becoming an influential person *was* on my list. I always wanted to learn a lot, to learn faster, and to become better, and when I got familiar with venture capital, I saw that I could do exactly that. I always make decisions based on my long-term goals and gains, rather than short-term ones. And while I may still end up building another startup — these days, I can do more as an investor," Lu concluded.

Today, Lu Zhang is managing her second fund and has almost $130 million in total assets under management. She was lucky to have lead investors who eagerly signed her first checks for her first $17 million Fusion Fund I, and her second fund — Fusion Fund II — got oversubscribed and closed at $85 million.

"The word 'fusion' brings to mind a sense of energy. The idea came from the basis of nuclear fusion: small elements come together and result in huge energy and power. This is similar to what I do as a venture capitalist — investing in startups is a combination (or fusion) of tech, innovation, but also involves a mixture of other different elements, including culture. My company has a blend of tech, market, capital, and global investments, so Fusion Fund felt like the right name for where we were and where were going. Just like nuclear fusion, the combination of different elements can result in explosive growth that isn't possible from just single components," Lu revealed the meaning of her name choice.

"Combining my entrepreneurial and investing experience, I realized that it is not easy for a medtech entrepreneur to find a VC investor, because tough tech requires a pretty deep understanding from the investor's side as well. I decided that I want to be a buddy for such entrepreneurs on the dark side," Lu went on explaining the reasoning behind starting her own fund in 2014.

"At Fenox, I was working on later-stage companies, but I really enjoyed working with early-stage founders, and in the meantime, I was able to see lots of amazing technologies at their earliest stage. Venture capital tremendously broadened my horizon," she said. "I learned a lot about the tech world and innovations, but I also realized that not only am I passionate about them, but I am also quite good at recognizing them."

With the recent changes in the political relationship between the US and China, Lu believes that the US is fostering an 'anti-immigrant, anti-international' image for Silicon Valley. "People are more about perceptions, than regulations. More and more people have started seeing the United States as a very unfriendly country towards immigrants, and it hurts Silicon Valley the most, because 50% of the founders here are immigrants," she added.

When it came to her own experience, Lu admitted that she had seen it all. "People have challenged me due to my gender, my nationality, and my young age, but I have never taken it personally. Instead, I treat it as yet another life challenge, and the stronger the challenge I face, the stronger my motivation to prove that I can make it happen. So whoever doubted me, helped me become stronger, better, and able to move farther and faster. I was working in healthcare where people need to have gray hair in order to be respected, and I sold my company at the age of 23. That helped me a lot to avoid that 'crisis of confidence', which many women encounter today.

"These days, VC has witnessed a growing number of women enrolling in this industry, and so have the tech industry and entrepreneurship in general. This is a process of awakening. It is by showing the industry what we can do, that the prejudice will be removed. Innovation needs diversity — it is important to keep the ecosystem diversified with people of different backgrounds, in order to motivate the innovation to happen."

ABOUT THE AUTHOR

Renata George is an entrepreneur turned VC.
She currently works in corporate venturing.

Aside from operating a venture fund, Renata makes venture capital education more accessible, and is passionate about advancing women and representatives of minority groups in the venture capital industry. She is the editor-in-chief of www.vc.academy, producer for www.women.vc and www.all.vc.

After selling her business in Europe, she started investing as an angel investor and raised a VC fund in the United States in 2011. She then joined another VC firm in Singapore, and established a strategic corporate venture arm for an Asian unicorn startup.

Along the way, Ms George helped various tech companies to raise ~USD $30M from state institutions, as well as ~USD $20M from venture capital investors.

As an entrepreneur, she built one of the most successful media network franchises in Eastern Europe, and timely exited the business in 2008.

Ms George is a frequent speaker and active advisor to startups. She was featured on Forbes.com lists "Millennial Women Venture Investors" and "The Top Women in Venture Capital and Angel Investing".

She has authored two other books "Venture Capital Mindset" (2018) and "The Manual for Finding a Perfect Mentor for Entrepreneurs" (2013), and co-authored a course on venture capital and entrepreneurship (2014)

www.renata.vc

CPSIA information can be obtained
at www.ICGtesting.com
Printed in the USA
BVHW041904140619
551057BV00003B/6/P